Good Governance, Democratic Societies and Globalisation

Good Governance, Democratic Societies and Globalisation

EDITORS

Surendra Munshi
Biju Paul Abraham

Sage Publications Inc.   Sage Publications Ltd

Good governance, democratic societies and globalisation/edited by Surendra Munshi, Biju Paul Abraham.

SAGE Publications
New Delhi/Thousand Oaks/London

First published in 2004 by

Sage Publications India Pvt Ltd
B-42, Panchsheel Enclave
New Delhi 110 017

Sage Publications Inc.
2455 Teller Road
Thousand Oaks, California 91320

Sage Publications Ltd
1 Oliver's Yard, 55 City Road
London EC1Y 1SP

Published by Tejeshwar Singh for Sage Publications India Pvt Ltd, typeset in 10/12 Ushwerwood Medium at S.R. Enterprises, New Delhi, and printed at Chaman Enterprises, New Delhi.

Library of Congress Cataloging-in-Publication Data

Good governance, democratic societies and globalisation/edited by Surendra Munshi, Biju Paul Abraham.
    p. cm.
    Includes bibliographical references and index.
    1. Public administration—Europe. 2. Europe—Politics and government. 3. Europe—Economic policy. 4. Public administration—India. 5. India—Politics and government. 6. India—Economic policy. 7. Public administration—Cross-cultural studies. 8. Globalisation. 9. Democracy. I. Title: Good governance, democratic societies and globalisation. II. Munshi, Surendra. III. Abraham, Biju Paul.
JN94.A58G66 351.4—dc22   2004   2003017081

ISBN: 0-7619-9848-9 (US-Hb)   81-7829-315-3 (India-Hb)

Sage Production Team: Parul Nayyar, Sushanta Gayen and Santosh Rawat

CONTENTS

This book is the outcome of an international conference that was held at the Indian Institute of Management Calcutta from 25 to 27 April 2002. The papers presented at the Conference are included here, with the exception of one paper. These papers went through revisions after the Conference. To these papers has been added an introduction that not only outlines the concern that was behind the design of the Conference but also provides an important outcome of the Conference. We have tried to take a broader view of good governance, going beyond disciplinary and other demarcations. This will be borne out by the coverage of the papers as well as by the profile of contributors.

The Conference was organised as part of the European Union (EU)–India Economic Cross-Cultural Programme (ECCP) and was on 'Good Governance in Democratic Societies in Cross-Cultural Perspective'. The following institutions and persons were involved in the project: the Indian Institute of Management Calcutta was represented by Professor Surendra Munshi and Dr Biju Paul Abraham; Professor Diane Reyniers and Professor Peter Abell represented the Interdisciplinary Institute of Management, London School of Economics; Professor Hellmut Wollmann represented Humboldt University, Berlin; Professor Rudi Schmidt represented the Friedrich Schiller University, Jena; Professor Sergio Bortolani represented Scuola di Amministrazione Aziendale (SAA), University of Turin; and Professor Abram De Swaan represented the Amsterdam School for Social Science Research. The Indian Institute of Management Calcutta was the coordinating institution of the network.

We are thankful to our partners for their support. They stood by us throughout the duration of the project. Their contribution to the project was significant at all stages. We could not have asked for better partners. Other contributors to the Conference represented here have also earned our gratitude. Our thanks are due to those doctoral

students of our Institute who took the responsibility of acting
as rapporteurs of the Conference: Shamama Afreen, Debabrata
Chattopadhyay, Nilanjan Ghosh, Runa Sarkar, Manish Singhal, and
Munish Thakur. Runa Sarkar and Munish Thakur contributed in a
significant manner even after the conference in collating the
rapporteurs' reports. Our research assistants, Soma Chaudhuri and
later Anupama Muhuri, proved excellent in their work and gave us
invaluable research assistance.

We are grateful to the European Community represented by the
European Commission for the award of the financial grant that made
this project possible. This book has been produced with the financial assistance of the European Community. The views expressed
herein are those of the authors and can therefore in no way be
taken to reflect the official opinion of the European Community. The
Indian Institute of Management Calcutta offered a supportive environment for carrying out the project. We are thankful to Professor
Amitava Bose and Professor Ranjan Ghosh for their support. Thanks
are due to the staff members of the Institute, especially Mr K.A.
Ahmed, who were in one way or the other involved in the project.

For a competent handling of the publication plan of the book we
are grateful to SAGE, especially to Debjani M. Dutta who was entrusted
with the task of publication. To the anonymous reviewer appointed
by the publisher, our thanks for a detailed report on the book that
proved useful to us.

Surendra Munshi
Biju Paul Abraham

INTRODUCTION[1]

SURENDRA MUNSHI AND BIJU PAUL ABRAHAM

The task of this introduction is to spell out the concern that was behind the design of the Conference in which the chapters collected here were presented. This concern may be broadly identified as the issue of good governance in democratic societies in the context of globalisation. India and the European Union are viewed in a comparative perspective to see what the two unions can learn from each other. The collapse of the Soviet Union and its allies in Eastern Europe has shown that the model of socialism that was adopted in these countries with the massive role that was assigned to the state in all spheres has not worked. Moreover, the pressure that is imposed by the processes of globalisation implies a reduced role of the state, especially in the economic sphere. While an argument is advanced for reducing the role of the state, the importance of ensuring that the state carries out its responsibilities towards its citizens is also observed. Thus, for example, the current Indian scene is characterised by a tendency to let the market operate in a relatively free manner, but no political party can afford to leave out concern for the poor from its rhetoric.

It is useful to pay attention to experiences and debates in different societies and to bring them into discussion in a comparative perspective. It makes greater sense for the present purpose to compare India with Europe rather than with one European country, for in terms of size and population alone India and Europe are more comparable than, say, India and Holland. Then there is this significant effort (going back in time perhaps to Churchill's call for 'a kind of the United States of Europe' in 1946) to build the European Union which was created, following successive treaties, by the *Treaty on European*

Union which came into force in 1993. The role of Jean Monnet and Robert Schuman is noteworthy in this context. In India, it was in 1947 that Jawaharlal Nehru made his famous *Tryst with Destiny* speech when he hailed India awakening to freedom and discovering herself again. The Union of India has been in existence for more than 50 years now. There is much that these two unions that represent old histories, rich cultures and new aspirations can learn from each other. A comparative perspective offers the possibility of reducing ethnocentrism and raises questions that are relevant across societies. These questions are to be asked with the awareness that the comparative method need not be reduced to area studies in the Third World, but may be fruitfully utilised across the developed/developing divide. The choice of democratic societies reflects not only the value choices made by India and the European societies under discussion here, but also the consideration that democratic societies provide a formal condition for building consensus among citizens in a free manner. This has significance for the consideration of good governance. A final point needs to be made in this context. Much of the discussion on good governance has been carried out in a segregated manner, maintaining disciplinary and other demarcations. It is necessary to cross these boundaries and take a broader view. This is the reason why chapters on issues of governance, administrative reforms and corporate governance have been put together. They have bearing on each other as will be hopefully evident on reading the book. For good governance, administrative reforms provide a mechanism of governing, and it can well be argued that corporate governance, in spite of its specificity, suggests good governance at the level of corporation which in turn is dependent on good governance at the macro level.

Yet another task of this introduction is to present what has been drawn from the chapters. Though it will be misleading to claim that the chapters constitute a unity, what is remarkable is the extent to which the 20 voices presented here lend themselves to becoming one distinct voice through a careful analysis of the chapters, even though there are differences among them as is to be expected. Abstracting from their individual concerns, an attempt is made to formulate inductively an alternative view that has been called the *heterogeneity thesis*. This is in contrast to the *homogenisation thesis* that has been constructed from an examination of an influential trend in current thought. It can be said safely that the alternative view formulated here belongs to all the authors and yet to none wholly. No attempt is made here to provide detailed summaries of all the chapters. This introduction draws from these chapters but does not claim to speak for them, for the authors are capable of doing that for themselves.

THE CONTEXT OF GLOBALISATION

In a celebrated article which brought Francis Fukuyama (1989) instant international fame, he announces the 'triumph of the West' and argues that the United States and, following in its footsteps, Japan, have been able 'to create a truly universal consumer culture that has become both a symbol and an underpinning of the universal homogeneous state' (p. 10). Not only have all possible 'contradictions' in human life been resolved or are likely to be resolved in the context of this way of life, but there also is a total exhaustion of any alternative to it. Marxism has been discredited. Fukuyama argues that hardly anyone believes in it any longer in the Soviet Union. In China, Maoism does not show the path of the Asian future; rather it presents an 'anachronism' with the mainland Chinese envying the prosperity of the Chinese abroad. We have thus reached the end of history and must face the 'prospect of centuries of boredom' ahead. It is useful here to look upon Fukuyama's article concerning the end of history as a document that represents a characteristic worldview that found its confirmation around the time the Tiananmen Square massacre took place and the Berlin Wall fell. It goes to his credit that he captured well the spirit of the time in his article. More recently, Fukuyama (2001) asserts that time is on the side of modernity and there is no lack of the will of the United States to prevail.

The march of modernity is presented as 'an unabashed victory of economic and political liberalism' (Fukuyama 1989: 3). When discussing modernity, it makes sense to consider that if modern refers to something pertaining to the present and recent times, it needs to be contrasted with something that existed earlier. While in philology it is customary to divide the history of living languages into the three periods of 'old', 'middle', and 'modern', it is common in social sciences to contrast between 'traditional' and 'modern' societies. If time is on the side of modernity, so is logic. It is believed that modernity operates with its own logic, replacing traditional societies and creating a homogeneous world. Indeed, Fukuyama does mention the need for understanding 'the economic logic of marketization' (1989: 13). The need to understand logic was earlier conveyed by reference to the 'logic of industrialism' (Kerr 1960) which was believed to promote convergence in the world. More recently, globalisation has become a popular word that has been associated with growing interdependence of different societies in what is believed to be the emerging single society of all human beings. In economic terms, globalisation has been associated with a remarkable increase in global activities accompanied by a reduction of national barriers since the 1980s. An integrating world economy is characterised by such features as international trade, foreign investment, labour mobility, global networks, and cultural homogenisation. It is common to talk of globalisation of production as well as products. Large multinational companies integrate their production across different nations and sell globally. This is best illustrated by the automobile industry where major companies dominate the world market through efficient production and marketing networks. These marketing networks are promoted by global advertising that makes the products visible and creates brand identities. Several institutional arrangements at different levels, which culminated in the creation of the World Trade Organisation (WTO) in 1995, provide the institutional framework for the new system, informed by the 'Washington Consensus' that is concerned with policy recommendations for greater integration within a liberalised global economy.

The term globalisation is used in two different ways. While it is used to describe a process of increasing integration in the world economy, it is also used in a normative sense to prescribe a strategy for this integration (Nayyar 2001). In its positive sense, globalisation is evident in the integration of global markets, rapid advances in communication technology and the spread of what has been called 'mass culture'. Globalisation in this sense is viewed as inevitable. It is believed that the 'new economy', driven by recent developments in technology, brings in an economy that goes beyond its previous limitations (Gates 1995: 1999). This position is contested but it is the use of the term in its normative sense that has proved more controversial. It is when the generalised use of commodities at a global level is seen not only as inevitable but also as beneficial, or when the argument is developed that the market need not be regulated but instead should be allowed to operate as the guiding principle for individual and collective action that we enter into a highly contested territory. Often the choice is formulated in terms of individual freedom and collective solidarity (Berthoud 1997). An attempt has been made to reconcile the Westernised mode of consumption and stable community within the process of globalisation using the metaphors of the Lexus and the olive tree with the argument that globalisation represents the deepest aspiration of the people (Friedman 1999). But this is far from convincing. A moral argument is made by Jagdish Bhagwati (2000) in 'Globalization: A Moral Imperative'. He argues here that certain economic freedoms are basic to prosperity and are therefore of 'the highest moral value'. Markets serve by providing incentives to produce and they can strengthen democracy by providing means of sustenance outside government structures, and by including excluded groups such as women and the poor.

Returning to Fukuyama and the spirit that he captured in his article in 1989, it needs to be noted that he has remained loyal to this spirit. He argues after the tragedy of September 11 that the West has won. His response to the tragedy is clear. 'I believe that in the end I remain right: modernity is a very powerful freight train that will not be derailed by recent events, however painful. Democracy and free markets will continue to expand as the dominant organising principles for much of the world' (Fukuyama 2001). His argument about free market and universal consumer culture, the convergence theory of Clark Kerr and the views of the proponents of globalisation ('globalists' like Bhagwati) add up to a thesis that may be called here the *homogenisation thesis*, for all of them suggest the appearance of a homogeneous world. An attempt will be made now to draw from the criticism that has been brought against these constituents to develop a critique of the thesis. The editors of *The National Interest* invited six comments on Fukuyama's article and they were published in the same issue. Some of the questions that arise from these comments are interesting. Can the West remain unaffected by war and poverty in the rest of the world (Hassner 1989)? Can the United States remain unaffected by its problems within, such as the problem of black poverty (Himmelfarb 1989) or the problem that arises from its practice of democracy (Kristol 1989)? Can we overlook the increasing salience of ethnicity in industrial societies (Moynihan 1989)? Yet another question can be formulated in the context of the recent book of Fukuyama (2002) on the consequences of the biotechnology revolution. Is the thesis regarding the end of history sustainable considering that scientific advancement has not ended? Indeed, he seems to be in favour of regulation in the face of what unregulated human biotechnology can mean to all of us. As far as the will of the United States is concerned (to which Fukuyama approvingly refers), it has not always been beneficial for the rest of the world. This is well illustrated by *The National Security Strategy of the United States* of President George W. Bush where the 'pre-emptive' action of the United States is contemplated in the defence of 'freedom, democracy and free enterprise', serving American values and interests (White House 2002).

The convergence theory has been criticised for upholding technological imperatives and neglecting historical contingencies. Indeed, some of the criticism brought earlier against the modernisation theory has been brought against the views of the 'globalists'. Many points of criticism against their views can be seen as the error of simplification. Heterogeneity arising out of different historical and contemporary contexts is overlooked, just as the fact that the same policy prescriptions when implemented in different contexts have widely varying outcomes depending on the nature of economic and political institutions is ignored (Green and Griffith 2002). The error of simplification gets expressed in terms of not only unrecognised heterogeneity and divergence but also the unrecognised issue of conflict. One of the biggest problems that globalisation is faced with is the confrontation between 'globalised culture' and heterogeneous societies with different cultures, languages and historical experiences. The fear of cultural erosion is apparent not just in the developing world but the developed world as well, especially Europe (Friedman 1994). The spread of the culture of fast-food restaurants of American origin ('McDonaldization' as in Ritzer 1996) and one language (English) through global empires of mass media have given rise to resistance and protests that try to assert regional, ethnic or religious identities in opposition to this process of integration. In the developing world the resistance takes the form of communal or fundamentalist movements that try to resist integration, at times through violent means, and retreat to 'purer' and more exclusive forms or religious identities (Appadurai 1998; Barber 1996). While the impact of many of these movements is largely confined within the nation-state, they do spill over into conflict with other states and cultures. An important thesis in this regard is the thesis of the clash of civilisations (Huntington 1996). In the developed world assertion of identity usually takes the form of protests against immigration as an effort to protect domestic cultures by trying to keep out those who are dissimilar—the other.

Yet another error that can be identified is the error arising out of the neglect of power and political choice. Globalisation of domestic policy has had a detrimental effect on the location of political and economic power within nations. The increasing loss of domestic sovereignty caused by the expanding power of multilateral financial institutions such as the International Monetary Fund (IMF) and the World Bank, or multilateral trading institutions such as the WTO, has meant national governments ceding some of their powers relating to economic and social policy-making without being able to ensure that procedures are in place to guarantee that these decisions are arrived at democratically (Atik 2001). Ideally, officials representing national governments involved in the policy-making process of these multilateral organisations should present national concerns. But the process of 'political capture' has often been at work to ensure that negotiating positions taken by bureaucrats representing national governments reflect not national concerns but the concerns of special interest groups who are effective in lobbying governments (Anderson and Cavenagh 2000). The choices that are foisted on many developing countries deny any voice to civil society in general, and marginalised groups in particular, in the policies that are to be implemented, apparently for their benefit. It is this 'democratic deficit' in decision-making processes both within nations and multilateral institutions that has led to a large number of protests. Anti-globalisation protests that were seen in Seattle, Davos, Genoa and most recently in Washington reflect concerns at a global level regarding the level of democracy both nationally and internationally (Desai and Said 2001). Groups belonging to civil society express concern over the fact that, while globalisation was supposed to have helped the poor escape from chronic poverty, the benefits of globalisation have gone to an affluent few. Nearly a quarter of the population of the world continues to live in poverty, with indications that the condition of the poorest has deteriorated. It is important to take the warning of Joseph Stiglitz (2002) seriously: 'If globalization continues to be conducted in the way that it has been in the past, if we continue to fail to learn from our mistakes, globalization will not only not succeed in promoting development, but will continue to create poverty and instability' (p. 248).

The errors of simplification and the neglect of the issue of power and political choice lead to the unresolved issue of the role of the state. While discussing the problem of defining the role of the state in the context of reforms, John Kenneth Galbraith (1973) once said, 'The role of the government, when one contemplates reform, is a dual one. The government is a major part of the problem; it is also central to the remedy' (p. 242). Ever since the rise of the neo-liberal political forces in the West in the late 1970s and early 1980s, the state as an institution has been seen as a problem, not as a part of the remedy. The idea, initially put forward by Margaret Thatcher in Britain and by Ronald Reagan in the United States, that the all-pervasive state was stifling individual initiative and hindering economic progress, grew increasingly popular as the 1980s progressed (Robinson 2001). This position does not recognise that the state is confronted with three different challenges in the face of globalisation. First, the ability of the states to maintain expensive welfare systems is restricted by globalisation and the need to keep costs low, though some states have done better than others in this respect (Garrett 1998). Second, the state is often unable to respond positively to demands placed on it by domestic constituencies because it has surrendered the power to take such decisions to multilateral institutions (Sassen 1996). Third, the devolution of power to regional or federal units means that the benefits of economic growth may flow unevenly to different regions of the same nation-state (Sala 1994). The power of the nation-state is 'eroding from above by globalisation and from below by devolution' (Ostry 1998). On the relevance of the state it is important to consider the views of Eric Hobsbawm (1996). He has argued that the state is becoming even more relevant as the process of market-led globalisation moves further ahead. As a greater proportion of newly created wealth flows into the hands of a small minority, the role of the state in the equitable distribution of wealth becomes more important than ever. Others have suggested that though the state has shed some of its power to market forces, the state and the market are complementary institutions and this calls for a constant review of the relationship between them (Bhaduri and Nayyar 1996). A changed role of the state is not to be confused with a reduced role of the state. It is instructive to read Elmar Altvater and Birgit Mahnkopf (2002) on this point.

THE ISSUE OF GOOD GOVERNANCE

With the end of the Cold War the term 'good governance' came into circulation, which signified prescriptions by donor agencies for carrying out economic and political reforms by recipient countries. These prescriptions were presented by international donor agencies such as the World Bank and the IMF as 'conditionalities' and were expected to be met with compliance. They have proved controversial. Barber Conable (1991), who was the President of the World Bank in the early 1990s, emphasised four objectives that had to be achieved for increasing economic growth. They were: increased government investment in education, health care and nutrition; greater competition in domestic markets; greater integration of the domestic economy with the global economy; and the creation of a stable macro-economic environment.

It is remarkable that the recommendations of the World Bank and the IMF mirror neo-liberal economic principles that were popular in the United States throughout the 1980s. Thus, competition in the domestic economy is to be achieved by privatising state monopolies and removing barriers to foreign investment. While integration of the domestic economy with the global economy is to be achieved by lowering or eliminating tariff and non-tariff trade barriers, a stable macro-economic environment is to be created by reducing budget deficits through the reduction of subsidies and welfare spending. Increased investment in social services is to be funded by resources obtained from privatisation of state enterprises and reduction in subsidies. Many analysts in the developing world have argued that the World Bank and the IMF are trying to impose Western neo-liberal economic policies on economies which are not yet ready for them (Guhan 1998). Their prescriptions have been the same for all countries in spite of their differences in terms of economic and social development, or type of governmental system. This 'one world consensus' has generated controversy with many suspecting the motives that underlie these prescriptions (Waelbroeck 1998). Some argue that the linking of development assistance to implementation of neo-liberal economic policies is an attempt to 'ideologise' the development process in the developing world (Mishra and Mishra 2002). The concept has even been seen as a 'symbol of recolonisation and new Imperialism' (Bandyopadhyay 1996). Though the World Bank and the IMF are not expected to interfere in the internal political processes of member states, many of the conditionalities involve not just economic reform but political reform as well. Officials of the World Bank and the IMF insist that these reforms are necessary if their economic mandate is to be fulfilled. According to Michael Camdessus (1998), a former Director, 'the IMF's role in governance issues has been evolving over the years, and good governance has taken on increasing importance in our traditional mandate of promoting economic stability and what I call high-quality growth'. The fact that both the World Bank and the IMF prescribe almost the same conditions for aid also reflects the remarkable unanimity of views within the developed world about the direction that economic policy in the developing world should take. The structure of the World Bank and the IMF and the distribution of voting rights within its decision-making structures mean that decisions are in effect taken by the countries of the Organisation for Economic Cooperation and Development (OECD). Neo-liberal economic policies have, however, not been confined to the agenda of the World Bank and the IMF. A greater emphasis on neo-liberal economic reform is apparent in prescriptions for economic growth that have been made by institutions in the developed world as well. The OECD recommendations on economic policy have included decentralisation of government authority, privatisation of some of its activities, introduction of better cost-effective ways of delivering services, such as contracting out of government services, and the use of market mechanisms to improve competition (Lewis 1998).

Yet another context in which the term governance appears is in the discussion of 'progressive governance' in the United States. It proved successful in the presidential campaign of Bill Clinton. In response to the demands of the 'new economy', the Democratic Leadership Council (DLC) proposed that 'the free market, regulated in the public interest, is the best engine of general prosperity' (DLC 1990). Later, it was clarified that progressive governance sought 'a third choice that replaces the left's reflexive defense of the bureaucratic status quo and counters the right's destructive bid to simply dismantle government' (DLC 1996). The progressive governance move sought to respond to the major challenges posed to the traditional state by globalisation (Latham 1998). The third choice became the Third Way in Europe, especially under the leadership of Tony

Blair. It seeks to go beyond neo-liberalism and traditional social democracy, and recognising that redistributive policies favoured by the traditional welfare state are no longer sustainable, accepts a higher level of economic inequality. Although it aims to offer equality of opportunity, civic participation and inclusion as a substitute for the reduced emphasis on equitable distribution of wealth, it does not place any great emphasis on social justice (Ehrke 2000). Ralf Dahrendorf (1999) has something interesting to say on this point:

> Overall, the Third Way project has been described as a combination of neoliberal economics and social democratic social policy. That is not entirely fair. In some ways the key feature of this approach is implicit rather than explicit: its optimism. I call this "globalization plus"—accepting the needs of global markets but adding key elements of social well-being (p. 14).

The two contexts of governance identified here are related to the process of globalisation. While the donor perspective is directed towards greater integration of the domestic economy of recipient countries with the global economy, the concern with progressive governance is in important ways directed towards coping with globalisation in a manner that cushions its impact. Just as the proponents of globalisation promote the idea of homogenisation, advocates of reforms for good governance also provide homogeneous prescriptions. The major problem with such prescriptions is that they do not apply to different situations equally well. In a study of international and aboriginal perspectives on good governance, Tim Plumptre and John Graham (1999) indicate the problem of applying attributes of good governance to different situations.

> The emphasis given to different aspects of sound governance will vary in different settings because societies value outcomes differently. For example, in more utilitarian Western cultures, great store may be placed on efficiency. Elsewhere, a desire for harmony and consensus may override this value. Similarly, some cultures will give primacy to individual rights whereas others will place more stress on communal obligations. Some will accord priority to the 'objective' application of the rule of law, while others may accord more weight to tradition and clan in decisions. Some societies may see economic

growth as their primary goal while others may accord more importance to cultural richness and diversity. Determining what constitutes 'good governance' thus leads to a debate on values and cultural norms, and on desired social and economic outcomes. This in turn leads to questions about the role of government, how governments should relate to citizens, relationships between legislative, executive and judicial branches of government, and the roles of different sectors (pp. 11–12).

HONOURING HETEROGENEITY: AN ALTERNATIVE VIEW

If the *homogenisation thesis* lends itself to criticism because of prescriptions that are based on the error of simplification, then the first step towards gaining clarity is to take note of the complexity. This complexity is not only characterised by what is present but also by what is lacking. Our contributors note this complexity at societal, institutional and corporate levels and across different spheres. The European situation presents complexity. At the level of the European Union, as De Swaan shows, a 'peculiar political construct' has come into existence of which a special feature is that no European public space exists as yet. Europeans speak different languages and carry out debates within their respective national frameworks. This creates a 'democratic deficit' where policies are formulated without politics, without public participation or partisan moves by political representatives. In the discussion on De Swaan's paper, Jha observed that the absence of public space and political discussion was also to be observed at the international level in policy prescriptions by agencies such as the World Bank and the IMF. Liberatore confirms that a certain degree of homogeneity that is assumed by most notions of 'demos' is lacking in the European Union. The experience of the European Union, moreover, shows that democracy may be reached through diverse paths. This should lead to respect for diversity. In his chapter, Martell discusses divergences within the Third Way over issues such as community, inclusion and equality and argues that the Third Way agenda will be different in different countries. This is because, in spite of globalisation, national differences matter and different countries follow different models of capitalism. The complexity of the Indian situation gets expressed, as Sinha shows, in such terms as the insufficient transformation of economy and society, the failure of good, or even functional governance, and yet the persistence of democratic practice. Indeed, if Jha is followed, it is in the very structure of Indian democracy that the growing 'ungovernability' of India is embedded. Mathur pointed out during the discussion that instability in India was due to the contradiction between political and economic spheres. Marginal groups that were gaining access to political participation were still denied economic participation. He was of the opinion that economic reforms were unlikely to succeed because the reform agenda was not in congruence with our ethos.

A number of chapters in this book discuss the heterogeneous nature of societies and institutions where reforms are being attempted, and the impact of this heterogeneity on the process of reforms itself. Responding to the Anglo-Saxon model which enjoys hegemony in the field, Wollmann takes a broad comparative view and considers the convergence theory which maintains that the forces of globalisation are leading to homogenisation across countries. While accepting that powerful forces are at work in this direction, especially in view of the role of such international bodies as the World Bank and the OECD, he argues that country-specific features such as institutional and cultural boundaries have their impact, and this will persist. Going into the German case in the context of the European experience, Roeber argues that even with respect to one country it is important to take a differentiated view. Thus, the situation in Germany varies at different levels of government with local government having taken a lead in administrative reforms in comparison with what has been achieved at the levels of the state and the federal government. During the discussion that followed the presentation of his paper, Roeber highlighted the political context of public administration. While public administration performs its public role, its functions are based on law. Abraham also writes in his chapter that administrative reforms depend largely on the constitutional and institutional context within which they take place. They cannot be understood outside this context. Agnihotri and Dar point out that in the implementation of administrative reforms in India, the states seem to have done better than the central government.

At the corporate level, Seth takes a comparative view and argues that only by understanding how and why governance systems came into existence as they did in different national contexts can we develop a suitable yardstick for measuring the appropriateness of different reform initiatives. Bhattacharyya says in his chapter that institutions that are developed to protect the interests of financiers are influenced by the ownership structure of publicly traded companies and also by the stage of economic development and the culture and ethos of a society. One reason why there is interest in studying corporate governance is the lack of uniformity in this respect in different countries. With respect to Germany, Schmidt shows that, while under the impact of globalisation German corporate governance is undergoing change, resistance to this change comes from traditional German practices of cooperative structure based on the principles of co-determination, delegation and trust. The chapter by Abell and Reyniers is interesting in this context. They analyse the participation by employed labour in both the management and the ownership of productive assets of the firms, highlighting the inherent difficulties in establishing its inferiority or superiority in terms of efficiency and performance over traditional capitalist firms. In the discussion that took place after the paper was presented, Roeber noted the decline of such practices in Germany and elsewhere in view of low returns. One of the participants, however, said that this model was still valid and there were successful examples in India.

The error of simplification includes the unrecognised issue of conflict of interests. The presence of conflict is highlighted with respect to the Indian situation. Munshi brings into discussion Gunnar Myrdal's concept of the 'soft state' and asks the question: Can good governance be built on the basis of inequalities, vested interests in the status quo and indiscipline? Jha argues that there is a need to break the nexus between bad money and politics that lies at the heart of the 'predator' state. Mathur sees the need for political will for the success of administrative reforms in India. It is possible to misuse power by resisting change and demand for transparency. Dar noted in the discussion that the bureaucracy was equally responsible for the failure to implement administrative reforms. The administrative will to carry out reforms was needed.

This brings the role of the state into discussion. While the European Union is almost a world power, but without any military power or an effective foreign policy (De Swaan), or put differently, while it might appear to be a sort of 'supra state' without specific features associated with the state (Liberatore), at the level of the nation-state the concern with the state is more direct. It is in this context that the

Third Way becomes important. For the Britain of Blair the Third Way means going 'beyond old left and new right' which tries to match rights and responsibilities (Martell). As he said in the discussion on his paper, while the Third Way eases the transition brought by globalisation, globalist social democracy would be difficult to attain within the European Union, much less globally. In India the discussion needs to go beyond the issue of market freedom against state intervention (Munshi, Sinha). In this context, Dar mentioned during the discussion that in a situation where the state has not fulfilled its responsibilities, non-state organisations have a positive role to play. Rajan argues in his chapter that the social space that has opened up today offers an opportunity for all players, including activists, to work together on community issues. While there is awareness about the role of non-governmental organisations (NGOs), Mathur expressed his fear that this might mean their co-option into the government machinery as delivery agents.

The role of global institutions is important. Sinha observes that global economic integration involves some form of global governance, though present institutions, influenced as they are by the Washington Consensus, are not in a position to ensure equity and sustainability. The need for global institutions is also stressed by De Vincentiis who argues in her chapter that there is a need for supranational surveillance of the working of the global financial system. Competition leads to increased concentration and consolidation. Once the consolidation battle is over the danger arises that the global groups will exploit their world market power in a traditional oligopolistic fashion. This is the reason why many recognise that global competition laws, enforced by a supranational competition authority, dealing with issues such as anti-trust and abuse of dominant positions are required.

Two conceptual points need to be mentioned that arise out of this effort to honour heterogeneity. Noting that evaluation is involved in good governance, Munshi provides a middle ground between the arbitrariness of subjective evaluations and the excesses of objectivism by his concept of 'reflective evaluation'. It is the principle of thinking through one's value position and practice as a social actor, and it differs from conventional evaluation, particularly with respect to the criteria of evaluation which are not brought from outside but are drawn from the consensus of those directly involved. Reed provides in his chapter a conceptual analysis of corporate governance. It attempts to fulfil the goal of identifying the nature of the disputes in the field by first distinguishing between three basic approaches to the analysis of corporate governance and then identifying the issues that arise within each of these approaches. In taking up this goal, the underlying intent is to facilitate interaction and greater mutual understanding both within and across the different disciplines which take up the analysis of corporate governance. Finally, it is useful to go back to Liberatore who refers to the European experience and proposes for consideration, among others, the commonality and diversity of democratic systems for the purpose of global governance. If the Indian Union has already achieved what the European Union is struggling hard to achieve (Munshi), then it can also be said that this subcontinent torn by strife has much to learn from the European Union. The comparison between India and Europe holds out much promise at both the academic and policy levels. There is much to learn from each other.

NOTE

1. This introduction was circulated among all the contributors who were kind enough to offer us their comments. These comments were rather detailed in some cases. We are grateful for this benefit, even though we could not do equal justice to all the comments that we received, especially due to the constraints of space.

REFERENCES

Altvater, Elmar and Mahnkopf, Birgit. 2002. *Grenzen der Globalisierung: Oekonomie, Oekologie und Politik in der Weltgesellschaft*. Muenster: Wesfaelisches Dampfboot.

Anderson, Sarah and Cavenagh, John. 2000. *Top 200: The Rise of Corporate Global Power*. Washington, D.C.: Institute for Policy Studies.

Appadurai, Arjun. 1998. 'Dead Certainty: Ethnic Violence in the Era of Globalisation'. *Development and Change*, 29: 905–25.

Atik, Jeffrey. 2001. 'Democratising the WTO'. *The George Washington International Law Review*, 31: 451–72.

Barber, Benjamin R. 1996. *Jihad vs. McWorld: How the World is both Falling Apart and Coming Together—And What This Means for Democracy*. New York: Times Books.

Bandyopadhyay, D. 1996. 'Administration, Decentralisation and Good Governance'. *Economic and Political Weekly*, 31(44): 3109–14.

Berthoud, Gerald. 1997. 'Market', in Wolfgang Sachs (ed.). *The Development Dictionary: A Guide to Knowledge as Power*, pp. 94–117. Hyderabad: Orient Longman.

Bhaduri, Amit and Nayyar, Deepak. 1996. *The Intelligent Person's Guide to Liberalization*. New Delhi: Penguin.

Bhagwati, Jagdish. 2000. 'Globalization: A Moral Imperative'. *The Courier*, pp. 19–20. Paris: UNESCO.

Camdessus, Michael. 1998. 'The IMF and Good Governance'. Address to *Transparency International*. Paris. 21 January.

Conable, Barber. 1991. 'Foreword', in World Bank. *World Development Report 1991: The Challenge of Development*. New York: Oxford University Press.

Dahrendorf, Ralf. 1999. 'The Third Way and Liberty', *Foreign Affairs*, 78(5): 13–18.

Desai, Meghnad and Said, Yahia. 2001. 'The New Anti-Capitalist Movement: Money and Global Civil Society', in H. Anheir, M. Glasius and M. Kaldor (eds). *Global Civil Society 2001*, pp. 51–78. Oxford: Oxford University Press.

Democratic Leadership Council (DLC). 1990. *The New Orleans Declaration of 1990: Statement endorsed at the Fourth Annual Democratic Leadership Council Conference*. Available online at *http://www.ndol.org/*.

————. 1996. *The New Progressive Declaration: A Political Philosophy for the Information Age*.

Ehrke, Michael. 2000. 'Revision Revisited: The Third Way and European Social Democracy'. *Concepts and Transformation*, 5(1): 7–27.

Friedman, Jonathan. 1994. *Cultural Identity and Global Process*. London: Sage.

Friedman, Thomas. 1999. *The Lexus and the Olive Tree*. New York: Farrar Straus & Giroux.

Fukuyama, F. 1989. 'The End of History'. *The National Interest*, 16: 3–18.

————. 2001. 'The West has Won'. *The Guardian*. 11 October.

————. 2002. *Our Posthuman Future: Consequences of the Biotechnology Revolution*. New York: Farrar Straus & Giroux.

Galbraith, John K. 1973. *Economics and the Public Purpose*. Boston: Houghton Mifflin.

Garrett, Geoffrey. 1998. *Partisan Politics in the Global Economy*. New York: Cambridge University Press.

Gates, Bill. 1995. *The Road Ahead*. New York: Viking.

————1999. *Business@the Speed of Thought*. New York: Viking.

Green, Duncan and Griffith, Mathew. 2002. 'Globalization and its Discontents'. *International Affairs*, 78(1): 49–68.

Guhan, S. 1998. 'World Bank on Governance: A Critique'. *Economic and Political Weekly*, 33(4): 185–92.

Hassner, Pierre. 1989. 'Responses to Fukuyama'. *The National Interest*, 16: 22–24.

Himmelfarb, Gertrude. 1989. 'Responses to Fukuyama'. *The National Interest*, 16: 24–26.

Hobsbawm, E.J. 1996. 'The Future of the State'. *Development and Change*, 27: 267–78.

Huntington, Samuel P. 1996. *The Clash of Civilisations and the Remaking of the World Order*. New York: Simon and Schuster.

Kerr, Clark. 1960. *Industrialism and Industrial Man: The Problems of Labour and Management in Economic Growth*. Cambridge, M.A.: Harvard University Press.

Kristol, Irwing. 1989. 'Responses to Fukuyama'. *The National Interest*, 16: 26–28.

Latham, Mark. 1998. 'Economic Policy and the Third Way'. *The Australian Economic Review*, 31(4): 384–98.

Lewis, Norman Douglas. 1998. 'Good Governance: The UK Experience'. *Indian Journal of Public Administration*, XLIV (3): 616–25.

Mishra, S.N. and Mishra, Sweta. 2002. *Decentralised Governance*. Delhi: Shipra Publications.

Moynihan, Daniel Patrick. 1989. 'Responses to Fukuyama'. *The National Interest*, 16: 28–32.

Nayyar, Deepak. 2001. 'Globalization: What Does it Mean?', in K.S. Jomo and Shyamala Nagaraj (eds). *Globalization versus Development*, pp. 1–25. London: Palgarave.

Ostry, Slyvia. 1998. 'Globalization and the Nation-state: Erosion From Above'. *Timlin Lecture*. Regina: University of Saskatchewan.

Plumptre,Tim and Graham, John. 1999. *Governance and Good Governance: International and Aboriginal Perspective*. Canberra: Institute of Governance.

Ritzer, G. 1996. *The McDonaldization of Society*. Thousand Oaks, California: Pine Forge Press.

Robinson, William L. 2001. 'Social Theory and Globalization: The Rise of the Transnational State'. *Theory & Society*, 30: 157–200.

Sala, Vincent Della. 1994. 'Capital Blight? The Regulation of Financial Institutions in Italy and Canada'. *Governance: An International Journal of Policy & Administration*, 7(3): 244–64.

Sassen, Saskia. 1996. *Losing Control: Sovereignty in the Age of Globalization*. New York: Columbia University Press.

Stiglitz, Joseph. 2002. *Globalization and its Discontents*. London: Penguin.

Waelbroeck, J. 1998. 'Half a Century of Development Economics'. *The World Bank Economic Review*, 12(2): 323–52.

White House. 2002. *The National Security Strategy of the United States*. Washington, D.C.: US Government Publishing Office.

THE SOCIETAL CONTEXT OF GOVERNANCE

PART 1

THE SOCIAL CONTEXT OF GOVERNANCE

Three chapters in this part are devoted to Europe (De Swaan, Liberatore, Martell), two are devoted to India (Sinha, Jha), and the opening chapter (Munshi) is meant to provide an overview of the theme in comparative perspective.

Munshi locates the theme of good governance in Indian debate and also in the context of reinventing government. The debate in India on this point has considered, often critically, the stand of the World Bank on good governance. The issue of the legitimacy of the state and its role has also been raised, especially after the reforms introduced since 1991. The approach of reinventing government that was popularised in the United States by an influential publication in 1992 emphasised the need for bringing management into government and upheld 'the entrepreneurial spirit' for maximising productivity and effectiveness. It gave rise to the politics of the 'third choice' which became the Third Way in Europe. The 'three for the Third Way' were identified as Clinton, Blair and Schroeder. Munshi reconsiders the concept of good governance and notes that this concept does not lend itself to a normatively neutral treatment. He offers the principle of 'reflective evaluation' as a solution to the problem of arbitrariness of subjective evaluations and the excesses of objectivism. He concludes his chapter with a definition of good governance that is presented as an outcome of his analysis in this contested area.

De Swaan examines social, cultural and linguistic affairs in the European Union. He argues that policy in the European Union in many important fields is either the result of 'non-decision-making' or of seemingly neutral administrative implementation of general treaty principles. The first applies to the precarious field of language policy in the Union, where it can be shown that no stable decision is feasible. The second applies to social policy. Many rather sweeping measures like equality for male and female employees or the option to receive benefits or pensions when resident in other member countries seem to derive solely from the 'consistent' application of fundamental rules such as 'equal treatment' and 'free movement'. Cultural affairs are expressly left to the member states on the basis of the principle of subsidiarity, but are nevertheless dealt with indirectly as in trade matters or language issues. The Union does not interfere with the moral regimes in national societies that differ from the European pattern: they are eroded by the free movement of persons across borders (e.g., abortion or alcohol or even soft drugs). This is explained, in part, by the absence in the Union of politics in the sense of public debate and civil participation. A European public space does not exist yet. Political debate is almost entirely defined by national frontiers and barriers of language and culture.

Liberatore's chapter tries to simplify the complexity of the 'governance' debate by examining a specific context, the European Union, and a specific policy initiative, the White Paper on Governance issued by the European Commission in 2001. It keeps in focus the links between 'governance' and 'democracy'. Such links are not obvious and, in addition, take specific features in a supranational context such as the European Union. She examines the distinction between 'good governance' and 'democratic governance' and using the distinction between 'input legitimacy' and 'output legitimacy' describes some aspects of the White Paper, some responses to it and follow-up initiatives. The chapter discusses six issues: the relationship between representative institutions and civil society; possible trade-off between participation, efficiency and effectiveness; expertise and democracy; conditions for accountability and the chain of accountability; citizenship, 'demos' and public space; and governance, democracy and sustainable development. Some reflections are also offered on the relevance of such debate for global governance and the role of Europe in the international context.

Martell examines in his chapter the meaning of the Third Way and its relationship to the first and second ways, the old left and the new right. He outlines changing economic and social circumstances that have led to it and sketches out its values. His chapter discusses what the Third Way envisages in terms of the role for government and the balance between private and public provision. The chapter shows how there are divergences within the Third Way or rather between third ways over issues such as community, inclusion and equality. It argues that the Third Way combines left and right rather than goes beyond them, and that it accepts much of the ground laid by the new right but is not simply the continuation of neo-liberalism. At the same time the Third Way redefines as much as renews social democracy. Different attitudes to the Third Way in Europe are also discussed. Many governments in Europe are addressing comparable third-way agendas but differences in national institutions and cultures mean such agendas will turn out differently in different places. The Third Way is received differently in different countries as is shown by, for example, different responses to the Blair–Schroeder paper and to globalisation in Britain and Europe. Blair's Third Way may be too biased towards laissez-faire Anglo-American capitalism for many other governments in Europe.

Sinha argues in his chapter that compulsions emanating from global economic trends, along with a disillusionment about the government's interventionist role in development strategies, have led to a resurgence of faith in market-driven growth in a number of countries around the world. This tendency has been more pronounced since the collapse of the Soviet Union. India also embarked on a market-friendly strategy of development and initiated a series of policy reforms since 1991. The debate about development has shifted from national planning and industrial policy controls to facilitating markets and free trade. In the context of the changing contours of the debate, the role of the state and the range and quality of governance have received attention. Sinha's chapter addresses some basic issues pertaining to governance in India. The first issue is one of redefining the role of the state in a market-friendly environment. The second issue is how the transition to new and more effective governance mechanisms can be brought about in terms of legal and institutional structures. The third issue relates to locating market-friendly governance mechanisms in an age of international market integration that has a propensity to erode the autonomy of the nation-state. It is argued that a sense of equity and sustainability lies at the core of good governance in the age of globalisation. It is also argued that economic integration necessarily entails some version of global governance. However, the mechanism of global governance does not ensure that equity and sustainability are ensured.

Jha draws attention in his chapter to the political crisis facing the Indian Republic. He argues that this crisis is systemic. The central government has lost the power to govern due to the failings of the political and constitutional system. This growing ungovernability is embedded in the structure of Indian democracy. The very features of the Indian Constitution that were responsible for the success of nation-building during the first four decades of independence in India have become the main threats to it in the fifth decade. India succeeded in building a modern nation-state through democracy and the working of its federal system. As long as a single dominant party ruled the centre, there was a healthy balance between nation-building and ethnic accommodation. However, with the collapse of single-party governance at the centre and the separation of central elections from state elections, the balance between the two has been lost. India has become a classic example of the predator state. The developmental state in India can be restored by first restoring the power to govern to the central government, and second by breaking the nexus between bad money and politics that lies at the heart of the predator state. Jha suggests constitutional reforms for reuniting the central and state elections to ensure greater stability at the centre, and the reform of electoral finance to break the nexus between bad money, crime and politics for bringing back the developmental state in India.

CHAPTER 2

CONCERN FOR GOOD GOVERNANCE IN COMPARATIVE PERSPECTIVE

SURENDRA MUNSHI[1]

GOOD GOVERNANCE IN INDIAN DEBATE

In a critique of the approach of the World Bank to the issue of governance, S. Guhan (1998) points out that to define governance as 'the exercise of political power to manage a nation's affairs' carries neutrality too far. It allows both 'good' and 'bad' governance to qualify in so far as political will is exercised in the management of those affairs. True, the World Bank has elaborated later its conception of governance in terms of economic role for the state, a set of 'policy reforms' and other non-economic aspects such as transparency, accountability, participation, and responsiveness in the process of government. These features do not yet add up to a concern for the acceptable form of government. What the World Bank desires is an open economy, not necessarily an open polity. This is unacceptable, for to Guhan 'an open liberal democracy is the non-negotiable bedrock of what good governance must mean'. The second issue relates to democracy and development. Apart from its own intrinsic value, democracy could also have a positive relationship with human development. The criticism, then, of the World Bank is that 'it has not chosen, in clear and ringing tones, to take a stand against authoritarian regimes and squarely in favour of democratic ones' (Guhan 1998: 186). Other points of criticism can now be noted. The functional role of the state and the type of reforms that have been spelled out make it clear that what is of primary concern to the World Bank is the extent to which market replaces government. This raises a number of issues. The blueprint that the World Bank provides is 'narrowly techno-economic'. It is also not clear how useful standard prescriptions for liberalisation are going to be, especially in view of the fact that the evidence in favour of these prescriptions is far from conclusive. The World Bank falls back in the final analysis on the 'conditionalities' that it can impose through its lending operations. This is often seen as 'falling in line' on the part of developing societies. Finally, the World Bank is yet to recognise that governance at the national level cannot be separated from governance at the international level.

Guhan concludes by observing that the World Bank is capable of distorting the word 'governance', something that has already happened to two other mantras of the World Bank, 'economic reforms' and 'structural adjustment'. D. Bandyopadhyay (1996) expressed a concern of this kind earlier:

> I commend the concept of 'good governance' in its simple English meaning. But I have a strong objection to the term as it is being touted in recent years by multilateral and bilateral aid agencies as a part of precondition of aid or as a process of reform as condition of aid (p. 3109).

The paradox of neutrality as ideology where what appears as neutral at one level is seen as ideological at another can be discerned from these comments. Both Guhan and Bandyopadhyay question the credentials of the World Bank and the efficacy of its prescriptions from the point of view of developing societies. Indeed, they argue that governance is under threat conceptually and concretely by that very agency which appears to promote it.

The perception of threat has come in India from other sources as well. This can be seen from a number of books that have appeared during recent years. Rajni Kothari (1988) notes that in the period of social and political erosion during the last decade or so there has been a decline in the legitimacy of the state.

> It is the polarisation between a State increasingly unwilling to carry out its constitutional obligations and a people not knowing who else to turn to that is setting the stage for the growing incidence of violence, injustice, destruction of moderate modes

of dissent and articulation of people's discontent and disenchantment (p. iii).

Atul Kohli (1991) questions the ability of the state to maintain order and create conditions for the eradication of the unresolved problem of poverty. Bhabani Sen Gupta (1996) takes up this concern and writes that 'the crisis of governance is by and large written with the ink of political failure' (p. 41). This political failure is viewed in different ways, especially with reference to political parties that participate in democracy but are themselves undemocratic, and the growing hiatus between 'power' and 'people'.

The awareness of crisis in governance has come from the civil service as well. In November 1996, a conference of Chief Secretaries of all the states and union territories was held in New Delhi. The theme of the conference, inaugurated by the Prime Minister and presided over by the Cabinet Secretary, was 'An Agenda for Effective and Responsive Administration'. The three main areas of concern in this conference were ensuring administrative accountability, eliminating corruption in the civil service from within and making civil service more committed to the principles of the Constitution. A 'Discussion Note' for the conference, prepared by the Department of Administrative Reforms and Public Grievances of the Ministry of Personnel, Public Grievances and Pensions, New Delhi, November 1996, spells out these concerns (DARPG 1996a).

They are spelled out in the context of the recognised need for the government to be more 'caring and responsive', taking into account the requirements of economic growth as well as social justice. It is noted that the civil service in India, as a major instrument of the government, central as well as state, has a positive role to play even in this era of liberalisation. This role cannot be played well unless the civil service is restructured and reoriented, more so when it is generally perceived negatively by the people, especially by those who are not privileged. The civil service suffers from demoralisation, resulting in its failure at different levels. There is a need to overcome the 'eroded credibility and effectiveness' of the civil service. The accountability of the civil service requires going beyond performing assigned tasks and developing a 'consumer orientation to administration'. In view of the growing public perception that corruption in high places is on the increase and a nexus between politicians, criminals and bureaucrats exists, the value of governance is undermined. Attention has to be given to organisational as well as individual factors for cleaning up the civil service. Finally, it is noted, there is a need to adhere to the principles of the Constitution, such as secularism, justice and the rule of law. The Conference of Chief Secretaries endorsed the 'Discussion Note' and emphasised the urgent need for 'corrective efforts to arrest the present drift'. It was recognised that public confidence has to be restored and the public has to be empowered and involved at all levels. The admission of 'the crisis in administration' was clearly made. A document issued after the Conference lists the recommendations made by Chief Secretaries. These recommendations are listed under three headings: 'Responsive Administration', 'Cleansing the Civil Service' and 'Commitment to the Principles of the Constitution' (DARPG 1996b). The statement adopted at the Conference of Chief Ministers held on 24 May 1997 clearly expresses 'the need for ensuring responsive, accountable, transparent and people-friendly administration at all levels' and the need for 'necessary corrective steps . . . to arrest the present drift in the management of public services' (DARPG 1997: 3).

This brings us to an important issue concerning the Constitution of India. While there has been a serious effort to review the functioning of the Constitution, it is also argued with justification that it is not the Constitution but the manner in which it has been used which is at fault. Bandyopadhyay (1996) clearly states that what is needed for the substance of good governance is not to get influenced by the World Bank, but to 'reorient our economic and social policies on the basis of the principles enshrined in the Constitution' (p. 3114). The Constitution of India recognises the fundamental rights of citizens (Part–II) and also lays down in the part on the 'Directive Principles of State Policy' the principles fundamental to the governance of the country (Part–III). There is a clear recognition in these two parts in the Constitution of individual rights and of the 'the common good'.

To conclude this brief note on the issues that have a bearing on the theme of good governance which has been discussed in India in recent years, it is important to draw attention to the reforms that were introduced in 1991 and the broad manner in which they were discussed. Referring to the cover picture of the survey of the Indian economy that was published in *The Economist* in May 1991, Jean Drèze and Amartya Sen note that the study found the reason for India's economic predicament in 'ever-proliferating bureaucracy' and its 'licence raj'. These reforms did try to remove restrictions and they led to considerable debate in the country. Public opinion was divided, as it still is, between those who favoured market freedom and those who asked for state intervention. There has been a tendency to believe that liberalisation means the retreat of the state. Arguing in favour of taking the debate beyond market versus state, Drèze and Sen (1996) point out:

> While much energy has been spent on sorting out these issues, too little attention has been paid to what is *lacking* in the current orientation of economic policy in India. The removal of counter-productive regulations on domestic production and international trade can form a helpful *part* of a programme of participation and widely-shared growth, but it may achieve relatively little in the absence of more active public policy aimed at reducing the other social handicaps that shackle the Indian economy and reduce the well-being of the population. The absence of real reform in the field of basic education is a telling illustration of the government's neglect of that part of the agenda (pp. 187–88).

GOOD GOVERNANCE IN THE CONTEXT OF REINVENTING GOVERNMENT

At the request of President Bill Clinton, Vice President Al Gore, Jr. reviewed the performance of the federal government of the United States of America in 1993. The purpose of the review, as the title of the report that was submitted in the same year indicates, was to create a government that is result oriented, works better and costs less (Gore 1993). The report notes that only 20 per cent of the American people trust the federal government to act rightly most of the time. To reduce this 'trust deficit' then becomes an important objective of his initiative. For Gore (1994), the way to this goal is shown, as he spells out in the article 'The New Job of the Federal Executive', by two recent developments in management theory which are relevant to both the public and private sectors of management. These are indicated as a shift in the understanding of human capacity and an awareness of the new role of information technology in transforming the manager's job.

Gore notes that the distinction between those who work with their heads and those who work with their muscles that was assumed in the older theory and management hierarchies in actual practice is no longer valid. Drawing from the recent writings of a number of scholars, he argues that an important realisation today is that those who work manually are capable of having new ideas. Thus, organisations are capable of producing more if this potential is realised. The task of the executive, in government and industry alike, is 'to uncover this untapped potential'. With respect to the introduction of 'the information age', he notes that information technology makes it possible, like never before, to share information fast and across larger organisations. 'It is now possible for a president—whether of a company or of a country—to decentralize, yet at the same time keep field operations fully informed and accountable for results' (Gore 1994: 318). These developments together make it possible to transform the nature of management in the federal government. The role of the federal executive within the new management style is noted. It is characterised in the following manner: all employees may now be involved in developing 'a clear vision and a shared sense of mission'; cross-organisational teams may be created to have a more integrated organisation; employees may be empowered; customers may be put first and served the way they want; communication may be directed at all levels, including the level of front-line employees; red tape may be cut as subordinates suggest ways to improve their performance; and accountability may be established taking into account not just inputs but clear results.

Gore identifies two obstacles in having the challenge of change accepted: cynicism and culture. Cynicism shows in the attitude that looks upon this initiative as transitory. Culture refers to that work culture which offers security to federal employees. He argues that the structure of status and reward in the existing work culture 'limits individual accountability and protects against change'. Hence the need for a new culture that may serve 'the public interest'. The need is to 'reinvent government' that sets high levels of quality. Federal executives have a key role to play in this movement. Gore takes the challenge of turning this vision into reality, the vision of 'a reformed national government'. 'Over time', he writes confidently, 'old ways of thinking will fade and will be replaced by a new culture that promotes innovation and quality. A new face of government will appear—of leaders with vision, of employees newly empowered and newly motivated, and of customers newly satisfied' (Gore 1994: 321).

The Gore initiative, taken in the first year of the Clinton Adminis-tration, has produced its critics. The criticism of Peter Drucker (1995) deserves serious attention. Drucker admits that this initiative has produced results. He is yet critical of it because he thinks these results are not more than 'trivial' and that Gore's recommenda-tions, even though many in number, are not new. His main criticism is that the 'basic approach is wrong'. What is needed is not 'patch-ing', nor downsizing. Amputation before diagnosis, he warns, is as wrong in management as in surgery. For a radical change in the ways of the federal government, he recommends the introduction of 'continuous improvement' and 'benchmarking'. These practices, he argues, are of American origin, used first by the Bell Telephone System. They will require a clear statement of objectives regarding performance, quality and cost. More fundamentally, he recommends a change in the basic structure that requires 'rethinking' with the help of questions regarding the organisational mission, the way to redefine it and to pursue it, if at all it is to be retained. Performance or activities need to be evaluated not according to their intentions but according to their results. This brings Drucker to his abiding concern. Reinventing government means to him to question what governments—federal, state and local—can effectively do and what is best left for non-governmental ways to achieve. This does not mean that he subscribes to the view that governments should with-draw from all activities. He concludes:

> By now it has become clear that a developed country can nei-ther extend big government, as the (so-called) liberals want, nor abolish it and go back to 19th century innocence, as the (so-called) conservatives want. The government we need will have to transcend both groups. The megastate that this cen-tury built is bankrupt, morally as well as financially. It has not delivered. But its successor cannot be 'small government'. There are far too many tasks, domestically and internation-ally. We need *effective* government—and that is what the vot-ers in all developed countries are actually clamoring for (Drucker 1995: 15).

The critique of Henry Mintzberg (1996) needs to be taken into consideration now. The article chosen here serves as a critique of Gore and also implicitly of Drucker. He argues that what has triumphed in the West is not 'free enterprise' as against 'subversive' socialism, but rather the balance of different types of organisations, each with its own contribution to society. He identifies four types of organisations for this purpose: privately-owned organisations, those closely held or held in the form of market-traded shares; publicly-owned organisations (more suitably called state owned); cooperatively-owned organisations, such as agricultural cooperatives, mutual insurance companies; cooperative retail chains, and commercial enterprises owned by their employees; and non-owned organisations, frequently referred to as non-government organisations (NGOs) but also non-business and non-cooperative organisations (NBOs and NCOs) such as universities, hospitals, charity organisations, volunteer and activist organisations. To understand his argument it is important to take into account yet another classification that he brings into discussion for the purpose of clarification. In an explicit reference to Gore's official announcement that the American people are their customers, he raises the issue as to whether people relate with their governments as mere customers. We relate with our governments, he argues, under four hats: customer, client, citizen, and subject. While governments offer professional services, such as education, which put us in the role of clients, they provide us in our role as citizens services such as highways, social security and economic policy. Citizens benefit from the public infrastructure that the government provides. To our rights as citizens correspond our obligations as subjects such as of tax payments and of respecting government regulations. We wear more than one hat at times. Thus, for example, prisoners are clearly subjects who yet retain certain rights as citizens and also claims as clients when it comes to their rehabilitation insofar as this service is recognised as necessary. He writes:

> Customers are appropriately served by privately owned organizations, although cooperatively owned ones—such as mutual insurance companies—can often do the job effectively. Only in limited spheres is direct customer service a job for the state. When it comes to citizen and subject activities, we should stray beyond the state-ownership model only with a great deal of prudence. The trade-offs among conflicting interests in citizen activities and the necessary use of authority in subject activities mandate a clear role for the state (Mintzberg 1996: 78).

What about the client relationship? He acknowledges that this is a more complicated area, although his general preference seems to be for non-owned organisations or in certain cases cooperatively owned ones with public funding to ensure some distributional equity.

Mintzberg has turned out to be right about contesting the proposition that governments must become more like businesses. Indeed, the Gore initiative may be seen as part of what has been called the 'paradigm' of new public management or 'entrepreneurial management paradigm' that became fashionable in the Anglo-American world before Clinton assumed office. Indeed, a year before he launched the National Performance Review, a book appeared that made the approach popular under the name *Reinventing Government*. David Osborne and Ted Gaebler (1992) popularised yet another expression for the revolt against bureaucratic malaise, 'the entrepreneurial spirit'. This spirit is described as that of using 'resources in new ways to maximize productivity and effectiveness', or more plainly as that of managing to 'squeeze more bang out of every buck' (Osborne and Gaebler 1992: 35). This is how management is brought into government. The criticism of this approach mainly centres on the position taken by Mintzberg. It has been pointed out that in this approach 'customer' replaces 'citizen' without adequate recognition of the difference between public and private sectors (Savoie 2002). It has also been shown that the problem of bureaucracy in the United States is actually a problem of governance, arising out of the failure of electoral institutions (Meier 2002). Through a close look at the book and a subsequent publication, Daniel W. Williams (2000) concludes that these texts contain certain contradictory ideas and 'little is gained by attempting to apply this model of government'. This does not reduce the celebrity status of the principal author or the popularity of these texts. Osborne served as an advisor to the National Performance Review. His ideas have travelled far. One of the principles that he formulates in his *Reinventing Government* is that of catalytic government that undertakes 'steering rather than rowing'. Williams criticises this principle. He sees in this idea the old controversy of policy versus administration. He notes that the formulation of these functions as dichotomous was generally given up by mid-20th century. Yet it finds place in the Blair and Schroeder paper, 'Europe: The Third Way—Die New Mitte', in the following prescription: 'The state should not row but steer'. Ralf Dahrendorf (1999) finds this statement 'curious', apparently without seeing the connection with Osborne, and adds his own comments. This means that, he writes, 'it will no longer pay for things but will tell people what to do. Certainly, the British experience provides worrying illustrations of what this might mean' (Dahrendorf 1999: 16). Meanwhile, Gore's vision of a new face of government with customers newly satisfied did not find realisation. Research studies show that 'American confidence in government has declined', though this does not mean dissatisfaction with the United States or the democratic form of government (Nye 1997). Through a quarterly time series measure of trust in the national government in the United States from 1980 to 1997, it is found that there is a clear evidence of 'declining public trust in government' (Chanley et al. 2000).

It has been claimed that the idea of going beyond the traditional left debate in the dramatically changed condition of the 'new economy' goes back to Clinton's days as the Governor of Arkansas. It was then that, in a meeting of the Democratic Leadership Council held at New Orleans in 1990, a declaration was issued that came to be known as the New Orleans Declaration. This declaration became the guiding principle of his campaign and later of his presidential administration. This declaration later led to the Hyde Park Declaration when President Clinton looked back with confidence at the idea of a new citizen–government relationship based on a new understanding: opportunity for all, responsibility from all and community of all. This was supposed to be the outlook of the 'New Democrat' who wanted to bring the party closer to the centre to appeal to a wider constituency. New Democrats called for new politics, the politics of the dynamic centre, for the next decade to reflect new realities. Later, with the election of British Prime Minister Tony Blair, it was observed that politicians on both sides of the Atlantic were seeking a new middle ground. Indeed, Clinton, Gore and Blair met in 1997 in New York to find out what they had in common. Similar meetings that were run more like seminars than summits were held later at different places in which German Chancellor Gerhard Schroeder and Italian Prime Minister Romano Prodi also took part. Newsweek (1998) ran a story under the heading 'Three for the Third Way' in which the similarities between Clinton, Blair and Schroeder were pointed out. These similarities are seen by the participants themselves in their effort to define 'progressive governance' for the new century. Conservatives familiar with the ideology of Ronald Reagan, Margaret Thatcher and Helmut Kohl have remained sceptical of the New Way rhetoric. Criticism has come in from the perspective of the left as well. Thus, Alex Callinicos (2001) argues that Blair and Clinton do not challenge the logic of the market, rather they extend it. It is important to note here the criticism of Dahrendorf (1999) who points out the decline in the support for social democrats in Europe and argues that there are multiple ways in an open world, not just three ways. There are differences within the Third Way itself as the 'Rhenish' model differs from the 'Anglo-Saxon' model. As far as the managerialism of new public management is concerned, scholars have pointed out differences in different countries of Europe (Ridley 1996; Wollmann 2000).

RETHINKING GOOD GOVERNANCE

What can we learn from this brief look at the issues that arise from different contexts?

The section on India concluded with a quotation from Drèze and Sen. The distinction that they have drawn between governmental activities that are market complementary (when the state does what the market does not do) and those that are market excluding (when markets are not allowed to operate at all or freely) is important. To this may be added the distinction in governmental activities in terms of regulation and displacement. An argument against the displacement of a legitimate non-governmental activity by a governmental activity is not in itself an argument against regulation, which may in turn be considered in a differentiated manner, say as hard, moderate or soft, or seen differently as in old or new forms. That we cannot do away with all types of regulations is to be recognised. Governments are required to regulate in the public interest. Even when deregulation is on the agenda, new forms of regulation may be required or hard regulations may need to be replaced by soft regulations. This is as true of economic activity as of other areas of social life, such as health, education, environment, and so on. Indeed, past failures are to be assessed and lessons learnt from this assessment in a broader perspective. 'The failures can, thus', argue Drèze and Sen (1996), 'be scarcely seen simply as the result of an "overactive" government. What can be justifiably seen as overactivity in some fields has been inseparably accompanied by thoroughgoing *underactivity* in others' (p. 8). Good governance requires activity, activity that is free from the ills of overactivity and also underactivity.

This has to be taken into account along with three further considerations with respect to administration. It is good to remember what Gunnar Myrdal (1968) noted about three decades ago. He finds in the *Asian Drama* that the 'soft state' of this region is reluctant to push policies through implementation for reasons such as deficiencies in government, social and economic inequalities, and vested interests in the status quo. He also finds the ideal of 'democratic planning' here excludes 'social discipline' (pp. 66–67). This is as true of administration specifically as of the people in general. Discipline is at a discount in offices and also in national life. There is no reason why a democratic society cannot be a disciplined society. The second consideration relates to the broader context of administration. Who will reform those who have the responsibility of reforming the administration? Corruption at all levels and also the erosion of institutions, among which the civil service certainly counts as one of the most important modern institutions, along with the undermining of minimum standards of decent public behaviour are matters of grave concern for this country at this critical juncture. Administration by definition requires a clear determination of who performs what and how. This is to prevent arbitrary action. What is left of administration if arbitrary action motivated by personal or factional interests is imposed on the governmental machinery? What is left of ordered rule or the legitimacy of government in such a situation? The third consideration relates to the question of will. Is there the will to translate words into actions? It is important to keep in mind the distinction between problems arising from poor knowledge and distortions arising from weak or even perverted will. Could it be that good governance is to a large extent a victim of weak or even perverted will? Can good governance be built on the basis of inequalities, vested interests and indiscipline? It is useful to keep in mind that bad governance may be good business for those who stand to gain by it.

It is moreover clear that a narrow administrative view or a narrow managerial view does not adequately address the question of good governance, even though this does not mean internal reforms are not important. Indeed, the effort made by the Department of Administrative Reforms and Public Grievances that led to the conference of Chief Secretaries in November 1996 is to be appreciated. If India faces a crisis of governance that is accentuated by intolerant politics and terrorism, it is not going to be fully resolved by constituting commissions and having them produce long reports. Good governance is a political question as well and the problem also needs to be addressed politically. Both political will and administrative competence are needed for ensuring good governance. The problem has to be approached with an awareness of what is wrong and also what is right. There is much that is right as well. An awareness of it can be a source of a positive approach to the problems of Indian society at different levels. There is much that is right in the Indian Union, which has already achieved what the European Union is struggling hard to achieve.

As far as the Gore initiative for administrative reforms is concerned, it was directed towards reducing the 'trust deficit' by creating a federal government that is efficient. Gore undertook to improve the efficiency of his government by using the insights of management theory regarding human capacity and the role of information technology. His entire programme of decentralisation, let it not be overlooked, was based on the principle of tapping human capacity in the service of organisational goals while ensuring accountability down the line. Information technology makes it possible to decentralise without sacrificing accountability. Federal executives play a critical role in his scheme of things in 'empowering' employees, and Gore's challenge was to turn his vision into their mission. While the strength of his approach lies in his emphasis on efficiency (a government that works better and costs less), its weakness lies in not putting effectiveness in focus. What is important is not just achievement of goals but, as Drucker would argue, the determination of appropriate goals—'doing the right thing'. Even though Gore mentions motivated employees and satisfied customers for the new face of his government, these cannot be treated as the overall objectives of a government.

This is where Drucker's criticism appears valid. He is concerned with effectiveness. His consideration, however, turns out to be what a government can effectively do rather than what is the right thing for a government to do. While it may be true for a government, as for a person, that it is not right for them to do what they cannot do well, that is not the only criterion on the basis of which a choice of what is the right thing to do is usually made. In fact, Drucker admits that there are far too many tasks for a government of a developed country to perform. But these tasks are not subjected to a critical examination. We need to be clear about the basic tasks that the American government must perform. He admits we need a theory that we do not have at present, a theory of what a government can do. This is true. We also need a theory of what is the right thing to do for a government. This theory has to be developed not just on a factual basis. Yet, reading Drucker serves a useful purpose for us. We can draw from him two points: his support of such practices as continuous improvement and benchmarking which are meant to improve efficiency, and, second, his emphasis on rethinking, even though this is an activity that he has not himself carried out adequately regarding government. Indeed, it may well be argued that there is scope for rethinking on the issue of effectiveness. Drucker is famous for the distinction he makes elsewhere between 'priorities' and 'posteriorities', tasks that should not be done at all rather than done better or at a lower price. This distinction does not, however, help in the determination of what is the right thing to do unless certain decisions about broader goals have already been made. This is as true of individuals and organisations as of governments.

Mintzberg's classification of organisations and of the different hats that we wear in relation to our governments is a correct step towards a theory of what is the right thing to do for a government. More than having the satisfied customers of Gore's vision, it is important for governments in democratic societies to have responsibilities towards their citizens. This point needs to be developed further. The rights of citizens need to be recognised adequately, along with the awareness that these rights operate at individual and group levels. It was T.H. Marshall (1963) who argued that citizenship has now come to comprehend, besides legal and political rights, social rights as well, including the right to an appropriate standard of living. Along with the issue of citizenship in a democratic society, we need to consider the issue of the public interest. This is an issue that is closely related to the functioning of a democratic state. The public interest is not a simple aggregate of private interests. It is a recognition, as John Dewey (1927) showed, of the shared interest of a public in controlling the consequences of interactions among private parties, interactions which create the public as well as the consequences that need to be controlled by it. The public interest lends itself in principle to be stated in objective terms. It also provides a standard of evaluation of the policies and activities of those agencies which are created to serve it but may fail to do so, intentionally or otherwise (Long 1990). The government of a democratic state serves the public interest in a responsive manner. It controls the public and is controlled by it. This means it upholds the indivisible collective interest of the public and is in turn evaluated by it by the same standard. The public interest is not served by regulation alone. It requires the provision of public good as well, which cannot be supplied by the market, or which a particular government chooses to supply. These goods may provide, apart from direct benefits, indirect social benefits as well, which are ignored by private producers or suppliers. Thus, for example, Drèze and Sen have argued that education and health have significance beyond the immediate personal effects. Good governance has then to do with efficiency and more basically with such objectives of democratic governments as upholding the rights of individual citizens and promoting the public interest.

The 'trust deficit' can be reduced in the United States, India and elsewhere by creating a government that is efficient and also just. There is something to be learnt from Kautilya (1992) as well as Gandhi on this point. In his *Arthashastra*, a treatise on statecraft that was written not later than AD 150, Kautilya, much maligned as a teacher of unethical practices, formulates the following precept: 'In the happiness of his subjects lies the king's happiness; in their welfare his welfare. He shall not consider as good only that which pleases him but treat as beneficial to him whatever pleases his subjects' (p. x). Towards the end of his life Gandhi presented a moving idea:

I will give you a talisman. Whenever you are in doubt, or when the self becomes too much with you, apply the following test. Recall the face of the poorest and weakest man whom you may have seen, and ask yourself if the step you contemplate is going to be of any use to him. Will he gain anything by it? Will it restore him to a control over his life and destiny? In other words, will it lead to *swaraj* for the hungry and spiritually starving millions? Then you will find your doubts and yourself melting away (Iyer 1993: 418).

REFLECTIVE EVALUATION

Evaluation is thus involved. Governance cannot be confined to the factual description of governing by a person or group. It involves the state of being governed, the state of good order, or at least the effort to set in governance. Good governance, like good life, does not lend itself to a normatively neutral treatment. It involves governing according to legitimate principles. The *Oxford English Dictionary* has a quotation going back to 1656 which is relevant here: 'Wise Princes ought not to be admired for their Government, but Governance'. While this anticipates the current usage of differentiating 'government' from 'governance' with the hint of a linkage between wisdom and governance, it is recognised now that governance involves not only traditional structures and actors of government but also other actors (Rosenau 1992; Weiss 2000). It has led scholars to suggest the possibility of governance without government, though it might be justifiably argued that what is needed is government within governance (Bache 2000). Government within governance should suggest that governance is a broader concept and also that it is a concept that sets the normative basis of government. If evaluation is involved, how is this evaluation to be made? Gandhi's talisman brings clarity of meaning, but is not easy to apply. A less challenging consideration is proposed here. This is the principle of thinking through one's value position and practice as a social actor, called here reflective evaluation. Reflective evaluation should provide the middle ground between the arbitrariness of subjective evaluations and the excesses of objectivism. It differs from conventional evaluation, particularly with respect to the criteria of evaluation which are not brought from outside but are drawn from the consensus of those directly involved. It is based on this consensus, rather than the value position of an external agency. To be a genuine consensus, this consensus should be free from crippling conditions such as the imposition of the will of a dictator, represented by a person or a party. Though no ideal situation is assumed for the benefit of this consensus, it is expected that the public participation of citizens in a democratic society provides a formal condition for arriving at potential agreement in a free manner. Reflective evaluation involves the possibility of all social actors to effectively participate in reflection. It builds upon and in turn promotes a free society, without necessarily being confined to it.

The principle of reflective evaluation is presented here with the example of interface of government and industry in the context of democracy, bureaucracy and industrial society.

Modern democracies are no longer direct but indirect, and they operate through large bureaucracies. These features of modern democracies have a significant bearing on their nature and the manner in which they function. The indirect mode gives rise to politicians as representatives of the people who govern in the name of the people. Bureaucracies are manned by bureaucrats who occupy positions by virtue of rules that include the rules of eligibility for appointment to different offices. These bureaucrats function in accordance with specified rules that draw the boundaries of different administrative authorities. While it is important for the representatives to represent the people, a bureaucracy needs to function as machinery bound by a legal framework. The deviation arises, all too often sadly, when the representatives of the people fail to represent them or when bureaucrats fail to perform in the prescribed manner. The failure to represent the people may take different forms, including the practice of self-serving in the political activity, which is no longer in the interest of the people but lives off the people. Bureaucrats fail when they go beyond the limits of their offices or when they fail to do justice to their prescribed roles. A bureaucrat who seeks too much authority is as much to be faulted as the one who does not exercise the authority of his office. Bureaucrats and bureaucracies tend to develop vested interests over time. There is, moreover, the need for coordination among the politicians holding ministerial positions and the bureaucrats placed under them in different ministries of the government. Many of the problems of modern democracies arise from the failures of the representatives of the people and the bureaucrats who hold different administrative positions. The problems arise also from the faulty manner in which ministers and bureaucrats work together. Indeed, they may work together through an unholy alliance based on corruption, the most important factor that undermines good governance at different levels in the world.

Let us take a look at industry now. Industry refers quite plainly to diligence, useful work and different branches of trade or manufacture taken as a whole. This useful work is supposed to promote the material welfare of society. From the time of the Industrial Revolution we have seen the emergence of a new kind of society where industrial organisations have increasingly played a dominant role and where production has been increasingly carried out by machines. Industrial society is characterised by an advanced division of labour and class distinctions. Recent developments have seen the emergence of powerful multinational corporations that command vast resources and operate across national boundaries in global markets. Yet another feature of our times that needs to be noted is the intensification of technological change in recent years that has brought about significant changes leading to what some sociologists have termed as post-industrial society. Concern about modern society may range from normative consensus to alienation and anomie to positive beliefs that in the words of Comte represent 'the religion of humanity'.

What do we expect from the democratic state? We expect good governance. We expect it to be stable, efficient and legitimate. The democratic state is often criticised for its instability and inefficiency. It has, therefore, to strive hard to overcome these weaknesses within it. The strength, specific to its form from which it can draw, is the possibility of promoting individual rights and the public interest in accordance with the rule of law. The democratic state assumes constitutional legitimacy. It also assumes the value of the individual human being whose rights have to be protected. The democratic state is expected to create conditions that facilitate consensus formation, providing equal opportunities for citizens and providing possibilities of negotiations between the parties involved. It provides, so to speak, a level playing field. For the form and functioning of democratic societies, it is relevant to raise issues relating to the representation by politicians, the limits and the use of bureaucratic authority, constitutional legitimacy, the rights of citizens, and the public interest. With respect to industry in modern society, whether it is called industrial society or post-industrial society, the relevant issues are those regarding useful work, the material welfare of society and development. To what extent does democracy as it is practised endanger the principle of representation or the rights of citizens? To what extent has industrial society run up against its limit of development by threatening our planet and by it our very existence? Can we visualise an alternative model of society? Do democracy and the present form of industrial society go together? These questions that go into basic issues may be raised. They may be raised from different points of view, including basic value choices and their fulfilment.

Remaining confined to the task here, reflective evaluation in the context of democracy, bureaucracy and industrial society involves above all concern with the material welfare of society and sustainable development, along with the protection and promotion of individual rights and the public interest. These values arise as we have tried to see from the assumptions of industrialism and democracy. With respect to politicians and bureaucrats, not much is gained by stipulating that they should be honest and truthful. These values and similar other general values apply to them as much as to other members of society. What does apply to them specifically is the need to ensure that development is not retarded, nor allowed to proceed in a manner that sacrifices individual rights and the public interest that are to be served in an interactive manner. This needs emphasis in this era of globalisation that has meant concentration and strengthening of the power of capital in large corporations. These corporations may prove threatening not only to the general public but also to the national enterprise in a country like India. Professional managers can contribute by serving the interests of stakeholders and by ensuring that private gains are not at the cost of the public interest. To provide for sustainable development with social justice is admittedly a difficult task. In actual practice vested interests introduce distortions for their own benefit.

The context that has been identified here is broadly the context of a social formation that is both industrial and democratic. If one is located in a specific society that combines the features drawn from a social formation that is both industrial and democratic, and also if one accepts them for playing out a social role, then it is useful to know what the values embedded in this society are. Reflective evaluation then means gaining clarity about the implications of this acceptance and making a conscious choice. An analyst can serve by introducing his objective assessment of the values embedded in a society that can prove useful to the participants. This is not a case of inferring 'ought' from 'is', nor of agreeing on principles under an imaginary condition such as 'veil of ignorance' as in John Rawls, but of spelling out the value position that the participants have actually taken by virtue of accepting the values assumed by a society. If clarity, thus gained by reflection, shows up not equilibrium but contradictions and dilemmas that cannot be glossed over any longer and makes one's choices more difficult, so be it; for the unexamined life as we have been taught is not worth living.

In conclusion, it will be useful to provide a definition of good governance based on these considerations. It is advisable to arrive at it after an analysis in this contested area rather than begin with it in the form of a subjective declaration of preference. Good governance signifies a participative manner of governing that functions in a responsible, accountable and transparent manner based on the principles of efficiency, legitimacy and consensus for the purpose of promoting the rights of individual citizens and the public interest, thus indicating the exercise of political will for ensuring the material welfare of society and sustainable development with social justice.

NOTE

1. I am grateful to all those who gave me the benefit of their comments on an earlier draft, especially Abram De Swaan, Sudha Kaul, Pushpa Mishra, Darryl Reed, Anju Seth and Hellmut Wollmann.

REFERENCES

Bache, Ian. 2000. 'Government Within Governance: Network Steering in Yorkshire and the Humber'. *Public Administration: An International Quarterly,* 78(3): 575–92.

Bandyopadhyay, D. 1996. 'Administration, Decentralisation and Good Governance'. *Economic and Political Weekly,* 31(44): 3109–14.

Callinicos, Alex. 2001. *Against the Third Way.* Cambridge: Polity Press.

Chanley, Virginia A., Rudolph, Thomas J. and Rahn, Wendy M. 2000. 'The Origins and Consequences of Public Trust in Government: A Time Series Analysis'. *Public Opinion Quarterly,* 64(3): 239–56.

Dahrendorf, Ralf. 1999. 'The Third Way and Liberty'. *Foreign Affairs,* 78(5): 13–17.

Department of Administrative Reforms and Public Grievances (DARPG). 1996a. 'An Agenda for Effective and Responsive Administration: Discussion Note for the Conference of Chief Secretaries of States/UTs'. Department of Administration Reforms and Public Grievances, Ministry of Personnel, Public Grievances and Pensions, Government of India.

————. 1996b. 'Recommendations of the Conference of Chief Secretaries' (held on 20 November 1996). Department of Administrative Reforms and Public Grievances, Ministry of Personnel, Public Grievances and Pensions, Government of India.

————. 1997. 'An Action Plan for Effective and Responsive Administration: Statement Adopted at the Conference of Chief Ministers' (held on 24 May 1997). Department of Administrative Reforms and Public Grievances, Ministry of Personnel, Public Grievances and Pensions, Government of India.

Dewey, John. 1927. *The Public and Its Problems.* Denver: Holt.

Drèze, Jean and Sen, Amartya. 1996. *India: Economic Development and Social Opportunity.* Delhi: Oxford University Press.

Drucker, Peter. 1995. 'Really Reinventing Government'. *Span,* 36(12): 1–15.

Gore, Al Jr. 1993. *From Red Tape to Results: Creating a Government That Works Better and Costs Less.* Washington, D.C.: U.S. Superintendent of Documents.

Gore, Al Jr. 1994. 'The New Job of the Federal Executive'. *Public Administration Review*, 54(4): 317–21.

Guhan, S. 1998. 'World Bank on Governance: A Critique'. *Economic and Political Weekly*, 33(4): 185–92.

Iyer, Raghavan (ed.). 1993. *The Essential Writings of Mahatma Gandhi*. Delhi: Oxford University Press.

Kothari, Rajni. 1988. *State Against Democracy: In Search of Humane Governance*. Delhi: Ajanta Publications.

Kautilya. 1992. *The Arthashastra*. New Delhi: Penguin.

Kohli, Atul (ed.). 1991. *India's Democracy: An Analysis of Changing State–Society Relations*. Hyderabad: Orient Longman.

Long, Norton E. 1990. 'Conceptual Notes on the Public Interest for Public Administration and Policy Analysts'. *Administration & Society*, 22(2): 170–81.

Marshall, T.H. 1963. *Class, Citizenship and Social Development*, Chicago: Chicago University Press.

Meier, Kenneth J. 2002. 'Bureaucracy and Democracy: The Case for More Bureaucracy and Less Democracy', in Stephen P. Osborne (ed.). *Public Management: Critical Perspectives*, Vol. I, pp. 248–62. London and New York: Routledge.

Mintzberg, Henry. 1996. 'Managing Government, Governing Management'. *Harvard Business Review*, 74(3): 75–83.

Myrdal, Gunnar. 1968. *Asian Drama: An Inquiry into the Poverty of Nations*. Middlesex: Penguin.

Newsweek. 1998. 'Three for the Third Way'. *Newsweek*, 132(15): 8.

Nye, Joseph S., Jr. 1997. 'In Government We Don't Trust', *Foreign Policy*, 108: 99–111.

Osborne, David and Gaebler, Ted. 1992. *Reinventing Government: How the Entrepreneurial Spirit is Transforming the Public Sector*, New Delhi: Prentice-Hall of India.

Ridley, F.F. 1996. 'The New Public Management in Europe: Comparative Perspectives'. *Public Policy and Administration*, 11(1): 16–29.

Rosenau, James N. 1992. 'Governance, Order, and Change in World Politics', in James N. Rosenau and E.O. Czempiel (eds.). *Governance without Government: Order and Change in World Politics*, pp. 1–29. Cambridge: Cambridge University Press.

Savoie, Donald J. 2002. 'What is Wrong with the New Public Management', in Stephen P. Osborne (ed.). *Public Management: Critical Perspectives*, Vol. I, pp. 263–72. London and New York: Routledge.

Sen Gupta, Bhabani. 1996. *India: Problems of Governance*. Delhi: Konark Publishers.

Weiss, T.G. 2000. 'Governance, Good Governance and Global Governance: Conceptual and Actual Challenges'. *Third World Quarterly*, 21(5): 795–814.

Williams, Daniel W. 2000. 'Reinventing the Proverbs of Government'. *Public Administration Review*, 60(6): 522–34.

Wollmann, Hellmut. 2000. 'Comparing Institutional Development in Britain and Germany: (Persistent) Divergence or (Progressive) Convergence?', in Hellmut Wollmann and Eckhard Schroeter (eds.). *Comparing Public Sector Reform in Britain and Germany: Key Traditions and Trends in Modernisation*, pp. 1–26. Aldershot: Ashgate.

CHAPTER 3

POLICY WITHOUT POLITICS: SOCIAL, CULTURAL AND LINGUISTIC AFFAIRS IN THE EUROPEAN UNION

ABRAM DE SWAAN

A peculiar political construct has emerged from the combination of European states in the past half century: the European Union (EU) is more than a confederation, but less than a federation; more than just a free trade zone, but not quite an economic whole; almost a world power, but one without an army or an effective foreign policy of its own; with a common currency, the Euro, but with coins that reserve a different verso for each member state. And yet, taken together, in less than a lifetime, these are major achievements. The ambitions are even more grandiose: ever eastward. The Union is to expand to Central Europe, Eastern Europe, the Balkans and the Baltic States, one day Turkey, and maybe, in the end, even Russia.

Nevertheless, an uneasy mood reigns among the Europeans. The EU fascinates its citizens some of the time, irritates them most of the time and bores them the rest of the time. No doubt that is connected to the notorious democratic deficit of the Union. There is a Council of Ministers, in which the governments of the member states are represented, each supported by a freely elected parliamentary majority. There is a European Parliament, directly elected by the citizens of every country. There is a European Commission which must take into account the Parliament's majority. If, nonetheless, a democratic deficit remains, this is not so much due to the deficiencies of Europe's treaties and institutions, as it is the result of a cultural gap.

The Europeans do not speak the same language and hence do not understand each other well enough to differ. But quite apart from the confusion of tongues, in every member state opinions take shape within a national framework. What is passionately debated in one country is not even an issue in the neighbouring countries.

Hence, there is no question of a common European debate, a discussion that allows voices from all member states to disagree, but to disagree about the same issues, according to a common agenda of dissent. The political and cultural debate proceeds mainly in relative isolation within each national society even today. Abroad, it hardly meets response. In short, there is no such thing as a European public space, as yet.

As a consequence, political issues that concern the EU in its entirety are rarely discussed in public, but usually indoors, in the council rooms where the ministers meet one another or in the smoke-free offices of the Commission's bureaucrats. Every two years or so there is a plenary conference where the grand decisions of the congregating statesmen are announced to the citizenry of the EU. But the everyday politics, the day to day politicking, the polemics and discussions, the sound bites and the repartees that are part and parcel of democratic debate are reserved for the national arena and remain absent at the European level.

POLICY AS THE 'NECESSARY IMPLICATION' OF ACCEPTED PRINCIPLES

If in the EU there is no politics in the classic sense of public discussion and partisan manoeuvring by elected representatives, an impressive amount of policy is generated nevertheless. The EU is much ridiculed and maligned for the large number of rules and regulations it produces from day to day and from week to week. But these decisions are drafted by the officials of the Commission and their expert advisors; in most cases they need not even be confirmed by the European Parliament. The civil servants of the Commission can adopt these measures because they are presented as the necessary consequences of broad principles agreed upon in the major treaties that constitute the legal framework of the Union. They can also take those decisions by applying a legal competence that was initially intended for a different purpose. And finally, the civil servants, tacitly backed by their superiors, the European Commissioners and the national politicians, may decide to decide nothing at all and thus silently confirm the ongoing course of events as their policy by default: this is what Bachrach and Baratz (1963) have called 'non-decision-making'.

An avalanche of regulations was adopted as the unavoidable consequence of the 'principle of free movement' within the Union, which allows the unfettered circulation of persons, goods, services, and capital across the borders of the member states. As a matter of course, this principle required the 'harmonisation' (or, weaker, 'coordination') of the separate national regulations, e.g., each and every definition of goods under the customs legislation or the consumer legislation in all 15 separate member states. As the regulatory juggernaut rolled on, French cheeses or Spanish hams were under threat of sudden elimination, if they did not satisfy one regulatory requirement or another. The free movement of persons demanded similar harmonisation, not of the persons themselves but of the conditions under which they were expected to work and be paid. Here, and to the surprise of many, EU regulations touched upon the realm of 'social policy'. In the legislation of quite a few member states, for example, men were considered the 'breadwinners' of first instance and working women were not treated on equal terms. As the treaties expressly prohibit discrimination on the basis of gender and since national social regulations had to be brought into line, it 'logically' followed that women should be granted the same rights as men when it came to social and labour regulation. As a consequence, the rules issued by the European Commission caused a wave of emancipation, a minor social revolution in quite a few member states (Kjeldstad 2001; Sorensen 2001). But none of this was the result of activist intervention, of petitions or demonstrations. It hardly provoked intervention on the part of politicians from the member states. It 'just happened' as the inexorable consequence of the harmonisation of national regulations. In this manner, this most controversial intersection of gender politics and social policy was quietly depoliticised, apparently without design on anyone's part.

EXAMPLES

Much in the same manner, the European Court issued a series of verdicts that in their overall consequences much strengthened the rights of citizens vis-à-vis the authorities, again as the unavoidable implication of the rules embodied in the founding treaty, especially the Rome Treaty. Here, judge-made law operated in much the same manner as the rules made by the Brussels bureaucrats, not as the outcome of contested political choice, but as the necessary implication of existing treaty principles.

European regulation has proceeded in another manner also. The EU agencies were eager to bend the rules to apply them to fields they had not been intended for. This 'detournement' turned out to be quite effective in cultural matters which were expressly ruled out under the existing agreements as pertaining to the competence of the member states. This follows from the so-called 'subsidiarity principle' which leaves to the member states all those matters that need not be regulated at the Union level because they do not affect the free movement of persons, services, goods, and capital. Religious issues are a clear example of a subject matter better left to the member states, or maybe even to be entirely avoided by the state within the framework of an overall guarantee of the freedom of expression and belief.

The same abstention applies, in principle, to cultural matters. However, it increasingly appeared that decisions pertaining to free trade did indeed touch upon interests of a cultural character. Thus, the French policy of setting quota for the broadcasting of songs with foreign instead of French lyrics, or of imposing a quota for American films shown on TV or of subsidising French films, appeared to go against the general principles of free economic competition. These cases were among the rare instances that did generate a public debate that transcended national frontiers. It was finally decided to allow the exemption of cultural goods from the free trade regime: Article 128 of the Maastricht Treaty expressly states that cultural considerations may be taken into account when regulating the circulation of certain goods. A similar 'cultural exemption' allowed fixed sales prices for books, a practice that would otherwise have been ruled out as an infraction upon the principle of free competition (which would have allowed booksellers to set whatever price they saw as right).

POLICY AS THE OUTCOME OF 'NONDECISIONS'

There is yet another way in which the EU works upon the national societies of the member states, once again without politics but in this case also without policy. The four freedoms of the movement of persons, capital, commodities, and services have created entirely unintended effects in the realm of 'moral regulation' in the separate countries. In her enlightening study of the regimes governing abortion, drugs and alcohol in Ireland, the Netherlands, Finland and Sweden respectively, Paulette Kurzer (2001) has demonstrated that the 'exceptionalist' regimes in these countries were subtly transformed by the individual movements that Kurzer calls 'sin tourism'. Irish women cross the sea to have an abortion in the United Kingdom (UK) or elsewhere, Finns and Swedes travel abroad to profit from the more liberal liquor laws on the European mainland, and 'drug tourists' flock to the Netherlands to enjoy soft drugs in the coffee shops tolerated there and even purchase hard drugs (which are illegal in the Netherlands too). As a result, the more restrictive regimes in the first three countries are tacitly undermined and the more tolerant regime prevailing in the Netherlands provides a free haven for visitors from neighbouring countries with stricter regulations and harsher penalties. This in turn forced the Dutch authorities to take action against motorised peddlers recruiting clients on the highways leading from the borders to the main cities.

These disparities in moral regulation in adjacent countries have provoked not just border-crossing 'sin tourism', but also vivid and sometimes acrimonious debate across borders (thus, the French have criticised the Dutch for their drug policies and disqualified the Netherlands at some point as a 'narco-état'). Interestingly enough, as Kurzer points out, the EU has not tried to bring these deviant moral regimes into line as it has attempted in other fields, e.g., consumer legislation, safety rules or social policy. Rather, it has left each country to pursue its own policies. Nevertheless, the net effect of individual movements has been to diminish the discrepancies between the various regimes. Similar unintended effects of the increased movement throughout the Union have prompted more intensive collaboration between the police in various countries. One is reminded of the attempts to coordinate anti-terrorism efforts (collaboration hampered by the concerns of national governments that their particular liberties might be threatened by concerted police action, e.g., the successful effort by the Dutch to exempt drug traffic from the new policing agreements after September 11 and equally effective Italian attempts to respect the restrictions on the prosecution of corruption cases peculiar to that country). The massive movement of football fans across the continent also inspired increased coordination and reciprocal assistance in crowd control and the exclusion of known hooligans. The protest demonstrations at the occasion of encounters of European leaders and other major international conferences have equally provoked collaboration between security services and police authorities of the various countries, prompting preventive arrests and exclusionary measures.

The liberalisation of movement following the Schengen accords in combination with the overall growth of travel due to lower air and train fares and increasing automobile traffic has rendered national borders more and more porous. In fact, it is well-nigh impossible to effectively maintain a more restrictive policy of moral regulation when adjacent countries offer a more liberal regime to the traveller. Capital may gravitate to the countries with the highest profit rates; many individuals will flock to the member states with the most liberal regimes. And this holds true, even if the Union does not meddle with those regimes at all or precisely because it prefers not to intervene. As a result, the abstinence of the Union in matters of national or regional culture is unintentionally accompanied by a subtle erosion of moral restrictions in the separate member states. Liberals can easily live with this state of affairs: people who so choose may travel and pursue their particular happiness in member states that allow it, at the cost of some displacement, while nations that prefer to restrict these liberties may continue to do so without unduly frustrating their dissident citizens. For conservatives who desire to protect their fellow citizens against temptation, the free movement towards the most tolerant places may appear to undo the imposition of moral standards. On the other hand, liberals on their part have viewed the international collaboration of police authorities as a movement towards the lowest common denominator of the rule of law.

DEPOLITICISED SOCIAL POLICY

The four freedoms, or rather the four restrictions on the competence of states to impose limits on the movement of goods, capital, services and persons, will increase mobility of labourers and may provoke 'welfare tourism'. This would require states to either exclude migrants from their benefits, or allow all residents—including new and temporary residents—to profit from them, which may require mutual arrangements on the provision of benefits among states with intense traffic of persons. Alternatively, it might lead to a further individualisation of drawing rights through private insurance. Finally, it may persuade the Union and the member states to create an all-Union social regime for workers moving from one country to another (Hagen 1992). Ten years later, it appears that workers in the member states have become much less mobile than expected at the time. The migrant workers still are overwhelmingly citizens from outside the EU, from the Mediterranean countries, Africa and Asia, and from the candidate member states in East and Central Europe. The citizens of the Union mostly stay put. One partial explanation for this lack of labour mobility may be the housing market which overwhelmingly protects long-time residents through rent-subsides, subsidised home purchase and long waiting lists for the most attractive housing provided by building associations. The widely feared process of 'social dumping' of the least insured workers gravitating to countries with a more generous system where they drive out expensive, well-insured workers did not materialise. This is also explained by the higher level of qualification and labour discipline among workers in the wealthier economies which tend to be those with the most elaborate welfare systems: the more expensive workers may also be the more productive hands. Nor did a 'negative spiral' manifest itself in which the most elaborate welfare systems would have had to be adapted to the more restrictive levels of their competitors. This is partly the result of strong labour unions in most EU countries and intricate systems of mutual consultation among organised workers and employers, partly also because of a general consensus within the EU that globalisation and privatisation should not unduly dismantle the 'European social model'.

Finally, the treaty principles of 'non-discrimination' have spawned administrative and judicial decisions that bolster existing social entitlements and even impose new rights. Leibfried and Pierson (1995: 437ff.) explain the avoidance of a lowest common denominator, a downward spiral in social policy from the institutional characteristics of the European decision-making process: fragmented, multilevelled, prone to package-deals, from the special position of the Court and of the Commission. As a result, women have acquired a stronger position as social regulations may no longer differentiate between gender but must treat all 'earners' or 'breadwinners' equally. Also, guarantees of workers' health and security have improved across the board as the more advanced standards were applied to countries that had been lagging in this respect, rather than the other way round. At this point in time, Hagen's prognosis seems to be confirmed: 'A gradual convergence of social standards within the Community will consequently emerge, with decentralised bargaining between labour and capital (within the single states) as the driving force' (1992: 292).

> To the extent that individual rights will be granted, it will probably take place as a continuation of the present silent acceptance of rulings of the European Court of Justice. By passing sentences based on the general intentions of EC declarations, its rulings are predictably pro-integration; and by declaring the direct applicability of EC laws within the member states, national legislation has to be amended without any discussions in the national parliament or disruptive voting in the European Council (ibid.: 301).

But this also makes for a 'depoliticisation' of decision-making in the Union, an avoidance of politics while making policy. Already in 1994, Leibfried and Pierson (1994: 48) had written that '. . . European social intervention is likely to turn to regulatory or Court-centred mechanisms. EC social policy will be likely to take the form of mandates for national action'. Wolfgang Streeck (1995: 399) mentions 'the Court's impressive capacity to make supranational law that overrides national law and binds national policy'. Yet, it was never the intention of the Court to make social policy, but rather to insert transnational civil rights (embodied in the various treaties) into the separate legal systems of member states.

Stephan Leibfried and Paul Pierson (1994: 411) summarise the process in the following words: 'What is emerging in Europe is a multileveled, highly fragmented system in which policy "develops" but is beyond the firm control of any single political authority'. Member states suspicious of one another and wary of granting their competitors much influence allowed agencies of the EU to function rather autonomously: 'In many cases, then, they created institutions that even they cannot control' (p. 435). And these institutions on their part 'are always looking to enhance their own powers' (p. 435). As a result the EU has been 'highly interventionist' in imposing health and safety standards for products and production processes (p. 437). The European Court of Justice, with its activist interpretation of the treaty texts, adds its weight to this policy process. As a result the less wealthy and more laggard Southern welfare states were not only especially forced to control inflation and budget deficits, but also came under pressure from the EU institutions to heed the needs of the elderly and the disabled to promote gender equality and social inclusion, and to help reconcile the demands of family care with those of working life (Guillén and Álvarez 2001: 125). On the whole, the rather autonomous interventions of the Court and the Commission thus pursued social policies, while keeping politics at arm's length.

The Language Question: No Politics, No Policies

Although the present Union must live with 11 'official' languages, and in a few years may have to cope with another half a dozen, this predicament has so far evoked much discussion, but no political debate, let alone regulatory action. The issue appears so divisive that the parties concerned prefer to avoid it. The European Union proclaimed the year 2001 the 'year of languages' and used the occasion to promote language learning, but skirted the vexing issue of which languages should be the chosen means of all-European communication. Instead, it advocated that students learn many different languages, not exactly the best way to solve the barriers to communication in Babylonian Europe. Moreover, it was a somewhat disingenuous advice to students who might want to improve their position on the single labour market, which otherwise is the main preoccupation of the Commission. As if 11, or 15, or 20 languages were not enough, the Commission has adopted the cause of regional, immigrant and minority languages. It might, on the contrary, have occupied itself with improving the opportunities of minorities, migrants and inhabitants of the regions. This could have facilitated their becoming fluent in the national language and the major media of transnational communication, a policy more likely to increase the much-vaunted mobility and to promote the much-desired integration. But that would have required the Commission, or rather the Council, to make an explicit choice among languages and single out one or a few of them as the media of communication *par excellence*. As I have demonstrated elsewhere, such an explicit decision would have been impossible to reach (De Swaan 2001: 169–71).

In fact, the Union long ago decided not to decide and let matters run their—entirely predictable—course. It inherited French as the 'working language' from the European Coal and Steel Community. Once the United Kingdom acceded as a member, English was accepted as the second working language, gradually growing in importance until its position equalled and even surpassed that of French in oral and written communication within the Commission's bureaucracy. These two working languages are used in the meetings of the less important committees and in the everyday affairs of the Commission's administration. Germany has repeatedly demanded the adoption of German as the third working language with increasing insistence. And recently after a clash with the Finnish presidency, German may be tolerated next to French and English, although few civil servants there speak it as a second language. But the use of a few working languages leaves intact the principle of equal entitlement for all languages of the member states, embodied in the Treaty of Rome. In public meetings of the Council of Ministers, of the European Parliament and of its major committees, the official languages of all member states may be used and all externally binding decisions by the Commission's bureaucracy must also be phrased in all these languages. This requirement imposes an enormous logistic burden on the translation services of the Commission and exacts a huge financial toll—for the Commission alone, €325 million or 30 per cent of the internal budget; for the entire Union machinery some €700 million (De Swaan 2001: 172). Individual parliamentarians and bureaucrats may have complained about the persistent confusion of tongues, but no serious reform proposal was ever tabled. (There was a heated discussion about the languages to be used in the European patent bureau which ended with the acceptance of the five most numerous languages and the exclusion of the sixth, Dutch.)

In the meantime, some 90 per cent of all high school students in the Union now learn English, and throughout the EU English is by far the most used language in communication across borders. Since World War II, the position of French as a European lingua franca has been steadily eroded and, except in Central Europe, German lost what transnational functions it once had. Perversely, the continued acceptance of all official languages of the member states as media of the Union and the encouragement of the languages of migrants, minorities and regions have only worked in favour of English. As the number of languages used increases, the confusion grows proportionally (or rather by the second power), and the one most widely spoken language will increasingly be perceived as the only solution: the more languages, the more English (a lesson learned time and again in postcolonial societies that wanted to adopt an indigenous language as their official medium but could not come to a decision which one to single out and therefore had to accept them all, so that soon the ex-colonial language returned as the only efficient means of nation-wide and official communication). The French, who may have understood this paradox, did indeed advocate the official use of a small number of languages, hoping that such a restricted language regime might be efficient enough to prevent the stampede towards English. But if such a proposal had ever been debated and put to the vote it would have been rejected as either too unwieldy or too exclusive. For the same reasons, even if the Germans were successful in their campaign to have their language adopted as the third working language, they would still fail to achieve their objective. Predictably, the Spanish, with the second largest language after English, not in the EU but in the world, would insist on the adoption of Spanish in an equal position. So would the Italians, founding members of the Community and heirs to a great literary tradition. Even the Dutch, notorious for their modesty (or indifference) in this respect would be prodded into claiming equal treatment, if only by the member states next in line for inclusion of their language.

Under these conditions, the language issue in the EU can not be openly debated and settled by political means. But it need not be. The dynamics of the European language constellation are such that if no decision is ever taken, the outcome will still be the predominance of English as the medium of transnational communication in civil society, of everyday practice in the bureaucracy and more and more also of parliamentary deliberation. As a parliamentary culture develops in the European Parliament, members will want to persuade their peers directly, rather than through the muzzle of translation. Most of them will turn to English, some may abide with French, and they will revert to their national language only to address their own electorate over the heads of the parliamentarians.

In the case of the language issue, non-decision-making amounts to a tacit, latent decision: to let matters take their course and allow

English to prevail in the European Union. All else is either *naiveté*, make-believe, or a perverse way of accelerating the process by increasing the confusion.

DISCUSSION: POLICY, POLITICS AND GOVERNANCE

By avoiding the politicisation of a broad range of issues, all of them prone to elicit intense and heated conflict, the EU has maintained a low level of controversy, but also a low level of electoral interest and citizens' participation in social, cultural and language affairs. It was not immobility that kept these matters depoliticised. Quite to the contrary, the EU did affect many of these issues; sometimes passively, as on the language issue, quite often with an activist momentum, as in the regulation of social rights. At other times, the institutions of the Union took no direct action, but other measures they had put in place did have indirect effects, desired or not, intended or not, that all went in a specific direction, as in the case of deviant national 'moral regulation' that was eroded through increased mobility across borders. In all these cases, politics in the sense of public debate and open partisan action by elected representatives hardly played a role. In the case of social policy, European bureaucrats and the European Court regularly filled the void by issuing regulations that appeared to be no more than the necessary implications of treaty principles adopted by the member states. In moral affairs they stayed clear of explicit intervention in national regimes, but saw the citizens of one country seeking solace under the regime of another, in the process dulling the sharp edges of the deviant regime. The language question, too, was mostly avoided and left to follow its internal dynamics, towards English. In other cultural matters, the competence granted to the institutions of the EU was subtly bent to apply in other matters than they had been intended for.

Yet, in most cases, the aggregate outcome was rather consistent, almost as if there had been an explicit policy. Apparently, the EU could do without politics in these instances. Nevertheless, a price was paid for this depoliticisation. The citizens of the EU were never consulted on the matter, they were hardly aware of the decisions and nondecisions that shaped the issue, and as a consequence they felt no involvement, let alone any responsibility. This is part of the explanation for the notorious 'democratic deficit' of the EU and that deficit in turn explains in part the scarcity of explicit politics in the EU.

The absence of politics in the government of Europe reflects a certain style of governance. That expression itself has only recently become current, it is not mentioned even in major dictionaries before the 1980s. 'Governance' refers to 'government', 'rule' or 'administration', both in politics and business, *and* it is almost always used in an evaluative, even a judgemental context, especially by the United Nations and its agencies. 'Good governance' refers to corporate or governmental 'administration' that is not corrupt, technically competent, legally correct, efficient in its implementation and oriented towards the interests of its citizens, customers or employees. In this sense, the term can also be applied to characterise the government of Europe.

European policy is made by administrators and judges, by professionals and experts, often presented as no more than the inexorable consequences of treaties accepted unanimously by the governments of the member states, sometimes the outcome of a policy of abstention on the part of the decision makers. The word most often used to qualify and disqualify this style of rule is 'bureaucratic'. The next most frequent characterisation is 'technocratic' and indeed, by its sheer size and complexity, the tangle of rules is well-nigh inextricable: only administrative specialists and technical professionals can find their way through the regulatory labyrinth. The EU style of governance is also autocratic, but in a complex, two-tiered fashion. The EU is legalistic to a fault, and its constituting laws are deeply steeped in the legalistic tradition of human rights, civil, political, social, and even cultural. The member states are constitutional democracies without exception. That is a condition for their accession to the Union. The final decisions are taken by a Council of Ministers who each represent a government supported by a parliamentary majority elected by all adult voters in free and open elections.

However, the major decisions are taken by unanimity and that in itself requires deliberations and negotiations that allow great scope for any member state that threatens to veto the proposal. Moreover, the European agenda is hardly an issue during the elections of the European Parliament; usually people vote according to their preferences for the national parties, while European policies are rarely discussed in domestic politics. Once a decision has been taken, it is left to the

Commission and its high-ranking officials to elaborate the rules and regulations that are supposed to follow from it. The result is a style of governance that is authoritarian under the rule of law, *rechtsstaatlich*, but not democratic, in the sense of participatory or deliberative. At times, the style of governance in the EU has been *immobiliste*: the unanimity requirement prevented any strong initiative or innovation. It is a surprising feature that under these conditions the EU has been capable of rather radical transformations nevertheless: the establishment of a common market, the introduction of the Euro, the inclusion of Southern states first and at present the opening towards the East. Even during periods of immobility, the free movement of persons made for quite incisive mutual adaptations, as citizens went shopping to profit from more permissive moral regimes in neighbouring countries when drugs, alcohol or abortion were concerned. Moreover, the courts used their competence to strengthen the rights of citizens vis-à-vis governments and employers. Administrators exploited existing regulations to further free movement and open competition, sometimes in a quite radical manner.

The EU has its problems of corruption and ineptitude, but in the technical sense it is well governed, quite efficient and thoroughly legalistic. The citizens are reasonably well served especially in their capacity as producers, consumers, employees and travellers. In terms of its governance, the EU may be rated quite positively. But as political subjects, its citizens figure only in the background of the overall picture. This is in part, but not entirely, an institutional shortcoming: the Council is not elected and requires unanimity or qualified majorities among ministers who are supported by elected majorities in their home countries but have no direct electoral mandate on European issues. The Commission is not elected. The European Parliament consists of representatives elected in their home countries, but rarely on European campaign issues, while the Parliament itself has relatively restricted authority. But the real weakness of the Union is its deficient political culture, a consequence of language barriers that are all too obvious and of cultural obstacles that are equally formidable but much less evident. So far, the politicians, journalists and intellectuals whose calling it is to pursue the debate on public affairs find it almost impossible to communicate across national borders. The political system is still overwhelmingly oriented towards national issues. Universities and the printed media, the natural havens of the intellectuals, are also very much national institutions. The gravity of national culture operates to pull journalists, writers and academics back within their domestic societies. There are hardly any media outlets or career possibilities in the European realm. In short, there is no 'cultural opportunity structure' that allows intellectuals to function at the European level (De Swaan 2002). This, more than anything else, explains the paltry state of the European public sphere. The weakness of the European Union resides not in the quality of its governance but of its politics. This is one fault that the grand administrators of the Union cannot correct by themselves. It is the task of the intellectuals and the politicians in Europe to bring about a public sphere across borders, to overcome the gravitational pull of domestic societies and to engage one another in a truly European, public and political debate.

REFERENCES

Bachrach, Peter and Baratz, Morton S. 1963. 'Decisions and Nondecisions: An Analytical Framework'. *American Political Science Review,* 57(3): 632–42.

De Swaan, Abram. 2001. *Words of the World: The Global Language System.* Cambridge, UK: Polity Press.

———. 2002. 'The European Void: The Democratic Deficit as a Cultural Lack'. *European Studies Newsletter,* 331: 4–5. 5 and 6 June. New York: Center for European Studies.

Guillén, Ana M. and Álvarez, Santuago. 2001. 'Globalization and the Southern Welfare States', in Robert Sykes, Bruno Palier and Pauline M. Prior (eds.). *Globalization and European Welfare States: Challenges and Change,* pp. 103–26. Basingstoke, New York: Palgrave.

Hagen, Kare. 1992. 'The Social Dimension: A Quest for a European Welfare State', in Zsuzsa Ferge and Jon Eivind Kolberg (eds.). *Social Policy in a Changing Europe,* pp. 281–303. Boulder, CO: Campus/Westview.

Kjeldstad, Randi. 2001. 'Gender Politics and Gender Equality', in Miko Kautto, Johan Fritzell, Bjorn Hvinden, Jon Kvist and Hannu Uusitalo (eds.). *Nordic Welfare States in the European Context,* pp. 66–97. London: Routledge.

Kurzer, Paulette. 2001. *Markets and Moral Regulation; Cultural Change in the European Union.* Cambridge, UK: Cambridge University Press.

Leibfried, Stephan and Pierson, Paul. 1994. 'The Prospects for Social Europe', in Abram De Swaan (ed.). *Social Policy Beyond Borders; The Social Question in Transnational Perspective,* pp. 59–82. Amsterdam: Amsterdam University Press.

Leibfried, Stephan and Pierson, Paul. 1995. 'The Dynamics of Social Policy Integration', in Stephan Leibfried and Paul Pierson (eds.). *European Social Policy: Between Fragmentation and Integration,* pp. 432–65. Washington, D.C.: Brookings Institution.

Sorensen, Annemette. 2001. 'Gender Equality in Earnings at Work and Home', in Miko Kautto, Johan Fritzell, Bjorn Hvinden, Jon Kvist and Hannu Uusitalo (eds.). *Nordic Welfare States in the European Context*, pp. 98–115. London: Routledge.

Streeck, Wolfgang. 1995. 'From Market Making to State Building? Reflections on the Political Economy of European Social Policy', in Stephan Leibfried and Paul Pierson (eds.). *European Social Policy: Between Fragmentation and Integration*, pp. 389–432. Washington, D.C.: The Brookings Institution Press.

CHAPTER 4

GOVERNANCE AND DEMOCRACY:
REFLECTIONS ON THE EUROPEAN DEBATE

ANGELA LIBERATORE[1]

PREAMBLE: EUROPEAN GOVERNANCE WITHOUT A EUROPEAN STATE?

When examining the debate on governance in a supranational context such as the European Union (EU), it is important to note that the
questions related to the responsibility of states and governments in
formulating and implementing public policies and delivering public goods take very specific features. With its institutional setting
and wealth of legislation (that takes priority—in case of difference—
over legislation of member states), the EU goes much beyond any
international organisation in exercising regulatory functions. Sometimes it is even considered as a sort of 'suprastate' comprising an
'executive' (as the European Commission is often portrayed), two
legislative bodies (the Council of Ministers and the European Parliament), a judiciary (the European Court of Justice), a European Ombudsman, and various other executive (e.g., agencies) and consultative
bodies (e.g., Economic and Social Committee, Committee of Regions).
It is, however, important to note that the state analogy is not fully
accurate when analysing the EU. One does not need to be an
intergovernmentalist (I am not) to acknowledge that not only does
the EU lack some specific state features (such as the 'monopoly over
legitimate means of coercion') but also that the EU decision-making process is a multilevel game which is *sui generis* rather than a mere
expansion of a federal (state) arrangement.

Such features of the EU do not make irrelevant the important questions of what governance functions public authorities should retain, how the interplay between private and public actors can lead to more effective results rather than 'abdication' of responsibility, and how accountability is built and implemented in a governance system. On the contrary, the EU case is of interest also for scholars and policy makers—and any concerned citizen—working on the role of states in new governance arrangements. After all, the increasing role of the private sector in regulation (e.g., with voluntary agreements and other forms of co-regulation) is far from being a peculiar EU phenomenon. Also, with the erosion of some important state's formerly unique competences, any state faces some of the dilemmas that a supranational, non-state organisation like the EU is experiencing. As a case of such 'erosion', one can take the exclusive competence for decision over movements of persons, goods, capital and services within state borders. This is not only limited by European legislation for EU member states, but is limited for any country which is a party to the World Trade Organisation (WTO) and often also for countries who are not.

By focusing on the issue of democracy, this contribution will not pursue a full analysis of the issues noted above, but rather incorporate them in the discussion.

Change is a key word in addressing the above issues, and the analysis will try to point to dynamics rather than assuming static 'equilibrium'. Again, this is almost obvious when examining such in-progress and experimental setting as the EU (Laffan et al. 2000), especially during a period of unprecedented enlargement and of deep debate on the future of Europe and on the related institutional reforms. More broadly, such dynamic perspective also applies to governance actors and processes.

THE WHITE PAPER ON GOVERNANCE AND ITS CHALLENGES

When the European Commission's President, Romano Prodi, announced 'promoting new forms of European governance' as first priority in the Strategic Objectives for the period 2000–2005, expectations and questions emerged. The word 'governance' itself was not one immediately understandable, nor palatable, to many; and supporters and detractors of European integration could read such priority—with fear or happiness—as moving towards a 'super-government' or diluting European legal competencies and policy functions.

The challenges ahead became clear as soon as actual work on this priority was initiated. What does 'governance' actually mean, for whom, and how does it apply to the European Union? Is this a matter that complements or overlaps with the agenda on institutional reform of the Nice Inter-Governmental Conference (IGC)? And, from a more 'internal' perspective, how was the White Paper on Governance to relate to the ongoing administrative reform of the European Commission? Finally, and most important, which changes in European governance could help in meeting the challenges of enlargement, dealing with the expansion of competencies (with the two new 'pillars'—Justice and Home Affairs, and Common Foreign and Security Policy—added with the Maastricht Treaty) and responding to the needs of EU citizens? Each of these questions was hard to settle. 'Governance' was taken as mainly dealing with the way in which decisions and policies are made and implemented; that is, to focus on 'how' rather than 'who'. This was partly due to the mandate of the White Paper, which was supposed to be based on the current treaty of the EU (rather than suggesting changes) and was not intended to 'interfere' with the debate on institutional reform of the IGC. However, it is quite obvious that one cannot discuss the 'how' in full abstraction from the 'who'; again, given the parallel debate at the IGC, the Commission undertook to focus on its own role in governance while also addressing other institutions. How to respond to increasing competencies (some of them quite 'split'[2]), enlargement and the need of citizens was then to be addressed in such framework. It is useful to keep such 'background' in mind when discussing the achievements and shortcomings of the White Paper and the issue of democracy.

Of course the Commission was not starting from zero. Preliminary work had been undertaken by the Forward Studies Unit: a series of workshops resulted in proceedings published once the work on the White Paper had started (De Schutter et al. 2001). In addition, the issue of *global governance* was familiar to the services working in the areas of trade and external relations, the notion of *corporate governance* was familiar to services handling economic affairs and industrial policy, *environmental governance* was upfront in the Commission's work on international environmental agreements, and research on *governance and citizenship* had been started by the

Directorate General (DG), Research. Nevertheless, putting all these streams in dialogue—plus others to be listened to, and accounted for, from other institutions, civil society, etc.—did not prove to be easy. In addition, as part of the 'diagnosis' work, a report on perceptions of Europe by citizens in EU countries and candidate countries was commissioned (OPTEM 2001). This report seems to indicate a paradox. On the one hand, citizens expect a strong Europe, capable of tackling common problems within the Union, and of taking a stand in face of regional conflicts and global issues; on the other hand, distrust in European as well as national institutions is widespread.

A small 'governance team', led by Jerome Vignon,[3] was established within the Secretariat General, a Work Programme was adopted on 11 October 2000 (SEC [2000] 1547/7), and 12 Working Groups were appointed around the six main areas of the Work Programme with the involvement of about 100 officials. Such groups and areas are listed in Table 4.1.

The text of the White Paper, the reports of the Working Groups, and a synthesis on the consultations held with other European institutions, local and regional authorities, civil society organisations, researchers, etc., during the work that led to the White Paper are published on the

Table 4.1

1. *Enhancing and enriching the public debate on Europe*
    a. Building the European public area
    b. Democratising expertise and establishing European scientific references
2. *Handling the preparation and implementation processes*
    a. Formalising the right to be involved
    b. Transparency of evaluation
    c. Better lawmaking
3. *Improving the exercise of European responsibilities through decentralisation*
    a. Horizontal decentralisation (agencies)
    b. Vertical decentralisation
4. *Coherence and cooperation in a networked Europe*
    a. Convergence of national policies
    b. Organisation structures for Trans-European networks
    c. Linking the various levels—European, national, regional and local
5. *Strengthening the Union's contribution to world governance*
    a. Applying the European strategy of sustainable development on the world stage
6. *Strengthening the integration and strategic dimension of Union policies across the continent*
    a. Defining the framework for a debate on the policies the Union needs

Commission's website: *http://europa.eu.int/comm/governance/index_en.htm*. This website also hosts the responses received on the White Paper during the period of consultation running from its publication to the deadline of 31 March 2002. The White Paper indeed gave rise to a rather broad debate,[4] including important criticisms. The reflections offered in this contribution do not try to synthesise such debate, but contribute to it. Of course, I do not claim 'neutrality' in such discussion: on top of the subjective values and biases of any author, I was involved in some preparatory work for the White Paper and must share responsibility for it while not necessarily subscribing to every word in it.

GOVERNANCE AND DEMOCRACY IN THE WHITE PAPER

The link between governance and democracy has been at the core of the effort: 'enhancing democracy in Europe' is indeed the 'motto' that appears in the Work Programme for the White Paper. The White Paper itself (European Commission 2001) starts with a diagnosis of problems affecting democracies today, such as alienation of citizens, loss of confidence in institutions and politics—especially acute at the EU level. It then suggests that 'Democratic institutions and representatives of the people, at both national and European levels, can and must try to connect Europe with its citizens. This is the starting condition for more effective and relevant policies' (White Paper: 3). It goes on to identify principles of 'good governance': openness, participation, accountability, effectiveness and coherence. These are expected to complement the principles of subsidiarity (concerning the level of actions taken) and proportionality (of the measure decided in relation to the problem to be tackled). Specific proposals are then developed, ranging from the adoption of minimum standards for consultation to guidelines to make more open and accountable the use of expert advice, codification of rules concerning the handling of legal complaints, etc.

The follow up of such proposals—that took the form of three Communications in June 2002 on better lawmaking and of other measures published in December the same year[5]—are discussed in the relevant sections below. Proposals on the reform of the overall institutional setting of the EU were beyond the mandate of the White

Paper, even though the Nice Summit of December 2000—where a debate on the future of Europe and ambitious reforms were called for—raised expectations in that direction.

It is useful to note that 'good governance' is a concept often used (e.g., by the World Bank) to indicate some integrity of public action, as against corruption and fraud. In principle there can be non-democratic governments that are non-corrupted and surely there are democracies deeply affected by corruption. Therefore, to aim at good, democratic governance involves some additional requirements, mainly in relation to legitimacy. We can consider the first three principles identified in the White Paper as components of 'input legitimacy' of policies and institutions, and the other two as components of 'output legitimacy'. Issues of openness, participation and accountability are at the core of notions of democracy, and lack of effectiveness and coherence are identified among the threats to the credibility and stability of democratic institutions. While legitimacy is not a synonym of democracy (Olsen 1999), surely a 'non-legitimate democracy' sounds a contradiction in terms; at the same time, different perspectives exist as to whether democratic legitimacy is mainly or exclusively a matter of process (input) or of results (outputs), or both. Clearly the White Paper tries to address both. Some critics (e.g., Eriksen 2001; Wind 2001) argue that the balance 'bends' towards efficiency (output) rather than accountability (input). Others note that more attention should have been devoted to the substance of policies in order to effectively manage the increased diversity that is being brought about by the EU enlargement (Scharpf 2001).

More to the roots, different views exist as to whether it is really necessary and possible to 'democratise' the EU, with strong arguments being made that this is indeed both necessary and feasible under certain conditions (Schmitter 2000). The White Paper can be seen as a significant policy component in such debate. For example, someone could interpret the White Paper as assuming that the EU is already fully democratic when it says

> These results have been achieved by democratic means. The Union is built on the rule of law, it can draw on the Charter of Fundamental Rights, and it has a double democratic mandate through a Parliament representing the EU citizens and a Council representing the elected governments of the member states (European Commission 2001: 7).

But of course there would not be a White Paper if there were no problems related to the very working—and citizens' trust in—democratic institutions within European countries and at the European level. On the other hand, those who believe that that the EU cannot or should not be democratic can consider the efforts toward openness, accountability, etc., as addressing a wrong 'target'. Finally, the very definition of democratisation can vary: is it mainly a matter of 'majoritarianism', plus protection of minorities, and/or a matter of constitutional guarantees and principles with an important role for non-majoritarian institutions (Majone 1996)?

The debate is not only analytical, but also normative. My normative stand, to make it explicit, is that the EU needs further democratisation. European policies and legislation affect the everyday life of people in fields as different as health, environment, mobility and social protection, thus citizens are supposed to have a say on how they are made. In addition, the EU is far from a merely economic organisation and is increasingly establishing itself as a political entity, which clearly claims to be part of the democracy 'family' (e.g., in its requirements towards candidate countries); its democratic features need, therefore, to be developed in the changing context.

Some issues pertaining to 'democratising European governance' and addressed in the White Paper include the following: the relations between consultation of civil society and role of representative institutions; possible trade-offs between participation, efficiency and effectiveness; role of expertise; conditions for and chains of accountability. Also present, while in a less explicit way, are the relations between citizenship, 'demos' and public space, and the relations between governance, democracy and sustainable development.

CIVIL SOCIETY AND REPRESENTATIVE INSTITUTIONS

Involvement of civil society in decision making can be seen as a key feature of 'governance' itself, where the question 'who governs' is not that simple to answer. Critics of the very notion of 'governance' even consider that it hides a trend towards privatisation of government. In addition, one must note that 'civil society' is far from uniquely defined. In the definition used in the White Paper— borrowing from the Economic and Social Committee—it refers to any non-state actor (from grassroot organisations to large corporations). Alternatively it can refer to a space of actors between, and distinct from, state and market (see Crouch et al. 2001).

Participation by civil society is not bad or good in itself. Participation of citizens—as individuals as well as collectively organised—in decisions affecting their lives is a (quasi) obvious feature of democracy. On the other hand, participation of *some* actors of civil society or lack of proper procedures to check how participation happens and what its results are can indeed lead to an 'oligarchist' governance rather than a democratic one. Literature on 'regulatory capture' of public authorities by vested, private interests can be seen as a case in point (see Stigler 1971; Wilson 1980). Participatory governance acknowledges that there is a multiplicity of actors who hold interests, rights and competencies in public choice and public policy; at the same time it raises important issues of entitlements—who decides who is entitled to participate, in which form (Grote and Gbikpi 2001)? In the EU context, the matter is (as usual) more complex than at national and local levels. 'Umbrella organisations' based in Brussels, while not necessarily being the closest to their 'constituencies' (whether consumers, farmers, patients, women or others), often have more chances to be consulted. At the same time, the relations with representative institutions occur at various levels; and it is to be noted that national Parliaments are pushing for stronger involvement in European affairs—at times in cooperation, and others in competition, with the European Parliament. In the White Paper, some proposals are made to clarify who is consulted, when and how. At the same time the importance of the representative institutions (European and national Parliaments) is stressed. The assumption is that participative and representative democracy are complementary rather than mutually exclusive, and that 'good'/'democratic' governance needs both.

The report of the European Parliament on the White Paper (EP 304.289, 28/11/02, rapporteur: MEP Sylvia Kaufmann) indicates that such complementarity is not to be taken for granted. By pointing to the fact that organised civil society is inevitably sectoral and does not have the legitimacy that comes from popular election, the Parliament is accurate indeed. At the same time, it seems to assert its own role in an almost 'zero-sum-game' approach where elected representatives seem to lose if non-elected civil society organisations come 'to the table'. In times of low turn out at elections and of distrust in formal institutions, the contrary might be the case if the proper framework is developed. Also, by inviting the Commission to avoid adding a further level of bureaucracy in terms of 'accredited organisations', the Parliament points to a real risk. However, it perhaps disregards the attempt to build some transparency and accountability in the ongoing—and ever increasing—informal consultations that take place at the various stages of policy formulation.

As a specific follow up to the White Paper and the comments by the European Parliament and others on this issue, the Commission published on 5 June 2002 a Communication on 'principles and minimum standards of consultation of interested parties by the Commission' (COM. [2002] 277 final). In such a consultation document, it is stressed that 'there is no contradiction between wide consultations and the concept of representative democracy', and also that it is necessary to 'reduce the risk of the policymakers just listening to one side of the argument or of particular groups getting privileged access' (p. 5). Some minimum standards for consultations are then proposed, aimed at guaranteeing openness and accountability, effectiveness and coherence. They include clear content of the consultation, publication (including on the Internet), sufficient time for responses, acknowledgement of receipt of contributions and publication of the feedback, specific elements for 'focused consultation'. In addition a database on formal and consultative bodies (CONECCS–Consultation, the European Commission and Civil Society) is available on the Internet: *http://europa.eu.int/comm/civil_society/coneccs/index.htm*.

Surely the relations between civil society and representative institutions will continue to raise policy, societal and scholarly attention. The Convention established after the Nice Summit to develop proposals for the future institutional setting of the EU will necessarily face some of these issues, and the study of democracy at any level cannot disregard the relations between civil society and representative institutions.

TRADEOFFS BETWEEN PARTICIPATION, EFFICIENCY AND EFFECTIVENESS

It is often considered that participation is inefficient as it takes a lot of time and energy, and it is questioned whether it is effective in bringing about better results. With regard to the potential trade-offs between participation, efficiency and effectiveness, experience and research in mediation of public disputes and in policy implementation provide interesting evidence on the importance of involving 'target' sectors/'stakeholders' as early as possible in the policy formulation process so as to prevent decisional impasse and implementation failures (Downing and Hanf 1983; Susskind and Cruikshank 1987; Weidner 1995). In other words, it may look less 'efficient'—i.e., take longer—to formulate a policy by increasing consultation and (which is a step beyond) participation. However, it can avoid not just delays in implementation (which would lead to a sort of 'time balance' between formulation and implementation), but total failure in getting anything decided for implementation. In other words, participation can enhance effectiveness by allowing decisions that are actually put in practice.

Similarly, political failures can be explained—at least in some cases—as resulting from lack of consultation and participation at an early stage. For example, some observers interpret in this way the negative results of the first Irish referendum on the ratification of the Nice Treaty. Whether it was not clear earlier or whether better consultation and debate would lead to a different result in terms of 'yes' or 'no', at least more citizens would have had a genuine interest in the matter and participated in the vote (Sinnott 2001). The second referendum, characterised by intense debate, led to more participation and eventually to a success of the 'yes' campaign. The White Paper advances proposals on legislative simplification while insisting on consultation and participation. The option of regulating completely behind closed doors is normally not available due to the many interests that claim an involvement; and, when it is pursued, it is at odds with democratic processes. Therefore, finding a balance between simplification and participation is one of the challenges ahead. Such a challenge is understood, while not solved, by the White Paper, and by the follow up Communication on an Action Plan for simplifying and improving the regulatory environment of 5 June 2002 (COM [2002] 278 final).

The June Communication acknowledges the importance of consultation as a way of improving the quality of legislative proposals, and reference is made to the related Communication on minimum standards for consultation. It was also planned to expand the explanatory memoranda accompanying legislative proposals to include an account of the consultations held and results obtained, as well as the impact assessment carried out, the reasons for choosing the proposed instrument and the budgetary implications. At the same time the necessity of simplifying and reducing the volume of community legislation, to make the regulation more attuned to a user's requirements, facilitate implementation in the member states and save time and reduce costs for companies and public authorities is stressed. The possible tension between wide consultation (where diverse interests and viewpoints may lead to multiple requirements) and simplification (which involves the reduction of requirements to the 'basics') is not explicitly mentioned in the Communication. However, one can extrapolate a 'rule of thumb' that could be used to settle such tension when looking at the proposal to withdraw legislative proposals if amendments introduced by the European Parliament and/or Council denature the proposal or add complexity incompatible with the proposal's objectives. By extension, if consultation would only lead to denature or add 'too much' complexity to proposals, the Commission could either reject them or withdraw a proposal before even presenting it to the legislative institutions. The ultimate goal stressed in the Communication is to ensure a high level of legal certainty across the EU, also after enlargement, and indeed it is only through effective implementation of common rules that such legal certainty can be strengthened. As discussed above, this is compatible, rather than at odds, with participation, while not immediately compatible with time and economic efficiency at the formulation stage.

EXPERTISE, TECHNOCRACY AND DEMOCRACY

European policy-making, and European institutions—especially the Commission—are often portrayed as 'technocratic', or at least as heavily based on expertise and relatively shielded from public debate. Indeed, regulatory policy-making in the European Union is strongly based on the mobilisation of in-house expertise as well as expertise provided by a variety of sources: from experts appointed by member states to consultants and independent researchers. With regard to the former, the system of expert committees has been described as one of the most opaque areas of community decision-making and proposals for its reform were made (see Joerges and Vos 1999; Schaefer et al. 2002). With regard to the latter, a variety of mechanisms for gathering experts' inputs are used: from formal scientific committees (e.g., in the field of food safety) to commissioned studies and informal hearings and workshops.

While most analysts agree on the need to increase the transparency of the committee system, few so far had pointed to the broader issue of making the overall process of mobilisation and use of expertise more open and accountable, let alone 'democratising expertise' itself. This is what the White Paper calls for. As I was the rapporteur of the working group on 'Democratising Expertise', let me refer to our document (Liberatore 2001) with only a few comments.

First of all, it is necessary to address the paradox of expertise being a resource that is increasingly sought for policy-making and, at the same time, being increasingly contested (as controversies over nuclear power, biotechnology and food safety demonstrate). This paradox is far from being uniquely relevant to the EU (indeed it is widespread beyond Europe as well), but it takes important features in such a context. Should the EU resort less to expertise (be less 'technocratic') and risk losing one of its main resources and be then labelled as incompetent? Or should it disregard the controversies surrounding many areas of expert advice and be charged with myopia or top-down selection of (preferred) advice? Surely, reforming the way expertise is mobilised and used seems a more fruitful option. Second, a plurality of expertise sources must be acknowledged—from natural to social sciences, from theoretical to practical knowledge—as part of the broader pluralism in democratic debate. Third, while expertise—by definition—involves degrees of specialisation that are not universally shared, it does not mean that it is the exclusive prerogative of an elite that can only be judged by the elite itself; the way problems are defined—and options suggested—can benefit from broader scrutiny. Fourth, democratising expertise should not be understood as 'majority voting in science'; it is rather about due process in terms of guaranteeing plurality, openness and accountability in the way expertise is mobilised and used for policy-making.

As a follow up to the White Paper, and following the Science and Society Action Plan issued in December 2001 (COM [2001] 428 final), a working group was established to define principles and guidelines for the collection and use of expertise. The results of such work forms part of the second 'package' of Communications intended to implement the proposals on the White Paper, that is the Communication on the collection and use of expert advice (COM [2002] 713 final).

Accountability and Responsibility

Accountability is a term that requires many specifications, namely whose accountability to whom and how. Elected representatives are accountable to the citizens is the first answer; such representatives can be sanctioned by the electors by non-renewal of mandate. And governments, of course, are accountable to parliaments and the citizens who, again, are supposed to be able to sanction them.

All this assumes that citizens are indeed interested, actively participating and are granted access to clear procedures for making politicians stick to their promises. But how does accountability work if distrust emerges and leads to low turnout in elections and decline in other ways—petitions, demonstrations, etc.—of 'sanctioning' governments and parliaments? Or if the chain of accountability is not clear and shifting of responsibility is allowed leading to nobody actually appearing in charge? Another aspect is, of course, accountability as legally 'sanctionable' (liability) by the judiciary; here the connotation of democracy as being based on the rule of law comes into play and access to justice becomes a crucial right to be granted.

Accountability is one of the key arguments in discourses over the 'democratic deficit' of the EU. The White Paper makes some proposals to enhance accountability by making it easier to 'trace back' who did what and when in the policy process. It also stresses that all EU institutions need to play the game in their function of control (Parliament), legislation (Council and Parliament), implementation (authorities in the member states), 'watchdog' (Ombudsman), etc. The relative roles of European institutions and the clarification of the 'chain of accountability' could only be addressed in the White Paper (which was supposed to assume no change in the treaty) by suggesting to 'revitalise the community method'.

Admittedly, this approach was bound to attract criticisms that range from lack of innovation to perceived willingness to further 'centralise power' in the Commission (e.g., when stressing that the Commission has unique responsibility for initiating legislation). When comparing the EU with national democracy, the obvious criticism is regarding the peculiarity and even non-accountability of a non-elected institution being the initiator of legislation. Here it is worth pointing to the need to have one institution representing the 'common European interest' instead of national ones and noting the far from transparent procedures in the Council of Ministers (formerly the unique legislator and then with the Maastricht treaty—co-legislator with the European Parliament). Also the charge of 'centralism' could be mitigated by the White Paper's emphasis on decentralisation: 'horizontal'—through agencies, and 'vertical—e.g., through 'target based, tripartite contracts' between local authorities, national ones and the Commission. However, issues of accountability are again raised concerning the working of agencies or of tripartite contracts. In its Communication on Better Lawmaking of June 2002, the Commission calls for an inter-institutional agreement (between the European Commission, Council and Parliament) to clarify their respective responsibilities. This indicates that the issue of accountability and responsibility of European (public) authorities, while still not settled, is firmly on the agenda.

CITIZENSHIP, 'DEMOS' AND THE PUBLIC SPHERE

A point emphasised by those who think that the EU cannot be democratised is that it lacks a 'demos'. Of course what a 'demos' is depends on definitions, but it is true that a certain degree of homogeneity—as implicit in most notions of 'demos'—is lacking in the EU (and, we may add, fortunately we have such diversity!). Then the point is whether a different notion of 'demos' can be developed (see Zuern 1999) or whether we can 'simply' have a democracy with a polity and a citizenry based on democratic principles where a public space for debate is developed—eventually across 'demoi'. Strong arguments can be put forward to support such options, including the need to counteract the potential for conflicts coming from ethnically-based definitions of citizenship (e.g., Weiler et al. 1995).

Since 'enhancing public debate on Europe' was a key focus of the White Paper, it seems fair to say that regardless of whether a 'European demos' can be envisaged or not, surely a (democratic) public space is what is being aimed at. Such a 'European public space' can be understood as the processes and institutions that allow for public debate and deliberation on issues that are of common interest across countries and—quite often—across levels of responsibility and policy sectors.

A growing literature is being devoted to this subject and raises important issues with regard to the feasibility and possible features of a European public sphere in a context characterised by many different languages, nationally oriented mass media and political discourses, diverse interests and cultures (e.g., Calhoun 1992; De Swaan 1993; Schlesinger 1995) (a number of European research projects are ongoing in the public sphere, coordinated by A. Bora, L. Giorgi, R. Koopmans, T. Risse and others[6]). Empirical evidence can be found of transnational debates and mobilisation on European issues (e.g., European campaigns—mainly organised by non-governmental organisations—on environment protection, food safety, anti-racism, social protection standards, role of the EU in the WTO). In addition, some European issues are debated as such by the national media and political parties (e.g., introduction and stability of the Euro; BSE crisis and responses to it; migration and diverse assessments of the need for coordinated European policies). It seems fair to say that a European public space can be hardly expected to be a 'stand alone' one: it will need to be nurtured by public debates taking place at local and national levels on issues of common 'European' interest, and recognised as such. This is shown also by the proceedings of the Convention on the future institutional setting of the EU. While the Convention should respond to the need to 'open up' the diplomatic/behind closed door process of the Inter-Governmental Conferences, it can provide an arena for a truly European debate only if its work and agenda are discussed not only 'in Brussels' but also in local and national contexts.

It is interesting to note that while there are temptations to interpret the need for public debate in the mere sense of engaging in 'public relations', the policy debate surrounding the White Paper on Governance seems receptive to arguments that stress the need to provide for procedures for 'real' debate, including the above-mentioned proposal for minimum standards of consultation.

GOVERNANCE AND SUSTAINABLE DEVELOPMENT

In parallel with the drafting of the White Paper, the Commission developed an EU Strategy for Sustainable Development (COM [2001] 264 final) for submission at the Council meeting in Goetheborg. Since they were working in parallel, the two documents contain some cross-referencing while not substantially linking governance and sustainable development. Nevertheless, governance and sustainable development share a number of features and in one of the follow ups to the White Paper—the Communication on Impact Assessment—this is recognised, as discussed in the final paragraph of this section. Let me expand on those shared features since—as Amartya Sen wrote—'development is freedom' (Sen 1999) and it is thus necessary to link issues of governance with issues of (sustainable) development. Governance and sustainable development are broad concepts with an appearance of 'apple pie'—who does not want governance, namely good governance, and a development that is sustainable?—but they also involve tensions and conflicts. Both reflect different cultures and experiences and sometimes are hard to translate in languages other than English; in spite of such diversity, however, these concepts share a global outreach. And they are not just 'concepts'. Programmes to promote good governance have been launched at various levels, from local to global or—more often—from global actors and institutions to national and local ones. Agendas, policies and strategies intended to foster sustainable development have decades of history.

In spite of a wealth of reflection as well as action on governance and on sustainable development, the interactions between the two need further exploration. Six main links can be identified: enhancing democracy and participation; overcoming 'sectoralisation'; managing public goods; tackling distributive aspects; avoiding 'short-termism'; and articulating levels.

Enhancing democracy and participation is not an automatic outcome of debating 'governance'. As discussed earlier, the debate on governance is closely related to improving civil society participation in policy-making, matching this with strong representative institutions, increasing openness. All this is relevant for pursuing sustainable development policies; Agenda 21 and Local Agenda 21 already stressed the importance of participation, and the pursuit of economic, social and ecological compatibility requires that all views be put 'on the table' and that decision made be checked and challenged.

Overcoming 'sectoralisation' of policies is a basic ingredient for tackling the complexity and interdependence of environmental, economic and social processes. It is also a challenge to current governance modes where sectoral policies, administrative structures and political agendas tend to exclude 'cross-cutting' issues from consideration. Integrating environmental considerations in other policies has been a useful approach introduced in European policy-making. The next step is even more ambitious and calls for integrating economic, social and ecological aspects of sustainable development 'upstream'. Since 'integrating everything with everything else' is clearly impossible, defining the key interfaces and priorities is a must.

Managing public goods is another link between governance and sustainable development. Even if the definition of 'public good' is not to be taken for granted, it is clear that the ability of governments and of governance structures to guarantee universal access to vital resources is a key element of their effectiveness and legitimacy. This raises important issues with regard to the shape and impact of privatisation policies as well as to the diverse contributions—by countries, economic sectors and social groups—to the depletion and protection of global public goods.

Tackling distributive aspects is an old problem. Such a problem, however, assumes new features when environmental and sustainable development constraints come into the picture. The possibility to simply 'expand the cake'—e.g., through uncontrolled use of natural resources, postponement of decision to later generations—is not feasible. Equitably sharing 'the cake' becomes then an issue that cannot be shifted nor postponed and that involves important governance issues, e.g., the balanced representation of interests within and between countries, the identification of instruments to allocate resources, the assessment of economic, social as well as environmental costs. In a transnational context such as the EU, distributive aspects between and within countries and sectors are being reassessed in the light of enlargement, globalisation, as well as sustainable development.

Avoiding 'short-termism' in policy-making is a key challenge for governance. Not only electoral cycles but also investment cycles (which are crucial when deciding on issues such as infrastructures) tend to be too short to deal with long-term changes and take care of future generations as sustainable development principles prescribe. Again, this seems to be a specifically tough challenge for democratic governance where 'constituencies' are present and decisions are made to respond to interests that find a 'voice' in the political and economic sphere.

Articulating levels is an obvious but still difficult task in the context of 'multilevel governance' which spans from local to global. The tendency is to stick to a 'clear', often rigid, definition of competencies at the expense of working out the interfaces and synergies. Lessons from the environmental movement motto 'think globally, act locally' (and vice versa) are still to become part of new governance arrangements. Articulation of levels is a key issue in settings like the EU where the principle of subsidiarity is at the core of policy debate and implementation.

The Communication of 5 June 2002 on Impact Assessment (COM [2002] 276 final) provides a step forward in tackling some of the above issues, namely overcoming sectoralisation through an integrated assessment of economic, ecological and social impacts of proposed measures. In addition the Communication on 'tripartite contracts' (COM [2002] 709 final) explicitly acknowledges the need to articulate levels of responsibility as appropriate to specific issues and circumstances.

GLOBAL GOVERNANCE, SECURITY AND THE ROLE OF EUROPE

I would like to conclude my contribution by trying to go beyond a potentially 'Eurocentric' perspective while sticking to the task of a chapter on European governance. 'The EU's contribution to global governance' is after all one of the chapters of the White Paper, and it proposes, inter alia, to promote a discussion on the reform of global institutions and improve dialogue with 'third countries' actors. From a more personal point of view, I would like to offer three main points for consideration: commonality and diversities of democracy systems and governance arrangements; accountability of institutions, including global institutions; governance capacity for the prevention and resolution of conflicts.

Democracy can take many forms and shapes while being based on some shared, basic elements such as respect for fundamental rights, rule of law, political competition, checks and balances. In addition, democracy is a process that may involve diverse transition paths (as shown by transitions to democracy from fascist regimes and from communist ones) and is never to be taken for granted even in its 'mature' stages. The EU can, therefore, contribute to its own democratisation and support democratisation in other parts of the world by respecting diversity and, at the same time, continuously monitoring democracy within its own borders. This applies, for example, in relation to the rise of the far right and of xenophobic trends, the introduction of some restrictions of civil liberties following the terrorist attack of September 11.

The accountability of global institutions (increasingly challenged by vocal social movements, often labelled as 'anti-globalisation' movements) is clearly an issue to be tackled. If it is already hard to 'democratise' a setting like the EU, it is probably a 'mission impossible' to aim at 'democratising the international system'. This is partly due to the fact that non-democratic countries are part of it and would not subscribe to its democratisation; and even if all the world was run by democratic governments, it is hard to conceive a workable 'global democratic system'. Still, chains and procedures of accountability can and should be developed for institutions that have an important influence in economic matters as well as in other fields (e.g., labour standards, health care). The EU can share its experience in developing accountability for transnational institutions.

Last but not least, (Western) Europe was blessed by decades of peace after the destruction caused by World War II. Not all areas of the world had the same 'luck', and in addition violent conflicts— including within Europe, as in the Balkans, or in its neighbourhood, as in the Middle East—remind us that security and stability cannot be taken for granted. It has been demonstrated that democracy allows for the negotiation of different interests and values through rules for social dialogue, legislation for protection of minorities, etc. At the same time, democracies are not necessarily 'peaceful' as war interventions in Vietnam, Iraq and other areas show. Some democratically elected governments have resorted to military occupation of other's territories, with the related infringement of fundamental rights that should be a basic requirement for a democracy. Therefore, the development of democratic governance capacity to prevent and resolve conflicts seems a difficult but urgent task. And it is an honour to be able to address such an appeal in a book resulting from a conference hosted in the country of Mahatma Gandhi.

NOTES

1. The opinions expressed are those of the author and do not necessarily represent the views of the European Commission.

2. The two new 'pillars' are much more 'intergovernmental' (that is, mainly in the hands of the Council of Ministers) than the original 'Community' pillar where policy initiative is the responsibility of the Commission.
3. Former aide to former Commission's President Jacques Delors and coordinator of another influential White Paper on 'Growth, Competitiveness and Employment'.
4. The Internet-based consultation following the publication of the White Paper includes less than 300 responses: this is surely not an impressive number, but it must be noted that most responses are collective ones (by local and regional authorities, national Parliaments, non-governmental organisations [NGOs], business organisations, universities) each resulting from broader debate. In addition, the consultations held during the preparation of the White Paper were extensive and debates relating the White Paper to the work of the Convention continue.
5. The follow up Communications of 5 June 2002 include: an Action Plan on simplifying and improving the regulatory environment; general principles and minimum standards for consultation of interested parties by the Commission; impact assessment of policy proposals. The Communications published on 11 December 2002 tackle the role of agencies, the reform of committees, the collection and use of expertise and the tripartite contracts between Commission, states and local authorities.
6. Alfons Bora et al., 'Participation and the Dynamics of Social Positioning. The Case of Biotechnology'; Liana Giorgi et al., 'The European Public Space Observatory: Assembling Information that Allows the Monitoring of European Diversity'; R. Koopmans et al., 'The Transformation of Political Mobilisation and Communication in European Public Sphere'; Thomas Risse et al., 'Europeanization, Collective Identities and Public Discourses'. Such research projects are supported by DG Research of the European Commission, under the Key Action 'Improving the socio-economic knowledge base'; for further information: *http://www.cordis.lu/improving/socio-economic/home.htm*.

REFERENCES

Calhoun, C. (ed.). 1992. *Habermas and the Public Sphere*. Cambridge MA: MIT Press

Crouch, Colin, Eder, K. and Tambini, D. (eds). 2001. *Citizenship, Markets, and the State*. Oxford: Oxford University Press.

De Schutter, O., Lebessis, N. and Paterson, J. (eds). *Governance in the European Union*. Luxembourg: Office for Official Publications of the European Communities.

De Swaan, Abram. 1993. 'The Evolving European Language System: A Theory of Communication Potential and Language Competition'. *International Political Science Review*, 14(3): 241–55.

Downing, P.B. and Hanf, K. (eds). 1983. *Implementing Pollution Laws*. Boston: Kluwer-Nijhoff.

Eriksen, Erik O. 2001. 'Democratic or Technocratic Governance?', in C. Joerges, Y. Meny, J. Weiler (eds). *Mountain or Molehill? A Critical Appraisal of the Commission White Paper on Governance*, pp. 61–72. Florence and Harvard Law School: European University Institute.

European Commission. 2001. *European Governance. A White Paper*. COM 428, available at http://europa.eu.int/comm/governance/white-paper/index_en.htm.

Grote, Jürgen and Gbikpi, Bernard (eds). 2001. *Participatory Governance: Political and Societal Implications*. Opladen: Leske-Budrich.

Joerges, Christian and Vos, Ellen (eds). 1999. *EU Committees: Social Regulation, Law and Politics*. Oxford and Portland: Hart Publishing.

Laffan, Brigid, O'Donnell, Rory and Smith, Michael. 2000. *Europe's Experimental Union: Rethinking Integration*. London and New York: Routledge.

Liberatore, Angela (Rapporteur). 2001. Report of the Working Group. *Democratising Expertise and Establishing Scientific Reference Systems*. Brussels: European Commission. *http://europa.eu.int/comm/governance/areas/index_en.htm*.

Majone, Giandomenico. 1996. 'Temporal Consistency and Policy Credibility: Why Democracies Need Non-majoritarian Institutions'. *Working Paper*. Florence: European University Institute.

Olsen, Johan. 1999. 'Organizing European Institutions for Governance', in A. Liberatore (ed.). *Governance and Citizenship in Europe: Some Research Directions*. Brussels: European Commission.

OPTEM. 2001. *Perceptions of the European Union: A Qualitative Study of the Public's Attitudes to and Expectations of the European Union in the 15 Member States and the 9 Candidate Countries*. Brussels: OPTEM for the European Commission.

Schaefer, Guenter et al. 2002. *Governance by Committees*. Final Report of a Research Project Funded by the European Commission. Mimeo.

Scharpf, Fritz. 2001. 'European Governance: Common Concerns vs the Challenge of Diversity', in C. Joerges, Y. Meny and J.Weiler (eds). *Mountain or Molehill? A Critical Appraisal of the Commission White Paper on Governance*, pp. 1–12. Florence and Harvard Law School: European University Institute.

Schlesinger, Philip. 1995. Europeanisation and the Media: National Identity and the Public Sphere. *Working Paper No. 7*. Oslo: The Norwegian Research Council.

Schmitter, Philippe. 2000. *How to Democratise the European Union . . . and Why Bother?* Lanham and Oxford: Rowman & Littlefield.

Sen, Amartya. 1999. *Development as Freedom*. Oxford: Oxford University Press.

Sinnott, Richard. 2001. 'It Couldn't Happen Here? Support for Integration and Orientations to Participation in the Member States in the Light of the Irish Nice Referendum'. Paper at the Conference on *Unity and Diversity*, co-organised by the Belgian Presidency of the EU and the European Commission. 29–30 October 2001.

Stigler, Georges. 1971. 'The Theory of Economic Regulation'. *Bell Journal of Economics and Management Science*, 6(2): 3–21.

Susskind, Larry and Cruikshank, J. 1987. *Breaking the Impasse: Consensual Approaches to Resolving Public Disputes*. New York: Basic Books.

Weidner, Helmut. 1995. 'Mediation as a Policy Instrument', in B. Dente (ed.). *Environmental Policy in Search of New Instruments*. Kluwer: Dordrecht.

Weiler, Joseph, Haltern, U. and Mayer, F. 1995. 'European Democracy and its Critique. Five Uneasy Pieces'. *Working Paper*. Florence: European University Institute.

Wilson, James. 1980. *The Politics of Regulation*. New York: Basic Books.

Wind, Marlene. 2001. 'Bridging the Gap Between the Governed and the Governing?', in C. Joerges, Y. Meny and J. Weiler (eds). *Mountain or Molehill? A Critical Appraisal of the Commission White Paper on Governance,* pp. 185–93. Florence and Harvard Law School, Cambridge MA: European University Institute.

Zuern, Michael. 1999. 'The Social Prerequisites of European Democracy', in A. Liberatore (ed.). *Governance and Citizenship in Europe. Some Research Directions*. Brussels: European Commission.

CHAPTER 5

NATIONAL DIFFERENCES AND THE RETHINKING OF SOCIAL DEMOCRACY: THIRD WAYS IN EUROPE

LUKE MARTELL

The idea of the Third Way emerged from centre–left rethinking in the 1980s, especially in the United States of America (USA) and United Kingdom (UK). It also caught on elsewhere in Europe and in other parts of the world. In this chapter, I will discuss what the Third Way involves, how it differs from the first and second ways, old-style social democracy and neo-liberalism, and how it compares to other social democratic responses to social changes such as globalisation. I will discuss the values of the Third Way and what it envisages as the role for government. I will argue that while common Third Way agendas are popular across Europe, how they turn out will vary according to national institutions and cultures, and that many variations in Third Ways can be linked to left–right divides. In the UK, New Labour's Third Way has tried to tackle social exclusion and the failure of public services, but the adoption of an Anglo-American neo-liberal economic model undermines goals such as equality, the eradication of poverty and responsiveness to stakeholders other than shareholders. In the era of globalisation and the Third Way, national differences and left and right still matter.[1]

OLD LEFT AND NEW RIGHT: THE FIRST AND SECOND WAYS

Let me start with Britain. New Labour in Britain defines the Third Way as 'beyond old left and new right' (see, e.g., Blair 1998). 'Old left' means the post-war politics of Keynesian egalitarianism and state and corporatist forms of economic and welfare governance within a mixed economy. Third-wayers criticise the 'old left' for being too statist, too concerned with redistribution and tax-and-spend policies and not enough with the creation of wealth, too willing to grant rights without expecting responsibilities in return and too liberal about social behaviour and the family. The Third Way is about finding alternatives to state provision and government control, promoting wealth creation by accepting inequalities and being fiscally 'prudent', and expecting responsibilities in return for rights.

'New right' means neo-liberal Thatcherite conservatism. New Labour says that new right Conservative governments were wrong to automatically favour market solutions against state intervention and to value individual gain over wider social values. New Labour argues for a Third Way in favour of wealth creation *and* social justice, the market *and* the community, that is, positive about private enterprise but without necessarily always favouring market solutions and which sees an active role for government—for example, in welfare to work strategies to attack poverty.

Third-Way advocates argue that politics has to respond to significant social changes. Post-war social democracy has been undermined by globalisation. In particular, Keynesian economic management to achieve full employment is seen as redundant in the context of a global economy. Capital is globally mobile and so governments need to adjust their policies to be business-friendly and promote skills to attract investment. Consumers buy goods from all over the world, so pouring money into your own national economy to promote demand, Keynesian style, could just stimulate the buying of overseas rather than domestic goods. The global economy is increasingly interdependent so governments need to promote free trade, rather than protectionism and regulation, to stimulate growth. Hence economic policies which give businesses special treatment, the promotion of economic stability and liberalisation and an educated workforce to attract investment. Meanwhile, individuals need the education and training appropriate for an economy increasingly based on new information and communication technologies. In these circumstances, for the Third Way, the priorities of both right and left, economic success and social justice, can be squared. Government promotes economic growth by creating stable economic conditions and an educated workforce. Simultaneously, its interventions to promote workers' skills increase opportunities for individuals and promote social inclusion. The Third Way mixes both right and left aims.

So globalisation provides a major part of the context for the Third Way rethinking of social democracy. What about the values that the Third Way promotes? Tony Blair (1998) has tended to identify two main values of the Third Way—equal opportunities and community (see also Giddens 1998; Latham 2001; Le Grand 1998; White 1998).

The Third Way's perspective on equal opportunities is that they require certain resources to be achieved. These resources include things like educational opportunities and access to the labour market. This goes beyond the 'new right' in seeing opportunities as not just freedom from state coercion but also something that needs positive resources. It also goes beyond the 'old left' who are accused of being concerned with equal outcomes rather than fair opportunities, with end-states rather than starting-gates.

Blair advocates a meritocratic approach. For him inequality is an important incentive in a market economy and often deserved. White and Giaimo (2001) argue that this can be seen as a 'Left Thatcherism'—'an ideology which says that we should try to ensure citizens roughly equal initial endowments of marketable assets and then let the free market rip' (p. 216). For Merkel (2001), the British Third Way is shifting social democracy 'to the recognition of societal inequality as a legitimate and functional stratification pattern in highly developed market economies under the conditions of globalised economic transactions' (p. 50). Supporters of the Third Way 'seem fully prepared to accept greater income inequality as a market and policy outcome. Their acceptance ends only at the point where this leads to voluntary and involuntary exclusion in the higher and lower strata of society' (Merkel 2001: 53). Giddens (2002) argues that more equal outcomes are required for equal opportunities to be achieved. Inequalities in economic outcomes are a basis for unequal opportunities. For Callinicos (2001), New Labour's neo-liberalism has led them to abandon the redistributional egalitarianism necessary for equality of opportunity: the tension between Labour's neo-liberalism and their egalitarianism has been resolved in favour of the former.

So New Labour's focus is more on opportunities than more equal outcomes. As far as opportunity goes, their concern is mostly with greater chances for those excluded from minimum opportunities rather than with equalising opportunities. This can lead to greater equality of opportunities as those excluded from fair chances get better access to them and so more equal opportunities relative to others. But this approach is oriented to *inclusion* into the world of opportunities as much as to *equality* of opportunity within it. On the basis of minimum opportunities for the socially excluded there still remain inequalities in opportunities. Ronald Dworkin (2001) argues that the Third Way has replaced 'equality' as an objective with 'sufficiency', in which 'once those minimal standards are met, government has no further obligation to make people equal in anything' (p. 172).

The second value the British Third Way tends to emphasise is responsibility or community. For Blair, 'responsibility' means that people should not just claim rights from the state but also accept their responsibilities as citizens, parents and members of communities. This is reflected in government policies which expect obligations from welfare claimants, parents and children. Third-Way approaches to community differ from more traditional social democratic ideas of community (see Driver and Martell 1997). The latter see community as being based in greater equality and in the universal experience of welfare, health and education and stress, rhetorically at least, the obligations of business to the community. The Third Way is based more on opportunities than greater equality of outcomes. It retains an emphasis on universal, collective services such as health and education, but some of its policies make them more selective and targeted. The Third Way has a more business-friendly tone that stresses moral community and work as the basis of inclusion as well as the more traditional social and economic bases of community. Responsibility of the citizen to the state is emphasised more than the obligations required from business. The latter is more part of the ideas of traditional social democracy than of the Third Way.

THE THIRD WAY AND THE ROLE FOR GOVERNMENT

How about ways in which such value goals are achieved? Advocates of the Third Way argue that they are pragmatic about the role for government in achieving their objectives—committed to what works best rather than to any ideological predispositions of left or right about the preferability of state and market or public and private provision (e.g., Blair 1998). For Blair, when times change, so must the means to achieve centre–left values. The values, in his view at least, are fixed, but how they are achieved is open to change. Pragmatism about means is what makes the Third Way neither 'old left' nor 'new right', while sticking to the important values is what is said to give it its enduring centre–left character.

The role for government in a market society—the balance of state and market and of public and private provision—has long been a concern of the left. Le Grand (1998) says that what makes New Labour novel on such questions is that it is pragmatic about them. It has no prior commitment to the public sector, as the 'old left' did, or the private sector, as the 'new right' did. Yet one thing the Third Way does tend to stick to is that active government is important, although it tends away from the 'old left' on this by not seeing it always in terms of direct state provision and from the 'new right' by being more positive about active government and less automatically biased to market solutions.

The role for government in the Third Way has a number of characteristics:

- government working in partnership with the private and voluntary sectors, e.g., the government's 'New Deal' which funds things like training on private sector jobs, and public–private cooperation in health and education, such as in hospital building or private sector school management;
- government acting as a guarantor but not a direct provider of public goods or of basic standards, e.g., the introduction of a minimum wage guaranteed by government but paid by employers;
- 'joined up government', i.e., government departments and agencies working together across departmental boundaries, as with the role of a central social exclusion unit in coordinating policy across government departments on this issue;
- the welfare state helping individuals off social security and into work rather than leaving it just to market forces or government provision of welfare or jobs;
- government providing goods, such as childcare, education and training, to improve opportunities;
- government targeting social policy on the socially excluded while at the same time encouraging greater individual responsibility for welfare provision (e.g., obligations on welfare claimants to take training or work experience).

The Third Way is different here from the 'old left' by finding forms of active government other than state ownership or the direct provision of things like welfare and jobs—the new way is 'steering not rowing'. It is different from the 'new right' in its emphasis on public intervention and not just leaving things to the market or individual self-help.

I would like to stress, though, my argument that not only has the role of government and the means of achieving ends under the Third Way changed, but, contrary to what is sometimes claimed by its proponents, the values and objectives of the Third Way have also done so. For instance, I have mentioned above the shift from egalitarian objectives to minimum opportunities and social inclusion. Plant (2001) argues that New Labour stresses the means for achieving goals as what has happened and so glosses over change in the goals themselves. Changing means affects the ends they are intended to achieve. So a shift from public ownership, Keynesianism and redistribution affects whether centre–left ends such as equality can be pursued. Preferences for private ownership, supply-side economics and inclusion strategies are less likely to be conducive to egalitarianism than to minimum opportunities. Likewise a shift away from ideas of universal welfare and the comprehensive ideal in education affects whether equality and community can be achieved. Targeted welfare and a pluralistic education system undermine egalitarianism as a goal and take away means for achieving community.

THE THIRD WAY, LEFT AND RIGHT

The Third Way involves the combination rather than transcendence of left and right. The Third Way is not left or right or something completely different from them, but combines them. It involves social justice *and* economic efficiency, rights *and* responsibilities, the market economy *and* social cohesion. Social justice, for instance, can be pursued by ensuring everyone has the education and training needed to give them opportunities. This also helps with economic dynamism by providing a skilled workforce which can attract investment and be more productive.

So the Third Way is more a mix of left and right than something that synthesises or goes beyond them. The problem is that in such combinations there have to be trade-offs and the Third Way often appears to try to combine contradictory principles. Compatibility or reciprocity between different principles may sometimes be possible, but often what is involved are contrary interests. It is not as easy to be all things to all people as Third Way politicians like to make out.

Because it combines such different and often competing principles, the Third Way cannot be said to be a coherent philosophy. There is no systematic guide to action or on which principles should be favoured in circumstances where they clash. So the Third Way is more of a framework than a philosophy, a space between alternatives within which policy can be developed rather than a clear guide to policy-making (Giddens 2001; White 2001). What should be chosen between contrary principles is left undecided. So, in economic policy the commitment to minimum opportunities may conflict with the commitment to a successful market economy. Choosing the market economy is one reason why egalitarianism has been downgraded in Labour's approach. Giddens (2001) supports egalitarianism, the European social model and global economic regulation including policies such as taxes on currency speculation. But he rejects demand management and a role for the government in supporting ailing industries, and supports flexible labour markets. But such an approach seems to avoid the way in which some of the more left-wing commitments expressed here clash with some of the more pro-market ones, and the way in which this is likely to lead to one side negating the other in actual practice.

Some of these conflicts are resolved by the right wing winning out over the left-wing preferences they contradict, and for some the Third Way is just a disguise for the adoption of a right-wing consensus in politics (Hall 1994, 1998; Hall and Jacques 1997; Hay 1999). In Britain, the political agenda shifted to the right under Mrs. Thatcher and the main parties now occupy a similar post-Thatcherite terrain. Labour has adopted policies that favour low inflation, spending limits, privatisation and deregulation, stability and other conditions favourable to private business, such as low corporate taxes. Criticisms of Blair from other European social democrats are often that he is too right wing. Certainly the neo-liberalism of the Anglo-American model causes inequality and poverty and is responsive to the short-term interests of shareholders at the expense of longer-term interests and wider stakeholders. But in other public policy areas—the introduction of a minimum wage, the signing of the Social chapter, constitutional reform, increases in taxation to fund improved public services, public spending on health and education, the scale of the New Deal—it is possible to identify left-wing sentiments. These suggest that while there has been a shift to the right in social democracy, it has not been a complete one.

So there is a mixture of left and right in the space between the old left and the new right. In this complex mixture, there is room for a number of Third Ways, some of which could be more left or more right (see White 1998). Differences are sometimes over equality and divide along left and right lines. Leftists would like to see a greater redistribution of income and wealth rather than of just opportunities (Hattersley 1997a, 1997b; Levitas 1999). There are also Third Ways to the right, such as Blair's. So left and right divisions have not been left behind and continue to be relevant. Versions of the Third Way are more left or right, more or less social democratic. Criticisms and defences of Blair's Third Way also often break down along such lines.

Such differences also characterise reforms to social democracy beyond the United Kingdom and affect how the Third Way is received elsewhere. Between Britain and other parts of Europe there are differences over what the Third Way should be about. These are often affected by differences in national institutions and cultures as well as by left–right divisions, but these national and political dimensions are also often linked.

COMMONALTIES IN THIRD WAYS IN THE USA AND ACROSS EUROPE

Some other centre–left parties were pursuing Third-Way policies before Blair. Similarities may result from shared processes of globalisation, European integration or welfare crisis leading to the same sort of political conclusions (Giddens 1998; Sassoon 1999). I will look first at common patterns in Third Ways across Britain, USA and Europe, before moving on to examine the way national institutions and cultures lead Third Ways to take different forms in different places.

Bill Clinton and Tony Blair both came to power after years of neo-liberal government in their respective countries, believing that modernisation and a move to the centre ground was necessary for a return to power. They both emphasised social changes such as globalisation and the rise of the information economy and policies of welfare reform, economic stability and fiscal prudence. Robert Reich (1997), former Secretary of Labour under Clinton, argues that in Western Europe and USA there have been programmes of reducing budget deficits, deregulation or privatisation, an acceptance of economic globalisation, and flexible labour markets and reductions in welfare. The US Democrats and New Labour, he argues, have both been committed to reducing burdens on business and have accepted the growth of inequality.

But there is also a commitment to active government which has made the British and US approaches Third Ways, not old left but also more interventionist than neo-liberalism (Jaenicke 2000). The US and UK Third Way governments have pursued social inclusion through education and training, support for families with children, and making sure that work is worthwhile for the poor, through tax credits for instance. Both Clinton and Blair's welfare reforms have also required obligations in return for welfare rights and limits on benefits.

In Europe in the 1980s and 1990s, low inflation and stability replaced Keynesianism and full employment as policy goals. Before Tony Blair became Labour leader, the Dutch social democrats had adopted a pragmatic approach to the market and were pursuing deregulation, privatisation and internal markets. They were practising sound public finances, tax reductions, promoting the work ethic, increasing flexibility and training initiatives in the labour market, and reallocations of funding from social security to areas such as education (de Beus 1999).

Nationalisation has generally been discarded by European social democrats. Many have advocated partnership between business and government and have pursued privatisation programmes (Sassoon 1999). Swedish social democrats have long been open to private enterprise and undogmatic about state ownership as well as open to free trade and international competition (Lindgren 1999). Beyond Britain, social democrats have proposed active government, rather than direct state intervention or *laissez-faire*, lower business taxes, labour market flexibility and restrictions on public expenditure. Keeping inflation down, fiscal stability and curbing tax-and-spend policies have been the general commitments, along with supply-side measures, subsidies and incentives to tackle unemployment. Small businesses and innovation in hi-tech sectors have been promoted.

Beyond the French socialists' policy for a 35-hour week, some see differences from Blair as often not fundamental (e.g., Sassoon 1999). For instance, Jospin's reductions to the working week led to agreements on labour market flexibility. The British are reluctant to increase income taxes while in Germany taxes are seen as too high and the tax system in need of restructuring. The principle of central bank independence is accepted, implemented in Sweden at the same time as in the UK, and part of the German scene long before that (ibid.). Social democrats across Europe have wished to pursue reforms to international financial organisations.

Comparable agendas of welfare reform have been discussed by social democrats across Europe (Vandenbroucke 2001). The Swedes developed 'workfare' and active labour market policies based on education and training. They support universalism but have shifted away from the idea that the state should shoulder all the costs. Fiscal problems and increases in the numbers of pensioners and students led Swedish social democrats to limit rises in social security (Lindgren 1999). Employment has been seen by many European social democrats as the basis of welfare reform. People, it is thought, need a 'hand up' into paid work rather than the 'handouts' of welfare payments. It has been perceived that welfare needs to be more responsive to changes in the family and gender roles and more attuned to balancing work and family life. Welfare has been seen as being as much about investment in education as spending on benefits (Vandenbroucke 2001). Britain as well as the German Social Democratic Party (SPD) have also advocated imposing obligations on the unemployed. The advocacy of toughness on crime, the linking of rights to responsibilities and education, and training as routes to employment and equal opportunities have been advocated across European Social Democratic parties.

THIRD WAYS AND NATIONAL DIFFERENCES

Despite these commonalties and common pressures such as globalisation and European integration, national differences remain important. While Clift (2001) says that 'European social democratic parties are more similar now than at any time this century' (p. 71), he also states that differences between social democratic parties in Europe are the most notable feature. Vandenbroucke (2001) stresses convergence across European social democratic parties on policy agendas but divergence in national models and policies (see also Kelly 1999; Lovecy 2000; Martell et al. 2001; White 2001: Part III). To some social democrats in Europe New Labour is seen as having gone too far in its modernisation. Blair has tried to promote liberalisation and free trade, labour market flexibility, welfare reform and cuts in business regulations to European social democrats. But many have been reluctant about this agenda, seeing it as too much of a concession to the neo-liberal right and inappropriate in less free market contexts outside the UK.

The British Third Way has often been contrasted with the social democracy of those such as the former French Prime Minister Lionel Jospin who has been more open to labour market regulation and public spending on job creation. Some social democrats among the Italians, French and Germans, if not all of their party leaders, have argued for demand management at a European level to create jobs, while the British Third Way has focused more on advocating supply-side measures, arguing that globalisation has made Keynesianism redundant (Clift 2001; Giddens 1994, 1998; Vandenbroucke 2001). In qualifiying this, though, it has to be said that the European Central Bank with the support of social democratic governments has pursued a conservative monetary policy in recent years, while it is central banks in the UK and US that have pursued a more active and growth-oriented monetary policy by cutting interest rates. British Chancellor Gordon Brown has come under pressure from elsewhere in Europe to restrict government spending on decaying public services in the UK. In Britain it is through private sector jobs that inclusion in the job market is seen as occurring, while social democrats like the French have put greater emphasis on public sector job creation. The French socialist policy has been to decrease the average working week to 35 hours while the British maximum is 48 hours.

Germany's social market encourages goals that go beyond inclusion, equality of opportunity and *laissez-faire* to a more collaborative approach (Meyer 1999). In France, Germany, Sweden and elsewhere, trade unions are more important than in the UK. New Labour has attempted to distance itself from the unions, which are seen as an electoral liability and very weak after years of Thatcherism. In the

Netherlands and Sweden, political culture is more social democratic and emphasises consensus and continuity unlike the competitive individualism and Conservative domination of politics in Britain (van den Anker 2001).

Let me give some illustrations of these differences in political culture. A hostile takeover bid for German mobile phone operator Mannesman launched by British mobile company Vodaphone caused considerable outrage in Germany. In Britain, such events are more normal and attract less attention. Similarly the paper jointly authored by British Prime Minister Blair and German Chancellor Gerhard Schroeder (1999) provoked noisy opposition in Germany, and Schroeder subsequently tried to distance himself from some of the paper's arguments. In Britain, the paper slipped by almost unnoticed. Its arguments were too neo-liberal for Germany; in the UK its neo-liberalism was far from exceptional after 20 years of Conservative rule. When British firm Marks and Spencer decided to close its stores in France, the lack of consultation with workers was condemned by French politicians, workers and shoppers. Such lack of consultation is not such an unexpected part of economic life in the UK. The liberalisation of labour laws brought thousands on to the streets of Italy. Labour market flexibility is part of British normality.

When it comes to welfare, problems are different in different parts of Europe. Pensions are a high priority in the debate in Italy, Sweden, Germany and France. In Britain, spending on health services is seen as too low, but in Germany as too high. Unemployment dominates concerns in Germany and France more than in the UK where poverty and exclusion are more of a focus, partly because of inequality in the UK, low paid work and low rates of benefit (Kelly 1999). The Swedes are more attached to the universal nature of welfare than some other countries (Lindgren 1999). Foreign policy and approaches to the European Union (EU) vary. Britain emphasises national incentives to attract mobile capital as a response to globalisation and has tended to err against moves towards a stronger social model in Europe, seeing this as imposing burdens on business. The British and Swedes are open to economic globalisation but more cautious about European political integration than some other countries. Britain is more pro-America than some other European countries and Blair has been interventionist and active in military coordination, for instance in the Kosovo war, the creation of a European defence identity and the war against Afghanistan. Other social democrats in Europe have remained neutral, true to national traditions or been more hesitant about international military intervention or support for the US.

WHY NATIONAL THIRD WAYS? MODELS OF CAPITALISM

So Third Ways and the rethinking of social democracy share commonalties in policy agendas but also vary in the forms they take in different European nations. I want to look now at explanations for this variation. Different historical economies, social structures, political systems and cultures affect the form Third Ways take (Martell et al. 2001; Vandenbroucke 1998, 2001). The USA and UK share an Anglo-American tradition of capitalism: individualistic, *laissez-faire* and with limited government; flexible, less regulated with weak unions and with a market-based and short-termist financial system. This model has relatively low unemployment but high inequality and poverty.

This contrasts with 'Rhenish' capitalism elsewhere in Europe where economic and political culture is more collaborative and corporatist, unions are more important, finance is less market-based and longer term, and work is more skilled, secure and better paid— more of a 'social market' (Albert 1993; Hutton 1995). In Germany and other European countries there are more statist or collaborative political cultures reflected, for example, in references in the Blair–Schroeder document to partnership with the trade unions which rarely play a part in New Labour discourse. France has a tradition of centralised government and state involvement in public services. In Sweden and the Netherlands, political culture is social democratic, consensual and solidaristic, in contrast to the more conservative, competitive and individualist culture of Anglo-Americanism.

Another factor in national political differences has been the effects of neo-liberalism in the US and UK. Conservative reforms in Britain in the 1980s introduced fiscal conservatism, anti-inflationary policies, tough trade union legislation, large-scale privatisation, deregulation of the labour market and reforms to health, education and housing. Blair's Third Way is a post-Thatcherite project, defined by inheritance of this Thatcherite legacy, and often an acceptance or even continuation of it, alongside a reaction against it in policies geared towards political devolution and social inclusion (Driver and Martell 1998). The approach of the US democrats has been shaped by a similar neo-liberal inheritance. Such a neo-liberal background is not shared in other European countries. Other governments of the right in the 1980s did not carry out experiments as radical as those in Britain and the US. Blair's rhetoric is more pro-market and friendly to private business than that of others in Europe because of the Thatcherite inheritance and its shifting of the political ground to the free market right. This inheritance also makes Blair more left wing in the UK than he would be in other European countries— reforms which may seem unimpressive from a left-wing view in other countries (the introduction of a minimum wage or devolved assemblies, for instance) constitute a shift to the left and to greater pluralism in the UK.

WHY NATIONAL THIRD WAYS? POLITICAL INFLUENCES

But economic culture is not all of the story of why Third Ways may vary in Europe. The first-past-the-post British political system gives Blair an absolute majority of seats. He does not have to compromise with left wing or green coalition partners as in France, Germany, Italy, Denmark and Sweden to secure a parliamentary majority. Moreover, there are no significant parties to the left of Labour in the UK, so Labour does not have to appeal to more left-wing voters because such voters have no other significant left parties to vote for. Blair has great freedom to determine his own agenda and is less constrained by left wing or green partners or competition from the left for votes. The bigger role for demand management and environmental concerns in the Blair–Schroeder document than they would get in New Labour statements of the Third Way is in part a reflection of the role of the left and greens in the German government. Similarly Jospin's more 'socialist' rhetoric was, to some extent, an attempt to keep his five party centre–left coalition together (Bouvet and Michel 2001).

The British electoral system also created greater pressure to modernise than it would for other left parties in proportional systems who get a small vote in elections. When Labour received only 27.6 per cent of the vote in the 1983 General Elections, it was a long,

long way from power in a first-past-the-post system. Drastic action was seen to be needed to make it electable again. But when the French socialists came into government with 26.5 per cent of the vote in 1997, the electoral system allowed them to govern in a coalition—major modernisation of policy was not such a pressure (Lovecy 2000).

Germany has an electoral system that encourages coalitions, but also has other pressures that have sent its Third Way in nationally specific directions. The SPD is a decentralised party, making it more complex for a leader to carry out policy reforms like those in Britain between 1987 and 1997. There is a devolved Laender system of government and strong interest groups representing employers and unions so that power is diffused and there are many potential obstacles to reform (Busch and Manow 2001). Similarly, the consensual culture I have mentioned in the Netherlands is embodied there in a system of politics that requires coalitions and negotiation with formally empowered non-state organised interests. The Dutch Social Democratic Party (PvdA) is less autonomous when it comes to policy reform and is restrained by the need to pursue change in a negotiated way (Hemerijck and Visser 2001).

CONCLUSIONS

The British Labour Party is further down the road to taking social democracy in a neo-liberal direction. In other countries, such as Germany, the government has to combine a centrist image to get votes with a more radical appeal to coalition partners, and it is constrained by the social market culture and the devolved nature of the German political system. In Britain there is a more centralised state, an electoral system which places less obstacles in the way of modernisers, and a *laissez-faire* economic culture (Lees 2001). The Netherlands has consensual norms that counteract more economically liberal developments in social democracy. In France, there has been a pride in French exceptionalism and the statist and public sector tradition and a need to hold together a coalition of the left.

Some social democrats in Britain such as Will Hutton (1995) argue for Tony Blair to adopt more of a social market approach from Germany. There are industrialists and SPD modernisers in Germany who would like a bit more Anglo-American competitive individualism to make the German economy more dynamic. But sadly, in my view, Hutton's arguments are not well received in the British Labour Party and Schroeder's collaboration with Blair had to be downplayed in Germany because of the more *social* nature of the market economy there. Blair has been keener on exporting Anglo-Americanism to Europe than importing a German-style stakeholder model once advocated by him (Blair 1996; Driver and Martell 1998: 51–60). I have sympathy with Hutton's arguments because while New Labour has made significant steps towards tackling social exclusion and the failure of public services, the Anglo-American model they have adopted favours short-term shareholder interests over longer term and wider stakeholder interests, and tends to reproduce and accentuate the inequality and poverty the New Labour government aims to reduce. The British Third Way genuinely attempts to marry economic efficiency and social justice, but sometimes the former undermines the latter.

Social democratic parties in Europe have pursued neo-liberal programmes alongside continuing social democratic concerns for social inclusion. But the contexts have varied so the outcomes of similar agendas differ: dependent on factors such as whether control in political systems is centralised or devolved; the extent to which modernisers monopolise power or share it; and historical traditions of statism, consensus or economic liberalism. So Third Ways between neo-liberalism and old-style social democracy are different Third Ways rather than just one. The Third Way is diverse and contested. National factors lead to divergence and different reforms to social democracy. Sometimes these divergences between Third Ways happen not only on the basis of national traditions and cultures, but also, at the same time, on left and right lines. In the era of globalisation and the Third Way, national differences and left and right still matter.

| NOTE

1. This paper is based on joint research done with Stephen Driver (see Driver and Martell 2002), though I must add that I am responsible for the views expressed here.

Albert, M. 1993. *Capitalism against Capitalism*. London: Whurr.

Blair, T. 1996. Speech to the Singapore Business Community. 8 January.

———. 1998. *The Third Way: New Politics for the New Century*. London: The Fabian Society.

Blair, T. and Schroeder, G. 1999. *Europe: The Third Way—Die Neue Mitte*. London: Labour Party.

Bouvet, L. and Michel, F. 2001. 'Pluralism and the Future of the French Left', in S. White (ed.). *New Labour: The Progressive Future?* pp. 209–13. Basingstoke: Palgrave.

Busch, A. and Manow, P. 2001. 'The SPD and the Neue Mitte in Germany', in S. White (ed.). *New Labour: The Progressive Future?* pp. 175–90. Basingstoke: Palgrave.

Callinicos, A. 2001. *Against the Third Way: An Anti-Capitalist Critique*. Cambridge: Polity Press.

Clift, B. 2001. 'New Labour's Third Way and European Social Democracy', in S. Ludlam and M. Smith (eds). *New Labour in Government*, pp. 55–73. Basingstoke: Palgrave.

de Beus, J. 1999. 'The Politics of Consensual Well-being: The Dutch Left Greets the Twenty-First Century', in G. Kelly (ed.). *The New European Left*, pp. 59–68. London: The Labour Party.

Driver, S. and Martell, L. 1997. 'New Labour's Communitarianisms'. *Critical Social Policy*, 17(3): 27–46.

———. 1998. *New Labour: Politics after Thatcherism*. Cambridge: Polity Press.

———. 2002. *Blair's Britain*. Cambridge. Polity Press.

Dworkin, R. 2001. 'Does Equality Matter?', in A. Giddens (ed.). *The Global Third Way Debate*. Cambridge: Polity Press.

Giddens, A. 1994. *Beyond Left and Right*. Cambridge: Polity Press.

———. 1998. *The Third Way: The Renewal of Social Democracy*. Cambridge: Polity Press.

———. 2001. *The Global Third Way Debate*. Cambridge: Polity Press.

———. 2002. *What Next for New Labour?* Cambridge: Polity Press.

Hall, S. 1994. 'Son of Margaret'. *New Statesman*. 6 October.

———. 1998. 'The Great Moving Nowhere Show', *Marxism Today*. November/December.

Hall, S. and Jacques, M. 1997. 'Blair: Is He the Greatest Tory Since Thatcher?' *The Observer*. 13 April.

Hattersley, R. 1997a. 'Just One Per Cent on Top Tax Wouldn't Hurt'. *Guardian*. 24 June.

———. 1997b. 'Why I'm no Longer Loyal to Labour'. *Guardian*. 26 July.

Hay, C. 1999. *The Political Economy of New Labour*. Manchester: Manchester University Press.

Hemerijck, A. and Visser, J. 2001. 'Dutch Lessons in Social Pragmatism', in S. White (ed.). *New Labour: The Progressive Future?* Basingstoke: Palgrave.

Hutton, W. 1995. *The State We're In*. London: Jonathan Cape.

Jaenicke, D. 2000. 'New Labour and the Clinton Presidency', in D. Coates and P. Lawler (eds). *New Labour in Power*, pp. 34–49. Manchester: Manchester University Press.

Kelly, G. (ed.). 1999. *The New European Left*. London: Fabian Society.

Latham, M. 2001. 'The Third Way: An Outline', in A. Giddens (ed.). *The Global Third Way Debate*, pp. 25–36. Cambridge: Polity Press.

Lees, C. 2001. 'Social Democracy and the Structures of Governance in Britain and Germany: How Institutions and Norms Shape Political Innovation', in L. Martell, Christien van der Anker, Matthew Browne, Stephanie Hoopes, Phil Larkin, Charles Lees, Francis McGowan and Neil Stammers (eds). *Social Democracy: Global and National Perspectives,* pp. 160–79. Basingstoke: Palgrave.

Le Grand, J. 1998. 'The Third Way Begins with Cora'. *New Statesman.* 6 March.

Levitas, R. 1999. *The Inclusive Society? Social Exclusion and New Labour*. Basingstoke: Macmillan.

Lindgren, A-M. 1999. 'Swedish Social Democracy in Transition', in G. Kelly, (ed.). *The New European Left*, pp. 45–79. London: The Fabian Society.

Lovecy, J. 2000. 'New Labour and the "Left that is Left" in Western Europe', in D. Coates and P. Lawler (eds). *New Labour in Power*, pp. 49–65. Manchester: Manchester University Press.

Martell, L., van der Anker, Christien, Browne, Matthew, Hooper, Stephanie, Larkin, Phil, Lees, Charles, McGowan, Francis and Stammers, Neil (eds), 2001. *Social Democracy: Global and National Perspectives.* Basingstoke: Palgrave.

Merkel, W. 2001. 'The Third Ways of Social Democracy', in A. Giddens (ed.). *The Global Third Way Debate,* pp. 50–74. Cambridge: Polity Press.

Meyer, T. 1999. 'From Godesborg to the Neue Mitte: The New Social Democracy in Germany', in G. Kelly (ed.). *The New European Left*. London: Fabian Society.

Plant, R. 2001. 'Blair and Ideology', in A. Seldon (ed.). *The Blair Effect*, pp. 20–35. London: Little Brown.

Reich, R. 1997. *Locked in the Cabinet*. New York: Knopf.

Sassoon, D. 1999. 'Introduction: Convergence, Continuity and Change on the European Left', in G. Kelly (ed.). *The New European Left*. London: Fabian Society.

van den Anker, C. 2001. 'Dutch Social Democracy and the Polder Model', in L. Martell, Christien van den Anker, Matthew Browne, Stephanie Hoopes, Phil Larkin, Charles Lees, Francis McGrowan and Neil Stammers (eds). *Social Democracy: Global and National Perspectives*, pp. 129–60. Basingstoke: Palgrave.

Vandenbroucke, F. 1998. *Globalisation, Inequality and Social Democracy*. London: IPPR.

————. 2001. 'European Social Democracy and the Third Way: Convergence, Divisions and Shared Questions', in S. White (ed.). *New Labour: The Progressive Future?* pp. 161–75. Basingstoke: Palgrave.

White, S. 1998. 'Interpreting the Third Way: Not One Road, but Many'. *Renewal*, 6(2): 17–30.

————. 2001. *New Labour: The Progressive Future?* Basingstoke: Palgrave.

White, S. and Giaimo, S. 2001. 'Conclusion: New Labour and the Uncertain Future of Progressive Politics', in S. White (ed.). *New Labour: The Progressive Future?* pp. 213–23. Basingstoke: Palgrave.

CHAPTER 6

GOOD GOVERNANCE, MARKET-FRIENDLY
GLOBALISATION AND THE CHANGING SPACE
OF STATE INTERVENTION: THE CASE OF INDIA

ANUP SINHA[1]

There is a Swedish proverb that says, when a blind man carries a lame man both go forward. The proverb is remarkably appropriate in the context of the debate about markets and the state. There are two things worthy of note here. The first is that despite the imperfections of both, the combination serves a purpose. The second observation is that the combination must be quite specific, in the sense that a lame man carrying a blind man would be terribly inadequate in attaining the aim of moving forward.

The debate about the role of the government in promoting economic development is as old as economics itself. Classical scholars had stressed the importance of the enabling role of government. There have been differences of opinion, though, on the degree and depth of this enabling role, especially in terms of what the state ought to do as well as what the state ought not to do. Historical evidence suggests that societies that were late starters in the process of modern industrialisation have witnessed a more active role of the state in the development process than the countries that were the early leaders. Twentieth-century success stories like Japan and many other Asian economies have had strong governments that took an active interest in promoting and organising economic growth. However, there are numerous other instances too, where the state did assume an important role in the control and allocation of resources and in the creation of incentive structures for investment, but failed to promote adequate transformations. Even in places where growth did occur under the aegis of strong state controls, the issue of the state's ability to sustain that growth came to the fore with the dramatic collapse of the Soviet Union and the East European economies.

The closing decades of the 20th century witnessed a steady resurgence of faith in markets, with the state's role as economic strategist and planner coming under increasing scrutiny and criticism. Government failures have received more attention than market failures as the possible root cause of the lack of adequate economic development. The conventional wisdom about economic development has had a perceptible shift; from state interventions being perceived as essential to another extreme where the state is supposed to have a minimal role. The latter position is often referred to as the Washington Consensus, which argues for unregulated markets and free trade with conservative fiscal and monetary policies for macro-economic stability as the fit-all formula for global development. This shift has, perforce, put into new focus the somewhat old debate about markets and the state. The more specific questions of importance being raised are: what constitutes good governance in the context of economic development? What are the constraints in achieving good governance?

In seeking answers to these questions it is worth noting that in this context, governance has two distinct but interrelated aspects. The first is the content of policies and strategies that define the priorities for action. For instance, the macro-economic policies of the state, its programme to enable investments and accumulation, and its approach to distributive justice, all combine to set the action agenda. The second aspect is the quality of the institutions of governance, the rules and processes through which policies are formed and implemented. Here the issues pertain to the participation and voice of the governed along with the transparency and accountability of the institutions and offices of governance. It is obvious that when one talks of good governance one really has an ideal in mind that is difficult to specify in great detail and accuracy. However, what is often actually meant is searching for functional governance that can serve the purpose of promoting material development that is both equitable in some socially accepted sense and sustainable into some foreseeable future. Functionally good governance may be far from being ideal, and to that extent can be changed and improved. Such improvements, in turn, are likely to have positive effects in expanding the choice of feasible policies.

A recent paper (Morris 2001) has raised the question of causality: is development constrained by the lack of good governance, or is good governance constrained by unsuccessful developmental efforts? I have defined governance as constituting both policies and processes, and hence development to be the consequential outcome of governance. Yet development and governance are related in a fundamental way as outcomes of development have positive feedback effects on governance. In reality both can be highly imperfect, and both can be improved. Governance is of important instrumental value in achieving economic development. It is also of intrinsic value to the extent that it defines the quality of institutions in a society, their efficiency, transparency and accountability.

THE FAILURE OF FUNCTIONAL GOVERNANCE

The content of governance in India since political independence was based on an active role for the state in what Prime Minister Nehru had described as attaining the commanding heights of the economy. Economic planning would create infrastructure and capital goods to ensure the crowding-in of private investment. Private investment would be controlled and directed into priority areas through a complex set of controls on prices, locations, capacities, technologies, over and above the more standard instruments of tax-subsidy, monetary policy controls over interest rates and credit rationing schemes. The aim was to develop a sound industrial base that would reduce India's dependence on foreign sources of supply and simultaneously feed the domestic market with a larger variety of goods and services. Thus, in an essential way, this strategy was inward looking, with global competition and export markets having no critical role in the overall design of strategy.[2] The quality of governance would be dependent on the bureaucracy. The Indian Constitution envisaged a federal, plural polity with the usual institutions of parliamentary democracy and decentralised government being well enshrined along with universal franchise. Private property and voluntary exchange in markets (some of which would be tightly regulated) were guaranteed.

The economic history of independent India displayed both the strengths and vulnerabilities of this approach to development. The state was able to mobilise sizeable resources for the construction of an impressive industrial sector. Economic growth was steady and uninterrupted, though the average rate of growth and the rate of growth of per capita income were inadequate on two counts. More as a rule rather than an exception, the targets for economic growth were unfulfilled. Inadequate growth coupled with demographic pressures failed to reduce poverty and acute economic deprivations in any substantial way. However, despite the controls and pervasive state interventions, a private sector of industrialists and entrepreneurs emerged as the leaders of a nascent middle-class different frcm the old colonial middle-class. Indeed the controls actually contributed to the growth of this class through assured and protected markets and cheap subsidised inputs. This emerging group was more self-assured, articulate, with an outlook that was both materialistic and global. This group, as part of its growing self-assurance, sought more freedoms from state controls.

The inadequacy of economic growth also led to shortages, congestion-costs and uncertainties that led to significant increases in the opportunistic behaviour of the powerful organised sections of the economy. Distributional coalitions (see Bardhan 1986, 2001) fighting for a larger share of a slowly growing pie led to a negative feedback effect on the quality of the institutions of governance. Government institutions, of all arms and functions, led the way to steady deterioration of every institution in the public as well as private realms. Economic fractures in a socially heterogeneous country led to corruption and inefficiencies and an attitude of callousness.

The failure of good, or even functional, governance in India has economic, political and social dimensions. There is a large hiatus between the written law, the political claims and ground reality of deprivations and poverty. Constitutional guarantees remain unfulfilled and laws unimplemented with a regularity that is awesome. Public services are abysmally poor and inadequate. Basic needs of education, health care and sanitation, clean drinking water, minimum insurance against malnutrition and hunger remain beyond the reach of more than half the population.

Yet there is a long and growing list of small and diverse programmes targeted directly for the poor and vulnerable.[3] These programmes have failed to create the expected impact on poverty for a variety of reasons. Without significant land redistribution in agriculture, sustaining any welfare improving measure becomes extremely difficult. The total quantum of resources used as a proportion of national income is still very inadequate. Leakage stemming from corruption and faulty project planning, moreover, could be very high as to render these programmes completely ineffective. In a similar fashion, indirect and inefficient subsidies are doled out from the government's budget at all levels of governance. Perhaps nowhere is the wastage of resources so obvious than in subsidies given to infrastructural services such as power, water, irrigation and food. Economists seldom agree with one another. But this is one area where there is almost universal agreement that the design and administration of subsidies in India can be vastly improved (see Morris 2001, 2002a). Over and above these, government contracts are made with little care for public interest. Together with acute shortages in infrastructural facilities, these interventions described above help nurture corruption and contribute to serious failures of good governance. According to Morris (2002b), they serve the purpose of buying up dissent amongst the excluded and deprived. The economic resources that constitute the political games in distributional coalitions are state sponsored. The developmental outcomes of governance mechanisms have been inadequate, inefficient and extremely unevenly distributed, representing a classic case of systematic private gains at public expense.

It was in the decade of the 1980s that the national government began to feel the pressures of a combination of effects. One was the growing voice of discontent with economic controls, not only from the rising class of domestic entrepreneurs, but also from groups and classes at the margin of the distributional coalition. Then there were increasing global pressures to integrate with international markets, especially the lure of revolutionary changes in information and communications technologies. Finally, the collapse of the Soviet system removed an important frame of reference from the apparatus of policy-making. The balance of payments crisis of 1991 (coupled with some sharp developments on the political front) led to the acceptance of the Washington Consensus as economic policy. The multilateral agencies like the International Monetary Fund (IMF) and the World Bank set the agenda for deep changes in the content of governance in terms of economic policies. Indeed in 1991, if one were to look around the world and search for national examples of high economic performance, all such would be economies *primarily* driven by markets. It is important to stress the word primarily, because in all economies the state does play a role (though the role may not be the one envisaged in the Washington Consensus), and it would be impossible to identify an economy that is purely market driven or purely state controlled. What is often overlooked, however, is the fact that while almost all (China could be an arguable exception) high-performing economies were primarily market driven, all market-driven economies were certainly not high performing. In other words, it is quite clear that allowing markets to function is certainly not sufficient for ensuring economic growth. There must be a certain chemistry of governance, opportunities and free markets that catalyses development.

MARKET FAILURES AND COORDINATION PROBLEMS

The process of economic reforms initiated in 1991 by the Government of India accepted the stabilisation and structural adjustment package of the IMF and World Bank. The decade of the 1990s witnessed a sharp change in economic policies. The decade also witnessed all three major political formations in India, the Bharatiya Janata Party (BJP)-led National Democratic Alliance (NDA), the Janata Dal-led Third Force, and of course the Indian National Congress, enjoying separate stints in office in New Delhi. The polity has, by and large, accepted the overall thrust of the policy prescriptions, namely decontrol of the private sector, privatisation of the public sector and opening up of domestic markets. The implementation of these would require a stable macro-economic environment brought about by a tight control over fiscal deficits including tax reforms and cutbacks in subsidies and public investments, a conservative monetary policy for curbing inflation and a movement towards a flexible exchange rate regime.[4] Despite the declared commitment to policy reforms and substantial new legislative enactment, India's track record has been quite mediocre (see Parikh 1997, 1999).

Market-friendly economic reforms do imply a serious reduction in the negative role of the state in restricting and controlling markets through a complicated set of licences and permits. What then is supposed to be the new role of governance in terms of content as well as processes? In terms of the content of governance, the policy prescriptions heavily emphasise the dismantling of the apparatus of control over the private sector and market activities. Little wonder that the prescriptions of the Washington Consensus are taken, once the reform measures are implemented, to imply no strategic role of the state beyond national defence, law and order, and legitimisation of private property and contracts. There are many who argue persuasively (see Sen 2000) for the state not merely dismantling the apparatus of control, but complementing it with a switch of attention and resources to areas hitherto neglected. This would entail an active role of the state in promoting services in sectors such as education and health.

It is important to understand the need for having active and efficient governance in some particular sectors. Markets have a proven track record of efficient allocation of resources in most activities where private gains and costs conform closely to social gains and costs. However, this statement neither claims that markets are efficient for *all* activities, nor does it imply anything about the fairness of market outcomes. There are markets that fail (where private cost-benefits are significantly different from social cost-benefits), markets that are imperfect or incomplete, and markets that are missing. Many such shortcomings of markets are particularly stark in poor and less developed economies (Mookherjee and Ray 2001). In all these instances it is possible to make a case for governing markets. One quick example will suffice. The market for narcotics provides opportunities for substantial private gains. Yet, no government in the world permits legal trade in narcotics. The reason is that the perceived social costs (negative returns) are extremely high compared to private gains. Whether governments have been able to successfully curb illegal trade is a distinctly different matter.

As a parallel example, consider the possibilities of private investments in primary education and basic health care in a poor tribal village in some remote corner of India. One does not have to appreciate the finer points of economic theory to realise that private gains are expected to be extremely low from the point of view of the investor, yet the social gains from a school or a health care centre could be substantial. There will be a lot of potential demand for both types of services that are not backed up with purchasing power. Poor people do not have the franchise to vote with their 'dollars' so lucidly described in elementary economics textbooks. Dwelling on this particular example a little longer, one might argue that the social needs for which the perceived returns are deemed to be high is a moral one based on notions of equality and justice. Indeed it is, and in my opinion a very valid one.[5] What is often forgotten is that there are strong economic reasons too for acquiring basic capabilities such as education and health. Consider a situation where market-friendly reforms work wonders in creating job opportunities. If half the population is malnourished and illiterate then it is possible to think of situations where there may be a real shortage of labour equipped with even the bare minimum capabilities of education and health. In an economy such as India's, so richly endowed with labour, this situation would be a cruel twist of fate! And if markets fail in societies where people live in abject poverty, good governance requires that market failures be countered with successful alternative arrangements for providing these services.

India's track record in this regard has always been poor. Compared to not only the developed countries of the world, but also to all the emerging market economies of South-East Asia and East Asia, India's spending on primary education and health has been far too low. On top of it the quality and delivery of such services has been far too poor (see Harriss-White 1999; Shariff 1999). This has been true since independence whether under a democratic socialism of *garibi hatao* or under more contemporary market-friendly regimes.

The second crucial sector where market friendliness could be inadequate is infrastructure. In the process of sustaining high rates of economic growth, the creation of additional capacity in infrastructure is obviously of paramount importance. A policy framework that enables investments in these areas is needed to attract private investments, both domestic and foreign. Infrastructure availability is a necessary condition for the rate of productive investment to increase. Markets, provided the state refrains from policies like reservation for the public sector and administered pricing, can take care of infrastructural investments because private returns can be attractive if suitable pricing policies are allowed. However, there is one crucial problem regarding the flow of such investments. In each area of infrastructure, investment is usually bulky and gestation periods typically long. Moreover, the need is to have large volumes of investment in *all* areas of infrastructure such as power, roads, telecommunications and port capacities, to ensure a balanced growth of facilities. Unless there is some degree of balanced growth, private investments that need to avail of infrastructure will be inadequate. For instance, India could have the best roadways in the world, but if there remains a shortage of power, private investments and market activity in general will be constrained.

The investment portfolio to meet the needs of a balanced growth in infrastructure in a country like India, where existing shortfalls are quite large, would be enormous. The market, left to its own mechanisms, is likely to take a long time in installing adequate capacity in all areas of requirements. Obviously, in such a situation, the resultant growth rate of the economy would be far lower than the case where investment flows are more balanced across different areas. If capacities are to be installed within a reasonable time span, then the state has to coordinate investment flows in terms of a loose but well-directed plan. Alternative exercises could be undertaken to study the feasibility of different rates of growth that could be sustained into the future. For instance, one could target a sustained growth rate of 7 per cent within a period of 15 years. On this basis, the investment profile for the creation of adequate capacity in the chosen time frame could be arrived at. The state would then have to devise suitable policies to attract private investments as well as, if the need arises, mobilise additional resources.

This strategic exercise would depend critically on the transparency and efficiency of the regulatory framework[6] that governs the conditions under which long-term investments are made. Infrastructure policies have been singularly muddle-headed in India. Despite a decade of reforms and the opening up of all sectors of infrastructure, investments have not been forthcoming to the extent necessary. Inadequacy of infrastructure is one of the chief constraints that limit the rate of growth of the economy. Astonishing sloth, corruption, and political tug-of-wars, with too frequent amendments and alterations, have marked India's regulatory policies.

INSTITUTIONAL FAILURES

I have argued for a positive set of interventions by the state especially in terms of promoting human capabilities and coordinating infrastructure over and above the roll back of the negative set of interventions that restricted rather than enabled markets. These issues pertain to the content of governance. A consensus on the role of government is much easier to arrive at. It is more difficult to implement those measures with reasonable efficiency. Processes, explicit regulations and laws, implicit rules that govern contracts, all may warrant changes to create a more suitable environment for the new set of enabling interventions. Institutional change is one of the most difficult aspects of development and according to many analysts constitute the most important constraint on economic development. Bardhan (2001) argues that the economic failure of India can be analysed not merely by the failure of the state at the national level, but also by the failure of smaller local institutions of governance independent of whether these institutions are formally run by the government or not.

The reasons why markets fail to deliver the expected outcomes are much better understood than the reasons why institutions fail. Getting to the core of government failures at both the central and decentralised levels is all about understanding why collective action in general and cooperation in particular fails. Collective action (cooperation out of self-interest) succeeds only under some restrictive configuration of perceived costs and benefits. The individuals should not be too myopic. The gains from universal cooperation must be substantial, the loss from unilateral cooperation small, and the gain from unilateral non-cooperation not too large. Above all, each individual must be confident that everyone else is rational and fully informed. Such conditions are difficult to fulfil in large heterogeneous collectivities. Strong social norms will be required to supplant self-interest in ensuring a desirable, intended consequence. In fact Elster (1989) argues that a solution to a generalised Prisoners' Dilemma would require a sufficiently large number of Kantians (who would do what would be best if all did it, *independent* of what others actually did) in the collectivity. It is quite evident that such changes in social norms and ethical positions cannot be legislated.

This is not to suggest, however, that legislative changes are irrelevant. There could be changes in the Constitution, or in the rules of democratic representation. For instance, Dutta (2000) has argued that fragmented national and provincial legislatures with unstable coalitions tend to be conservative in experimenting with major reforms. He has tried to demonstrate that by changing the representation rule in India from a plural to a proportional system could produce more stable governments, and hence the likelihood of systemic reforms would increase.

In making institutions more participatory, accountable and transparent, there is, first of all, a need to improve the credibility of commitments made by an institution at every level of governance (Sinha 2001). In India there is far too much of a gap between the letter of a law or a contract and what is actually done in practice. This gap widens with too much dependence on discretionary rather than on general rules of governance. Poor design, lobbying pressures and the ample possibilities of opportunistic behaviour, all contribute to a situation where every rule can be flouted without much cost, and every law can be made impotent by discretionary departures built into the enactment.

The second aspect of improving institutional performance is to appreciate and admit that large bureaucracies (public or corporate) do not always behave as a benevolent autocrat or a universal class with a shared objective. Governance structures in bureaus suffer from agency problems with the usual shortcomings of the conflict of interests between the group's overall aims and the objectives of smaller coalitions within the group, or that of some dominant individual within the group. In many cases it would be impossible to make the incentive structure fully compatible with the principal objective, but that does not imply that existing incentive structures cannot be improved upon.

Remediability is an aspect of institutional improvement that has been emphasised by Williamson (2001). A governance structure is said to be remediable if a better alternative can be fully described *and* found to be politically feasible. Sometimes what appears as a failure of governance in the sense of the principal objective of a rule remaining unfulfilled may have been designed to be ineffective to ensure an individual's or a smaller coalition's particular gains. In such cases an alternative is easy to describe but political feasibility remains difficult to establish. There could well be instances where an intended change cannot be implemented because of lobbying by the potential losers if the change is actually brought about. The losers could be small in absolute numbers but they could be organised with a political voice, and their per capita losses could be substantial. The potential winners could be many more in number but they could be spread out, unorganised, and not very certain about the expected size and incidence of the distribution of gains. In such cases, even if the alternative intended implied an unambiguous social or economic gain, there is a very strong likelihood of it getting stalled and obstructed.

The possibility of collective action failures and the difficulty in remedying institutional arrangements are quite well known. In economies such as India's the problem is made much more difficult by the stark social fragmentation and economic inequality in power and access to economic resources (Bardhan 2001). The lack of an encompassing interest of the state in the development of the country, coupled with the absence of an embedded autonomy that insulates the state from a complex set of pressures from particular interest groups, affect both macro as well as micro outcomes. At the macro level it become more difficult to establish and implement major policy transformations, and at the micro level the delivery and maintenance of crucial services such as education and health care, as well as physical infrastructure, become highly inadequate and inefficient.

The pervasive extent of institutional failures in India,[7] the culture of corruption and inefficiency along with a noisy, fragmented polity, are often used to argue about the irrelevance of a fragile democracy. It is even more tempting to argue that successful economies of Asia like South Korea, Singapore and post-reform China have had autocratic governments that have been able to articulate the nation's encompassing interests. This argument, however attractive it might seem, is not universally valid. Studies (Barro 1996; Przeworski 1995 amongst many others) that have tried to systematically look at the negative relationship between political freedom and economic performance have been unable to establish a strong trade-off. The argument for democracy lies in the intrinsic value of political and civil liberties as basic capabilities, as also in its instrumental value in promoting the voice people have in public affairs. Democratic institutions like a free press, therefore, serve the purpose of setting the agenda for change. The rapid growth of non-governmental organisations (NGOs) in India and elsewhere (even in non-democratic societies) illustrates the inherent need of citizens to seek representation of their interests beyond the ballot, as taxpayers, users of public goods, and in seeking participation in social and community affairs. These expressions of voice, participation (see World Bank 1997) and unpersecuted opposition, however imperfect, have demonstrated usefulness in preventing economic disasters. The political and economic incentives provided by democratic governance are of central importance in leveraging institutional improvements in India. However, there are strong forces of global economic change that impinge upon the feasible set of political and economic incentives.

One of the most important prescriptions of the IMF–World Bank economic reforms package is the opening up of the Indian economy in terms of reduced trade barriers and easier flows of international capital. The gains from free trade in goods and services are supposed to be substantial, for a hitherto inward-looking economy like India. The flow of goods and capital across international borders would help the domestic economy integrate into world markets and ensure a globally efficient allocation of resources. It would make the law of one price prevail, and market-determined exchange rates would provide the flexibility in foreign exchange markets that could cure chronic balance of payments difficulties associated with rapid development. Obtaining access to new technologies and adequate financial capital for investments would no longer remain an acute problem. This is the crux of globalisation. The Indian state is committed to integrating into world markets not from its programme of economic reforms alone, but also under the compulsions of being a member of the World Trade Organisation (WTO). India's international trade regime and the regulations governing foreign exchange markets have already undergone many changes in the last decade. More changes are likely in the near future if all obligations to the WTO are to be met.

The phenomenon of globalisation is debated quite passionately in different forums and in different discourses. The purpose is not to review the various arguments used and positions adopted in this regard (see Berger 2001; Thomas 2001). However, some observations about globalisation are in order before discussing the implications of current global compulsions for governance in India. First of all, globalisation is not something new. The dynamic of capitalism is accumulation and expansion. Capitalist market economies are by their very nature always under compulsions to grow. So globalisation is part of a continuing trend of growing international trade and capital movements since the advent of the Industrial Revolution.

Second, globalisation is far from complete in the sense that the law of one price for commodities does not prevail, capital mobility is imperfect in the sense that all arbitrage and speculative opportunities have not been exhausted and a single rate of interest does not prevail in the world economy. Labour mobility is still highly restricted, in the sense that wages have not been equalised globally. There is a deeper implication of this. Cross-border transaction costs are high because each nation's internal systems of law, regulation and social norms are distinct from one another. To this extent globalisation would remain incomplete and shallow, even if all rules and regulations governing international trade were made exactly the same across all countries. Global markets are not fully integrated (see Rodrik 2000). The process has been fragmentary and incomplete at best.

Another important aspect of globalisation worth mentioning is the nature of global capital movements. Financial institutional investors, sometimes also called Hedge Funds, are enormously rich in liquid wealth (see Krugman 2000). International capital markets are controlled by a handful of key players. Movements of capital can be enormously large in volume and can move at astonishing speed from one location to another. The decade of the 1990s has repeatedly shown that capital movements can exhibit unanticipated volatility. There is no central bank or government powerful and resourceful enough that can fully anticipate the movements and prevent economic crisis in terms of unemployment and bankruptcy. In such situations autonomous national economic policies (like monetary and fiscal) become much less potent. The incompleteness, the uncertainty, and the erosion of national autonomy in terms of policy-making associated with the contemporary stage of global integration have important implications for governance.

The process of moving towards higher degrees of market integration in goods and services, especially financial capital, has a tendency to open up productive opportunities for economic growth, but also carries with it significant instability and a dramatic rise in uncertainties (Sinha 2002). It can create oligopolistic markets comprising a handful of giant players and can erode the autonomy of the nation-state in terms of its control over domestic prices, output, employment levels and interest rates. Integration implies greater external compulsions to reform domestic institutions along the lines of those prevailing in the developed economies. In short, the nation-state faces increasing impotency in domestic economic control on the one hand and a rising pressure from external compulsions to conform to global trends on the other. Globalisation appears as an inexorable force.

It is in this sense that the nation-state faces a dilemma (Friedman 1999) and a crisis of identity. One possibility is that the state integrates with the global economy and yet retains some distinctive identity of its own. This can be achieved by shrinking the domain of mass politics in the sense of allowing universal franchise, political mobilisation and responding to domestic public opinion. The nation can survive by becoming a representative of global capitalism, facilitating free movements of goods and capital, reforming institutions and property rights to enable markets to efficiently allocate resources. In this case, the market outcomes may be efficient but are likely to be inequitable. The political agenda will be similar across contending political groups and parties with only shades of differences in opinion. Friedman describes this political difference as being similar to that of choosing between Pepsi and Coke.

The second possibility is that the nation-state chooses to minimise its economic relationships with the rest of the world, and concentrates on a kind of insular, inward-looking development strategy (Bird 2001). This could be under the aegis of a benevolent autocrat or under some kind of open polity allowing for mass politics like the Indian example of the past 50 years. The economic costs of isolation, in a world where integration is proceeding rapidly, could be substantial. The possibility of the loss of political rights and freedoms would add to social woes. This could be unsustainable in the long haul as borne out by the collapse of the Soviet Union and other East European economies.

A final possibility and perhaps a more ideal outcome of globalisation could be some kind of an international federal structure where the 20th century concept of a nation-state is fundamentally altered. This would require the emergence of a complete structure of global governance, of which the United Nations, World Bank, IMF and WTO could be a nascent configuration. The system would ideally have the potential to be responsive to the demands of universal franchise and political mobilisation. In other words, the structure of global governance would shift the agenda of change from national to the international domain, with constituent nations having almost identical institutions of law, contract and private property and regulatory frameworks.

Full international economic integration and the autonomy of the nation-state to control its own economy, and democratic mass politics that allow for a vibrant plurality are not simultaneously possible. At most combinations of any two of them seem feasible. What will emerge from current trends discernable in the global economy is difficult to predict. However, if market-friendly globalisation is to translate to a genuine bread and butter proposition for the overwhelming portion of the world's population, the global system has to be equitable and sustainable (see UNDP 1999).

GLOBAL GOVERNANCE AND EQUITY

Any consideration of good governance necessarily implies an underlying notion of justice and fairness. Very often a discussion of the ethical basis of governance is set in the context of a modern, industrialised, market society with a long history and a well-defined, materialist understanding of progress. The core of equity lies in reconciling individual advantage with a concern for all. Equity is then about balancing a set of individual rights with concerns of public utility, balancing private property with larger social considerations. It is in this sense that the freedom of the market and the authority of the state come into conflict, especially in situations where the rights of the rich stand uncomfortably against the needs of the poor.

The entire world, however, does not consist of industrialised market societies like those of North America or Western Europe. Societies, especially in developing, emerging economies are far more complex and heterogeneous. There are still tribal or ethnic societies where the concept of justice is based much more on solidarity, where private property rights are far less important. There are also hierarchical societies where maintaining a stable order is of paramount importance, and rights are based on social positions. In market societies the central institutions are private property and markets based on voluntary contracts. Each person is formally free to enter into contracts, and to acquire and dispose of property according to opportunities perceived to be the best. A market society is the product of contracts and voluntary associations into which individuals enter for their own advantage. The social order is not a constraint on human ambitions. In fact it is the opposite. The order which society possesses is the result of the underlying human wants and interests.

As market relations become more dominant through global integration, the universal demands for equal human rights, political equality and equality before the law become sharper. The global economy also faces a problem of ensuring that the material development process is sustainable into the future.[8] There are, for instance, serious environmental concerns arising out of global externalities created by material development. These problems also concern distributional ethics in a fundamental way, not merely intragenerational but more regarding the inter-generational equity. There is a limited carrying capacity of planet earth given technology and the rate of growth of population. Global governance must ensure that life support systems such as air, water and soil, to social fundamentals such as education and health care systems, are not jeopardised. In the long haul, new technologies, consumer preferences and investment strategies will have to reflect a deeper harmony with nature. The material consumption patterns of the richest 20 per cent in the world who consume roughly 80 per cent of resources cannot be emulated by all. Yet that is what growth and development is supposed to be all about.[9] The imagery of development is an enticing collage of greedy mechanisms and mechanised greed. Global distributional ethics, in this context, revolves around two fundamental questions: is today's development hurting someone now? Will today's development hurt those who will live here in the future?

Where formal notions of equality are absent, even recognising these needs can be an important matter. In a country like India, where most of the needs are formally recognised in the Constitution and the set of Legislative Acts, the demand is for a more universal *de facto* claim to these entitlements. However, as global integration proceeds, market outcomes in the distribution of material goods and services have become increasingly unequal. Most societies, including India, are far from being a pure type. The constraints of community and hierarchy are real, which adds another dimension to the tension between the egalitarian demands of political democracy and the distributionally inequitable possessive individualism of the market.

THE DOMINANT TREND OF CHANGE

Over the past decade, Indian polity has been able to forge a broad consensus amongst the major political formations regarding the need to carry out economic reforms on the lines of the Washington Consensus. India's commitment to carry out the IMF–World Bank stabilisation and structural adjustment programmes and its membership of the WTO has brought about major changes in the economy. Management of fiscal and monetary resources has received much attention. Rolling back of the licence and permit 'raj' has been quite significant.

Yet, despite this commitment and a broad consensus, India has had limited success in bringing about the desired degree and depth of change, constrained by the fragmentary nature of its polity and the inability of the government to bring about institutional remedies. Development of human capabilities continues to be constrained by the inadequacies of resource allocations and the inefficiencies of policy design. As the compulsions to integrate become sharper, the domain of politics continues to move away from substantial issues of economic policy and the positive role of the state. Issues of employment generation, inflation, the quantity and quality of public services and the growing disparities of income are all being displaced by questions of sub-national identities, group entitlements, religion, terrorism, nuclear capability, and foreign policy matters on the political agenda. Opening up of the economy, deregulating markets and having tighter fiscal and monetary management constitute the essence of national policy. The slowness of achieving these ends lie partly in the noisiness of an open, but fragmented polity, and partly in the complexities of relentless bargaining between coalitions representing the vested interests of different communities and hierarchies. The Indian economy is moving towards a tortuous integration with global markets where the government may have to compete with other national governments to attract foreign investments and trade flows. The national government is bound to find the task complicated by international compulsions on the one hand, and a long history of institutional failures on the other. The transition to a politically democratic, market-friendly economy, which is also integrated with the rest of the world, is likely to be painful and patchy.

Concluding Remarks

India, since political independence, has failed to transform its economy and society into a fully modern industrial one, despite having been able to hold on to political democracy. This is not to suggest that no economic or social changes have occurred. The insufficient transformation is evident on two counts. First, the extent of economic deprivation and poverty is too large to be acceptable by any yardstick. Second, there are many instances of economies around the world, especially in Asia, which have moved far ahead of India in terms of living standards in a very decisive fashion. The apparent reasons are not hard to find. It has been a story of the lack of good governance in terms of the content of economic policies and in institutional failures.

In the last two decades of the 20th century, there were strong internal and external compulsions of merging with a global economic system that was itself marked by major political changes and economic uncertainties. In choosing to pursue the economic policies of the Washington Consensus, India has been reducing the space of state intervention so as to enable markets to work more freely. However, there are three specific areas where the state should play a more (and not less) active role to ensure facilitation, coordination and correction of market failures. Specifically these entail serious attention towards institutional reforms in regulatory frameworks and incentive structures, improved use of resources (both in quantity and efficiency) in building fundamental capabilities in primary education and basic health, and a more coordinated effort in generating investments in physical infrastructure.

A related aspect of governance in a market economy that is open to free flows of trade and some international capital movements is a loss of autonomy in conducting domestic fiscal and monetary policies. This loss is not in form, but market integration substantially reduces the power of standard economic policies to address issues of unemployment, inflation and growth. One likely outcome is that India begins to concentrate in competing with other nation-states in attracting investments and trade. The domain of mass politics, so critical to good governance in democratic societies, has begun to shrink. The political agenda is changing quite rapidly from basic economic issues to regional, particularistic concerns of community, ethnicity and religion.

The lack of good governance affects the poorest 40 per cent (income distribution-wise) of India's population the worst. Here the extent of acute deprivation and destitution desperately needs active governance in creating fundamental capabilities. The next 40 per cent (relatively better off, but still very poor by international standards) is deprived from availing and creating market opportunities because of the inadequacies of physical infrastructure and inefficiencies of local institutions in harnessing dynamic energies into productive collective efforts. The top 20 per cent constitute the power elite and the primary constituents of the distributional coalition. The elite's material development has been significant, and it has benefited from planned interventions of the past and stands to benefit from a globalised economy of the future.

There is a nascent form of global governance already discernable, based on the Washington Consensus. There are a number of multilateral institutions that could serve the purpose of further developing such a governance structure. At the same time, there are numerous groups and organisations that are raising their voices over other important global concerns such as fairness in international trade, poverty alleviation and environmental protection. They are contesting the rising hegemony of the Washington Consensus. The structure and the ethical basis of future governance in an integrated world are, therefore, hard to predict just yet. Dominant global trends along with India's own experiment with international integration are far removed from the desirable features of good governance. The two most important features of any global governance structure are democracy and equity. Good governance must also ensure sustained development opportunities for the poor and deprived people of the world. It entails, amongst many other things, new economic policies and institutions, new life styles and preferences. Above all, it must be able to reconcile individual advantage nurtured by the market with a tolerant concern for all.

NOTES

1. The author is indebted to participants at the conference for comments, especially to Debashish Bhattacherjee, Kuldeep Mathur, Prem Shankar Jha and Annapurna Shaw for comments on the earlier draft.
2. For an extensive analysis of India's initial strategy see Joshi and Little (1994).
3. For an analysis of public policy aimed at alleviating poverty in India see Mahendra Dev and Ranade (1997, 1999).
4. For detailed analysis of the different dimensions of the economic reforms programme see Cassen and Joshi (1995) as well as Joshi and Little (1996). For a different and more critical view of the liberalisation process see Bhaduri and Nayyar (1996). The IMF–World Bank's logic underlying the Washington Consensus is well presented in World Bank (1991).

5. This is also discussed in Sinha (1998).
6. The regulatory frameworks for governing infrastructures in India are notorious for being inadequately designed and seem to indicate a high degree of instability as they are changed too frequently. On this see Morris (2001, 2002a).
7. For a collection of interesting discussions on institutional change in India see Kahkonen and Lanyi (2000). For more conceptual discussions on problems of contending approaches to issues as well as the need to create an institutional network that have both competitive and cooperative dimensions see Gnyawali and Madhavan (2001) and Townley (2002).
8. This of course is a very critical issue underlying the debate about sustainable development where the ethical positions of rich and poor confront one another in different layers of complexity. See Beladi et al. (2000), and Li and Lofgren (2000) for discussions on the simultaneous conflict between the North and the South, and between now and the future. For an Indian perspective on environmental regulations and problems see Dwivedi (1997).
9. However, there has been an increasing use of non-material ends of development in the economics literature, especially following the tradition built by Amartya Sen and others. For an interesting discussion on the dimensions of human development see Alkire (2002).

REFERENCES

Alkire, Sabina. 2002. 'Dimensions of Human Development'. *World Development*, 30(2): 181–205.
Bardhan, Pranab. 1986. *The Political Economy of Development in India*. Delhi: Oxford University Press.
———. 2001. 'The Nature of Institutional Impediments to Economic Development', in Satu Kahkonen and Mancur Olson (eds). *A New Institutional Approach to Economic Development*, pp. 245–67. New Delhi: Vistaar.
Barro, Robert J. 1996. *Getting it Right; Markets and Choices in a Free Society*. Cambridge, Mass.: MIT Press.
Beladi, H., Chau, N.H. and Khan, Ali M. 2000. 'North–South Investment Flows and Optimal Environmental Policies', *Journal of Environmental Economics and Management*, 40(3): 275–96.
Berger, Mark T. 2001. 'The Nation-state and the Challenge of Global Capitalism'. *Third World Quarterly*, 22(6): 889–907.
Bird, Graham. 2001. 'Conducting Macroeconomic Policy in Developing Countries: Piece of Cake or Mission Impossible?' *Third World Quarterly*, 22(1): 37–49.
Bhaduri, A. and Nayyar, D. 1996. *The Intelligent Person's Guide to Liberalization*. New Delhi: Penguin.
Cassen, Robert and Joshi, Vijay (eds). 1995. *India: The Future of Economic Reforms*. Delhi: Oxford University Press.

Dutta, Bhaskar. 2000. 'Fragmented Legislatures and Electoral Systems: The Indian Experience', in Satu Kahkonen and Anthony Lanyi (eds). *Institutions, Incentives and Economic Reforms in India,* pp. 77–100. New Delhi: Sage.

Dwivedi, O.P. 1997. *India's Environmental Policies, Programmes and Stewardship.* Great Britain: Macmillan.

Elster, J. 1989. *Nuts and Bolts for the Social Sciences.* Cambridge: Cambridge University Press.

Friedman, Thomas L. 1999. *The Lexus and The Olive Tree: Understanding Globalization.* New York: Farrar, Straus and Giroux.

Gnyawali, D.R. and Madhavan, R. 2001. 'Cooperative Networks and Competitive Dynamics: A Structural Embeddedness Perspective'. *Academy of Management Review,* 26(3): 431–45.

Harriss-White, Barbara. 1999. 'State, Market, Collective and Household Action in India's Social Sector', in Barbara Harriss-White and S. Subramanian (eds). *Illfare in India,* pp. 303–28. New Delhi: Sage.

Joshi, Vijay and Little, I.M.D. 1994. *India: Macroeconomics and Political Economy 1964–1991.* Delhi: Oxford University Press.

———. 1996. *India's Economic Reforms 1991–2001.* Delhi: Oxford University Press.

Kahkonen, Satu and Lanyi, Anthony (eds). 2000. *Institutions, Incentives and Economic Reforms in India.* New Delhi: Sage.

Krugman, Paul. 2000. *The Return of Depression Economics.* Harmondsworth: Penguin.

Li, Chuan-Zhong and Lofgren, Karl-Gustaf. 2000. 'Renewable Resources and Economic Sustainability: A Dynamic Analysis with Heterogeneous Time Preferences'. *Journal of Environmental Economics and Management,* 40(3): 236–50.

Mahendra Dev, S. and Ranade, Ajit. 1997. 'Poverty and Public Policy: A Mixed Record', in Kirit Parikh (ed.). *India Development Report 1997,* pp. 61–76. Delhi: Oxford University Press.

———. 1999. 'Persisting Poverty and Social Insecurity: A Selective Assessment', in Kirit Parikh (ed.). *India Development Report 1999–2000.* Delhi: Oxford University Press.

Mookherjee, Dilip and Ray, Debraj (eds). 2001. *Readings in the Theory of Economic Development.* Oxford: Blackwell.

Morris, Sebastian (ed.). 2001. *India Infrastructure Report 2001: Issues in Regulation and Market Structure.* For 3iNetwork. Delhi: Oxford University Press.

———. 2002a. *India Infrastructure Report: Governance Issues for Commercialization.* For 3iNetwork. Delhi: Oxford University Press.

———. 2002b. 'The Challenge to Governance in India', in Sebastian Morris (eds). *India Infrastructure Report 2002: Governance Issues For Commercialization,* pp. 15–36. For 3iNetwork. Delhi: Oxford University Press.

Parikh, Kirit (ed.). 1997. *India Development Report 1997.* Delhi: Oxford University Press.

———. 1999. *India Development Report 1999.* Delhi: Oxford University Press

Przeworski, Adam. 1995. *Sustainable Democracy.* Cambridge: Cambridge University Press.

Rodrik, Dani. 2000. 'How Far will International Integration Go?' *Journal of Economic Perspectives,* 14(1): 177–86.

Sen, Amartya. 2000. *Development as Freedom*. Delhi: Oxford University Press.

Shariff, Abusaleh. 1999. *India: Human Development Report*. NCAER, Delhi: Oxford University Press.

Sinha, Anup. 1998. 'Economic Reforms: Unaimed Opulence or Sustainable Growth?' *Decision,* 25(1–4): 1–10.

———. 2001. 'Economic Development in India: The Need for Institutional Reform', in Satu Kahkonen and Mancur Olson (eds). *A New Institutional Approach to Economic Development*, pp. 284–88. New Delhi: Vistaar.

———. 2002. 'A Century of Crisis'. *The Telegraph* (Kolkata). January 23.

Thomas, Caroline. 2001. 'Global Governance, Development and Human Security; Exploring the Links'. *Third World Quarterly,* 22(2):159–76.

Townley, Barbara. 2002. 'The Role of Competing Rationalities in Institutional Change'. *Academy of Management Journal,* 45(1): 163–79.

UNDP. 1999. *Human Development Report*. Delhi: Oxford University Press.

Williamson, Oliver E. 2001. 'Economic Institutions and Development: A View from the Bottom', in Satu Kahkonen and Mancur Olson (eds). *A New Institutional Approach to Economic Development,* pp. 92–118. New Delhi: Vistaar.

World Bank. 1991. *World Development Report*. Delhi: Oxford University Press.

———. 1997. *World Development Report*. Delhi: Oxford University Press.

CHAPTER 7

INDIA: FROM DEVELOPMENTAL TO PREDATOR STATE

PREM SHANKAR JHA[1]

The Indian republic is facing a political and constitutional crisis that is as sudden as it is confusing. With terrifying suddenness, the central government of the country has lost the power to govern. Intellectuals and media persons thrashing around for an explanation have, one and all, blamed individuals for New Delhi's malaise. At present the finger of blame is being pointed at Prime Minister Vajpayee, at Home Minister Advani, at Finance Minister Yashwant Sinha, at the contradictions within the Sangh Parivar and the tension between the Bharatiya Janata Party (BJP) and the Rashtriya Swayamsevak Sangh (RSS). Most of the finger pointers have forgotten that in 1997 they were levelling exactly the same charges at the United Front (UF) government and looking to the failings of Prime Minister Inder Gujral and the contradictions between the United Front and the Left Front, to provide an answer. Opposition politicians have muddied the waters by adopting these arguments and turning them into political weapons.

The political crisis is not born out of the failure of the Gujarat government to cope with the communal riots that engulfed the state on 28 February 2002, or of New Delhi's reluctance to take it to task for its calculated ambivalence towards the rioters. On the contrary, the Gujarat riots are only one, albeit the most, visible symptom of a far more pervasive failure of governance and nation-building in the country as a whole. Gujarat has revealed the political dimensions of this failure. But the growing weakness of the centre has been visible in the realm of economic policy for more than five years. So far very few people seem to have realised that there is a direct link between the failure of governance in Gujarat and the growing fiscal deficit and chronic stagnation in which the economy is locked. Few people have realised that the crisis India faces is systemic. It is a product not of the failings of individuals but of the political and constitutional system. The idea is even harder to grasp because the Constitution that is failing India today is the same one that has been responsible for its success in nation-building during the first five decades of independence.

The country got a hint of the crisis of governance in August 2001 when, seemingly out of the blue, Mr Vajpayee threatened to resign his premiership. Most people dismissed it as a politician's trick to bring his party and his coalition into line behind him. This interpretation diverted attention away from the real cause, which was that as Prime Minister he was the first to realise that India had become ungovernable. All that he, or any future prime minister, could do was to pretend not to see where the country was headed and make grandiose claims of progress at home to fool the voters and abroad to make the world believe that India was still a country of some consequence. Mr Vajpayee had, in all probability, grown tired of the game. Nowhere is the gap between performance and pretence more apparent than in the state of the economy. Till almost the end of 2001, the Finance Minister Yashwant Sinha continued to harp on India having attained one of the highest growth rates in the world during the 1990s, when in fact the trend growth rate had dropped rapidly after 1996–97, and for the four year period 1997–2001, was a full 2 per cent below the rate for 1993–97. He did this despite the fact that during the first nine months of 2001–2 industrial growth fell to a paltry 2.3 per cent, consumer demand had stopped growing, and inflation had virtually disappeared, a sure sign of deep slump in the economy.

This lack of growth is causing the most dangerous development that the country faces. Employment in the organised sector has stopped growing. While the number of job seekers is rising by 2.5 per cent per year, the growth of employment in this sector fell to 0.46 per cent in 1998, to 0.04 per cent in 1999, to –0.15 per cent in 2000 and –0.38 per cent in 2001. In all, 672,000 educated entrants into the job market have tried to find jobs every year, but only 17,000 have succeeded. In the four years of the National Democratic Alliance (NDA) rule, therefore, India has added 2.7 million young people to the educated unemployed. If the economy does not revive, in the next three years it will add another 2 million. With such a record the

NDA will not have even a ghost of a chance of coming back to power in 2004.

This paralysis has descended upon the economy not because of the Vajpayee government's inaction, but in spite of its every effort to break its grip. For more than two years, the Prime Minister and Mr Sinha have known that the root cause of the slowing of growth, the lack of investment and the disappearance of new jobs, is the unbearable fiscal deficit. This has forced the government to borrow unprecedented sums of money from the banking system, pushed up real interest rates (interest rates minus inflation) first to 5 and 6, and in the past one year to 8 and 9 per cent, and made new investment impossible. During all of this time, they have done their best to persuade their partners in the NDA, especially those that rule various states, to cooperate in bringing down the deficit by cutting down the size of the bureaucracy, raising prices and tariffs and reducing the theft of power and other services provided by the state. But all these efforts have failed.

The reason is the refusal of the BJP's allies in the NDA to go along with any central policy that might make them unpopular in their home states. The complete defeat of every measure proposed in the budget for 2000–1 to bring down the fiscal deficit and bestow a measure of autonomy on private industry is a case in point. The three most important were the discontinuation of unlimited food procurement by the centre at high, politically inspired support prices; the deregulation of oil product prices next year; and an amendment of the industrial disputes act to permit retrenchment of workers in all but the largest enterprises without the permission of the central and state governments. They have all failed.

The first was sabotaged by the Punjab and Haryana governments which announced that they would buy all the wheat the farmers wanted to sell them, and then forced the central government's Food Corporation of India (FCI) to buy it from them. As a result, instead of going down, the FCI's stocks have risen from 47 million tonnes in February to 60 million tonnes in June. Each tonne costs the central government Rs 5,000 a year to store and distribute, over its issue price. There are already murmurs of dissent over the decontrol of oil product prices, and the reform of labour laws has simply been forgotten.

To get an idea of the cost of rank political opportunism it is only necessary to point out that if only Mr Sinha were permitted to bring down the centre's fiscal deficit from 5.5 to 2 per cent of the gross domestic product (GDP), as his budget measures were intended to do, this would allow the government to divert over Rs 800 billion back from consumption into fixed investment without raising the deficit. This is sufficient to raise the additional power generating capacity from the present 2,500 MW per annum to 7,500 MW per annum, to build motorways and new ports, bridges, railway tracks and signalling systems. In short, it would have provided for completely modernising the economy, restoring the growth rate to 7.5 per cent and the rate of job growth to 2 per cent per annum without having to borrow a single dollar from abroad. What the end of dominant party democracy and the emergence of coalition rule at the centre has done, therefore, is to rob India of its future. In the political calculus of India's populist democracy, the smaller coalition partners' unwillingness to support the measures proposed by the finance minister to cut the fiscal deficit makes eminent sense. They fear that while they will have to shoulder the blame for the hardships that fiscal and labour reforms might impose in the short run, the lion's share of the credit for the gains that might accrue in the longer run will go to the BJP. This unwillingness gets a centre–state dimension and, therefore, gets reinforced when the prime minister and other senior members of the central cabinet are drawn from the BJP, while leaders of one or more of the minor parties, like Chandrababu Naidu and Parkash Singh Badal, are the chief ministers of state governments.

The NDA's experience since 1998 is not unique and is certainly not an aberration. On the contrary, it exactly mirrors the experience of the UF between 1996 and 1998. Despite having agreed to make a reduction of government spending and control of the fiscal deficit a central plank of the Front's Common Minimum Programme, the Communist Party of India (Marxist) (CPI [M]) lost no time in repudiating Finance Minister P. Chidambaram's effort in July 1996 to cut down the government's consumption and reduce the size of the bureaucracy through superannuation. It followed this up, days later, by refusing to go long with a rise in oil product prices to offset the rise in the international price of crude oil. Most commentators ascribed the CPI (M)'s cussedness to the party's mindless rearguard action against economic liberalisation. Few noticed that while this may have been what motivated its ideologues in the UF's steering committee, it did not explain the willingness of committed reformers like Jyoti Basu, the Chief Minister of West Bengal, to go along with obstructionist policies that he knew perfectly well would harm the economy in the long run.

The conflict between the interests of major and minor parties was laid bare by the inexplicable disappearance of Mr Chidambaram from New Delhi a year later when a cabinet subcommittee, of which he was a key member, was in the final stages of negotiating the details of salary increases awarded by the Fifth Pay Commission with the central government employees' trade unions. Agonised calls from the Prime Minister's Office to Chennai elicited the explanation that he had been summoned to Chennai by the leader of the Tamil Maanila Congress, G.K. Moopanar, and warned on pain of expulsion from the Party not to return to Delhi till the negotiations were over.[2] Without Mr Chidambaram to apply the brakes, the sub-committee tamely gave the employees 40 per cent more than the Pay Commission had recommended! In the process it bankrupted the state governments. Today only one state, Karnataka, is able to cover its employees' salaries and pensions out of its current revenues. All the others are borrowing from the central government against memoranda of intent in which they promise to put their house in order, or dreaming up new stratagems, such as borrowing through their state enterprises to finance current consumption. Nor are things improving. In September, Mr Arun Shourie announced that 13 states did not have the money to pay the salaries of their civil servants this year.

STRUCTURAL CAUSES OF GROWING UNGOVERNABILITY

This growing ungovernability is not a transitory phenomenon. On the contrary, its causes are embedded in the very structure of Indian democracy. Like Britain, India has a simple majority voting system. As in Britain, by enlarging the ratio of seats to votes of the largest party and doing the opposite to smaller parties this system has exerted remorseless pressure on the latter to merge with their immediate political neighbours in order to stay alive. As in Britain, over time this has tended to create two major parties or coalitions.

But the similarities have ended there. Unlike Britain, India is a federal and not a unitary democracy. Over 11 or more elections, the simple majority voting system has created two stable parties or coalitions in most states. But in the very act of doing so it has ensured that there will be a multiplicity of small parties at the centre. It has done this by allowing each party or coalition that is well entrenched in a state to translate its hold on the vote there into a small but stable number of seats in the Lok Sabha. Since each small party at the centre has a secure political base in the state, it is under no compulsion to merge itself with a political neighbour in order to survive or better its chances of capturing power. This makes it largely immune to the pressure that the simple majority voting system exerts on small parties to merge themselves with their neighbours to create a two-party system in the central legislature. Not surprisingly, in the last Lok Sabha elections there were no fewer than 63 recognised political parties in the fray. As a result, unlike the British Parliament in which coalition governments have been rare and transitory, in India coalition governments are here to stay.

India's ungovernability has been heightened by the separation of central from state elections that took place in 1971. Coalitions can gain stability, cohesion and effectiveness if they stay and work together for long enough. But in India this has been made virtually impossible by the occurrence of elections to one or more state assemblies every year. This has made sure that at no time are all the members of a coalition free from the pressures of electoral politics. As a result it has become virtually impossible for any coalition government to adopt policies that will yield dividends only after an initial period of dislocation. Economic development is precisely one such area for, in its essence, it involves extracting savings from the public in the short run to enhance investment and augment output, productivity and employment in the long run.

The separation of central and state elections had begun to undermine the capacity of the central government to govern even before the disappearance of one-party government at the centre. It was widely believed even within the Congress Party that, if the Party lost the November 1993 state elections in the four states where BJP governments had been dismissed in the wake of the Babri Masjid demolition, the Rao government would have no option but to resign. This was mercifully not put to the test, but the Central government's capacity to govern remained unimpaired only for another year. Most people attribute the collapse of economic reform to the exit of the Congress. But in actual fact it occurred in December 1994 after two shock defeats the Congress suffered in the Andhra and Karnataka state elections in that month. One of the two subcommittees the Congress set up to analyse the causes of the defeat reported that it had been caused by high inflation. When in May 1995, inflation touched 11.1 per cent, the Party decided that this had gone too far. Inflation had to be curbed by any means whatever. There followed a tightening of money supply that pushed all money rates (overnight interest rates between banks) to 60 per cent. The rise in interest rates knocked the bottom out of the share market and overall raised the cost of investment. Investment fell by 40 per cent in 1995–96. Industrial growth fell from a peak of 16.2 per cent in January to March 1996 to 3 per cent in November. We have remained in a slump ever since. With the disappearance of the one-party government in 1996, probably never to return, both the baneful influences described above have begun to work in tandem with one another. That is the real reason why the Vajpayee government has been unable to make any dent in the problems and challenges before the nation. No government will ever do any better.

In sum, the replacement of single party with coalition governments at the centre has weakened national governance till it is now endangering the unity of the nation. Today India is like a giant ship becalmed in a tranquil sea. It is in no immediate danger of breaking up. But it has no motor and no rudder.

There is an element of Greek tragedy in what is happening now. For the very same features of the Indian Constitution that were responsible for India's phenomenal success in nation-building during the first four decades of its independence have become the main threats to it in the fifth. India is the only country in history that has by and large succeeded in building a modern nation-state through democracy. Without exception, all the other successful modern states were built through the use of coercive power. India did this by accommodating the demands of the country's various ethnic groups and movements and allowing them full play through the working of its federal system. So long as a single, dominant party ruled the centre there was a healthy balance between nation-building and ethnic accommodation. But ethnic accommodation led inevitably to the rise of ethnic, one-state parties. With the collapse of single-party governance at the centre, and the separation of central from state elections, the balance between the two has been lost. Today the compulsions of development and stability are pulling policy in opposite directions, and stability is winning out.

Unfortunately, this stability is an illusion. Without development, there can be no jobs, and without the hope of a stable job in the future, young people have nothing to look forward to. So far they have been giving vent to their disillusionment by throwing out government after government in successive elections. That is the cause of the so-called protest vote, or the anti-incumbency factor that has been noted by political analysts over the past 20 years. In fact the real reason for the Congress Party's surprise defeat in 1994 in Andhra and Karnataka was that this was the first election in which the newly enfranchised 18 to 21-year-old voters turned out in strength to vote. Overall, one in three of the people who voted in the two states in 1994 had never voted before. Very few of the new voters voted for the Congress.

The growing instability of the electorate is reflected in the growing fragility of coalition governments. The awareness that they are not likely to last for more than a single term in office has gradually altered the very objectives of securing power. In the heyday of single-party dominance, the purpose of capturing power was to make and implement policies that would strengthen the nation and enlarge the national cake. Rightly or wrongly, the state was seen as the main instrument for achieving this goal. But as impotent coalitions have replaced the stable single-party government and the political time horizon has shortened, the goals underlying the pursuit of power have changed. Unable to make any changes to the condition of the people, political leaders are increasingly seeking power in order to parcel out the wealth of the state among themselves. This is the reason for the rampant corruption and kickbacks of the kind exposed by the Tehelka team, and the uncontrolled burgeoning of subsidies in the last dozen years.

There is a vicious circle built into this process. The more the state foregoes development in favour of predation, the more rapidly will it lose whatever legitimacy it enjoys in the eyes of the people. The more rapidly it does so, the shorter becomes its life. The shorter its life, the greater its tendency to prey upon the state during the time in office. In the end this leads to what students of Africa's political economy have called 'clientelism'—the construction of coalitions of interests that come together with the express purpose of robbing the state. In states like Bihar and Assam, this process is already virtually complete and bandits have begun to run parallel governments, extorting 'taxes' from the people. The cancer could spread, but fear of this happening is more likely to make the better off states take action to insulate themselves. Such action could end by dismembering the Indian State.

A revealing example is the perversion of the public distribution system for foodgrains that had gone virtually unnoticed till the central government found itself sitting, in the middle of 2001, on 60 million tonnes of foodgrains, of which 18 million tonnes had rotted for want of buyers. This happened even while the Vajpayee government was being severely criticised for allowing starvation deaths to take place in Orissa and elsewhere. The government defended itself in Parliament by pointing out that the centre could only allocate the foodgrains and lower their price. It was up to the states to take the grain and actually distribute it. If starvation deaths had occurred it was because they had failed to do so. What escaped notice was that both the ever-rising government purchases and the declining offtake are the outcome of the rise of a predator state.

In 2000–1, the output of foodgrains fell by 6.3 per cent but the procurement of foodgrains went up from 30.8 million tonnes to 35.5 million tonnes. In April to June 2001, the procurement of wheat from the Rabi crop rose by another 27 per cent. Government purchases accounted for 96 per cent of all the wheat brought to the market. The state thus literally crowded out the private sector from the foodgrains trade by offering a price that bore no relation to the market. The foodgrains then remained in the government's depots because the offtake from the ration shops, which had fallen from 17.1 million tonnes in 1999 to 12.1 million tonnes in 2000, showed only a small rise in the first half of 2001. Left-wing critics of the 'right-wing' BJP ascribed the sharp drop in offtake to the Finance Minister's decision in March 2000 to sharply raise the issue price of foodgrains sold through the ration shops to above-the-poverty-line families. But offtake had in fact been falling far short of procurement in every year since 1993. Between 1993 and 2000, the centre procured 212.8 million tonnes of foodgrains, but the states sold only 129.3 million tonnes. This was the genesis of the centre's food mountain. The starvation deaths and malnutrition were therefore a man-made tragedy.

How has a public distribution system that was originally designed to protect the poor against extortionate pricing during times of drought been turned into an engine of death? A closer examination shows that it is the product of each state-centred party in the ruling coalition adopting a 'me first and the devil take the hindmost' policy. The bulk of the rice and upto 86 per cent of the wheat that the centre procures comes from just two states, Punjab and Haryana. These states jack up support prices at will and evade the responsibility of selling their grain by forcing the centre to buy it from them. The opposite happens in the food deficit states. Since the distribution of even freely supplied foodgrains involves some cost to them, they prefer to minimise their offtake from the centre's allocation. When forced by the centre to take up at least some of their quota, they set rules for its sale that are designed to discourage purchase from the ration shops. Some of the balance finds its way into the black market, but in a final contemptuous slap in the face of the central government, some is sold back to it as grain 'procured' by the state government.

This is the classic behaviour of the predator state. Every one gains—the government and farmers of the grain surplus states, the government of the deficit states and the corrupt employees of the public distribution system. Only the consumers lose and the poorest among them die. Such predatory behaviour is ubiquitous. Almost a third of the power generated in the country is stolen outright. Another 30 per cent is sold to supposed agriculturists at a tenth of its cost of production. In reality, around two-thirds of the power sold to the rural sector is consumed by small industrialists and a new class of well-to-do farmers in their homes. To cover the deficit the state governments have hiked power tariffs relentlessly for the remaining one-third of the power they generate till industry and honest consumers in the urban domestic sector now pay some of the highest power tariffs in the world. In the same way, four-fifths of the fertiliser subsidy goes not to the farmers in whose name it is regularly renewed, but to the manufacturers who have gold plated their capital costs in ways too numerous to relate. Three-quarters of the subsidy on kerosene goes not to the rural poor who supposedly use it as a cooking fuel but to adulterators of gasoline and diesel and to smugglers who ship it out from Bihar and Bengal to Nepal and Bangladesh.

Predatory extortion has now become a way of life for all but a tiny handful of people in the state and central bureaucracies. Kickbacks are mandatory in every sale to a government organisation, whether it is for a rural development project costing a few million rupees, a power plant or an aircraft carrier. Kickbacks are indeed the reason why state governments regularly start new infrastructure projects, but never complete them. For the lion's share of the kickback has to be paid 'up front'. After that the government loses interest in the project. For any private company, whether Indian or foreign, entering a business in which the state might be even peripherally involved has become a nightmare, because deals that were closed with a previous government are regularly 'reopened' to negotiate a fresh kickback every time there is a change of government. That is why in every privatisation bid announced by the NDA government so far, prospective foreign buyers have come, examined the conditions in which business is conducted in India and withdrawn.

As the Indian democratic system has evolved, the millstones of the predator state have ground ever finer. Today it is not only projects, government purchases and large companies that are being regularly preyed upon. Preying upon individuals has become the order of the day. Whether one wants a water or power connection, a telephone or power line repaired, a building permit or a completion certificate; whether one wants to draw one's own pension or obtain a tax refund, or simply obtain an income tax clearance certificate, one must first pay a 'private cess' to concerned petty officials. These petty officials in turn pay huge bribes to their political bosses to be transferred to choice posts in which opportunities for enriching oneself through bribes abound. This predator state constitutes the largest and most powerful vested interest against any change in any law, especially any change towards economic liberalisation or an increase in production and productivity which could ease the conditions of scarcity in which it thrives. It is thus the submerged part of the iceberg that has destroyed nation-building and made India progressively more ungovernable over the last three decades.

The above analysis of the structural changes that underlie the decline of the developmental state and the rise of the predator state in India, and the decline of central power in the face of rising assertiveness by the states, makes it exceedingly unlikely that, even with the best will in the world, any future government will be able to restore a sense of national purpose to the central government in India. Yet if one fails to do so, India will unavoidably splinter into pieces one day in the near future, as it has done so often in the past. If this challenge is to be met, the first imperative is to restore the power to govern to the central government. The second is to break the nexus between bad money and politics that lies at the heart of the predator state. Theoretically the balance between direction and accommodation in the Indian nation-state can be restored if India returns once more to being a dominant party democracy with one, or at most two, national parties dominating both the centre and the states. But since it is most unlikely that one party will ever again dominate national politics, the only alternative is to make constitutional changes that will give coalition governments at the centre that stability and cohesion that will enable them to frame developmental policies once more.

REUNITE CENTRAL AND STATE ELECTIONS

The only alternative is to reunite central and state elections. This needs an amendment to the Constitution which could run somewhat as follows: 'If a state government falls in less than the five years of its normal life, it shall come under President's Rule for the period that remains. If the central government falls in less than five years, all state governments will also hold fresh elections at the same time as the new election to Parliament.' At first sight, these provisions seem draconian, even unfair. Is a long period of President's Rule not a denial of the peoples' right to be ruled by their own representatives? And isn't it doubly unfair to force a new election on a stable state government simply because the central government coalition has broken down? Isn't this, moreover, denying to the states that assured five-year span that they need to implement developmental policies? And is it right to force state legislators to spend still more money on elections that they have played no part in bringing about? Will the resulting decrease in the stability of the state governments not strengthen the predatory behaviour in them even as it weakens it at the centre?

A closer look at the effect that such a reform will have on the political system shows, however, that like Article 16 of the French Fifth Republic, its very enactment will make its invocation unnecessary, for it will eliminate instability not only at the centre but also in the states. The objections cited above relate to situations that can admittedly arise in theory, but will be made extremely rare by the reform itself. State governments first became unstable only after the 1967 assembly and parliamentary elections. The cause was the loss of power in six major states by the Congress, its replacement by shaky coalitions of political parties and groups that had no experience of either governing or of working together, and a determined bid by the Congress to bring these governments down by enticing groups within them to defect. In nine cases out of 10, defections were secured either by offering the defector a large sum of money or a ministership in the next government. Rajiv Gandhi succeeded in controlling the epidemic of defections to a considerable extent by enacting the Anti-Defection Bill with the unanimous support of all political parties, in 1985. But defections have continued at less frequent intervals both in the states and, in the past six years, at the centre. In all cases, the bait has remained the same.

Reuniting assembly and parliamentary elections will remove this lure. Once a Member of Legislative Assembly (MLA) in a state assembly knows that defection will not bring him money or a ministership but a long period of President's Rule, he will defect only on issues of conscience. Defections will then become exceedingly rare. Even in those rare cases where defections occur because of genuine political differences, there is a betrayal of a popular mandate. It is, therefore, still desirable not to allow the defectors to become part of a new government until they have obtained a fresh mandate. But what about the premature fall of a government at the centre? Since under the Constitution another election will have to be held within six months, will forcing all state assemblies to dissolve at the same time not impose a completely unwarranted punishment upon all of them? Once again, a close examination shows that while this eventuality cannot be ruled out in theory, it is exceedingly unlikely to arise in practice. Four central governments have fallen in the 1990s. Three were minority governments that fell because one or other large national party that was supporting them from the outside withdrew its support. These were the governments of Mr V.P. Singh in 1990, Mr Chandrashekhar in 1991 and Mr Gujral in 1998. This form of government formation was characteristic of the very early stages of dissolution of the dominant party system. With the rise and stabilisation of the NDA over the past three years, its day may well be past. But even if it recurs, the reunification of central and state elections will exert a powerful check on the withdrawal of support by an outside party. This is because the hope of capturing power in the next parliamentary election will have to be weighed against the threat of losing power in the states where it is currently in power. In practice the one will cancel out the other. This will not happen only in a situation where there is a minority government at the centre supported by a party that is large enough to count in the central parliament but is not in power in any state. That was not true of the BJP when it withdrew support from the V.P. Singh government in 1990, or of the Congress when it did the same to the Chandrashekhar and Gujral governments. Such a conjunction is, therefore, unlikely to occur in Indian politics.

The experience of the past three years of coalition government under Mr Vajpayee's NDA has thrown up two other reasons why a coalition can fail. The first was the withdrawal from the first NDA by Smt. Jayalalitha and the All India Anna Dravida Munnetra Kazhagam (AIADMK) in March 1999. She did so partly because of serious political differences with the BJP and the Samata Party over the dismissal of the Chief of Naval Staff Vishnu Bhagwat, but mainly because she expected to become a part of a Congress-led coalition government in New Delhi. Had the Congress succeeded in forming a government, there would have been no fresh election at the centre. It was only the Congress' miscalculation of the support it enjoyed in the Opposition that forced another election on the country. The second type of defection that can occur was exemplified by the Trinamool Congress' decision to leave the NDA just before the West Bengal elections in 2001. It did so because its leader, Smt. Mamata Banerjee, was worried that the harsh economic measures that the government unveiled in the budget for 2001–2 (but could not implement) would adversely affect her Party's chances in the state election. The decision to leave was taken with great reluctance, it split the Party and eventually forced her to come back. The fears that impelled Smt. Banerjee to defect are precisely the ones that reunifying central and state elections will eliminate. All in all, therefore, defections from coalition governments at the centre are likely to take place only when the defecting party is virtually certain that it will immediately return to power as part of a rival coalition. It will be for the voters to judge the morality of such a change of horses. But the defection itself will not trigger another general election, and will, therefore, pose little threat to the state assemblies.

REFORM OF ELECTORAL FINANCE

The constitutional reform described in detail above will go a long way towards rooting out the predatory state and bringing back the developmental one in India. Greater stability at the centre and the assurance that barring truly unusual developments a government will complete its five years in office will give coalitions time to jell to formulate policies in the expectation that they will be around to garner their electoral benefits. But to complete the return to the developmental state a second reform is absolutely essential. This is the reform of electoral finance. The damage that was done by the 1970 ban on corporate donations, and the doubling of electoral expenses that followed the separation of central from state elections a year later, has already been described above. Reuniting central and state elections will virtually halve electoral expenses and undo a great deal of it. But only the institution of a state fund for financing elections will start the process of breaking the nexus that has developed between black money, organised crime and politics, especially in the states. The proposal to set up such a fund is far from new. It was made first by a group of Congress Members of Parliament (MPs) to Mrs. Indira Gandhi as far back as 1971. She promised to consider it but lost the election in March 1977. Since then the demand has surfaced repeatedly, usually in the Opposition. But the very same parties that raised the demand showed an inexplicable lack of enthusiasm for it once they came to power. As a result bills have been introduced in Parliament for a reform of electoral finance more than once but been allowed to lapse. The ones that have been passed have made only cosmetic changes to the existing, by and large criminal, process. At present virtually every political party is committed on paper to the reform of electoral finance. A Bill, based on the report of a committee headed by Mr Indrajit Gupta of the Left Front, is waiting to be tabled. Apart from establishing modalities for state funding, it is also expected to make corporate donations to political parties tax deductible. One can only hope that the bill will provide sufficient funds for political parties to free them from the need to raise money from dubious sources.

NOTES

1. The economic statistics presented in this chapter have been obtained from (a) the Economic Surveys issued annually by the Ministry of Finance, Government of India. In particular the Surveys for the years 1999–2000, 2000–1 and 2001–2, (b) The Centre for Monitoring the Indian Economy (CMIE),

monthly reports entitled 'Monthly Review of the Indian Economy' and (c) CMIE periodic reports on Agriculture, the Energy sector, Central and State Finances, and Infrastructure. However, the argument developed on their basis is entirely my own.
2. Told to the author by a senior member of the Prime Minister's Office on condition of anonymity.

PART II

ADMINISTRATIVE REFORMS

The opening chapter (Abraham) in this part is meant to provide an overview of the theme of administrative reforms in India and Europe in a comparative perspective. While the chapter by Wollmann examines public-sector reforms in international perspective, paying special attention to Germany and France, Roeber compares administrative reforms in Germany with other European countries. Three chapters are devoted to India, two of them being concerned with bureaucracy (Mathur, Agnihotri and Dar) and one with non-governmental organisations (NGOs) in the process of reform (Rajan).

Abraham in his chapter argues that the organisation and functions of the state have changed significantly since the 1970s, both in India and Europe, reflecting a worldwide trend. While in the 1980s, the very need for a proactive state was questioned in much of the Western world, especially in the United States and Great Britain, in the developing world the state was still looked upon as the prime entity that could deliver rapid economic growth and improvements in the quality of life. However, the ability of the state to deliver was severely hampered in the 1990s by the deep fiscal crisis that it found itself in. While entrusting the non-governmental, or private, sector with the delivery of services was seen as one possible solution to this fiscal crisis, it created new problems of overstaffing and retraining public officials to manage service delivery (capacity-building). The chapter analyses administrative reforms that have been undertaken to deal with these challenges in India and Europe in comparative perspective, looking at differences both in the context and process of reforms. It examines the politics of reforms in both Europe and India and analyses the reasons why some countries have been able to move ahead more rapidly than others. It concludes that the nature, extent and success of administrative reforms depend to a very large extent on the constitutional and institutional context within which reforms take place.

Wollmann's chapter discusses variations in current public sector reforms internationally, going beyond the debate and practice in the Anglo-Saxon and Scandinavian countries and including particularly Germany and France. It tries to explain the observed variance of reform trajectories by using an analytical scheme in which country-specific 'starting conditions' (from where the reform track of a country 'takes off') and the 'discourse coalitions' are given particular attention as explanatory factors. In conclusion, the chapter discusses the question whether in the comparative perspective the modernisation trajectories of countries and country families are showing institutional convergence or divergence. The chapter argues that although convergence is certainly going on, significant divergence does (and will probably continue to) persist.

In a complementary chapter, Roeber gives an overview of recent approaches to public-sector modernisation in Germany and discusses these approaches in the context of European developments. According to different politico-administrative tiers in a federal state like Germany, the 'reform picture' varies considerably. Local authorities are still in a leading position compared to the 16 states and the federal government, although the latter have been trying hard to close at least some of the reform gaps. Despite all efforts, Germany is still regarded administratively as a 'reform laggard', though whether rightly or wrongly remains to be discussed. For this reason German reform concepts and experiences are scrutinised with special reference to mainstream tendencies in European public-sector modernisation.

Mathur shows in his chapter that the concern about administrative reform in India is not something new. What is new is the context in which it is being discussed now. Administrative reforms at present seek to reduce the scope of state intervention but at the same time expect a change in the quality of intervention in the chosen sectors. This reform movement has been triggered by the wave of policies of liberalisation and structural adjustment prompted by international financial agencies. Administrative reforms are also being attempted in response to the pressure from society. There has been a deepening of democracy and reforms in the process of decentralisation involving giving greater powers to the panchayats which show dissatisfaction with the way in which the government functions. This has led to the building of pressures for reform from below. The present endeavour of administrative reforms can be looked at more optimistically because rising social pressure from rural society may help to neutralise the reforms that may be undertaken to benefit the privileged. Mathur argues that a high degree of bureaucratic autonomy and capacity may not necessarily lead to development because bureaucracy, as seen in Indian experience and elsewhere, has not been able to rise above its interests. On the other hand, the market may not be the only answer for it cannot help those who are excluded from it because of various limitations. The solution lies in multiple institutions responding to the needs of society.

The chapter by Agnihotri and Dar presents the views of two socially responsible civil servants on the recent initiatives in governance reforms of the Government of India as well as some selected Indian states. Focusing on some critical issues and critical success factors, an analysis of the current reform initiatives is undertaken. This analysis reveals that a modicum of success has been achieved in respect to only a few of the items. Several initiatives have yet to reach the requisite level of maturity. In some cases, the states have stolen a march over the central government. International experience also confirms that in a rapidly changing world, the state is under pressure to become more effective but is not yet adapting swiftly enough to the demand. Some of the critical issues facing Indian reforms comprise evolving a consensus regarding the nature of India's nascent democracy, lack of people's faith in the agencies of governance and their effectiveness, and erratic trend affecting the capacity to govern. The issue of handling public grievances has the potential to provide a measure of our democratic maturity. The administrative structure needs to have the courage to face up to the realities of the situation and build its confidence in engaging the citizenry in a meaningful dialogue for the resolution of the problem.

Rajan, in his chapter, considers NGOs as partners in the process of reform. He notes that the need for participatory governance has made their involvement mandatory in all development programmes. This change has produced many forms of NGOs with several agendas, dictated by left ideology, self-interest, power politics or just style. But the social space that has opened up today offers a unique opportunity for all players—government, corporation, academia or grassroots activist—to put their heads together on developmental, environmental or community issues.

CHAPTER 8

Administrative Reform in India and Europe: A Comparative Perspective

Biju Paul Abraham

Few would contest the claim that public perceptions of the role and functions of the state have changed significantly worldwide since the 1970s. Once considered an institution that was indispensable for ensuring economic growth, an equitable distribution of wealth and sustained improvements in standards of living, the state later became identified as one of the main obstacles to continued progress. In the 1980s, the very need for a proactive state was questioned in much of the Western world, especially in the United States and Great Britain by the 'New Right'. In the 1990s, though there was an acceptance of the fact that the state was still relevant (Hobsbawm 1996), there was also the realisation that in a rapidly globalising world where competing supranational power structures were emerging, the state had to be 'reinvented' if it was to fulfil its tasks.

Changing perceptions have altered the image of the state in the developing world as well, though in a very different sense. The state here is still looked upon as the only entity that can ensure rapid economic growth and improvements in the quality of life, though its ability to deliver these have been severely hampered by the deep fiscal crisis that it finds itself in. While entrusting the non-governmental, or private, sector with the delivery of services might seem to be an answer to this fiscal problem, it creates new problems of retraining public officials to manage service delivery (capacity-building) rather than providing it themselves. It also creates the problem of surplus staff, made redundant by the fact that you need far fewer officials to manage a service than to deliver it.

This chapter considers the issue of administrative reform to deal with these challenges in comparative perspective, looking at the differences in the context and process of reform in India and three European countries, the UK, Germany and the Netherlands. While perceptions of the role of the state vary in these countries, as does the process of reform itself, the common feature is that reform is being undertaken within a democratic framework. The intention here is not so much to draw lessons from these different experiences as to analyse reforms so that the process and nature of the reforms that are taking place can be better understood. This chapter addresses three questions:

- What prompted the move towards administrative reform?
- To what extent did reform efforts succeed, and can the success or failure of reforms be attributed to political or institutional factors?
- Can the experience of reform in Europe help to identify conditions under which reform efforts in India are likely to succeed?

The chapter concludes that even though the experience of reform in Europe and India vary very widely, the European experience does provide some indications as to why reform efforts in India have not been very successful, and also the conditions that are necessary for effective reform to be possible in the Indian context.

THE POLITICS OF REFORM

Initiatives for administrative reform have almost always been triggered by political or economic factors, not by administrative bodies attempting to make themselves more efficient. This is because reform measures have been initiated either in response to the sustained attack that the traditional state has found itself under ever since the 1980s from right-wing groups intent on reducing government power, or by the fear of negative electoral consequences of public dissatisfaction with government-provided services.

A large body of literature has emerged over the last two decades which analyses administrative reforms that have taken place worldwide in comparative perspective (Kickert 1997; Naschod 1996; Pollitt and Bouchaert 2000). Though the nature and speed of reform varies from country to county, depending on the different political and institutional environments within which they take place, almost all analysts agree that these reform processes have certain common features. These include restructuring of public service organisations through contractual or semi-contractual arrangements, outsourcing of public services with an emphasis on developing competition in delivery of services, cost reduction, greater use of managerial techniques, and a customer orientation in provision of public services (Clark 2000).

Traditionally, the state through its administrative functions balanced private interests with broader societal concerns and thereby provided the political stability necessary to ensure investment and growth. Where private investment was not forthcoming, the state even stepped in and took on an entrepreneurial role and made the investments that were necessary. However, by the early 1980s, the ability of the state to fulfil its administrative and entrepreneurial role was circumscribed by two factors. First, the administrative state expanded to the extent that administrative agencies spent a lot of time administering themselves rather than fulfilling their economic or societal functions. Second, the cost of administration reduced the funds available for fulfilling the entrepreneurial role and drew resources away from private investment. Both the factors made the administrative agencies of government a tempting target for attack. The economic functions of the government—whether it is deciding on the allocation of resources, mediating a fair distribution of the fruits of economic growth or taking on itself an entrepreneurial role—have been attacked by right-wing interest groups who believe that market-driven forces, operating in a global environment, can deliver sustained economic growth, provided they are free of state intervention.

The drive to reform government, both in India and the West, was also motivated by the fact that governments felt they had to continue to be relevant in a world that is not very dependent on their regulatory activities. In the 1990s, an increasing amount of domestic legislation was the result of multilateral agreements, especially economic agreements. The desire to 'secure their own continued existence' forces the state to devise a role for itself that justifies its existence (Bardouille 2000: 82). This change in role means that the state no longer attempts to become a welfare state, but increasingly becomes an entity that enforces rules, which are set at the supranational level. The state then transforms itself into an oversight agency which ensures that internationally set rules are followed.

While the crisis that was facing the state was similar in India to what it was in the West, the response has been different. Many of the differences are attributable to the differing political conditions in which these reforms were formulated. In most Western democracies, the 1980s was a period when the state was under sustained attack. The idea that governments had become too big, too costly and a serious constraint on economic growth was propounded by the 'New Right' especially in the US and the UK (Ridley 1996). Government bureaucracies were accused of being too expensive, unresponsive, moribund and incapable of adapting to changed circumstances. Ronald Reagan in the US, Margaret Thatcher in the UK and Brian Mulrooney in Canada found that this political pitch had wide support among the public. They argued that the government had become too big to do any good and that the growth of government was due to the 'budget maximising' behaviour of bureaucrats (Saint-Martin 2001: 578). The only way out was to privatise and contract out services and downsize the civil service.

Political parties that sought to replace these right-wing governments, the Democrats in the US and the Labour Party in the UK in particular, began to look for an alternative vision for the state where the state would have a significant role, but not the one that it had until the 1970s. It is in countries where the anti-government movement has been strong that a coherent alternative vision has emerged. In countries where the role of the bureaucracy has not been effectively challenged, the reform movement has been proportionately diffuse.

In the US and Europe, the response was to 'reinvent government' and make it more relevant for the modern world. The term was coined by two management consultants, David Osborne and Ted Gaebler in their book *Reinventing Government: How the Entrepreneurial State is Transfroming the Public Sector*. In their book, Osborne and Gaebler called for a 'paradigm shift' from a Weberian model of public administration to an entrepreneurial government.

In India, the attempt at reform has not been as revolutionary as in Europe or the US. Often devised in response to external pressure or public dissatisfaction, reforms have stressed economic deregulation, privatisation of public enterprises and reform of administrative mechanisms to ensure that they are responsive to public demands.

REFORMS AND THE UNITARY STATE:
THE EXPERIENCE OF THE UNITED KINGDOM

Of all the European countries, Britain is unique in terms of the comprehensive nature of public service reform. Reform in Britain has emphasised the assertion of political will over the bureaucracy, the use of market mechanisms as administrative techniques and the protection of the consumers from the abuses of a bureaucracy that cites the public interest to cover up high-cost, low quality services. Clark identifies three distinct phases of reform. In the first phase (1979–82) reform was dominated by cost-reduction measures aimed at reducing public spending. In the next phase (1982–87) the stress was on the efficiency and performance of government agencies providing public services. Since 1987, there has been an attempt to bring about fundamental reforms in government agencies and departments so as to bring about changes in the culture of these organisations (Clark 2000). Government policy has been centred on three approaches, corporate-style management, client orientation and market competition (Kickert 2002). According to R. Austin, the changes were made so that 'public service is no longer the service of the public as a collective, but rather the service of the individual consumer of specific and limited public services' (Austin 1997: 23). The predominant strategies have been the use of market-style mechanisms, decentralisation of the management and delivery of services, and an emphasis on ensuring responsiveness through the Citizens Charter (Clark 2000). In terms of reforms to the civil service, the reforms included the New Steps programme of 1988 for 'agencification' of public services, and market testing, a competitive tendering system for privatising part of the work of government departments. The process of reform saw the bureaucracy being divided into core central departments and a network of executive agencies to deliver services. By 1995, 63 per cent of all civil servants were working in agencies, rather than directly for the government (Pollitt 2002). The system of civil service employment was also modified with agency heads, who were recruited in open competition—allowed to set agency-specific terms and conditions in terms of pay and service norms.

The importance of the Thatcherite agenda in bringing about these changes cannot be denied, but at the same time they should not be overstated. Extensive reform was possible because of the favourable institutional context in which these reforms were carried out. In a government structure that was unitary in character and operated without a written constitution, the Conservative governments of Thatcher and Major were able to introduce radical changes by which local authorities were deprived of their power and services were provided by private agencies, or contracted out under the management of the central government. Reform of the civil service in Britain was comparatively easy because reform measures did not need legislation or parliamentary approval. Decisions related to reforms could be enforced by the government under the Crown Prerogative. Radical reforms such as the creation of executive agencies with private sector style chief executive officers (CEOs), and the recruitment to top posts in the civil service through an open competitive process in which those outside the civil service could be considered and the contractual employment of civil servants could be enforced without any need for parliamentary approval (Ridley 1996: 23–24).

REFORM IN GERMANY: THE IMPACT OF SUBSIDIARITY

Reforms in Germany have been far less far-reaching in nature and have been done mostly at the local government level. Reform efforts in Germany, especially reform efforts as part of 'New Public Management', were initiated in the late 1980s, much later than the reform process in both the US and the UK. Wollmann identifies three reasons for the delay. First, administrators and experts felt that there was nothing wrong with the administrative system and that it was quite effective by international standards. Second, some of the reform efforts that were relevant for other countries, such as reform of the monopoly that local authorities had over service delivery, were not relevant to Germany because the local government in Germany had already been contracting delivery to non-profit organisations. Third, it was culturally more difficult for Germans to adopt corporate management practices in government, unlike in the US and the UK (Wollmann 2000).

Reform was adopted because of the growing fear that Germany, economically dependent on exports, would lose her economic competitiveness internationally. The objectives of reform both at the level of administration and public enterprises was modernisation to effectively deal with competition (Wollmann 1997). However, unlike Britain, there was no comprehensive programme to reform administration at all levels, central, state and local. Reforms at the federal government and state government level were largely confined to debate and limited changes in training programmes for middle and senior officials (Clark 2000). There are two reasons why reform is more successful at the local and not at the federal or state level. First, the rights of the German Civil Service, both at the federal and state level, are written into the Constitution and its reform requires constitutional amendments, a difficult task at the best of times. Reform is constrained by the fact that even matters related to administrative procedures are part of constitutional law and cannot easily be changed by governments as in the case of Britain. Second, the principle of subsidiarity which is the cardinal feature of local government in Germany, ensures that effective reform can be carried out at the local level without any reference to the state or federal government, and even if reforms do not take place at these higher levels.

Local government in Germany follows a pattern where local government and state administrative structures coexist, with the state administration having very few areas of administrative power. State functions are thus integrated locally, and state administrative power is kept well outside local administrative structures. This ensures effective decentralisation of administrative powers (Wollmann 1997). At the local level, even though there are differences in method, local authorities have accepted the 'New Steering Model' developed by the *Kommunale Gemeinschaftsstelle* (KGSt), the consulting agency for local governments. The main features of the model include the separation of policy-making and administration, with elected councillors deciding on strategy and performance standards, a system of central management with clearly defined objectives, performance targets and result-oriented budgets, and the outsourcing or privatisation of service delivery (Jann 1997).

This model has proved to be very effective at the local level. The process of administrative modernisation in Germany can be characterised as a 'bottom-up' model where reform at the local level does not necessarily go hand in hand or require administrative modernisation at the state and federal level (Klages and Loffles 1998).

Reform of civil service law, which is part of the German Constitution, has been a low priority for political parties. Though the debate on civil service reform has resumed in the last five years, mainly due to public pressure, there seems little hope that reform will happen anytime soon (Schroeter and Wollmann 1997). The federal legislature and the federal government are responsible for civil service reform. Unlike the Westminster Model followed in the UK and India, public servants are very well represented in the German Parliament and would effectively resist reforms seen as inimical to their interests (Clark 2000). 'Bureaucrat-bashing' is still not a part of political discourse in Germany, unlike the UK or the US. Government reports on civil service reform in the 1990s have spoken of the 'outstanding quality and achievements of the professional civil service', which seems to imply that no major changes were needed (Schroeter and Wollmann 1997: 195). Reforms have mainly involved measures to strengthen the principle of merit and to provide financial incentives for taking up jobs with the government rather than in the private sector (Roeber 1996).

COOPERATIVE REFORM IN THE NETHERLANDS: THE EXPERIENCE OF THE 'POLDER' MODEL

While much of Europe was struggling with the high costs of social welfare, low levels of economic growth and record levels of unemployment, the 'Polder Model' followed by the Netherlands seemed to offer much hope (Peet 2002). Though it was inspired in part by reform experiences in the US and the UK, the path that has been followed has been uniquely Dutch (Bekkers and Zouridis 1999). The Model, with its strong emphasis on consensus, seemed to provide ways in which government, both at the central and local levels, could reduce costs and improve services through negotiated agreements with unions over reform, avoiding the confrontation that marked reform in Britain or the ineffectiveness at the state or federal level that was the main feature of reform in Germany.

The Dutch government redistributed national income through policy interventions to a much greater extent than other European states. In the early 1990s, 61 per cent of national income was redistributed through the public sector, and of this 35 per cent was by way of state-controlled payments (Van de Ven 1994). These included expenses on social security, unemployment benefits, sickness benefits, disablement benefits, child allowances and old-age pensions. There were also transfers by way of consumer subsidies for transport and heavy subsidies for the housing and property sector that involved tax deductible loans for housing and subsidised rent for commercial properties.

When in the early 1990s these heavy subsidisation and transfer payments became difficult to sustain financially, a process of reform was initiated. However, the Dutch reform model was different from the British and the German model, and even the US model, in terms of its emphasis, not just on reform of institutions and processes but also on the reform of the relationship between the government and interest groups in society. Historically, the Dutch government had been organised into a three-level system known as a 'decentralized unitary state' (Lips and Owen 2000). Three levels of legitimised sovereign authority exists, each elected democratically. Dutch administrative organisations are also required to maintain uniformity in both organisation and function, with local communities being empowered and authorised to carry out tasks, similar to state, province and local governments. Rather than rely on a mere managerial approach to the problem of reform and just reform administration, the Dutch model recognised that effective reform of the administrative structure of the government could not be carried out without simultaneously reforming the relationship between government and society (Kickert 2002). Effective reform has meant not just the government withdrawing from certain sectors, as was the case in the US and UK, or reform just at the local level as in Germany. It has involved the government, increasing its role in many areas of popular concern if that was felt to be necessary. In the 1990s, while the government has reduced its role in several important areas such as the provision of housing or industrial subsidies, it has increased its interventionist role in such areas as environmental protection (ibid.). Dutch reform has stressed three principles, effectiveness of delivery, efficiency of task performance and the quality of representative administration (Lips and Owen 2000). While the first two principles are common to other administrative reform attempts, the principle of representative administration is uniquely Dutch.

It must, however, be recognised that the representative character of Dutch administration, with a strong emphasis on cooperative solutions, has historical roots. The Dutch political system is based on a system of consensus with almost all governments being coalitions. The desire for consensus decision-making extends to interest groups within the Dutch political system as well (see De Swaan 1988). The economic crisis of the early 1980s prompted Dutch business associations and the trade unions to sign the Wassenaar Agreement, under which the unions agreed to wage restraint in return for the Dutch business creating more jobs. Institutional mechanisms exist to mediate disputes between various interest groups. The Social and Economic Council (SER), which was set up in the 1950s, provides a méchanism for wide consultations between employees and employers (Peet 2002). It is this unique emphasis on consensus that has enabled the Netherlands to manage the problems of reform to an extent not possible in other democracies.

ADMINISTRATIVE REFORM IN INDIA: THE PROBLEMS OF MISMATCHED REFORM

Administrative reforms to ensure 'good governance' in India has occurred within the context of rapid economic and social changes that have occurred since the late 1980s. Economically, the advent of liberalisation has seen the state distancing itself from various aspects of administration that had hitherto been its forte: economic planning, infrastructure development and industrial licensing. The move away from traditional areas of operation has partly been justified by the need to lay greater stress on the improvement of the quality of life of the citizens. The move from a capital-centred development approach to a people-centred approach has also been necessitated by the increasing electoral assertiveness of hitherto underprivileged sections of Indian society.

The process of reform began with economic policy and gradually spread to administrative functions as it became clear that economic reform without changes in administration would fail to deliver the economic or political returns that the government was hoping for. Economic reforms began in 1991, in response to a deep economic crisis that the country faced. The crisis was brought about by economic stagnation and consecutive years of poor productivity growth, both of which led to rising inflation and a severe foreign exchange crisis. At one stage during the crisis, foreign exchange reserves were just enough to pay for 10 days' imports (Ahluwalia and Little 1998). It was the immediacy and severity of the crisis that made the government initiate a process of far-reaching reform. Over a period of a year, the licensing system was largely dismantled, import protection afforded to Indian industry was reduced and moves initiated to reform and, if necessary, privatise public-sector enterprises. However, the process of reform was lopsided, with the state governments largely reluctant to introduce complementary reforms of their own which were necessary if the reform process was to be fully effective. State governments were more relaxed in their attitudes to reform for two reasons. First, the economic crisis was a crisis of the centre, not of the states. Second, while the central government might have been willing to pay a political price for reforms because of the severity of the crisis and the need to secure aid from abroad, state governments were under no such compulsion. State-level political leaders were unwilling to introduce reforms for fear of immediate and adverse political consequences. As Jenkins (1999: 126) says, 'though economic reform was initiated (and its most visible elements largely orchestrated) by national elites in New Delhi, state-level politicians and political-systems have a key role to play in managing its implications, and contributing to its sustainability. They absorb much of the political burden'.

The fate of administrative reform in the 1990s was similar. Decades of slow, but steady, economic growth and the rapid spread of communication facilities had made the people more aware of their rights than ever before. This also led to demands that the system of administration be made both efficient and responsive to the needs of the people. The most vocal demands were for speedy delivery of services, elimination of corruption in government functioning, prompt action on complaints received from the public, and the active participation of the people in the formulation of programmes aimed at their welfare. The government responded to these demands by initiating a debate on the nature and extent of reforms needed to make the administrative system more responsive and caring. In a Discussion Note prepared by the Department of Administrative Reforms and Public Grievances (DARPG) of the Ministry of Personnel for the Conference of Chief Secretaries held in New Delhi in November 1996, it was admitted that the administrative system as it exists faces a 'crisis of credibility' which can be overcome only by 'reinventing' government at all levels and redefining its goals and responsibilities (DARPG 1996). Such an exercise would involve the identification of the precise role of the government in relation to the governed, the demarcation of functions between the central, state and local governments, the allocation of resources to enable each level of government to carry out its duties effectively, and the structural reform of ministries and departments to increase efficiency and effectiveness.

The government also tried to make the administrative system more responsive and participatory by decentralising the administration. The most significant reform carried out through the early 1990s was the 73rd and 74th Amendments to the Constitution which gave Panchayati Raj institutions the status of constitutional bodies. The Amendments also devolved some powers and responsibilities to panchayats with regard to the formulation of plans for economic development and social justice, and their implementation. However, the successful functioning of local self-governing institutions such as the panchayats has been hampered by the inability of many states to transfer substantive powers to them (Bandyopadhyay 1996). State governments, with a few exceptions like West Bengal and Kerala, have been reluctant to transfer administrative responsibilities and financial resources to the panchayats, and this has prevented these institutions from realising their full potential. Analysts have warned of the distinct possibility that in the absence of enabling legislation at the state level, the Panchayati Raj institutions would simply add another layer of bureaucracy in the administrative system without ensuring people's participation in the government at the grassroots level (Drèze and Sen 1995).

The ineffectiveness of decentralisation of powers is not just the result of the states not devolving power to the local level. It is also caused by the centre not devolving enough power and resources to the states. In India, there are two main methods of transferring resources from the centre to the states. The Planning Commission decides the plan allocations (for capital expenditure) while revenue allocations are determined by the finance commissions constituted once every five years. Chelliah points out that 84.1 per cent of total grants come from the Planning Commission, with the central government providing very little by way of support to the states for revenue expenditure. The ability of states to collect their own revenue is also limited by Constitutional provisions relating to revenue sharing. Chelliah suggests that effective devolution is possible only if residuary powers are given to the states and centre–state relations restructured through constitutional amendments (Chelliah 1998).

An additional problem was the large number of programmes at the local level that were initiated, and in some cases even closely controlled, directly by the central government. In the 1970s, a number of special rural development programmes were launched by the government to improve economic conditions in rural areas. These included poverty alleviation, employment generation and regional development programmes. There were also specific development programmes targeted at particular groups (Jain 1999). The dependence of local governments on resources passed on from the centre and states, and an administrative structure that did not accept the principle of subsidiarity, meant that the local government could not legislate on or implement policy that was solely its concern. This resulted in a situation where reform was, in effect, ineffective. Review committees set up by the government itself have identified the lack of effective decentralisation and accountability at the local level as being the main impediments to successful implementation of such programmes (Mathur 1995, 2001).

REFORMS IN COMPARATIVE PERSPECTIVE

A comparative analysis of the process of reform in India and Europe suggests that there is very little that each could learn from the other as far as reforms themselves are concerned. The political, social and economic contexts within which these reforms are undertaken are too different for the experience of reform in one country to be directly relevant for the other. However, there is a lot that could be learnt as far as the process of reform itself is concerned. The experience of reform in Europe suggests that certain political and institutional conditions are necessary if reforms are to succeed. These conditions do not, as yet, exist in India.

The experience of reform in the UK under successive Conservative governments, and also in the US during the presidency of Ronald Reagan, suggests that reforms can be pushed through only by a government that is determined to push through the process of reform. In both countries, governments that initiated reform had come into power with a mandate to reduce the role of the government and introduce administrative reform. This political will to reform has been lacking in India, with the consensus view across the political spectrum being that the state has to continue to play a major interventionary role in both the economic and social sectors. Reform has been imposed on reluctant governments either by popular disenchantment with existing systems, or by pressure from international agencies.

There are differences in the institutional context of reform as well. Reforms succeeded in the UK mainly within a unitary structure where the central government could force reform on local governments through the Crown Prerogative. In Germany, reforms succeeded at the local level mainly because their success was not dependent on complementary reform at the state or central level. The principle of subsidiarity meant that local governments were fully competent to reform their procedures and modes of service delivery without the need for complementary reform at the state or federal level. In the Netherlands, it was essentially a cooperative framework, involving the central and local governments, as well as trade unions and civil society that delivered successful reform.

The process of reform in India is hampered by the constitutional structure that defines the Indian Union. In the absence of the principle of subsidiarity that would have left state and local governments free to decide on matters that they are fully capable of legislating on, successful reform at the local and state levels is hampered by the need for similar reform at the central level. Similarly, reforms at the central level are hampered by the inability of state or local governments to carry out complementary reform. The mismatch between action at the central, state and local government levels is very often caused by a mismatch in the felt political need for reform. When the central government feels the need to reform, often in response to economic crisis or political pressure from below, state governments are very often reluctant to respond, fearing political costs that they would have to be incur. Reforms at the state level, designed in response to political or economic necessity, are similarly circumscribed by the unwillingness, or inability, of the central government to enact complementary reform simultaneously. The Indian experience would suggest that successful reform is possible only when all levels of the governance structure work with the citizens for modernising the state and administration (Jain 2001). This might involve changes to the existing constitutional structure so that the principle of subsidiarity is enshrined in it. When institutions and communities at the local level become genuinely independent, both in terms of access to resources as well as in terms of taking decisions on policy, governance could become more participatory and reforms more effective.

REFERENCES

Ahluwalia, I.J. and Little, I.M.D. (eds). 1998. *India's Economic Reforms and Development: Essays for Manmohan Singh*. Delhi: Oxford University Press.

Austin, R. 1997. 'Administrative Law's Reaction to the Changing Concepts of Public Service', in P. Leyland and T. Woods (eds). *Administrative Law Facing the Future: Old Constraints and New Horoizons'*. London: Blackstone Press.

Bandyopadhyay, D. 1996. 'Administration, Decentralisation and Good Governance'. *Economic and Political Weekly*, 31(44): 3109–14.

Bardouille, Nand C. 2000. 'The Transformation of Governance Paradigms and Modalities: Insights into the Marketization of the Public Service in Response to Globalization'. *The Round Table*, 353: 81–106.

Bekkers, Victor J.J.M and Zouridis, Stavros. 1999. 'Electronic Service Delivery in Public Administration: Some Trends and Issues'. *International Review of Adminsitrative Sciences*, 65 (2): 183–95.

Chelliah, Raja J. 1998. 'Liberalization, Economic Reforms and Centre–State Relaitons', in I.J. Ahluwalia and I.M.D. Little (eds). *India's Economic Reforms and Development: Essays for Manmohan Singh*, pp. 344–74. Delhi: Oxford University Press.

Clark, David. 2000. 'Public Service Reform: A Comparative West European Perspective'. *West European Politics*, 23 (3): 25–44.

Department of Administrative Reforms and Public Grievances, Ministry of Personnel (DARPG). 1996. *An Agenda for Effective and Responsive Administration*. New Delhi: Government of India.

De Swaan. 1988. *In the Care of the State*. London: Polity Press.

Drèze J. and Sen, Amartya. 1995. *India: Economic Development and Social Opportunity*. Delhi: Oxford University Press.

Hobsbawm, E.J. 1996. 'The Future of the State'. *Development & Change*, 27: 267–78.

Jain, R.B. 1999. 'Citizen Participation in Development Administration: Experiences of India'. *International Review of Administrative Sciences*, 65: 381–94.

————. 2001. 'Towards Good Governance: A Half Century of India's Administrative Development'. *International Journal of Public Administration*, 24: 1299–1334.

Jann, W. 1997. 'Public Management Reform in Germany: A Revolution Without a Theory?', in W. Kickert (ed.). *Public Management and Administrative Reform in Western Europe*, pp. 81–100. Cheltenham: Edward Elgar.

Jenkins, Rob. 1999. *Democratic Politics and Economic Reform in India*. Cambridge University Press

Kickert, W. (ed.). 1997. *Public Management and Administrative Reform in Western Europe*. Cheltenham: Edward Elgar.

Kickert, Walter J.M. 2002. 'Public Governance in the Netherlands: An Alternative to Anglo-American "Managerialism"', in Stephen Osborne (ed.). *Public Management, Critical Perspective*, Vol. 2, pp. 184–207. London/New York: Routledge.

Klages, Helmut and Loffles, Elke. 1998. 'New Public Management in Germany: The Implementation Process of the New Steering Model', *International Review of Administrative Science*, 64: 41–59.

Lips, Anna M.B. and Owen, C. James. 2000. 'Reinventing Urban Government in the Netherlands: An American Perspective'. *International Journal of Public Administration*, 23 (1): 149–73.

Mathur, Kuldeep. 1995. 'Politics and Implementation of Integrated Rural Development Programmes'. *Economic and Political Weekly*, 41 and 42: 2703–8.

———. 2001. 'Strengthening Bureaucracy: State and Development in India', in Niraja Gopal Jayal and Sudha Pai (eds). *Democratic Governance in India: Challenges of Poverty, Development and Identity*, pp. 109–31. New Delhi: Sage.

Naschod, Frieder. 1996. *New Frontiers in Public Sector Management: Trends and Issues in State and Local Government in Europe*, New York: Walter de Gruyter.

Osborne, D. and Gaebler, T. 1992. *Reinventing Governments: How the Enterpreneurial Spirit is Transforming the Public Sector*. Reading, Mass.: Adison Wesley.

Peet, John. 2002. 'A Survey of the Netherlands'. *The Economist*, 363 (8271).

Pollitt, Christopher. 2002. 'Justification by Work or by Faith? Evaluating the New Public Management', in Stephan Osborne (ed.). *Public Management, Critical Perspective,* Vol. 2, pp. 315–41. London/New York: Routledge.

Pollitt, C. and Bouchaert, G. (eds). 2000. *Public Management Reform: A Comparative Analysis*. Oxford: Oxford University Press.

Ridley, F.F. 1996. 'The New Public Management in Europe: Comparative Perspectives'. *Public Policy and Administration,* 11(1): 16–29.

Roeber, Manfred. 1996. 'Country Study "Germany"', in D. Farnham, S. Horton, J. Barlow and A. Hondegham (eds). *New Public Managers in Europe. Public Servants in Transition*, pp. 169–93. London: Macmillan.

Saint-Martin, Denis. 2001. 'How the Reinventing Government Movement in Public Administration was Exported from the US to Other Countries'. *International Journal of Public Administration*, 24(6): 573–604.

Schroeter, Eckhard and Wollmann, Hellmut. 1997. 'Public Sector Reforms in Germany: Whence and Where? A Case of Ambivalance'. *Administrative Studies/Hallinnon Tutkimus*, 3:184–200.

Van de Ven, A.T.L.M .1994. 'The Changing Role of Government in Public Enterprises: Dutch Experiences'. *International Review of Administrative Sciences*, 60: 371–83.

Wollmann, Hellmut. 1997. 'Modernization of the Public Sector and Public Adminstration in the Federal Republic of Germany—(Mostly) A Story of Fragmented Incrementalism', in Muramatsu, Michio and Frieder Naschold (eds). *State and Administration in Japan and Germany: A Comparative Perspective on Continuity and Change,* pp. 79–103. Berlin: De Gruyter.

———. 2000. 'Comparing Institutional Development in Britain and Germany: (Persistent) Divergence or (Progressing) Convergence?', in Hellmut Wollmann and Eckhard Schroeter. *Comparing Public Sector Reform in Britian and Germany: Key Traditions and Trends of Modernization*, pp. 1–26. Aldershot: Ashgate.

CHAPTER 9

POLICY CHANGE IN PUBLIC-SECTOR
REFORMS IN COMPARATIVE PERSPECTIVE:
BETWEEN CONVERGENCE AND DIVERGENCE

HELLMUT WOLLMANN

Since the 1980s, major policy changes in public-sector reforms have occurred throughout the Organisation for Economic Cooperation and Development (OECD) countries—with a considerable variance across countries in the timing, scope and focus of such reforms. In dealing with this development in a comparative perspective, the chapter will proceed in three steps.

First, nutshell profiles of the development and current state of public-sector reform in a number of key OECD countries will be sketched in order to identify the degree of institutional variance among them. Then, after submitting a hypothetical explanatory scheme and analytically singling out some crucial dimensions of public-sector reform policies, the attempt will be made to 'explain' these dimensions of variance. Finally, the question will be taken up as to whether the countries' trajectories show convergence or divergence.

VARIANCE OF PUBLIC-SECTOR REFORMS

DISTINCTION BETWEEN 'TRADITIONAL' AND NPM-GUIDED REFORMS

At the outset, a distinction should be made between 'traditional' reforms and reforms explicitly inspired and guided by 'New Public Management' (NPM).

Traditional reforms originated in earlier reform periods, particularly during the 1960s and 1970s. Reflecting the *zeitgeist* of that period, they were conceptually geared to the idea of strengthening the political and administrative structures of the advanced welfare state and often bore social-democratic handwriting. Typically, they were directed at the intergovernmental setting (by devolving political as well as administrative responsibilities on lower government levels), at 'modernising' the political and administrative capacities at all levels of government (by introducing planning, information and evaluation procedures), at enhancing the administrative capacity and efficiency of local level government (by local-level territorial reform and amalgamation), and, not least, at enhancing citizen participation. Their primary frame of reference was the political/administrative system and the citizen in his/her political role. In the recent upsurge of public-sector reforms, such traditional reform concepts and components have been given a new push.

By contrast, NPM is the offspring of a wider neo-liberal policy debate which is directed at dismantling the advanced (allegedly overgrown) welfare state and its public sector by reducing it to a 'lean', if not 'minimal state'. Within this broader ideological and political grasp, an array of demands, concepts and recipes have been formulated, first in Great Britain (UK) and in New Zealand, for which the label NPM has attained wide currency (see Hood 1991). Far from forming a theoretically consistent body of ideas and concepts, NPM can rather be likened to a 'shopping basket' (Pollitt 1995) of (in part contradictory) concepts (see Aucoin 1990). On the one hand, NPM draws on private-sector-derived managerialism ('let managers manage') which tends to devolve responsibilities and resources within administrative units, thus promoting autonomous processes with decentralising, if not centrifugal, tendencies. On the other hand, NPM borrows from institutional economics and its suspicion of the innate disposition of (private as well as public) bureaucracies to expand in size and spending; the remedy to this is seen in strengthening external political control with centralising implications. Furthermore, the creation of markets and quasi-markets, primarily through competition, is writ large. The common frame of reference in NPM thinking is essentially the private sector and market competition, with the citizen envisaged largely in a 'client'/ 'consumer' role.

In taking an internationally comparative view, the chapter will select a sample of countries which, on the one hand, includes some of the 'usual suspects' addressed in such debate, to wit, the UK, New Zealand, the United States of America and also Sweden. On the other hand, France and Germany shall be dealt with as two less discussed Continental European cases. The empirical information for this discussion will be mainly gathered from the comparative monograph by Christopher Pollitt and Geert Bouckaert (2000), as well as from articles in the edited books by Christensen and Laegreid (2001b) and Wollmann (2003a).

THE POLICY CHANGES IN PUBLIC-SECTOR REFORMS IN COMPARATIVE PERSPECTIVE

In order to identify and 'categorise' the variance in policy changes and modernisation trajectories between the countries under consideration here, we shall follow a typology that has been proposed in Pollitt and Bouckaert (2000), in which the distinction is made between *maintaining, modernising* and *marketising/minimising* profiles of modernisation trajectories. While a maintaining country can be seen as largely retaining its existing political and administrative structures, the modernising type exhibits significant changes without abandoning essential features in its traditional structures. The marketising/minirnising type can be seen as substantively remoulding the existing administrative structures in the pursuit of NPM modernisation.

The NPM-guided reforms have no doubt been pushed furthest in the UK since the early 1980s. A wave of privatisation of state-owned companies (such as British Telecom) was followed by the creation of ('Next Steps') central agencies (designed to decentralise hitherto Whitehall-centred administrative functions), by marketisation ('compulsory competitive tendering'), by ensuing 'outsourcing' (and 'quangoisation') of service provision and by introducing performance management and measurement (recently, under the Blair government, by establishing a 'best value' regime) (Pollitt and Bouckaert 2000: 273ff.). In sum, these NPM-guided reform measures can be brought, in accordance with Pollitt and Bouckaert, under the marketising category. In view of its 'agencification' and widespread performance management regime. New Zealand (see Halligan 2003), where NPM is said to have had 'its true start' (Kettl 2000: 8), can also be given the marketising tag.

In USA, on the federal level, the modernisation debate and some practical measures have centred around introducing managerialist tools and performance management in federal agencies (see Christensen et al. 2003). Hence, USA may be rated as (managerialist) modernising.

Sweden has experienced a duality of changes, as during the 1980s steps were taken in the pursuit of traditional reforms to further decentralising (devolving) state functions to the local authorities and to enlarge their autonomy. At the same time, NPM-guided reform measures were embarked upon by introducing performance management in the (traditional) central agencies, purchaser–provider split concepts for health care provision at the county level and market-testing of social services at the local level (see Pollitt and Bouckaert 2000: 264ff.). Thus, Sweden can be ranked as an (advanced) moderniser.

France has also seen a duality of changes. In the early 1980s, the central government made its historic move to decentralise the country's centralist ('Napoleonic') structure. Since the late 1980s, the French governments, both socialist and conservative, have pushed managerialist concepts to make its (traditionally legalist and hierarchical) public administration more flexible. In sum, France can also be rated as an (advanced) moderniser.

Germany conspicuously abstained from NPM-inspired reforms well unto the late 1980s. When in the early 1990s NPM concepts were finally turned to, typically at first by the local authorities, managerialist concepts addressing the rigidity of (traditionally legalist and hierarchical) public administration had been in the fore, with the local government level taking an early lead. Hence, Germany has exhibited a profile between maintaining and increasingly modernising itself.

Explaining Variance

Conceptual Framework

Without going into a more detailed conceptual discussion at this point (see Wollmann 2003b for further references, particularly on 'neo-institutionalism'; see Peters 1995), in our subsequent argument the following explanatory factors will be taken into consideration:

- The *socio-economic and budgetary situation and context* which sways upon the decision-making.
- The *starting conditions* (in terms of the state of the public sector and of public administration) in view of which the decision-making takes place.
- The institutional and cultural traditions which may impinge upon the decision-making (which is highlighted by *historical institutionalism*).
- The *institutional setting* (such as unitary or federal government structure) within which decision-making takes place.
- The relevant *political actors* and actor constellations that determine decision-making (which is emphasised by *actor-centred institutionalism*).
- The (professional, academic, etc.) *discourses and discourse communities*, including the *international discourse*, which may influence decision-making.

In the following section, some crucial dimensions of decision-making and implementation of public-sector reforms will be singled out and 'causal interpretations' will be tried out.

THE 'TAKE-OFF' DECISION ON PUBLIC-SECTOR REFORMS

The take-off decision to embark upon (large-scale) public sector reforms has in most cases been triggered by an economic and budgetary crisis which led or even compelled the political decision-makers, regardless of political party complexion, to seek remedy in (far-ranging) public-sector reforms, largely of the NPM persuasion. In most cases the adoption of public-sector reforms went hand in hand with a broader neo-liberal reorientation of the welfare state and economic policies.

The most conspicuous example of the overpowering influence of the budgetary situation on the government's decision to turn to neo-liberal economic policies and, at the same time, to NPM-guided public-sector reforms can be inspected in New Zealand. It was the Labour Party that having won the election of 1984 over the conservative National Party largely on a pro-'old' welfare state campaign shifted, in view of a desperate budgetary situation, (literally overnight) to neo-liberal economic policies, including stringent public-sector reforms.

Another revealing example can be seen in the French socialists in the early 1980s. They had hardly decided in 1981 to start a massive programme of nationalising key industries (in the pursuit of 'old' socialist ideas) when, not later than 1983, under the impression of the international economic environment, they performed a dramatic policy change and began a neo-liberal reorientation (see Schmidt 2000). In the late 1980s, the socialist Prime Minister Rocard introduced the first NPM-guided public-sector reform programme (see Postif 1996: 215).

In Sweden, it was under the impression of an economic and budgetary crisis that the Social Democrats, returning to power in 1982, embarked upon significant neo-liberal modifications of the famed Swedish Welfare State and upon administrative reforms.

Germany makes for another striking case. After the country had stayed conspicuously aloof from the NPM-guided public-sector reforms, it was the ever-worsening budgetary situation in the wake of the mounting costs of Unification that finally broke the ground for the adoption of NPM-oriented public-sector reforms.

The US is a kind of deviant case in that on the federal government level managerialist reforms have been propagated, while (and although) the country found itself in a relatively comfortable economic and budgetary situation. In this case the development may be explained by the typical personal involvement of recent presidents in federal government reforms (as an 'actor-centred' factor) as well as by the country's managerialist tradition (as a 'cultural tradition' factor).

CONCEPTUAL SCOPE AND INSTRUMENT MIX OF PUBLIC-SECTOR REFORMS

The conceptual scope and mix of public-sector reforms is significantly determined by the country-specific starting conditions and the modernisation needs (or 'leads') which follow from them (for a conceptual emphasis on country-specific starting conditions see Wright 1994).

In the UK, the public sector was characterised, in the late 1970s, by a wide scope of state-owned (nationalised) companies, by a high degree of governmental and administrative centralisation (at the Whitehall level in the traditional absence of an administrative meso level), and by a quasi-monopoly of the public sector in the delivery of health and social services. Against this background it was plausible, if not compelling, that the NPM concepts called for the devolution of central government functions to the newly created ('Next Steps') agencies as well as for the market-testing and 'outsourcing' of services hitherto entirely delivered by public-sector personnel proper. The same applies to New Zealand (whose extreme degree of administrative centrality is mirrored in almost 90 per cent of public-sector personnel being employed by the central government).

Sweden's starting conditions, towards the end of the 1970s, were characterised by a high degree of decentralisation—with the time-honoured largely autonomously operating central agencies carrying out most of the administrative state functions, and with the local authorities traditionally playing a politically as well as functionally strong role. County and municipal personnel have traditionally delivered the health and social services almost entirely. Against these starting conditions, reform measures have been pursued since the 1980s on two tracks. On the one hand, linking up with and stepping up the country's decentralisation tradition, further public functions were devolved to the local authorities and their autonomy was enlarged (through the Local Government Act of 1991). On the other hand, in reaction to the quasi-monopoly of public delivery, NPM-derived concepts have been introduced, purchaser–provider split in health delivery on the county level and market-testing, vouchers, etc., in the municipalities (see Montin 2000).

France was, in the late 1970s, marked by her traditional unitary and ('Napoleonic') centralist government structure as well as by a legalist hierarchical administrative model. In view of these starting conditions, two tracks of reforms ensued. Since the 1980s, legislation and measures to decentralise and deconcentrate political and administrative functions have been effected in order to overcome the country's high degree of centralisation. Since the late 1980s, NPM-guided managerialist reforms have been pushed by socialist as well as conservative governments for remedying the inflexibility in traditional administrative structures.

In Germany, too, the starting conditions significantly account for the course and focus of administrative modernisation. In the German federal system, federal legislation and policies are almost entirely implemented by the Laender (and, within the Laender, by the local authorities). In this one might detect a form of (in NPM jargon) 'agencification'. Primary health care has long since been provided by private medical doctors with the would-be patient having free choice among them (by means of a kind of insurance-based voucher system). Hospitals have been operated by a plurality of institutions (churches, red cross, municipalities, etc.). Furthermore, the majority of the social services (kindergartens, homes for the elderly, etc.) have, under the so-called subsidiarity principle, been provided by non-public, not-for-profit welfare ('charitable') organisations, historically affiliated with the churches and the labour movement. Thus, in the field of social services, the local authorities have traditionally focused on an, in current NPM parlance, 'enabling' function. Against these starting conditions, it should not be surprising that little attention was given in Germany to key NPM concepts such as agencification and outsourcing of health and social services. When NPM finally made its entry into the German modernisation debate, the interest was on managerialist concepts (in the so-called New Steering Model) that seemed apt to instil more flexibility and cost efficiency in the country's traditionally legalistic and hierarchical administrative world (see Wollmann 2000b, 2003b).

STYLE OF DECISION-MAKING IN PUBLIC-SECTOR REFORMS

The style of decision-making in public-sector reforms in a country (e.g., 'top down' or 'bottom up', 'wholesale' or 'fragmented') significantly hinges on the institutional setting of the country (unitary or federal, majoritarian single party ['Westminster'] government or multi-party coalition government, etc.).

The UK epitomises the type of unitary state 'Westminster' decision-making in which policy changes on public-sector reforms for the entire country can be decided by a simple majority vote in Parliament and can be enforced 'top down'. This also applies to New Zealand.

By contrast, in federal countries the federal competence on public-sector matters pertains, in principle, only to the federal level, while the other levels of government have the right to handle administrative reform matters on their own. Hence, for instance, in the US and in Germany, respectively the states, the Laender as well as the local government levels show a modernisation profile of their own. In fact, in Germany the local government level was first, in the early 1990s, to set off a new wave of administrative reform.

In Sweden, which is a unitary but highly decentralised state, a mixed picture can be found. While on the one hand, the central government has, mostly through national legislation, regulated important questions of public-sector reform, the local authorities, on the other hand, thanks to their traditional autonomy, have been self-standing actors in administrative reform matters.

POLITICAL RANGE AND PREMISES OF PUBLIC-SECTOR REFORMS

In the decision-making on policy change and policy formulation in public-sector reforms, the political parties, first of all the government, play a crucial role.

Besides the political parties as collective actors, powerful single actors have no doubt been crucial. The 'Conservative revolution' of 1979 in UK, which also triggered the wave of 'radical' public-sector reforms, was, to a large extent, the work of Mrs. Thatcher's single-handed leadership and of her personal neo-liberal beliefs. In New Zealand, the most important single actor was the Labour Finance Minister, Roger Douglas, who masterminded the country's (and Labour's!) new neo-liberal economic policy (nicknamed, after his first name, 'Rogernomics', see Schmidt 2000: 247) as well as a far-reaching public sector reform (see Halligan 2003). In the US, recent presidents have been personally interested in becoming (politically, electorally, if not historically) identified with a particular reform idea and label (such as Johnson's PPBS [Planning Programming Budgeting Systems], Nixon's MbO [Management by Objective], Carter's ZBB [Zero-Base-Budgeting] and Clinton's REGO ['reinventing government'] (see Kettl 2000: 26; Rockman 2001) which, within the US-typical groundswell of managerialism, has set off 'tides of reform' (Light 1997).

CONCEPTUAL AND THEORETICAL
PROFILE OF PUBLIC-SECTOR REFORMS

The conceptual focus and theoretical underpinning of public-sector reform can be significantly influenced by discourse and discourse communities and coalitions that have been involved in formulating, promoting and legitimating public-sector reform concepts by which such decision-making may be conceptually prepared, guided, accompanied, supported and/or legitimated (on discourse see Hall 1993; Schmidt 2000; Wittrock et al. 1991; Wollmann 2002; on 'advocacy coalitions' see Sabatier 1988).

For rendering the concept of discourse applicable to public-sector reform policy a number of distinctions seem useful.

First, a distinction can be made between the political discourse and debate on the one hand, and the professional as well as academic discourse on public-sector reforms on the other. Allowing for overlapping, while the former typically encompasses the political debate conducted within and by the political parties and political elites and also the media, the professional/academic discourse is identified with groups and individuals outside the political arena proper.

Second, within the professional/academic discourse arena, in turn, different (sub) communities and subgroups can be distinguished which, being premised on different normative and conceptual assumptions and guided by different disciplinary, professional, but also financial interests, may struggle among each other for gaining and retaining dominance ('dominant opinion') in the discourse.

Third, with regard to their possible access to and linkage with the political decision-making on public-sector reforms, the discourse communities may be distinguished according to their location in policy-close, administration-centred and 'at large' discourse communities. While the *policy-close* variant may be characterised as being convened and dominated by political actors, in the *administration-centred* one administrative actors prevail. By contrast, the *at large* variant embraces, on a voluntary, self-organised basis, academics, professionals, interest representatives and consultants.

Fourth, there is the international discourse arena and its relations with the national discourse arena and communities. The national discourse arena may be influenced by the dominant international discourse and international organisations supporting it. Hence, the national discourse may be shaped by international and transnational policy learning (see Dolowitz and Marsh 1996; Rose 1993) and imitation (*mimetic isomorphism*, DiMaggio and Powell 1991). In fact, since the 1980s, the international discourse on public-sector reform has been increasingly dominated by NPM and its wider neoliberal policy implications. On top of it, NPM has been adopted and propagated by influential international organisations, such as OECD, as the preferred, if not the only path to public-sector modernisation (see Naschold 1995: 69; Sahlin-Andersson 2001). The momentum of this international discourse and its implicit 'Anglo-Saxon-centricity' has been complemented by the hegemony of English as the lingua franca.

Turning to the analysis, cases of policy-close discourse communities can be found in the Anglo-Saxon countries. In UK, following 1979, Margaret Thatcher made it a point to keep the Whitehall top civil servants ('mandarins') (whom she suspected of impeding reforms) as well as university-based academics (whom she also mistrusted) out of the reform debate. Instead, she turned for advice to business leaders such as Derek Rayner (whom she appointed to chair a commission mandated to 'scrutinise' central government administration), as well as to New Right think-tanks (see Pollitt and Bouckaert 2000: 272ff.). Similarly in New Zealand, the Finance Minister convened a policy-centred discourse coalition, consisting of top officials from the Treasury and some handpicked neo-liberal university economists, constituting an almost 'secretive elite' (Halligan 2001: 85). As a result, New Zealand's NPM policy received a more pronouncedly theoretical imprint and wording (rational choice, principal/agent theory, etc.) than in any other country.

In USA, where recent presidents tended to resume personal leadership in federal level administrative reform matters, President Reagan, in pursuit of this goal to 'downsize (federal) government', typically appointed a prominent businessman to chair a commission ('Grace Commission') mandated to have the federal government operations checked, surveyed and reported on by private-sector economists (see Pollitt and Bouckaert 2000: 81). At the same time, New Right think-tanks were invited to advise the president. The Democratic President Bill Clinton (and his Vice-President Al Gore), too, turned primarily to private business advice on public-sector reform. In proclaiming to 're-invent government' the Clinton Administration explicitly borrowed the title of Osborne and Gaebler's 1992 bestseller and envisioned a 'business-like' government: 'lessons learned from America's best companies' (Gore 1997). While relying on the private business model and private-sector advice might at first sight not seem typical of a Democratic President, it was in reality a shrewdly calculated political and electoral move to occupy, if not 'steal', a traditionally Republican theme and discourse community (see Rockman 2001).

France offers the example of an administration-centred discourse and discourse coalition which essentially consists of top civil servants belonging to the administrative elites (*grands corps*) (see Pollitt and Bouckaert 2000: 54). An important discourse arena was provided by the *Association Services Publics*, which is a political club where top officials of the *grands corps* and academics meet to discuss administrative reform issues (see Clark 1998: 104). The shift, in the course of the 1980s, from traditional neo-Keynesian *dirigisme* to neo-liberal policy options was largely engineered from within the Finance Ministry (see Jobert and Theret 1994). The 'intra-elite' transfer of ideas has been supported by the cognitive and normative homogeneity which unites the members of the *grands corps* holding leading positions in politics, administration and economy.

Sweden can be seen as traditionally epitomising a broad ('at large') discourse on policy reforms which is characterised, amidst the country's time-honoured 'freedom of information', by a steady flow of governmental study reports (*SOU*) and by the practice of setting up commissions (*remiss*), consisting of governmental officials, interest group representatives and academics, whenever a new legislative proposal comes up (see Vedung 1997). On the issues of public-sector reforms three discourse communities have been distinguished (see Premfors 1998): the decentralists who, calling for further decentralisation of the country, are made up of representatives of local authorities, political scientists and the responsible ministry; the traditionists who, advocating cautious adaptations, can be found in the public-sector trade unions and the social ministry; and the economists who, in advocating far-reaching neo-liberal and NPM-related reforms, are made up of the conservative and liberal parties, the business sector and the Finance Ministry. At different phases different discourse communities prevailed. The reforms of the 1980s (ushering in a further functional strengthening of the local authorities) bore the handwriting of the decentralists. During the 1990s, the application of NPM-derived concepts (performance management, purchase–provider split, market-testing, etc.) has progressed which, besides the neo-liberal reorientation of the social democrats, can be attributed to the close ties which Sweden's pertinent discourse communities, not least thanks to the widespread knowledge of English in Sweden, entertained with the international (primarily Anglophone) debate, particularly with practitioners and academics in Great Britain regarding NPM concepts and practice.

Germany's story is about a conspicuous shift in the modernisation discourse (see Wollmann 2000b). Well into the late 1980s that discourse was dominated by traditional modernisers who, consisting of administrative practitioners, administrative lawyers and (marginally) social scientists, favoured continuous reformist adaptation within the accepted model of public administration. On the local level a crucial role was played by the *Kommunale Gemeinschaftsstelle* (KGSt), a municipally-funded, independent non-profit agency which, in advising the local authorities in organisational matters since 1949, had over the years advocated the traditional ('Max Weberian') model of legal rule-bound, hierarchical public administration. In doing so, KGSt lent legitimacy to the traditional administrative model which contributed to shielding the German debate from the international NPM discourse. In the early 1990s, this discourse constellation changed dramatically. First, KGSt made a radical strategy shift. All of a sudden severely criticising the traditional administrative model of (local) administration, KGSt put forward a 'New Steering Model' which drew heavily on NPM concepts, particularly on a variant that had been put in place in the Dutch city of Tilburg. Based on the prestige and credibility which KGSt had acquired over the years in the modernisation discourse, its strategy shift has been crucial in opening the German discourse arena to the international NPM debate. Another single event that was decisive in shattering and delegitimising the traditional administrative model was an international competition which, in 1993, was organised and funded by the Bertelsmann Foundation. The aim of this worldwide competition was to identify the most innovative cities in the field of administrative modernisation. When, as result of the competition, the New Zealand city of Christchurch and the US city of Phoenix, Arizona, came out on top while the German candidate cities ended at the very bottom, this was taken by many practitioners and academics as a devastating verdict on the viability of the traditional type of (local) administration. This development has been accompanied and mirrored by a conspicuous shift in the composition of the relevant discourse community. While in the past the (aforementioned) traditional reformers stood in the fore, now the centre stage in the discourse was taken over by economists, chief executives, NPM-sympathising academics and, last but not least, professionals from international consultancy firms who discovered and entered the German consultancy market. (It should be noticed that this shift in discourse arena coincided with the mounting budgetary crisis that, as was argued earlier, was crucial in triggering public-sector reforms.)

RECEPTIVITY FOR NPM IDEAS

Finally the supposition shall be taken up that a country's receptivity (or non-receptivity) to NPM ideas and concepts is influenced by its specific institutional and cultural traditions.

In USA, the recent reform message that the public sector should learn from private business and its managerialism found easy acceptance for reasons that are deeply ingrained in the country's history and culture. Since the very foundation of the country, American thinking has been significantly marked by a state-detached, if not anti-state, bias which was paraphrased by Dwight Waldo thus: 'We did not *want* a European-style state, we did not *need* a European-style state, and we did not *develop* a European-style state' (quoted from Stillman 1998: 172). Concomitantly, private-sector managerialism has been seen as a guideline for administrative reforms since the 19th-century progressivist and good government movements and has found its 'scientific' elevation in Fredrick W. Taylor's 'scientific management' (see Hood 1998: 16; Pollitt 1990: 15). Having said that, one should not forget that the progressive movement did not hesitate to borrow from Old Europe's, if not Prussia's, hierarchical bureaucratic model—in the attempt, in view of contemporary corrupt local governments, to create America's modern public administration (see Thompson 2003). President Ronald Reagan stood in a time-honoured American tradition when after 1980 he resumed the battle-cry against 'big government' and set on private-sector instruments (and advice) to cut down federal personnel and expenditures. Similarly the Democratic Clinton administration moved on traditional cultural and cognitive ground when he proclaimed the 'reinvention of government' on the formula of a 'business-like government'.

The UK presents a somewhat ambivalent case. On the one hand, in its more recent history since 1945 well up to the 1970s, the country's political and institutional development bearing the handwriting of the British Labour Party was characterised by the build-up and expansion of the advanced welfare state with an array of state-owned (nationalised) business companies, with a quasi-monopoly of the public sector in the delivery of health and social services and with public personnel body making up 20 per cent of the total number of employees (at the end of the 1970s). Pointedly put, post-war Great Britain somewhat exemplified the full-blown (centralist) welfare state. On the other hand, however, the British political and administrative tradition and culture has been rooted in the Common Law tradition in which, distinctly different from the Continental European Roman Law tradition, the state is legally or cognitively not recognised as a self-standing legal 'person'. In this sense, Britain could be called a 'state-less' country (see Dyson 1980: 53; Johnson 2000: 29). By the same logic, a divide and distinction between the state and society, between public law and private law is not made. Hence, key NPM concepts, geared to private-sector derived managerialism, marketisation, outsourcing and the like, had easy access and acceptance in the reform debate when the 'old' welfare state and its administrative structures came under fire (Wollmann 2000a).

By contrast, Germany is marked by a state and law tradition which was historically shaped by the Roman Law tradition (with its recognition of the state as a self-standing legal personality and its distinction of public and private law) and by the evolution of the *Rechtsstaat* tradition with its axiom to direct and control public administration by a codified set of legislative provisions and to put it under judicial review. By the same token, the ('Max Weberian') model of an (externally legal rule-bound and internally hierarchically-controlled) public administration has become and remained part and parcel of Germany's public administration tradition. It should be added that, reflecting the country's traumatic experience with tyrannical and law-negating government in the recent past, the *Rechtsstaat* has institutionally, legally and normatively been entrenched even more firmly in the post-war Federal Republic. Another important component in the country's political and institutional tradition can be seen in the existence of a politically and functionally strong local government based on a multi-function model. In sum, these institutional and cultural traditions have constituted barriers to an easy entry and acceptance of NPM concepts that are expressly 'imported' from the private sector and its different operational logic.

Sweden comes as an intriguingly mixed case. On the one hand, the country stands in a Roman Law and *Rechtsstaat* tradition which stems from its earlier historical links with Continental European, not least German, development. Furthermore, the country possesses a long tradition of highly decentralised government with politically as well as functionally strong local governments. On the other hand, Sweden has traditionally shown great pragmatism in reforming her institutions not least by learning from international experience. Particularly since World War II, Sweden has knit close cultural and

English language ties with the Anglo-Saxon world which eased the way to get to know, adopt and 'try out' NPM concepts, especially of British provenance.

(Progressing) Convergence or (Continuing) Divergence of the Countries' Trajectories?

In the conclusion, the question shall be taken up as to whether and to which degree the country trajectories of public-sector reforms in the countries under consideration in this chapter have shown convergence or divergence.

Summarising the arguments of this chapter and drawing on other pertinent internationally comparative sources (particularly Christensen and Laegreid 2001a; Pollitt and Bouckaert 2000; Wollmann 2003a) the following may, in conclusion, be said.

The countries' reform trajectories exhibit a great variance in the timing, the scope and instruments of public-sector reforms encompassing and mixing 'traditional' as well as NPM-guided reform strategies and elements. The variability and multi-faceted mix of the reform concepts and measures could be brought out even more clearly, if space allowed.

Put in a broad-brush manner, the trajectories of public sector on the one hand reveal a significant degree of convergence across countries. A few points should be highlighted.

- Public-sector reforms which have been initiated in all countries since the late 1970s (with a significant variance in time and scope) have been embedded in and driven by a more general policy change, which marked the departure from the 'old' welfare state and its underlying Keynesian policy and the advent of a neo-liberal reorientation in welfare state and economic policies. In this sense, the recent wave of public-sector reforms that can, on a larger or smaller scale, be observed in all countries can be interpreted as just one dimension of a more general and fundamental policy change.
- In concrete terms, there has been a move across countries to the devolution of political and administrative functions in the intergovernmental setting. This applies particularly to countries whose starting conditions were characterised

by the traditional profile of a unitary highly centralised state. So, in the early 1980s, France made a decisive step towards 'classical' decentralisation. In the late 1980s, Great Britain followed suit with the NPM-guided ('Next Steps') creation of central agencies. Sweden, which by tradition was already a highly decentralised country with politically and functionally strong local government levels, continued during the 1980s to further devolve state functions to the local authorities.

- Another general drive across countries was directed at dissolving the 'monopoly' of the public sector in the delivery of health and social services. This applies particularly to Great Britain and Sweden where as a result of the build-up of the post-war modern welfare state the health and social services had come to be almost entirely delivered by public-sector personnel. The reform concepts and instruments that have been put in place range from market-testing, voucher systems to outsourcing and (material) privatisation.
- In all countries, on different scales of conceptual and instrumental stringency, managerialist principles including performance management and procedures to evaluate performance outputs and results have been introduced. This applies not least to Germany and France whose starting conditions were characterised by the traditional existence of legal rule-bound hierarchical ('Max Weberian') bureaucracy.

While the institutional trajectories show conspicuous cross-country convergence, there can be no doubt that they, at least up to now, continue to exhibit significant divergence in important aspects.

First, this seems to hold true particularly for the law-applying and law-enforcing dimension and function of public administration which, in the countries with a *Rechtsstaat* tradition and an accepted emphasis on the legal regulation and judicial review of the operations of public administration, has a significantly greater institutional, cultural and normative salience than in the Anglo-Saxon Common Law countries (whereby the heavy dose of statute-law and judicial review in the US should, of course, not be ignored). Hence, a momentous segment of administrative functions and activities in *Rechtsstaat* tradition countries is bound to remain outside the attention and limelight of the NPM debate which (inasmuch as it emphasises market-testing and outsourcing) primarily envisages the provision of health and social services, that is, the service function of the state, leaving aside and out of sight the 'hard core' law-applying and law-enforcing function of the state. This aspect suggests continuing divergence between the Anglo-Saxon countries on the one hand, and Continental European countries, but, to a lesser degree, also Scandinavian countries, on the other hand.

Second, an important field of persisting divergence can be seen in the status and function that the local authorities have in the country's entire political and administrative system. In the international overview particularly, two groups of countries come in sight. On the one side, countries such as Germany and Sweden are traditionally characterised by politically as well as functionally strong local governments in which the local authorities play a crucial 'multi-functional' part in performing a wide array of public tasks. During the recent wave of public-sector reforms, there was a tendency to even further strengthen the political and functional role of local government. Because of this persisting political and functional strength, the local authorities in this group of countries are prone to place a political and functional limit to any 'excessive' outsourcing and privatisation of public functions. On the other side, in other countries such as the UK, the political and functional role of local government has been greatly reduced as a result of NPM-guided reforms and of accompanying local government-related measures. As an expression and a result of this enfeeblement of local government, the NPM-driven process of outsourcing and 'quangoisation' of public tasks could run rampant. Hence, also on this score, a relevant divergence between the countries with a persistently strong local government level and those with weak local authorities exists.

In summarising these aspects and features of divergence and in drawing on an ideal-type distinction submitted by Johan Olsen between a 'sovereign state' and a 'supermarket state' (see Olsen 1988), one might in an admittedly gross and simplified manner see the persistence of the 'sovereign state' in the profile of countries with a *Rechtsstaat* tradition plus politically and functionally strong local governments such as Germany and Sweden, while traces of the 'supermarket state' may be detected in the Anglo-Saxon countries with a 'marketisation' profile of public-sector reforms.

The further course of development is up for speculation and at best for 'informed guessing'.

Those who hold that there will be further convergence argue that internationally powerful forces and agents (such as the globalisation of the financial and economic markets) are bound to exert a degree of external determinism which is going to impose permanent, if not increasing, pressure, embodied and exercised by international organisations such as the OECD, on the national economies and states to adapt and converge (see Thoenig 2003). This argument may find a strong case in the European Union (EU) which has been pushing not only for formulating and enforcing (primarily economic) policies and related legal regulations (such as on market liberalisation) in 'one space without internal frontiers', but has also been, through the growing flux of EU regulations which need to be implemented by and within the members states, promoting 'one European administrative space' without having an explicit mandate and competence to interfere with the internal institutional matters of the member states.

In spite of these external—international as well as, in the case of the EU, inter-member state—pressures there is good reason to assume that the institutional variance and divergence is going to persist, at least in the foreseeable future. Notwithstanding the conspicuous policy and strategy change in public-sector reforms which took place throughout the countries at different points in time and on a different scale, the persistence of country-specific features has been conspicuous, which was demonstrated particularly by the salience of country-specific starting conditions and country-specific institutional and cultural traditions, if not 'path-dependencies'. There are no factors or developments in sight which could plausibly change these givens. It can finally be argued that, in view of the onrush of external factors prompting an international convergence and harmonisation of policies, the decisions on the (internal) institutions and the polity of a country will continue to be claimed (and jealously defended) by the national states and their governments (on all levels) as remaining the reserve and prerogative of intra-national, domestic policy and decision-making (for a similar argument see Koenig and Fuechtner 2000).

REFERENCES

Aucoin, Peter. 1990. 'Administrative Reform in Public Management: Paradigms, Principles, Paradoxes and Pendulums'. *Governance*, 3(2): 115–37.
Christensen, Tom and Laegreid, Per (eds). 2001a. *New Public Management*, pp. 59–79. Aldershot: Ashgate.

Christensen, Tom and Laegreid, Per (eds). 2001b. 'A Transformative Perspective on Administrative Reforms', in Tom Christensen and Per Laegreid (eds). *New Public Management*, pp. 13–39. Aldershot: Ashgate.

Christensen, Tom, Laegreid, Per and Wise, Lois. 2003. 'Assessing Public Sector Reforms in Norway, Sweden and the United States', in Hellmut Wollmann (ed.), *Evaluation in Public Sector Reform*, pp. 59–79. Cheltenham/Northampton: Edward Elgar.

Clark, David. 1998. 'The Modernization of the French Civil Service: Crisis, Change, and Continuity'. *Public Administration*, 76(1): 102–25.

DiMaggio, P.J. and Powell W.W. 1991. 'The Iron Cage Revisited: Institutional Isomorphism and Collective Rationality in Organisational Fields', in P.J. DiMaggio and W.W. Powell (eds). *The New Institutionalism in Organisational Analysis*, pp. 63–82. Chicago: University of Chicago Press.

Dolowitz, D. and Marsh, D. 1996, 'Who learns What from Whom? A Review of the Policy Transfer Literature'. *Political Studies*, 44(3): 343–57.

Dyson, Kenneth. 1980. *The State Traditions in Western Europe*. Oxford: Robertson.

Gore, Al. 1997. *Businesslike Government: Lessons Learned from America's Best Companies*. Washington, D.C.: National Performance Review.

Hall, Peter A. 1993. 'Policy Paradigms, Social Learning, and the State: The Case of Economic Making in Britain'. *Comparative Politics*, 25(3): 275–96.

Halligan, John. 2001. 'The Process of Reform in the Era of Public Sector Transformation', in Tom Christensen and Per Laegreid (eds). *New Public Management*, pp. 73–89. Aldershot: Ashgate.

———. 2003. 'Public Sector Modernization in Australia and New Zealand. An Evaluative Perspective', in Hellmut Wollmann (ed.), *Evaluation in Public Sector Reform*, pp. 80–103. Cheltenham/Northampton: Edward Elgar.

Hood, Christopher. 1991. 'A Public Management for All Seasons'. *Public Administration*, 69(1): 3–19.

———. 1998. *The Art of the State: Culture, Rhetoric and Public Management*. Oxford: Oxford University Press.

Jobert, B. and Theret, B. 1994. 'France, La Consecration Républicaine Du Néoliberalisme', in B. Jobert (ed.). *Le Tournant Néoliberal*. Paris: Harmattan.

Johnson, Nevil. 2000. 'State and Society in Britain: Some Contrasts with the German Experience', in Hellmut Wollmann and Eckhard Schroeter (eds). *Comparing Public Sector Reforms in Britain and Germany*, pp. 29–42. Aldershot: Ashgate.

Kettl, Donald F. 2000. *The Global Public Management Revolution*. Washington D.C.: Brookings.

Koenig, Klaus and Fuechtner, Natascha. 2000. *Schlanker Staat*. Baden-Baden: Nomos.

Light, Paul E. 1997. *The Tides of Reforms, 1945–1995*. New Haven: Yale University Press.

Montin, Stig. 2000. 'Between Fragmentation and Co-ordination: The Changing Role of Local Government in Sweden'. *Public Management*, 2(1): 1–23.

Naschold, Frieder. 1995. *Ergebnissteuerung, Wettbewerb, Qualitaetspolitik*. Berlin: Sigma.

Olsen, J.P. 1988. 'Administrative Reform and Theories of Organisation', in C. Campbell and Guy Peters (eds). *Organizing Governance: Governing Organisations*, pp. 233–54. Pittsburgh: University of Pittsburg Press.

Osborne, D. and Gaebler, T. 1992. *Reinventing Government: How the Entrepreneurial Spirit is Transforming the Public Sector*. Reading, Mass.: Adison Wesley.

Peters, Guy. 1995. 'Political institutions: Old and New', in Robert Goddin and Hans-Dieter Klingemann (eds). *A New Handbook on Political Science*, pp. 205–20. Oxford: Oxford University Press.

Pollitt, Christopher. 1990. *Managerialism and the Public Services: The Anglo-American Experience*. Oxford: Basil Blackwell.

———. 1995. 'Justification by Works or by Faith? Evaluating the New Public Management'. *Evaluation*, 1(2): 133–54.

Pollitt, Christopher and Bouckaert, Geert. 2000. *Public Management Reform*. Oxford: Oxford University Press.

Postif, Thierry. 1996. 'Public Sector Reform in France', in Jan-Erik Lane (ed.). *Public Sector Reform*, pp. 210–30. London: Sage.

Premfors, R. 1998. 'Reshaping the Democratic State: Swedish Experiences in a Comparative Perspective'. *Public Administration*, 76(1): 141–59.

Rockman, Bert. 2001. 'Politics by Other Means: Administrative Reform in the US'. *International Review of Public Administration*, 6(2): 1–15.

Rose, Richard. 1993. *Lesson Drawing in Public Policy*. New Jersey: Chatham House.

Sabatier, Paul. 1988. 'An Advocacy Coalition Framework of Policy Change and the Role of Policy-oriented Learning Therein'. *Policy Sciences*, 21: 129–68.

Sahlin-Andersson, Kerstin. 2001. 'National, International and Transnational Constructions of New Public Management', in Tom Christensen and Per Laegreid (eds). *New Public Management*, pp. 43–72. Aldershot: Ashgate.

Schmidt, Vivien A. 2000. 'Values and Discourse in the Politics of Adjustment', in Fritz W. Scharpf and Vivien Schmidt (eds). *Welfare and Work in the Open Economy*, Vol. 1, pp. 229–49. Oxford: Oxford University Press.

Stillman, Richard J. 1998. *Creating the American State*. Tuscaloosa/London: University of Alabama Press.

Thoenig, Jean-Claude. 2003. 'Learning from Evaluation Practice: The Case of Public-sector reforms', in Hellmut Wollmann (ed.), *Evaluation in Public Sector Reform*, pp. 209–30. Cheltenham/Northampton: Edward Elgar.

Thompson, Fred. 2003. 'Why a New Public Management? Why Now'. *Review of Public Personnel Administration*, 23.

Vedung, Evert. 1997. *Public Policy and Program Evaluation*. New Brunswick: Transaction.

Wittrock, Bjoern, Wagner, Peter and Wollmann, Hellmut. 1991. 'Social Science and the Modern State: Policy Knowledge and the Political Institutions in Western Europe and the United States', in Peter Wagner, Carol Weiss, Bjoern Wittrock and Hellmut Wollmann (eds). *Social Science and Modern States*, pp. 28–51. Cambridge: Cambridge University Press.

Wright, Vincent. 1994. 'Reshaping the State'. *West European Politics*, 17(1): 102–37.

Wollmann, Hellmut. 2000a. 'Comparing Institutional Development in Britain and Germany: (Persistent) Divergence or (Progressing) Convergence?', in

Hellmut Wollmann and Eckhard Schroeter (eds). *Comparing Public Sector Reform in Britain and Germany,* pp. 1–26. Aldershot: Ashgate.

———. 2000b. 'Local Government Modernization in Germany: Between Incrementalism and Reform Waves'. *Public Administration* 78(4): 915–36.

———. 2002, 'Verwaltungspolitische Reformdiskurse und—verlaeufe im internationalen Vergleich', in Klaus Koenig (Hrsg.), *Deutsche Verwaltung an der Wende zum 21 Jahrhundert,* pp. 489–524. Baden-Baden: Nomos.

———. (ed.). 2003a. *Evaluation in Public Sector Reform.* Aldershot: Elgar.

———. 2003b. 'Evaluation in public-sector reform: Trends, potentials and limits in international perspective', in Hellmut Wollmann (ed.), *Evaluation in Public-Sector Reform,* pp. 231–58. Cheltenham/Northampton: Edward Elgar.

CHAPTER 10

ADMINISTRATIVE REFORM IN GERMANY:
LEARNING FROM EUROPEAN EXPERIENCES

MANFRED ROEBER

INTRODUCTION

Germany is often regarded as a laggard—as far as administrative reform is concerned. Only some years after several other European countries had already conducted their reform initiatives and projects (see for example Banner and Reichard 1993), Germany, in the 1990s, started to modernise its public sector.[1] Mayors and top administrators in cities and local authorities realised that the traditional bureaucratic structure would no longer be able to meet future requirements for providing proper public services at reasonable costs for their citizens (Elcock 1998).

The reason for that diagnosis has been an emerging turbulent environment, particularly for local authorities. Challenges came from shifts in public duties (from regulatory functions to public service delivery which needs different organisational structures), demographic changes (the number of people older than 60 will nearly double in the next two decades), changing values in society (from materialism to post-materialism) and an increasingly competitive pressure (especially because of European Union legislation). Additionally, financial problems were beginning to loom ever larger on the horizon, internal management problems became more and more apparent, and work motivation and satisfaction began to crumble.

The German approach to management-oriented reform at the local level at the beginning of the 1990s has been very much influenced by the experience of Dutch local authorities, notably the city of Tilburg, which has been impressively successful in modernising its management system under severe financial problems during the 1980s. In general we can say that during the 1990s, modernisation of the public sector has mainly been an issue on the political agenda of the local government. Reform efforts at the state and federal levels have been lagging behind and have only gained some momentum in the second half of the 1990s (see also Reichard 2001). For that reason I will concentrate in my overview mainly on experiences with administrative reform at the local level.

CONSTITUTIONAL FRAMEWORK

Management reform in the public sector cannot be discussed without reference to the overall structure of the state. Compared to other European countries which are unitary states (with a high degree of centralisation like France till the 1980s and the United Kingdom, or with a fairly high degree of decentralisation like the Scandinavian countries), Germany is a federal state that gives considerable political and administrative power to its states (Laender) and to local authorities.

The 16 German states are sovereign parts of the Federal Republic with their own territories, constitutions, legislation, government, jurisdiction, administration and capitals. They are not just provinces or counties.

Local government in Germany is carried out in a two-tier system consisting of

- 324 counties which include all local authorities (without county boroughs) and 112 county boroughs which are independent from the counties, and
- about 14,000 local authorities and associations of small local authorities which all belong to a county.

Local government in the sense of local self-government is based on and safeguarded by Article 28 of the German Constitution ('Basic Law'): 'The local authorities must be guaranteed the right to regulate on their own responsibility all the affairs of the local government within the limits set by law'. It is defined by three concepts:

'general competence in local affairs', 'power to issue regulations for the respective local authority' and 'self-administration'. That means that many public services for the citizens are delivered at the local level—a significantly different situation compared to unified, centralised states in which 'central governments tend to be more heavily involved in the business of service delivery (education, health care, etc.) than do the central governments of federal decentralised states . . . ' (Pollitt and Bouckaert 2000: 43).

Adding to the high degree of vertical differentiation, the German politico-administrative system is also horizontally highly differentiated. An indicator for this is an extended system of public agencies (*Koerperschaften, Anstalten* and *Stiftungen*) as executing institutions—at federal as well as at the state level. They are responsible for special public duties—like the Federal Labour Corporation (*Bundesanstalt fuer Arbeit*) or the Federal Insurance Corporation for Salaried Employees (*Bundesversicherungsanstalt fuer Angestellte*). These agencies that are governed by public law and at arm's length have a higher degree of autonomy than for example the higher federal or state authorities. In their functions, the German agencies are more or less comparable to the British agencies established in the Next Steps Programme (Kemp 1990). And even at the local level, some municipalities provide more than 50 per cent of their services outside the city administration in public enterprises that are fully in the hand of the respective local authority. Furthermore, Germany has a very well-developed network of third sector non-profit organisations (either private or public quangos) (Wollmann 2001), which fulfil within the frame of the enabling state an increasing number of public duties (like social work or public health). This is due to the idea of subsidiarity which is no constitutional principle, but which is of considerable influence on the allocation of responsibilities for public duties and on the mode of service delivery.[2] This tendency is going to increase because of the present debate on core functions of the state, which most probably will result in many more public services being provided either by private or by partly state-run agencies, with the state remaining solely in the position of a 'principal'—steering the service delivery process.

Due to the extreme variety of politico-administrative institutions, it is impossible to identify a common type of administrative reform in Germany. At the state (Laender) level, different states still have different attitudes towards management-oriented reforms; public agencies even in the same state vary considerably in their efforts to modernise their administrative apparatus. And at the local level we can observe a patchwork of local authorities with extremely different stances towards reform (Reichard 1997; Schroeter and Wollmann 1997).

The still dominating administrative culture in Germany is based on the principles of the *Rechtsstaat* with its strong emphasis on legality. This culture is very much influenced by the Weberian ideal type of bureaucracy with a tall hierarchy of positions, functional specialisation, a system of strict rules, impersonal relationships, and a high degree of formalisation. Additionally the German administrative system is characterised by the relatively dominant role of administrative law that is, for example—in connection with constitutional and private law—the most important part in the curriculum for education and training for the civil service in Germany. That means that most of the public servants in Germany are not really able and ready to accept fundamental changes towards a new public management. Attempts, for example, to change and to tailor the curriculum in internal training institutions towards more management skills are still meeting with a lot of reservation and resistance from practitioners in the German bureaucracy, who are more or less captives of their traditional law-oriented mentalities. In many other European countries with long traditions in the *Rechtsstaat* (like the Netherlands and Scandinavian countries), the 'lawyerly dominance has been considerably diluted . . . (and) civil servants now come from a wide variety of disciplinary backgrounds . . . ' (Pollitt and Bouckaert 2000: 54).

MAIN STAGES OF ADMINISTRATIVE REFORM IN GERMANY

It seems quite helpful to realise that New Public Management (NPM) is not the very beginning of public-sector modernisation at all. Some advocates of NPM create the impression that administrative reform has been completely absent before 'reinventing government'. In Germany, we can identify, for example, different stages of reform over the last 50 years. It started with 'renovating' the legal system after the Nazi regime in the 1950s. In the 1950s and 1960s, a far-reaching territorial reform at the local level and attempts to decentralise administrative functions to lower levels of the system took place. After some modifications to the budgetary law (as a general law[3] setting the framework in which states and local authorities have to fulfil their financial and budgetary obligations) at the end of the 1960s, the focal subject during the 1970s was comprehensive planning approaches at federal and state levels (similar to the Planning Programming Budgeting Systems [PPBS] in the United States of America). Citizen participation in local town planning and improvements of citizen-friendly behaviour in service delivery were also equally emphasised. Parallel to developments in the UK and the US under the regimes of Margaret Thatcher and Ronald Reagan in the 1980s, deregulation, debureaucratisation (cutting red tape) and privatisation have been relatively high on the political agenda, but mainly at the level of 'talk' and not really at the level of 'decisions' and 'actions' (see, for these categories, Brunsson 1989).

At the beginning of the 1990s—after having overcome the most urgent difficulties in the process of German unification—the shortcomings and deficiencies of traditional bureaucracy became increasingly obvious in the context of the far-reaching changes in society that have been mentioned above. This has been true in particular for local authorities which—compared to federal and state institutions—have to deal directly with the problems of the citizens and which faced, especially at the beginning of the 1990s, increasing financial problems. For that reason it is no surprise that the driving force for administrative reform has come from the local level.

In general, the present aims of administrative reform in Germany are similar to those in other European countries. Efforts to modernise the public sector are mainly directed towards increased efficiency, reduced state functions, improved politico-administrative control, better steering capacities and strengthened administrative responsiveness. This is—all over Europe—nearly the same as far as the dimension of talk about administrative reform is concerned. In practice we can observe that different countries have placed major emphasis on different strategies as well as topics and instruments of administrative reform.

CHARACTERISTICS OF PRESENT PUBLIC-SECTOR MODERNISATION IN GERMANY

The modernisation of the public sector in Germany has very strongly been promoted by the 'Joint Local Government Agency' (*Kommunale*

Gemeinschaftsstelle [KGSt]), which is an independent consultancy agency organised by the voluntary membership of municipalities, counties and local authorities. The seminal contributions of the *Kommunale Gemeinschaftsstelle* have been influencing the process and progress of administrative reform in Germany considerably—and not only at the local level (Banner 1991, 1994; KGSt 1991, 1993; see also: *www.kgst.de/english/set_publications0.htm*). In accordance with the Tilburg Model in the Netherlands (Schrijvers 1993), the KGSt has made a proposal for a modern system of local government which has been labelled *Neues Steuerungsmodell* ('New Steering Model') and which concentrates reform efforts on the following elements of a new public management.

COMPANY-LIKE HOLDING STRUCTURE

Clear-cut Responsibilities between Politics and Administration: Referring to the often criticised mixture of political and administrative responsibilities—with the effect that councillors intervene too often in the implementation of programmes and administrators think too often in political categories—the KGSt pleaded for clear-cut responsibilities between politics and administration. Councillors should decide on general strategies, political priorities, objectives, performance standards, appropriate resources, and they should control the administration only along strategic lines. The administration should have full discretion on its resources, should be responsible for implementing political programmes and policies according to the strategies and objectives set by the council, and should have to report on the progress and realisation of programmes.

Contract Management: The council and the head of the administrative body (mayor, chief executive, and/or the heads of department as per the state's local government law) should agree on contracts on services or products (with regard to quantity, price, costs, quality and target groups) and on the budget for the local authority. Similar agreements have been planned between the head of department and the sections of department. To avoid discussions on too sophisticated and in the end practically useless models of contract management, one has to take into account the fact that the term 'contract' should not be used in a strict legal sense, but more as an operational arrangement.

General Shape of Administration

Integral Responsibilities for Decentralised Departments: On the basis of contract management with its well-defined objectives, performance standards and appropriate budgets, each department should get the responsibility for all management aspects (e.g., organisation, manpower planning, data processing and automation, cost accounting, deviation analysis and reporting) to fulfil its tasks. If possible, the congruence of responsibilities for tasks, resources and results should be established at each level of the department. It is expected that this system will provide a higher degree of clarity than the old bureaucratic system with its confused responsibilities.

Central Controlling Department: The traditionally powerful central units (like finance, organisation, personnel departments) would lose much of their power because they are regarded as one of the main causes for over-centralised bureaucratic procedures with their negative consequences on efficiency and effectiveness. The 'new type of central unit' should be directly attached to the chief executive officer of the authority, and it should become a small controlling department which has to fulfil similar functions like those of the 'holding staff' in the Tilburg Model. The model stipulates 'direct support of the political administrative bodies and governors; development of central standards and directions; coordination of the departments; development and improvement of planning and control systems; control and consolidation of the results and performances of the departments' (Schrijvers 1993: 597).

From Input Control to Output Control

Products: A key element of output-oriented management is to combine the 'countless' activities of administration to easily comprehensible products. The products must be specified with regard to quantity, quality, target groups and costs. And it must become clear to which goal each product has to contribute.

Integration of Products in a System of Cost Accounting: The prevailing classical annual budgetary planning with its limited political and economical scope is a classic example for input control in public administration. Product definition is regarded as the basis for a change from an input-oriented to an output-oriented budget. And it is indispensable for introducing modern business-like cost-accounting systems which allow for more clarity on cost effectiveness and which give each department more discretion on their financial resources (e.g., via block grants).

Quality Management: In German local government, the citizen and customer orientation and the quality of the service are still relatively weak. Comprehensive approaches like the Citizen's Charter in the UK (Cm 1599 1991) do not exist. Quality management as another very important element of output control must be improved. The KGSt Model refers to the systematic investigation of expectations to local services by citizens and companies. According to the KGSt proposal, helpful instruments of such an investigation can be regular surveys, analysis of citizens' complaints, suggestions for improvement by staff members, quality circles, etc. (for the general discussion on quality management and some additional ideas on citizens' participation in Germany, see Bertelsmann 1993 and Hill and Klages 1993).

COMPETITION

Competition is regarded in the KGSt Model as one of the key factors and driving forces in the modernisation process (especially at the local level), particularly as it would not make much sense to introduce company-like management structures in local authorities without establishing a conducive company-like competitive environment.

PRESENT STATE OF ADMINISTRATIVE REFORM IN GERMANY

Although there seems to be an idea of a blueprint in the form of the 'New Steering Model', in practice we can identify a colourful and varied patchwork of different reform strategies and reform instruments.

This is especially true for the whole politico-administrative system of Germany because—as already mentioned above—the pace of reform at the three levels (federation, states and local authorities) is still quite different. The local level is far ahead in modernising organisational structures and decision-making processes compared to the state and federal levels. There are, however, large differences in administrative reform among local authorities due to the high degree of political decentralisation in the frame of the federal system, which does not allow any attempt to design a master plan for all local authorities.

Nevertheless, certain German states have made some progress in administrative reform (see: *oecd_countryreport.pdf,* pp. 7–10, under *www.staat-modern.de*), and even at the federal level, some changes have taken place during the last few years. Examples are the Report of the Lean State Advisory Committee (1997), the Civil Service Reform Law, which was passed by Parliament (*Deutscher Bundestag*) in February 1997, and a comprehensive approach to introduce Electronic Government with far-reaching consequences for the citizens. At the end of 1999, the federal government had launched the programme 'Modern State—Modern Administration', which describes the enabling state as a guiding model for administrative modernisation at the federal level. This model refers to 'a new distribution of responsibilities, diversity of public administration, a firm orientation towards the citizens, and efficient and effective administration' (see: *oecd_countryreport.pdf*, under *www.staat-modern.de*). The programme contains altogether 38 projects (most of them still ongoing) covering the following main subjects: 'enhanced efficiency and acceptance of legislation', 'the federal government as a partner', 'a competitive, cost-efficient and transparent administrative system', and 'highly-motivated employees' (see: *moderner staat.pdf*, under *www.staat-modern.de*).

The overall picture for the local level can be drawn from surveys of the German Association of Cities (*Deutscher Staedtetag*).

Recent data from the last survey indicates that the picture has not changed significantly (see Table 10.1; Groemig 2001). It differs only in the respect that local authorities have obviously been trying to intensify their reform efforts.

The figures show that the main emphasis has been put on cost accounting (in connection with describing products as part of output-oriented budgeting and operational—and to a lesser extent—strategic controlling), on personnel management and on organisational development.

In organisational development, most German local authorities (and also some authorities at the state and federal levels) have redesigned their organisation structure in compliance with the general idea of the holding structure from large parent companies with their subsidiaries. But only concentrating on the organisation structure without analysing the processes of business engineering has

Table 10.1
Focus of Modernisation Activities of German Cities in 1996

Field of modernisation	Modernisation is realised	Modernisation is pursued	Modernisation is planned with high priority	Modernisation is planned with low priority	No modernisation in activities
Cost Accounting	2.4%	47.1%	37.1%	6.7%	6.7%
Personnel Development	6.7%	37.8%	37.1%	6.2%	12.4%
Organisational Development	6.7%	46.2%	28.6%	6.7%	11.9%
Contracting-out	7.1%	17.1%	23.3%	19.0%	33.3%
Politics and Administration	5.2%	21.0%	36.2%	11.9%	25.7%

Source: Groemig and Thielen 1996: 597.

very often been seen as a 'cosmetic' exercise during which, in the worst case, some authorities have only made amendments in their organisation charts and changed the signs on the doors of their offices. Meanwhile, there is an emerging consensus that even the best holding-structure will have no effect if there are no complementary changes in the modes of decision-making and business reengineering.

As far as personnel management is concerned, there is a slowly increasing awareness in German public administration that personnel is not only a cost factor, but also a productivity factor. No doubt, due to fiscal stress, personnel has to be reduced in absolute size, but at the same time it is necessary to motivate the staff better in order to unleash the hidden productivity potential (Roeber and Loeffler 2000). At present this new thinking manifests itself in two major streams of personnel management reforms in the German public administration. The reform of the Civil Service Law in 1997 has introduced some elements of flexible employment contracts, numerical flexibility, career mobility, and performance-oriented pay to increase the extrinsic motivation of civil servants in the state administration. On the local level, many municipalities experiment with 'soft' personnel management instruments such as employee surveys, employee dialogue and performance agreements between the superior and employees in order to improve the intrinsic motivation of public servants. Both forms of 'flexibilisation' still remain rather limited. In the state administration, the introduction of some limited pay flexibility lacks modern human resource management whereas at the local level municipalities with modern human resource management may not reward better individual productivity.

It is quite conspicuous—and not really surprising due to the fact that the reform impetus has been driven very strongly by increasing financial constraints—that cost accounting and budgetary reforms have been very high on the local reform agenda in the 1990s.[4] But financial management reforms in Germany are still behind developments in other European countries (like the Netherlands, Switzerland and UK) which have changed their accounting systems from traditional cash-based systems not only to double book-keeping, but also to accrual accounting systems 'with extended cost calculation supported by performance measurement systems' (Pollitt and Bouckaert 2000: 68). The necessity of cost-cutting still eclipses the reform process; and public employees are suspicious that administrative reform in general and financial management reform in particular are only disguised sophisticated and tricky strategies for cost reduction and downsizing.

But the German public sector faces a considerable and increasing risk of blundering into a 'cost trap' if administrative reform under heavy financial pressure does not include a severe debate on the core functions of public authorities. Unless the huge amount of public duties is scrutinised very carefully in order to reduce those functions, which are not really necessary, reform efforts are always under threat of losing their positive effects not only on effectiveness, but also on efficiency. Under these circumstances the important role of politicians cannot be overestimated. They are the ones who are legitimised and politically responsible for deciding on political priorities and 'posteriorities'.

The role of politicians is also very important as far as their commitment to the reform process is concerned. Despite a broad, political party–border crossing consensus on the aims of administrative reform, politicians so far show relatively little interest in practical reform issues and in a visible political support of reform ideas. Especially from Naschold's international research work (1997) we know quite well how important the interrelated roles of politicians and administrators for substantial improvements in administrative reform processes are. According to Naschold's results of empirical research, successful innovative strategies in the public sector are most likely when politicians play an active role in the reform process and when the role understanding of people at the top of administrative bodies is that of 'managers' and not of 'civil servants'. But even if politicians as well as top administrators play an active role in the modernisation process, the interface between politics and administration is still one of the most problematic issues in management-oriented administrative reforms in nearly all European countries. The reason for that lies in the different types of rationality in decision-making (maximising the share of the vote versus sustainable efficiency and effectiveness). Therefore, public-sector reformers begin to realise that administrative reform must not be considered without conducive political reforms. These political reforms should strengthen the position of politicians in such a way that they can concentrate on really important political issues and leave it to the administrative bodies to implement carefully designed and intensely discussed policies. In principle, we must discuss a new distribution of power between politicians and bureaucracy—with all opportunities, but also with all threats for the traditional model, which has provided a reasonable degree of democratic behaviour and an acceptable standard of public services.

For successful management-oriented reforms in the public sector, a key factor is trade unions. In Germany, public-sector trade unions played a very constructive and active role in the modernisation process from the very beginning. They stimulated the reform debate very early in the 1980s with their own proposals for more efficiency in the public sector and for improvements in service delivery. Although there can be no doubt that they did these under the impression of 'privatisation threats'—because an inflexible, inefficient and ineffective public service is much more vulnerable to drastic privatisation attempts from those political forces which are only interested in reducing the state to its core function ('skeleton state')—the moderate role of trade unions has been contributing a great deal to consensus-oriented procedures in administrative reforms and to significant improvements in cost-cutting and service delivery. Trade unions still play an important role in public-sector modernisation—even if some reform elements are combined with painful downsizing strategies. But, in general, the public-sector trade unions consider modernisation (even in connection with substantial cost-cuttings and restrictions in their traditional privileges) as the lesser evil, compared to the privatisation of public services.

In obvious contrast, especially with Anglo-Saxon reform countries, administrative reform in Germany has mainly been initiated from within (especially local) administrative bodies, and it was a bottom-up process (Klages and Loeffler 1995) without any interference from the federal level. The fact of the matter is, however, that

> public sector reform activities are bound to proceed in a disjointed and incrementalist rather than a comprehensive and 'whole-sale' manner. . . . It almost follows from the 'logic' of the German federal system . . . lacking a single, possibly centrally-located powerful protagonist and trend-setter in public sector reform matters and, instead, disposing of a multitude of such arenas and actors each interacting in its own right (Schroeter and Wollmann 1997: 188).

In general, Germany, France and the much more consensual countries like Sweden, Norway and the Netherlands have—unlike the Anglo-Saxon NPM countries—conducted their reform initiatives more from the bottom with more moderate speed and without establishing a whole host of new organisations (like agencies).

Another feature of administrative reform—which surprisingly does not fit into a common prejudice about Germans—is the fact that many local authorities, despite the general idea of the 'New Steering Model', did not have a master plan when they started their reform efforts. Single, relatively often disjointed projects or pilot projects have been the order of the day, without any integrated or comprehensive modernisation approach covering all parts of the local authority completely. A further critical point concerning the implementation of reform ideas and concepts is that some public authorities have not been able to establish a proper (reform) project management and that employees have not been sufficiently involved in the reform process.

Although the German system of public service provision is—according to the differentiated structure of the public sector—highly diversified with a considerable choice for citizens, experiences with attempts to put direct service provision of public services by local authorities or public agencies under external market pressure with direct competition between public authorities and private firms are so far relatively unknown in Germany (see the figures for 'contracting out' in Table 10.1, and for details Roeber 2000). Competition as a general attitude in the public service is—compared to the UK, for example—still relatively rare (Barlow and Roeber 1996).[5] Most public servants are still extremely suspicious of any competitive pressure in the public sector because they are afraid that competitive tendering for their services will be the first step to privatisation and not—as is often said—its alternative. Even mild forms of competition in the form of comparing different local authorities according to specific performance indicators (e.g., unit costs, promptness of decision-making) or internal market competition in the public sector have started relatively late.[6] In this context, it is also worth mentioning that customer orientation and emphasis on service delivery as integral parts of a total quality management is still one of the weak spots in administrative reform in Germany. Unfortunately, visible and perceptible improvements for the citizens have essentially taken place only in the form of one-stop-shops with citizen-friendly offices.[7] This is probably going to change because of recent developments in electronic government, which will reshape the interface between citizens and public administration considerably (with further consequences for process reengineering in public bureaucracies).

Despite a fairly long tradition in (representative) local democracy for nearly 200 years, Germany has so far been relatively cautious about giving more direct power to citizens in communal affairs, when compared especially with the Scandinavian countries. Discussions on the empowerment of citizens (*Buergerkommune*) have begun only very recently. They can be regarded as attempts to overcome the distinctive orientation of private management models as shining examples and to bring back the political dimension in the discourse on administrative reform (similar ideas can be identified in the present debate on public governance).

GERMAN REFORM IN THE EUROPEAN CONTEXT

Irrespective of all difficulties in portraying complex social realities through more or less simple typologies, we can identify at least three main focal points of local government modernisation in Europe (Naschold 1997; Naschold et al. 1997). These may be identified as internal modernisation (with special reference to cost accounting, budgeting, organisational and personnel management), democratisation of local government (with special reference to local government autonomy, decentralisation of government, roles and competencies of politicians and top administrators, the relationship between adminis-trative bodies and citizens) and market-oriented organisation devel-opments (with special reference to privatisation, market testing, compulsory competitive tendering, principal agent models).

As we have seen, the German approach to administrative reform is very strongly focused on internal rationalisation in order to in-crease public-sector productivity and achieve economic savings. Issues like strengthening local democracy (as, for example, in Scandi-navian countries) or competitive pressure (as in the UK) have so far played a minor role in the ongoing reform process. Some critics even say it is a reform from bureaucrats for bureaucrats which is barely interrelated with the spheres of politics, citizens and markets.

The reasons for reservations in Germany to adopt, especially the radical Anglo-Saxon reform philosophy, and to initiate dramatic changes in the public sector in the form of a paradigm shift from traditional Weberian bureaucracy to private-business-like arrange-ments can be seen inter alia in the following factors.

One of the main barriers for more management- or business-oriented reforms in Germany—which has been for more than 30 years much under discussion—seems to be the civil service law (which applies to civil servants) and respective labour conditions for public employees and workers. These regulations are more or less based on the traditional principles of a professional civil service (*hergebrachte Grundsaetze des Berufsbeamtentums*) which covers fea-tures like life-time main occupation and an appropriate salary ac-cording to the maintenance principle (*Alimentationsprinzip*), loyalty, political neutrality and moderation, complete dedication to public service (based on qualifications and the achievement principle), no right to strike, and subjection to special disciplinary regulations (Roeber 1996). The Civil Service Law can be regarded as an integral part of the Weberian model, which is—with its 'legal rule-bound hierarchical public administration' (Wollmann 2002: 11)—rooted in the tradition of the *Rechtsstaat* (see also Pollitt and Bouckaert 2000: 52–54). The law-oriented culture prevents administrative reformers in Germany from introducing far-reaching changes towards business-like management models for the public sector. A sudden spread of managerial professionalism with its business-like rationality in decision-making into the German public sector would be regarded as a 'clash of cultures'—with unforeseeable consequences for the stability of the politico-administrative system.

Another quite remarkable point seems to be the influence of the electoral system on strategies of administrative reform. In countries with proportional representation (and a relatively high likelihood of coalition governments like in Germany and in the Scandinavian countries), administrative reform manoeuvres are significantly less radical than in countries with a majority voting system ('first-past-the-post'). Governments with two or more parties seem to be more consensus oriented and seem to have moderating and integrative effects on the sweeping changes of the politico-administrative system. This constellation obviously prevents politicians and administrators from introducing radical reforms and initiating a dramatic shift from the traditional bureaucratic to a completely business-like paradigm.

Radical change—at least in the British case—has been influenced (Pollitt and Bouckaert 2000: 50; Rhodes 1997: 44) by a 'strong, directive and above all persistent, executive leadership' in combination with minimal constitutional barriers as far as political leadership is concerned, and by a clear and simple reform ideology. Germany does not have a similar consistent ideologically-driven role model of a 'modern' public sector. German politicians (even those from the conservative Christian Democratic Union and the 'market-radical' Liberal Democrats) and top administrators have been trying to follow the modernisation path very carefully and in a very cautious manner. There is still a relatively broad consensus that administrative reform must not erode the strength of traditional bureaucracy (like calculability, predictability, trust and propriety) for which the German bureaucracy has been especially famous.

CONVERGENCE, DIVERGENCE OR LEARNING FROM OTHER EXPERIENCES?

Despite an apparent inevitable tendency towards NPM (based either on radical approaches related to public choice theory or on more moderate models related to managerialism) (Reichard and Roeber 2001), the 'diversity of national regimes and practices' even in Europe is quite astonishing (Pollitt 2001: 935; Pollitt and Bouckaert 2000: Chapters 3 and 4). This nourishes some doubts about the overwhelming effects of globalisation and international competition on converging institutional arrangements in the public sector.

If it is true that there is far more talk about convergence than there is real convergence in action, then that can be explained in terms of normal organisational and political procedures— of people behaving rationally and straightforwardly within their own frames of reference and sets of incentives and symbols (Pollitt 2001: 934–35).

Administrative behaviour is obviously—despite more similarities in the prevailing philosophy of modernisation and in the use of management techniques—much more geared to basic state traditions, administrative cultures and constitutional roots of each country than expected.

Nevertheless, management-oriented reform is on the political agenda in all European countries. In order to get a better understanding of how this has happened and how the idea of a new public management has been disseminated (at least in Europe), it might be useful to refer to Powell and DiMaggio's (1991) typology of coercive, mimetic and normative isomorphism,[8] which represents an important contribution to the debate on social change. In general we can say that the spread of NPM ideas seems to be a mixture of mimetic and normative isomorphism. 'Mimetic' in the sense that without any doubt the international debate on public-sector reform in highly respected institutions like the World Bank or the Organisation for Economic Cooperation and Development (OECD) did have an effect on the perception of international benchmarks and best practice. 'Normative' in the sense that the community of management-oriented reformers (practitioners as well as scholars, consultants and politicians) has been growing over the past decade and has been able to constitute an increasing understanding of a common professional 'reform culture'.[9] These mutual perceptions may be a fertile 'breeding ground' for managing change and supporting organisational learning. But, as we have seen, the convergence in 'talk' has not found its expression in convergent decisions and actions (see also Pollitt 2001: 943–44).

This raises the question of to what extent and in which way countries can learn from each other as far as administrative modernisation is concerned. The idea that all countries learn from a certain blueprint and follow the same route of public sector modernisation (for example, in the sense that the strictly market-oriented and public-choice-based approach of the Anglo-Saxon countries is interpreted as the best practice and the best way) is obviously far too naïve. And it also seems absolutely unrealistic to believe—even in the European context—that reform concepts and experiences can be transferred from one country to another in the form of single-loop-learning. Pollitt's and Bouckaert's (2000) profound comparative analysis of 10 so-called reform countries provides impressive evidence of strong path-dependencies which result not only from different legacies and different starting points of administrative reform, but also from different ideas about the purpose of public-sector modernisation. Under these circumstances each country must find its own approach (which has to fit in the respective contextual environment) and must concentrate on what can finally be called the 'Frank Sinatra Doctrine' in Public Management: 'I did it my way'.

NOTES

1. The term 'public sector' covers core public administration, public agencies and private non-profit organisations.
2. The total workforce in the third sector is more than one million full-time employees (for details see Anheier et al. 1998).
3. General legislation is a characteristic feature of the complex system of inter-governmental relations between the federal government and the state governments due to different categories of federal legislation. These categories are exclusive legislation, concurrent legislation and general legislation. The federal level has the right of exclusive legislation in foreign affairs, defence, nationality law, trade and customs (Article 73 GG). Exclusive legislation of the states refers to (Article 70 GG) cultural matters, school education, broadcasting, police law and public order, local government law and special aspects of social services. Concurrent legislation will be used by the federation if uniformity for the Federal Republic is required (Article 74 GG); examples are civil law, criminal law, economic law, labour law, public welfare, social insurance including unemployment insurance, road and waterway traffic, and the most important taxes. General legislation comprises framework or skeleton laws which will be applied by the federal level if uniform enforcement of duties is required, e.g., civil service, film and press, town and country planning, identity cards and universities (Article 75 GG). In case of concurrent legislation, the state will only be free in legislation if the federal Diet does not make use of its legislative power. In case of general legislation the states must keep their own legislation within the limits of the federal framework law.
4. The focus on financial management has without any doubt been intensified by financial challenges and constraints in the context of German unification, which have been causing heavy financial burdens for all federal, state and local authorities.

5. Similar reservations with respect to market-type mechanisms can be observed in France and in the Scandinavian countries.
6. As far as benchmarking in the public sector is concerned, pioneering work has been done by the Bertelsmann Foundation and by the *Deutsche Hochschule für Verwaltungswissenschaften* in Speyer.
7. The one-stop-shop idea has played—apart from the United Kingdom—a prominent role, especially in the rural areas of France and of the Scandinavian countries.
8. Coercive isomorphism means that institutions can be forced by other institutions to behave in a certain manner. Mimetic isomorphism means that institutions copy concepts, which are regarded as modern or successful or just in fashion. Normative isomorphism means that organisational change is influenced by common perceptions and mentalities of professionals.
9. Coercive isomorphism is—apart from World Bank's structural adjustment programmes—the exception. Only some elements of the British approach can be classified as 'coercive'—for example, when local authorities have literally been forced overnight to accept the rigid regime of compulsory competitive tendering and to change their internal structures and procedures dramatically.

REFERENCES

Anheier, H.K. , Priller, E., Seibel, W. and Zimmer, A. 1998. *Der Dritte Sektor in Deutschland. Organisationen zwischen Staat und Markt im gesellschaftlichen Wandel*. 2nd edition. Berlin: Sigma.

Banner, G. 1991. 'Von der Behoerde zum Dienstleistungsunternehmen'. *Verwaltungsfuehrung/Organisation/Personal (VOP)*, 13: 6–11.

————. 1994. 'Neue Trends im kommunalen Management'. *Verwaltungsfuehrung/Organisation/Personal (VOP)*, 16: 5–12.

Banner, G. and Reichard, C. (eds). 1993. *Kommunale Managementkonzepte in Europa. Anregungen fuer die deutsche Reformdiskussion*. Stuttgart: Kohlhammer.

Barlow, J. and Roeber, M. 1996. 'Steering not Rowing. Co-ordination and Control in the Management of Public Services in Britain and Germany'. *The International Journal of Public Sector Management*, 9: 73–89.

Bertelsmann Foundation. 1993. *Democracy and Efficiency in Local Government*, Vol. I. Documentation of the International Research. Guetersloh: Bertelsmann Foundation Publishers.

Brunsson, N. 1989. *The Organisation of Hypocrisy: Talk, Decisions and Actions in Organisations*. Chichester: John Wiley.

Cm 1599. 1991. *Raising the Standard: The Citizen's Charter*. London: HMSO.

DiMaggio, P.J. and Powell, W.W. 1991. 'The Iron Cage Revisited: Institutional Isomorphism and Collective Rationality in Organizational Fields', in W.W. Powell, and P.J. DiMaggio (eds). *The New Institutionalism in Organizational Analysis*, pp. 63–82. Chicago: University of Chicago Press.

Elcock, H. 1998. 'German Lessons in Local Government: The Opportunities and Pitfalls of Managing Change'. *Local Government Studies*, 24: 41–59.

Groemig, E. 2001. 'Reform der Verwaltungen vor allem wegen Finanzkrise und überholter Strukturen'. *Der Staedtetag*, 3: 11–18.

Groemig, E. and Thielen, H. 1996. 'Staedte auf dem Reformweg. Zum Stand der Verwaltungsmodernisierung'. *Der Städtetag*, 9: 596–600.

Hill, H. and Klages, H. (eds). 1993. *Spitzenverwaltungen im Wettbewerb. Eine Dokumentation des 1. Speyerer Qualitaetswettbewerbs*. Baden-Baden: Nomos.

Kemp, P. 1990. 'Next Steps for the British Civil Service'. *Governance*, 3(2): 186–96.

Klages, H. and Loeffler, E. 1995. 'Administrative Modernization in Germany—A Big Qualitative Jump in Small Steps'. *International Review of Administrative Sciences*, 61(3): 373–83.

Kommunale Gemeinschaftsstelle (KGSt). 1991. *Dezentrale Ressourcenverantwortung: Ueberlegungen zu einem neuen Steuerungsmodell*. KGSt-Bericht 12/ 1991. Cologne: KGst-Publishers.

_____. 1993. *Das neue Steuerungsmodell: Begründung, Konturen, Umsetzung*. KGSt-Bericht 5/1993. Cologne: KGst-Publishers.

Lean State Advisory Committee. 1997. *Final Report*. Bonn: Federal Ministry of the Interior.

Naschold, F. 1997. *The Dialectics of Modernising Local Government. An Assessment for the Mid-90s and an Agenda for the 21st Century (Agenda 21)*. WZB discussion paper, FS II 97–205. Berlin.

Naschold, F., Oppen, M. and Wegener, A. (eds). 1997. *Innovative Kommunen*. Stuttgart: Kohlhammer.

Pollitt, C. 2001. 'Convergence: The Useful Myth?'. *Public Administration*, 79: 933–47.

Pollitt, C. and Bouckaert, G. 2000. *Public Management Reform. A Comparative Analysis*. Oxford: Oxford University Press.

Powell, W.W. and DiMaggio, P.J. (eds). 1991. *The New Institutionalism in Organizational Analysis*. Chicago: University of Chicago Press.

Reichard, C. 1997. 'Neues Steuerungsmodell: Local Reform in Germany', in W. Kickert (ed.). *Public Management and Administrative Reform in Western Europe*, pp. 59–79. Cheltenham: Edward Elgar.

_____. 2001. 'New Approaches to Public Management', in K. Koenig and H. Siedentopf (eds). *Public Administration in Germany*, pp. 541–56. Baden-Baden: Nomos.

Reichard, C. and Roeber, M. 2001. 'Konzept und Kritik des New Public Management', in E. Schroeter (ed.). *Empirische Policy—und Verwaltungsforschung. Lokale, nationale und internationale Perspektiven*, pp. 371–92. Opladen: Leske and Budrich.

Rhodes, R.A.W. 1997. 'Re-inventing Whitehall, 1979–1995', in W. Kickert (ed.). *Public Management and Administrative Reform in Western Europe*, pp. 43–58. Cheltenham: Edward Elgar.

Roeber, M. 1996. 'Country Study "Germany"', in D. Farnham, S. Horton, J. Barlow and A. Hondeghem (eds). *New Public Managers in Europe. Public Servants in Transition*, pp. 169–93. Houndmills and London: Macmillan Business.

Roeber, M. 2000. 'Competition—How Far Can You Go?'. *Public Management. An International Journal of Research and Theory,* 2: 311–35.

Roeber, M. and Loeffler, E. 2000. 'Germany: The Limitations of Flexibility Reforms', in D. Farnham and S. Horton (eds). *Human Resources Flexibilities in the Public Services. International Perspectives,* pp. 115–34. Houndmills and London: Macmillan Business.

Schrijvers, A.P.M. 1993. 'The Management of a Larger Town'. *Public Administration,* 71: 595–603.

Schroeter, E. and Wollmann, H. 1997. 'Public Sector Reforms in Germany: Whence and Where? A Case of Ambivalence'. *Administrative Studies/Hallinnon Tutkimus,* 3: 184–200.

Wollmann, H. 2001. 'Germany's Trajectory of Public Sector Modernisation: Continuities and Discontinuities'. *Policy & Politics,* 29: 151–69.

————. 2002 . 'The Variance of Public Sector Modernization in Different National Contexts. Convergence or Divergence?', Paper presented to the conference 'Good Governance in Democratic Societies in Cross-cultural Perspective'. Kolkata. 25–27 April 2002.

CHAPTER 11

ADMINISTRATIVE REFORM IN INDIA: POLICY PRESCRIPTIONS AND OUTCOMES

KULDEEP MATHUR

Concern about reforming public administration in India is not something new. What is new is the context in which it is being talked about today. The period beginning from 1991 is marked by the emergence of a liberal economic regime that is attempting to dismantle the centrally directed framework of economic development. It is also the beginning of the period when the international multilateral agencies have begun attaching conditionalities while giving aid. These conditionalities initially were limited to prescriptions on how the aid would be administered, but have gradually broadened their scope by suggesting reforms in the overall framework of governance itself. This is happening the world over. Reform is in the air and no country is left out of this global discourse. Changes in the intellectual climate that provided a new understanding of the role and scope of public administration propels this discourse while 'Reinventing Government' summarises and celebrates this new understanding.

When talking about the failure of the planned strategy of development, particularly in the achievements of the various five-year plans, the discussion usually veers around the impediments created by the inherited bureaucratic and administrative system of the British colonial days. The planners were quite conscious of the need for a different system to implement the planned objectives of development and wrote so in chapters of several plan documents. The government responded to this concern by appointing many committees to suggest changes in the system. In this expression of concern for administrative reform, public administration emerged as an academic discipline in India and provided the intellectual background for suggestions to improve public administration in practice. The intellectual analysis of the problems of public administration and nature of efforts at administrative reform are closely linked. The purpose of this chapter is to examine the efforts at administrative reform in India and analyse the context in which they were made. It is debatable whether these efforts made any substantive impact on the practice of public administration in India. The second part of the chapter will attempt to discuss some reasons why these efforts merely chanted the same litany of complaints against an ineffective administration without making any headway on the ground. Finally, the chapter will focus on the challenges facing the government in the post-economic reform period to see whether the experience will be different from the earlier one.

THE COLONIAL LEGACY

The building blocks for the study of public administration in India were provided by the contribution of many British administrators mainly belonging to the Indian Civil Service (ICS). Many of these contributions were in the nature of memoirs, and apart from being descriptive of the customs and manners of Indian society, were rich in detail of the working of the British Indian administration. One of the major outcomes of these writings was the creation of what has come to be known as the 'ICS mythology' and a romantic view of field administration. One of the premier representatives of the most romanticised version of the role of the ICS is 'The Guardians', the second volume of Philip Woodruff's well-known study, *The Men Who Ruled India* (1954). Even though Woodruff asserted that the term guardians was his own, several writers (ex-civil servants) joined him in perpetuating the myth of the altruistic characteristics of the ICS in which platonic guardianship and men being of superior virtue dominated. The love of outdoor life, commitment to the district and the welfare of its population, courage and daring in decision-making, independence and integrity were among the many other virtues that the ICS seemed to possess. The Indian members of the ICS helped in perpetuating these myths through their own writings in the post-independence era (see Chettur 1964; Panjabi 1965).

A number of scholars, particularly British, also joined in this chorus. A rhetorical question like the following was asked: 'How is it, that 760 British members of the ruling Indian Civil Service could as late as 1939, in the face of the massive force of India national movement led by Gandhi, held down 378 million Indians?' (quoted in Spangenburg 1976: 4). Such a question implied that the British had the skills to govern India. This assertion was based on three essential myths: the myth of the popularity of the civil service as a profession that attracted the best minds, the myth of efficiency in administering India and the myth of sacrificial *esprit de corps* of the ICS which ostensibly infused the government with the primary concern of working for the welfare of the people.

For the British, the perpetuation of this myth served many functions. It came as a defence of British imperialism in the court of world public opinion. Teddy Roosevelt, at the end of his second term as President in 1909, cited British administration in India as a prime example of overwhelming advancement achieved as a result of white or European rule among the 'peoples who dwell in the darker corners of the earth' (Spangenburg 1976: 7). It also helped assuage internal opinion in England, reassuring the British ruling classes that British rule was beneficial to India.

This myth not only survived but also prospered many years after independence. The basic framework of administration continued as if the colonial administrators had not departed at all. As an Indian journalist later remarked, 'this would be unbelievable were it not true', but Nehru and his colleagues sought to build 'a new India, a more egalitarian society . . . through the agency of those who had been the trained servants of imperialism—it is as if Lenin, on arrival in Russia, had promptly mustered the support of White Russians he could find' (quoted in Potter 1986: 2). What is paradoxical is that this myth has persisted well on to the 1980s, and has resulted in the general posture adopted by the civil servants and professionals in dealing with politicians and development processes.

The inability of the national leadership to bring about change in the early 1950s set the old system of administration in firm saddle. Nehru, writing much before independence, had said,

I am quite sure that no new order can be built up in India so long as the spirit of the ICS pervades our administration and our public services. That spirit of authoritarianism . . . cannot exist with freedom . . . . Therefore, it seems essential that the ICS and similar services must disappear completely as such before we can start real work on a new order (Nehru 1953: 8).

In the spring of 1964 Nehru was asked at a private meeting with some friends what he considered to be his greatest failure as India's first Prime Minister. He reportedly replied 'I could not change the administration, it is still colonial administration' (quoted in Potter 1986: 2).

The essential point is that the British administration upheld by its many myths survived and entrenched itself well into the postcolonial period. However, the introduction of the Community Development Programme first raised the demand of a new type of administrator who would be unrelated to the colonial one. The administrators began to be told that a programme of social change like that of community development could not be implemented successfully through colonial administrative structures and procedures. The administrators were exhorted to identify with rural life.

THE REFORM EFFORT

The emphasis on the schism between the old and the new gained scholarly attention really after Paul Appleby, a Professor at Syracuse University, was invited by the Government of India to report on Indian administration. He expressed the view that there was a dichotomy between bureaucratic dispositions and development needs in India (Appleby 1953). Some Ford Foundation experts reinforced this view when they recalled their work in community development programmes and commented that '. . . the inadequacies of the Indian bureaucracy are not due to the fact that it is bureaucracy but due to considerable fact that it carries too much baggage from the past' (Taylor et al. 1966: 579). This view gained further support when scholars like La Palombara (1963: 1) wrote 'Public Administration steeped in the tradition of the Indian Civil Service may be less useful as developmental administrators than those who are not so rigidly tied to the notions of bureaucratic status, hierarchy and impartiality'.

Simultaneously, the development administration movement was gaining momentum within the discipline of public administration.

This thrust had several dimensions among which at least two dominated. One was of professionalisation of administration through the acceptance of a management orientation. It was argued that management techniques and tools could be used successfully to improve the implementation of development programmes, and administrators must spend significant time and effort in learning these techniques and applying them. Improved education and training became the core efforts at professionalisation.

Another dimension of this movement had to do with the change of behavioural orientation of public administrators. This focus was aptly summed up by a leading contributor when he suggested that only by becoming less oligarchic, less technocratic, less stratified, closer to the administered and the managed, more deeply rooted in the aspirations and needs of the ordinary people, can public service become a force with which the people of a developing country may identify and in which they may have justified confidence (Gross 1974).

It was this message that the academics and consultants from the West, particularly the United States of America, brought to India and through financial and technical aid they influenced the theory and practice of public administration in the country. The Ford Foundation alone spent US$ 360,400 in grants to institutions and US$ 76,000 in providing consultants and specialists to improve public administration in India during 1951–62 (Braibanti 1966: 148). An important consequence of this financial and technical aid as well as the intellectual thrust of development administration was that it began to be believed that change in the colonial administrative system lies in changing the behaviour and professional capacity of the individual bureaucrat. This was possible through education and training programmes. Training institutions proliferated and studies that supported this broad argument multiplied. A large number of scholars was attracted to the field of development administration, motivated not only by scholarly reasons but also by the belief that administration was the instrument of change and administrative behaviour could be transformed without structural changes in the colonial administrative structure and procedure.

During the period 1952–66, policies of administrative reform were heavily influenced by the developments in disciplinary understanding of public administration in the US, and the perceptions of these academics and consultants of the problems of administration in developing countries like India. It was at the request of the Government of India that the Ford Foundation readily made available Professor Paul Appleby of Syracuse University to suggest changes in the administrative system in the country. He presented a Report in 1953 that set the tone of much of what was done later. What is important to note is that till 1966 no other committee was appointed to take a broad look at administration. As a consequence of the Appleby Report, organisation and methods divisions were established in each government department to take care of the everyday issues of procedural efficiency. Another recommendation of Paul Appleby to establish an Indian Institute of Public Administration was also accepted. This institute was supposed to take up reform measures on a continuous basis based on research studies.

In operational terms, the effort at administrative reform during this period was based on education and training programmes for civil servants. International aid was extensively utilised for this purpose. A large number of training institutions were established at both the central as well as state levels. The pattern of recruitment to the higher civil services was changed and the training system was also reformed.

A comprehensive examination of the Indian administrative system was undertaken with the appointment of the Administrative Reforms Commission in 1966. It was patterned after the Hoover Commission of the US, having a political and civil servant membership with experts coming in to write reports after study and research. The Commission worked over a period of four years making a total of 581 recommendations (Maheshwari 1993: 116). Little impact of the Commission was felt for no recommendations of consequence were accepted. The politicians who became members did not command prestige and influence with the government of the day. As a matter of fact, the government itself was in a flux. Lal Bahadur Shastri, the Prime Minister, who had appointed the Commission in 1965, suddenly died and Indira Gandhi took over. For the years up to 1971, she was fighting for her political survival, attending to crises and did not find time to reflect on administrative change. When the Commission finished its tasks, the country was facing a war for the liberation of Bangladesh, and subsequently was caught in the turmoil of the national Emergency. The ruling party was comfortable working with the existing administrative system and reforming it was not on the agenda of the political parties in the Opposition. The Administrative Reforms Commission just faded away leaving behind a pile of reports and frustration at the national inability to reform a colonial administrative system.

If during the early period of India's independence administration was seen as instrument of change, in the period after the Third Plan 1961–66, it began to be seen as an impediment to development. Plan performance had been poor and the policy makers saw lack of effective administration as a major contributing factor. As a matter of fact, in 1969, the Congress Party itself raised the issue of the inability of a neutral civil service to implement goals of development. It pleaded for a committed civil service. The question 'committed to what' was left open. A fierce debate followed in which retired and serving bureaucrats participated freely (see Chaturvedi 1971; Dubhashi 1971; *Seminar* 1973). No formal change took place but the practice of shifting bureaucrats on demands of political leadership began a practice that is spread widely in the system today. The period of Emergency when loyalty became an important criterion for holding a pivotal position in government was replicated when the Janata Party came to power defeating the Congress and Mrs. Gandhi. The return of the Congress and the defeat of the Janata Party in 1980 signalled the beginning of the process again. The practice has spawned what is colloquially known as the 'transfer industry' and the central government has begun to reflect what was confined to states only (Banik 2001). Formal acceptance of this idea would have transformed the role of the civil service but this did not happen. What could not be formalised was openly accepted in practice.

FAILURE OF THE REFORM EFFORT

One possible reason that administrative reform failed to make a dent in the inherited administrative system was the weakness on the conceptual front. No alternative was offered. What was offered was ways to improve the existing system. And these ways were too inconsequential. Intellectually, adherence to the Weberian Model and Taylorian norms of work considerably constrained the generation of alternatives. Overwhelming academic response to administrative problems was through analyses of structural attributes that caused bottlenecks in coordination or communication, or of the behavioural irritants that led to friction either in a team of bureaucrats only or one of bureaucrats and politicians. The prescription was already decided and not questioned, and therefore when the problems persisted, the solution was to increase the dosage of further division of labour and specialisation or tighten controls through improved lines of communications and authority.

The problem was that the empirical insights did not reflect the dominant concerns in the intellectual study of public administration where Weberian influences held the attention of most scholars who explained variations in administrative performance by examining issues of neutrality, training and professionalism, structure of hierarchies and processes of work, and behavioural orientations. Another source of explanation was the emphasis on the abilities and qualities of an individual and the belief that it was an individual who made the difference whatever be the structural constraints. A development-oriented bureaucrat implemented programmes well in spite of the prevailing administrative system. The memoirs of the civil servants are replete with illustrations that show how they as individuals dealt with new political issues (see for a recent example, Dar 1999).

Little concern for administrative reform was expressed in the 1970s and later. Severe indictment of the civil service was made by the Shah Commission of Inquiry, which reported that it carried out instructions from politicians and administrative heads on personal and political considerations. There were many cases where officers curried favour with politicians by doing what they thought the people in authority desired. In short, the evidence showed, as a journalist remarked, '(the Emergency was) the high watermark of the politicians' victory in the long drawn out struggle against the civil service' (quoted in Potter 1986: 157).

In the last two decades, the story of administration as an impediment to development has taken a drastic turn. If the beginning of the plan period saw an effort to strengthen state intervention as a recipe for triggering development, the 1980s ended with disastrous accounts of failures of regulatory and interventionist states and with strong pleas to dismantle state machinery and its roles. Neo-liberal economic theory tended to build its case on how rulers extract resources and invest them. It argued that rulers in interventionist states tend to use resources for their own benefit to the detriment of the development of their societies. The argument of state failure was based on how monopoly rents are created through the imposition of regulation and control of the economy. Political pressures dominate economic policy formulation and execution. A consequence of this system is that government machinery is used for personal interests. The policy recommendation that follows from this diagnosis is to minimise state intervention and to rely increasingly on markets for resource use and allocation.

RENEWED EFFORTS

The above diagnosis of the failure of the government in development led to a rethinking about the structure and role of public administration. A kind of revolution occurred and the focus shifted from control of bureaucracy and delivery of goods and services to increasingly privatise government and shape its role as an entrepreneur competing with other social groups and institutions to provide goods and services to the citizens. The book of Osborne and Gaebler, *Reinventing Government* (1992), was a landmark in the growth of ideas that have sought to build a new public administration. Public administration was admonished to 'steer rather than row', for 'those who steer the boat have far more power than those who row it' (Osborne and Gaebler 1992: 32). Since then, these ideas have swept across the world and the international/multilateral agencies have used them to influence public management of their economic aid programmes. The common theme in the myriad applications of these ideas has been the use of market mechanisms and terminology in which the relationship of public agencies and their customers is understood as based on self-interest, involving transactions similar to those occurring in the market place. Public managers are urged to steer not row their organisations, and they are challenged to find new and innovative ways to achieve results or to privatise functions previously provided by government (Denhardt and Denhardt 2000: 550). In this new world, the primary role of the government is not merely to direct the actions of the public through regulation and decree, nor is it merely to establish a set of rules and incentives through which people will be guided in the proper direction. Rather, the government becomes another player in the process of moving society in one direction or another. Where traditionally the government has responded to needs by saying 'yes, we can provide service' or 'no, we cannot', the new public service suggests that elected officials and public managers should respond to the requests of the citizens by saying 'let us work together to figure out what we are going to do, and then make it happen' (ibid.: 554).

Operationally these ideas have advocated (*a*) managerially-oriented administration, (*b*) reducing public budgets, (*c*) downsizing the government, (*d*) selective privatisation of public enterprises, (*e*) contracting out of services, (*f*) decentralisation, (*g*) transparency and accountability, and (*h*) emphasis on civil society institutions and non-governmental organisations (NGOs) to deliver goods and services.

When India embarked upon an ambitious programme of economic reform in 1991, the ideas about public administration reform had already entered the package of aid that was promised by the World Bank and the International Monetary Fund (IMF). It will be fair to say that they were reflecting a change in the disciplinary thrusts of public administration too. Country after country was deciding to change and reform their governments. There is little doubt that this change was being triggered by the wave of policies of structural adjustment and liberalisation prompted by a new globalisation that set in after the collapse of the Soviet Union. So while administrative reforms are profoundly domestic issues, the fact that they are being seen as part of the package of the 'new deal' makes them open to external pressures and influences. Reform is stylish today. And for more than one reason. Technological changes are calling for managerial changes. Information technology with its computer base has caught the imagination of both administrators and politicians. Demands for greater decentralisation are being met because of change in the political scenario. People's groups are becoming more aware of their rights and demanding improved government services that are transparent and accountable to them. This is apart from the influence that the international financial agencies are exercising on the government to reform to be eligible for more loan/aid and directly funding the NGOs to implement development programmes.

The effort at reducing the size of government began with successive budgets presented by the Union Finance Minister from 1992. The imperative need was to reduce the fiscal deficit and cut down on unproductive expenditure. In a bid to bring about fiscal prudence and austerity, the centre imposed a 10 per cent cut across the board in the number of sanctioned posts as on 1 January 1992. The Fifth Pay Commission that submitted its report contained a recommendation for a whopping one-third cut in government size in 10 years. The downsizing exercise was later taken up by the Expenditure Commission, which further recommended a cut in the number of sanctioned posts as on 1 January 2000. As a matter of fact, instructions for cutting sanctioned posts were renewed in 2000 directing a 10 per cent reduction in the posts created between 1992–99 (Raina 2002). Statistics maintained by the Ministry of Finance show that the pay and allowances bill of the central government was Rs 339.7779 billion for the year 1999–2000, showing a hike of Rs 315.6019 billion over the previous year. The number of central government civilian regular employees was 3.855 million on 1 March 2000 down from 3.907 million on 31 March 1999. There had been a decrease of 51,605 posts or of just 1.32 per cent (Mishra 2002). As one can see, there is very little impact of these efforts.

In 1996, a Chief Secretaries Conference reiterated the popular policy prescriptions for a responsive and effective administration. The Conference recognised that the public image of the bureaucracy was one of inaccessibility, indifference, procedure orientation, poor quality and sluggishness, corruption proneness, and non-accountability for result (Government of India 1996: 1). The Fifth Pay Commission (Government of India 1997) took the concerns of the Chief Secretaries, listed among many of its recommendations, the need to downsize the government and to bring about greater transparency and openness in government.

Two developments of significance took place. A Chief Minister's Conference endorsed the issue of transparency through citizens' right to information in 1997. In addition, the concept of a Citizen's Charter took shape. Both were a follow-up on the recommendations of the Pay Commission, which in turn was in a way responding to grassroots demands in villages of Rajasthan.

A people's organisation in Rajasthan, known as Mazdoor Kisan Shakti Sangathan (MKSS), has been in the vanguard of this struggle and forced the government to respond to the demands of information and accountability. As documented (in Roy et al. 2001), the people began to understand that their livelihood, wages and employment depended a great deal on the investments made by the government as a development agency. If these benefits were not coming, then they had the right to know where the investment occurred and how much of it was actually spent. The right to economic well-being got translated into right to information. As Roy et al. (2001) point out the struggle became for 'hamara paisa hamara hisab'. In other words, accountability became a critical issue in the public hearings organised in five blocks of four districts. Four demands were made: transparency of development spending, accountability, sanctity of social audit, and redressal. This campaign began in 1994 and gradually gained momentum, spreading to most parts of the state. It reached the level where assurances had to be provided by the Chief Minister (*The Statesman* 1998).

The essence of the campaign that steamrolled into a movement for the right to information was the *jan sunwai* (public hearing) where villagers assembled to testify whether the public works that have been met out of the expenditures certified by the government actually exist or not. The first *jan sunwai* was held in a village of Kot Kirana in 1994. Since then they have caught the imagination of the MKSS that has held them at several places. Beawar was the scene of a major event in April 1996. It was followed by a 40-day dharna in which activists were fed and sheltered by the public. Another 53-day dharna was organised at Jaipur (see Roy 2001). The Rajasthan government responded reluctantly but the Chief Minister ultimately announced that the people had the right to demand and receive details of expenditure on development works in their villages.

Three months after the event in Beawar, politicians, jurists, former bureaucrats, academics, and others joined in demanding the right to information legislation at a conference in New Delhi. A committee under the chairmanship of Justice P.B. Sawant was authorised to draft a model bill. The central government too came under pressure to introduce legislation in the Parliament that could be followed by the states.

The Government of India set up a Working Group on Right to Information and Promotion of Open and Transparent Government in 1997. The terms of reference of the Group included the examination of feasibility and need to introduce a full-fledged Right to Information Act so as to meet the needs of an open and responsive government. The Working Group placed its tasks within the broad framework of democracy and accountability and emphasised, 'democracy means choice and a sound and informed choice is possible only on the basis of knowledge' (Government of India 1997: 3). It also argued that transparency and openness in functioning have a cleansing effect on the operations of public agencies and approvingly quoted the saying that sunlight is the best disinfectant.

The Working Group accepted the following broad principles in the formulation of the legislation:

1. disclosure of information should be the rule and secrecy the exception;
2. the exceptions should be clearly defined; and
3. there should be an independent mechanism for adjudication of disputes between the citizens and public authorities.

A draft bill has been prepared which was put to public debate and now the proposed legislation is lying with the Parliament for approval.

Transparency in government also became an issue on the agenda of the Conference of Chief Ministers held on 24 May 1997. The Conference issued a statement that provided an Action Plan for Effective and Responsive Government at the central and state levels. In this statement, the Chief Ministers recognised that secrecy and lack of openness in transactions is largely responsible for corruption in official dealings. The government set for itself a time limit of three months to ensure easy access of the people to all information relating to government activities and decisions, except to the extent required to be excluded on specific grounds like national security. The statement also gave an assurance that the Report of the Working Group on Right to Information would be quickly examined and legislation introduced before the end of 1997. Political events have taken over and the Act has yet to come into existence.

It is clear from the above that this dimension of administrative reform that stresses transparency and right to information is an issue that has been spearheaded by the people. It is not a change attempted by a well-meaning and benign government. However, the struggle has not yet been enough to get legislation passed by the Parliament or the state legislatures. There has been resistance not only from the political leaders who swear by the name of democracy but also from the bureaucrats whose norms of work had been dictated by secrecy and confidentiality. The Rajasthan experience has shown that even the local-level administrators have found ways to thwart attempts at opening the administration closest to the people for scrutiny.

The reason for resistance is not far to seek. Much of the corruption that occurs in official dealings takes place under the cover of state-sanctioned secrecy. The norm has been to keep information away from the people on the pretext of guarding public interest. A large number of national scams occur because no one knows what is happening in the closets of the government. At the local level, even the information on muster rolls is deemed to be confidential. So the movement for information has as its genesis the fight against corruption and demand for accountability. The muster rolls carried false names in Rajasthan villages and this could be identified only by the local people and not by the audit parties sent by the government. It is for this reason that the proposed bill does not provide the full opening of the file of decisions to the public. Who advises what will not be told. The recent incident, widely reported in the press, when the Urban Development Minister's order for placing a particular file on land deals for public scrutiny was reversed by the bureaucrats shows the fear of open decision-making (see *The Statesman* 1998).

Information, then, is also associated with power that the government exercises. By restricting information, people in government become more powerful than those who are outside it. Thus, demand for transparency and information is also about sharing of power. It is possible to misuse power when it is concentrated rather than when it is shared among a broader stream of people. As information grows, the arbitrariness of government tends to reduce. But the resistance from the local-level functionaries is growing in response to the *jan sunwais* held by the MKSS in Rajasthan. A recent newspaper report of *The Hindu* (13 March 2002) mentions how over 240 *sarpanchas* have organised themselves and waited on the Chief Minister to resist further *sunwais*.

It is this kind of resistance that has delayed the actual passage of the bill. It is necessary for the Parliament to take early steps to pass the law on the right to information. Godbole (2001: 1423) rightfully fears that the longer the delay in the passage of the bill, the weaker and more anaemic it is likely to be. Each successive draft bill on the subject prepared by the central government is a watered down version of the earlier bill and is a bundle of compromises affected to accommodate the stiff opposition to the proposed measures at the political and bureaucratic levels.

The citizen's right to information has been coupled with the idea of the Citizen's Charter. The aim of the Charter is to make available to the citizen the information to demand accountability, transparency, quality, and choice of services by the government departments. It was first introduced in Britain in 1991 to streamline administration and make it citizen friendly. A Core group has been set up under the Chairmanship of Secretary (Personnel) for monitoring the progress of initiatives taken by ministries/departments with a substantial public interface. So far, 61 Charters have been formulated, which include 27 Charters for public sector banks and four Charters for hospitals (Agnihotri 2000: 126). For lack of effective monitoring, this has remained a paper exercise.

CONCLUDING REMARKS

Some lessons can be drawn from the experience of administrative reforms in India. Those who resisted change have derived great inspiration from the support that Sardar Patel, India's first Home Minister, gave in saving the ICS and the steel frame. At the time of India's partition, he warned that chaos would result if the Civil Service was removed from the scene. Nehru agreed and civil service reform was not on high priority at the time when riots and uprisings had to be handled to maintain the integrity of the country. Since then, one crisis or the other has taken precedence and administrative reform commanded little attention. When it did, it was an administrative matter to be handled by the administrators themselves. The committees and commissions that came to review administration had administrators themselves as members. The administrators, for purposes of feasibility of implementation, processed even the recommendations of the Administrative Reforms Commission, 1966–70, that had a wide range of consultations with people from various professions. One reason could be that the understanding of public administration was heavily influenced by a paradigm that was inward looking and perceived bureaucracy as a more or less autonomous instrument of implementing development policies and programmes.

Another could be that political leadership saw an advantage in maintaining the status quo while continuing to articulate the need for radical reforms for public rhetoric. Mrs. Gandhi and her group quickly saw that the civil service could be 'committed' while continuing the public posture of neutrality. The Emergency period and the subsequent years of 'transfer industry' are ample evidence of keeping to form rather than substance. Even in questions of downsizing the government, a mantra from 1992 the same evidence is forthcoming. The A-level positions continue to remain largely untouched

while all reforms—reduction of positions or contracting out principles are targeted at lower levels. The Indian Administrative Service (IAS) or the Indian Police Service (IPS), which have held critical
positions in government, have never been under scrutiny for reforms
in spite of public outcry against their role and behaviour. The only
time that a serious attempt was made was when the Administrative
Reforms Commission made the recommendation of delimiting areas
of specialisation in the secretariat and manning these areas from
personnel drawn from all sources through a mid-career competition to
include more specialists in the higher positions. This recommendation was scuttled and not accepted by the government when the
IAS itself sought specialisation through training and postings.

In the ultimate analysis, civil service reform in India has neither
enhanced efficiency nor the accountability of the civil service in
any meaningful manner. As far as the common citizen is concerned,
it has not been effective. If Maheshwari (1972: 55) commented that
India's efforts at reform have amounted to correction slips to the
inherited system, Das (1998: 213), himself an IAS officer, has gone a
step further to indict the reform effort, around a quarter of a century
later, by saying that they were not even correction slips—they were
more in the nature of endorsement slips. Probably the present time
of structural adjustment, liberalisation, technological imperatives
and grassroots pressures may provide the best confluence of forces
that can break bureaucratic resistance and promote political will to
make the administrative system more open to reform and change.

The impact of such a confluence of forces is not without risks,
however. The global advocates of reform have assumed that one
size fits all and any government could be improved by the magic of
market, privatisation, participation and efficiency. But the expectations of people of their governments are different in different societies
and they are critical in redesigning reform activities. Reinventing
government in the US is based on different assumptions and these
may not even hold in the UK. As Peters (2001: 167) points out, 'the
central problem for implementing public management reforms in
developing countries is that their success to some extent depends
on the existence of public service values and practices that support
accountability and effective management'. Deregulation and granting
autonomy may mean that the empowered decision-makers may use
the new-found freedom to serve themselves rather than the public.

India faces the major challenge of redesigning an administrative system that can sustain itself in an environment of globalisation

and economic reform. The earlier efforts were partly failures because they assumed an image of the administrative system that was divorced from reality. It was rigid for most people but very flexible for the privileged among them. Rules were flouted with impunity, privatisation of public office was common and procedures were discarded on many personal pretexts. The classic Riggsian formalism was at work. It is the common citizen who lost confidence in administration, and this has to be restored first. This cannot come about only through tinkering with administrative design. It challenges the basic issues of governance itself.

REFERENCES

Agnihotri, Vivek K. 2000. 'Government of India's Measures for Administrative Reforms', in Vinod Mehta (ed.). *Reforming Administration in India*, pp. 123–34. New Delhi: Indian Council of Social Science Research and Har Anand Publications.

Appleby, Paul. 1953. *Public Administration in India: Report of a Survey*. Delhi: Government of India.

Banik, Dan. 2001. 'The Transfer Raj: Indian Civil Servants on the Move'. *The European Journal Development Research*, 13(1): 106–34.

Braibanti, Ralph. 1966. 'Transnational Inducement of Administrative Reform', in J.D. Montgomery and W.J. Siffin (eds). *Approaches to Development, Politics and Change*, pp. 133–83. New York: McGraw-Hill.

Chaturvedi, M.K. 1971. 'Commitment in Civil Service'. *Indian Journal of Public Administration*, 17(1): 40–46.

Chettur, S.K. 1964. *The Steel Frame and I*. Bombay: Asia Publishing House.

Dar, R.K. (ed.). 1999. *Governance and the IAS: In Search of Resilience*. New Delhi: Tata McGraw-Hill.

Das, S.K. 1998. *Civil Service Reform & Structural Adjustment*. Delhi Oxford University Press.

Denhardt, Robert B. and Denhardt, Janet V. 2000. 'The New Public Service: Serving Rather than Steering'. *Public Administration Review*, 60(6): 549–59.

Dubhashi, P.R. 1971. 'Committed Bureaucracy', *Indian Journal of Public Administration*, 17(1): 33–39.

Godbole, Madhav. 2001. 'Right to Information. Write the Law Right'. *Economic and Political Weekly*, April 22: 1423–28.

Government of India. 1996. *Action Plan for Effective and Responsive Administration*. Statement Adopted at the Conference of Chief Ministers. New Delhi.

————. 1997. *Report of the Working Group on Right to Information and Promotion of Open and Transparent Government*. New Delhi: Department of Personnel and Administrative Reforms, Government of India.

Gross, P.M. 1974. 'The Limits of Development Administration in United Nations'. *Proceedings of the Inter-Regional Seminar on Organization and Administration of Development and Planning Agencies.* New York: United Nations.

La Palombara, J. (ed.). 1963. *Bureauçracy and Political Development.* Princeton: Princeton University Press.

Maheshwari, Shriram. 1972. *The Administrative Reforms Commission.* Agra: Laxmi Narain Agarwal.

Maheshwari, S.R. 1993. *Administrative Reform in India.* Delhi: Jawahar Publishers.

Mishra, D. 2002. 'Quality Government for Sound Economy'. *The Hindustan Times* (New Delhi). 8 February.

Nehru, Jawaharlal. 1953. *An Autobiography.* Oxford: Oxford University Press.

Osborne, David and Gaebler, Ted. 1992. *Reinventing Government: How the Entrepreneurial Spirit is Transforming the Public Sector.* New Delhi: Prentice-Hall.

Panjabi, K.L. (ed.). 1965. *Civil Servant in India.* Bombay: Bhartiya Vidya Bhawan.

Peters, Guy B. 2001. *The Future of Governing.* Lawrence: University Press of Kansas.

Potter, David C. 1986. *India's Political Administrators 1919–1983.* Oxford: Clarendon Press.

Raina, Jay. 2002. 'Downsizing May be Uphill Task'. *The Hindustan Times* (New Delhi). 8 February.

Roy, Aruna, Dey, Nikhil and Singh, Shanker. 2001. 'Demanding Accountability'. *Seminar.* April.

Roy, Bunker. 2001. *The Asian Age.* (New Delhi). 30 May.

Seminar. 1973. 'Committed Civil Service A Symposium'. *Seminar,* 168. August.

Spangenburg, Bradford. 1976. *British Bureaucracy in India: Status, Policy and the ICS, in the Late 19th Century.* Delhi: Manohar Book Service.

The Statesman. 1998. 'Bureaucrats Misled Cabinet on CVC Draft, Charges Jethmalani'. *The Statesman.*

Taylor, Carl C., Ensminger, Douglas, Johnson, Helen W. and Joyce, Jean. 1966. *India's Roots of Democracy.* New York: Praeger.

Woodruff, Philip. 1954. *The Men Who Ruled India.* London: Jonathan Cape.

CHAPTER 12

GOVERNANCE REFORMS IN INDIA: RESPONSIBLE CIVIL SERVANTS' VIEW FROM THE INSIDE

V.K. AGNIHOTRI AND R.K. DAR

THE HISTORICAL CONTEXT

Indian administration is a mix of diverse practices that have been assimilated over centuries. The classical tradition of statecraft is well documented in Kautilya's *Arthashastra*, which was written sometime between 321 and 300 BC. Proceeding from the premise that the state was an institutional necessity for human advancement, the book outlines how the state should be managed for the maximum happiness of its citizens. Perhaps this treatise should be regarded as a responsible civil servants' manual for those times, balancing the needs of daily operations and policy advisory functions of the civil services, with a rather high-minded view of kingship.

The administrative system in ancient India reached its pinnacle during the reign of Ashoka (273–232 BC). The main instrument of Ashokan administration was propagation of *Dhamma*, which has been variously described as 'Moral Order', 'a common Code of Conduct' or an 'Ethical Order'. One of the measures of administrative reforms undertaken by Ashoka was appointment of *Dhamma Mahamatyas* (ministers) for the propagation of *Dhamma*, redressing public grievances and distribution of charitable gifts among the subjects as well as foreigners. He also undertook measures for the welfare of women, judicial reforms relating to fair justice and uniformity in judicial procedures, opening of hospitals for human beings and animals, and programmes of public works. This tradition continued to flourish, with temporal modifications, till the beginning of the Islamic invasions.

The next major constituent of the Indian tradition in public administration was that of the Mughals, particularly as it evolved under Akbar (AD 1556–1605), an insight into which is provided by Abul Fazl's *Ain-i-Akbari* (AD 1590). The Mughal administration presented a combination of Indian and extra-Indian elements or, more correctly, it was the 'Perso-Arabic system in an Indian setting'. Generally speaking, in village administration and lower rungs of the official ladder, the earlier practice was allowed to prevail. The Mughal empire was a centralised despotism based on military power; it followed the policy of 'individualistic minimum interference', assuming responsibility only for law and order and revenue collection. It was a city-oriented and 'paper' government. Its officers had to maintain several records, such as copies of correspondence, nominal rolls, books of accounts in duplicate or triplicate, etc. (Maheshwari 2000).

The third and more recent influence on Indian Public Administration has been of the East India Company (1600–1858) as it stumbled into a power role, and the British Crown (1858–1947). This phase was marked by the maintenance of administrative continuity with the past and Indian adaptation of the old structures to the needs of the Company and the Crown. The British rulers left their mark in terms of political integration and administrative unification, rule of law and equality before law, a limited exposure to parliamentary democracy as well as local self-government, a merit-based civil service system, elaborate and relatively stable rules, procedures and regulations, consolidation of the district as the basic unit of administration, and the use of English as an official language (Maheshwari 2000).

During the long drawn out freedom struggle, Indian leaders and parties devoted considerable thought to the post-independence design of the state and its institutions, as well as to development planning policy options with an emphasis on the public sector. However, independence from the British Crown in 1947 came with extraordinarily violent convulsions and instability, linked to the largely unforeseen consequences of the partition of the country. Many of the more idealistic notions of local and regional democracy had to be abandoned, and a more centralised 'Union of States' came into existence than was foreseen. The Constitution finally included rather unusual provisions for extending protection to the permanent bureaucracy and for the creation of key All-India Services for civil and police administrative leadership.

Several measures were initiated to create new constitutional and administrative institutions and enterprises and to bring about administrative reforms soon after the country gained independence in 1947, especially in order to meet the challenges of development administration. More than 20 committees and commissions have been appointed to go into various aspects of public administration in India. Two major landmarks have been the report of Administrative Reforms Commission (Government of India 1970) and the Fifth Central Pay Commission (Government of India 1997b). Equally important was the contribution of the Balwantray Mehta Committee (Government of India 1957), which addressed the issues of decentralisation and structure of the Panchayati Raj institutions.

New impulses for reform, this time across a wide area, had their origin in the demands made by a modern minded and young Prime Minister (Rajiv Gandhi) in the mid-1980s who started to talk about preparing India for the 21st century and for strong local self-governing institutions. However, the real push for a major policy overhaul in the early 1990s came with the collapse of the antiquated foreign exchange regime and mounting budgetary crises. By now, governance reform was taking place across many sectors and in many places. The main theatres of the battles of reform are: redefinition of the role of the state and its enterprises; macro-economic policy formulation and interventions; reforms of financial systems and institutions; industrial policy and foreign investments regulations; sectoral initiatives in key infrastructure development-related areas like transport, power and communications; urban development and services; water resources management; the 'soft' areas of social development; management and reorientation of scientific and technological development regimes; and the management processes of the government.

One common factor that is forcing the pace of change in all public-funded or public-supported departments, institutions, industrial and commercial units, etc., is that of severe budgetary constraints being faced by the centre and the states, with governments having to borrow even to meet administrative and maintenance costs. At all points of the governmental structure there is a serious situation of far too many claimants clamouring for access to limited public funds.

A common exogenous factor is the changing information and communication technology situation. A new computer-savvy generation is rapidly coming up, even as an older generation has begun to come to terms with the technology. However, the critical mass of applications in government is not yet in sight.

Naturally, the central pressure point for the politician in power is the periodic electoral challenge in which the impact and value of relatively good or bad governance tends to register in a decisive way. The importance of performance, howsoever defined in the local contexts, is clearly seen in the return to power of incumbents in West Bengal and Madhya Pradesh in 2001 and the election losses of incumbents in 2002 in the states of Uttar Pradesh, Punjab and Uttaranchal.

Debates and questions in Parliament also involve scrutiny of reforms on a regular basis in different contexts and settings where the government seeks to explain and defend the working of initiatives for reforms in all fields.

The Judiciary is another source of reform even as it deliberates and decides, among others, on the rising numbers and range of Public Interest Litigation (PIL) applications being moved before it. Judicial orders have led to changes in many areas, notably so in respect to issues relating to the environment and social and individual rights.

Academia and intellectuals, the corporate sector representative associations, NGOs and other social activists, and the media are equal contributors of ideas and provide pressure for reforms.

From this very wide field, for the present chapter, the detailed examination in the following sections selects the segment that directly originates from and intends to impact on the vital internal management system of government; it is on this core that the administrative reform (AR) initiatives act. While the origin of the formal-legal administrative systems is in the 'virtual world' of various past policies and inherited or new laws, statutory rules and regulations, the 'real world' of their actual structural design and detail is mostly the product of the 'discretionary' exercise of executive powers by the government in the form of operating orders, directions, guidelines, instructions, etc., issued from time to time. These executive orders lay down the conditions for and parameters within which the innumerable organisations, agencies, institutions and enterprises of government and their respective personnel would function. It is this face that the external agents and citizens interact with. The devil is in these peculiar details.

The AR function in government, inter alia, covers the wage policy and structure, the human resource recruitment and management systems, the respective and comparative hierarchical structures and parities of various entities within the system, office procedures and codes, accounting, training, and to some extent also the broad general common purposes to be served by all organisations within the governmental ambit.

The monitoring or coordinating mechanisms for the AR actions across the board are not many, since it is in the nature of the vast and complex administrative system that most of the specialised operations remain internal to a sector or unit of administration, while only some may be system-wide. At the bureaucratic level, the AR function receives the highest system support through a central level committee under the Cabinet Secretary (the top-most post within the bureaucratic structure), and in the inter-state context by the many ad hoc conferences summoned by the various central ministries. A Conference of the Chief Secretaries of the States was also called in November 1996 by the Cabinet Secretary to evolve a common position on AR as such. At the political level, a Conference of Chief Ministers that focused on AR was held in May 1997, and it provided policy guidelines and pledged political support for the agreed agenda (Government of India 1997a), outlined below.

The Fifth Central Pay Commission (Government of India 1997b), though primarily set up to determine the pay scales and other perks of government employees, devoted almost one-tenth of its report to administrative reforms. It recommended jettisoning of redundant activities, including privatisation and contracting out, changes in work methods and environment, improvement in administrative productivity and enforcement of accountability, transparency, and effective redressal of citizen's grievances. It recommended 'reinventing' the government offices by adoption of level jumping and de-layering and reintroduction of small and business-like Desk Officer Systems.

Despite this seemingly extensive range of involvement in reform agendas, including an Action Plan derived from the politically and bureaucratically agreed agenda and priorities, when a questionnaire to update progress as in 2002 was sent out by the AR department of the central government, it brought back responses which gave a very bleak picture of reform, as is noted below. It, therefore, appears essential to squarely face the central question as to how to account for such an indifferent quality of response. Why were the results so weak? The detailed examination of the various initiatives may well provide some clues.

ACTION PLAN FOR EFFECTIVE AND RESPONSIVE GOVERNMENT

As noted above, the Government of India had convened a Conference of Chief Secretaries in November 1996 relating to the urgency of AR in the changed context of the 1990s. The ensuing national debate on the issue of governance culminated in an Action Plan for Effective and Responsive Government which was discussed and adopted at the Conference of Chief Ministers of the States in May 1997. The three main themes dealt with in the Action Plan were: (*i*) accountable and citizen-friendly government; (*ii*) transparency and right to information; and (*iii*) improving the performance and integrity of the public services (Government of India 1997a). The specific initiatives recommended under these themes in the Statement adopted at the Chief Ministers' Conference comprised: preparation of citizen's charters; strengthening of the machinery for redressal of public grievances; review of administrative laws; people's participation; decentralisation and devolution of powers (first theme); legislation on freedom of/right to information; setting up of information and facilitation counters; e-governance (second theme); granting statutory status to the Central Vigilance Commission; revamping of vigilance procedures; legislation on Lokpal; introduction of an award scheme for government employees; preparation of a professional Code of Ethics for civil servants, minimum tenures for civil servants (third theme), etc. Subsequent initiatives encompass: rightsizing the government, procedural reforms, greater focus on the use of information technology in government, dissemination of good practices, quality initiative in government, etc. (Agnihotri and Narula 2002).

The initiatives of AR do not encompass a holistic framework of linkages. The performance of the whole administrative system is difficult to assess, varying as it does with the specific context of each departmental or state situation, the local priorities laid down for various formations from time to time, the administrative structure, wide range of the tasks involved, etc. The development and use of a framework of linkages should enable identification of the direct and immediate context of a particular component of AR, its impact on related structures, as well as its significance for the total or ultimate picture of reforms. It may also throw light on the locus of the commentator or observer, and possibly also on the complexities which may be at work in the interpretation of events, or the energy and interest that may be bestowed on the proposals for reform.

Scanning the foregoing sequence and content of the AR processes in the Indian scene, a classification of reforms may be suggested as follows:

1. Reforms pertaining to the legal basis of government action. Falling in this category would be the measures pertaining to review of administrative laws, the constitutional amendments to impart stability to the rural and urban local self-governing institutions, and legislation for an effective set of vigilance bodies.

2. Comprehensive or specific reforms of administrative structure, size and design (allocation of work, numbers, status and hierarchy, linkages, etc.), and administrative procedures. The application of Total Quality Management (TQM) concepts would clearly be within the comprehensive reforms category. Programmes for modernisation also provide an example of comprehensive reform that may be applied in specific organisations. Depending on its design, the project to encourage the use of modern information and communication technology could be comprehensive (networked) or the stand-alone type. Rightsizing and rationalisation of departmental organisations and enterprises, which has been seen as motivated by budgetary considerations, could equally be part of wider concerns about the role of the state, or blocking of space which could be more appropriately opened to private, cooperative, community or joint partnerships. Procedural reforms in financial decentralisation and delegation of powers, personnel management, vigilance, etc., are essentially meant to speed up internal or inter-departmental operations.

3. Reforms for an improved work culture within the bureaucratic machine. These aim at improving the speed, performance and integrity of governmental functionaries and cover different aspects of the presumed major obstacles to

reform, including the inertia of the personnel in place. Many of the initiatives essentially aim at the creation of better systems of human resource management (HRM). Reference may be made here to the effort to develop and enforce a system of a professional Code of Ethics in different establishments, over and above the prescribed Conduct Rules; the incomplete deliberations regarding a policy for minimum tenures and transfers, which impinge upon the morale, expertise and overall effectiveness of the civil services; updating know-how through training and dissemination of good practices; systems for employee grievance removal, disputes resolution and reduction of litigation; and use of incentives and awards, as well as of disincentives through tighter disciplinary and vigilance processes.

4. Reforms for a more mature relationship between government and civil society. These include the all-important interface with citizens (right to information, redress of grievances, charters of rights to service); with local self-governance institutions (the municipalities and panchayats); with NGOs, registered associations (for instance, of residents of urban localities, or of businesses) and societies; with elected and other public representatives; with academia and intellectuals; with the media; etc.

EVALUATION OF RECENT REFORM INITIATIVES[1]

CENTRAL GOVERNMENT REFORM INITIATIVES

The implementation of the Action Plan for Effective and Responsive Government in the Central Government has been slow and in several cases unidimensional. Only 91 Citizen's Charters out of a possible 400 or more have so far been issued. It is reported that in a late surge 50 Charters are in the pipeline. However, the evaluation of these Charters, taken up some time ago, has revealed that the quality of these Charters is lacklustre. Several organisations have simply renamed their information brochures as Charters. There is also an absence of awareness about the Charters and the principles underlying them among the citizens as well as employees. If implemented in the right spirit, Citizen's Charters have the potential to bridge the gap between citizen's expectations and the quality of public service delivery through change of mindset of the service providers and discharge of their own responsibilities by the citizens.

An attempt has been made to strengthen the machinery for redress of public grievances. However, given the magnitude of the problem, the islands of success are strewn with startling moments of truth.

The review of laws, which was initially bogged down by a series of elections to the Parliament, has made some progress (against 1,641 laws to be repealed or amended, 404 have been repealed and 45 have been amended) but the decision of the ministries/departments not to repeal (819) and not to amend (72) leaves much to be desired.

The best thing that could have happened to promote people's participation and decentralisation has already happened, namely, the Constitutional Amendments. Beyond that, the central government has not been able to push the agenda very far despite various circulars and guidelines for devolution of powers, functions and resources.

The Freedom of Information Act 2002 has yet to be implemented and the Lokpal Bill has been languishing in Parliament. A study undertaken by the Department of Administrative Reforms and Public Grievances shows that most of the information and facilitation counters set up by the central government ministries and departments are non-functional. The award scheme has remained a nonstarter. Moreover, e-governance, which requires massive process reengineering and a change of mindset, is yet to take root. The pace of modernisation of central government offices has been slow. The initiative for rightsizing is yet to bear fruit despite the announcement of a liberal voluntary retirement scheme for surplus employees. The Code of Ethics for civil servants is in a limbo.

STATE GOVERNMENTS' REFORM INITIATIVES

A review of the data collected from the states reflects a wide range, from several serious attempts at reforms to business as usual in many other cases.

As regards Citizen's Charters, most of them relate to agriculture, animal husbandry and forests, education, electricity and power supply, finance and revenue, food and civil supplies, health, home and police administration, industries, labour and employment, local bodies, social welfare, transport and urban development. Very few states

(Andhra Pradesh and Karnataka) have gone through an extensive consultation process in development of the Charters. In a unique experiment, the government of Gujarat has decentralised issuing of Citizen's Charters to district and sub-district units of various departments. It has thus reported issuing 293 Citizen's Charters.

Only a few states have reported conducting training programmes to sensitise employees about their duties and responsibilities vis-à-vis Citizen's Charters (e.g., Andhra Pradesh, Assam and Karnataka). Creating awareness among the citizens through a multi-media campaign has, however, found favour with a large number of states (e.g., Assam, Gujarat, Karnataka, Kerala, Rajasthan and the Union Territory of Andaman and Nicobar Islands). As regards the review and monitoring of Citizen's Charters, only the government of Karnataka has contemplated appointing an independent agency for the purpose; the others have resorted to internal reviews and inspections. On the issue of accountability, the government of Rajasthan has reported that the employees are liable to transfer if they fail to meet the commitments enjoined by the Charters. Conducting exit polls has also been proposed.

With regard to public grievances, as stated earlier, a few states have made innovative institutional arrangements for their redressal as well as evaluation of the mechanism. To measure citizen's satisfaction, the government of Gujarat has appointed *lok praharis* (People's Watchmen). The government of Punjab measures citizen's satisfaction on the basis of the percentage of disposal of grievances, while the government of Karnataka relies on in-favour disposal of grievances for this purpose. One state has reported that since the number of formal complaints is limited, it is presumed that the grievances are being redressed.

Review of laws, rules and regulation has made little headway in the states, with only three of respondents (Gujarat, Karnataka and West Bengal) reporting concrete progress. The greatest convergence in replies to the questionnaires has been achieved with regard to assessing the impact of this exercise, with all the states drawing a blank.

Even though the Right to Information Act is in place in several states, its implementation leaves much to be desired. Maharashtra is the only state to report that a review of the Act is in progress, based on experience. Several states (e.g., Gujarat, Haryana, Nagaland, Punjab and West Bengal) have neither contemplated legislation nor issued any executive instructions to provide access to the citizens to government records. A large number of states have equated computerisation and hosting of websites with transparency.

The data collected, in general, reveals that with increasing sophistication of the information sought the replies tend to become vague and stereotyped. There are several yeses with no details. There are the usual 'instructions issued', 'from time to time', 'proposed to be done', 'under consideration', 'being examined', etc. Some of the gems, of course, are 'need not felt' and 'being done regularly' (for review of laws), 'adequate delegation' and 'information awaited' (for people's participation), etc.

There are indeed a few candid admissions. Thus, the government of Karnataka has reported that many Citizen's Charters have been framed without understanding their true purpose. The government of Maharashtra has admitted that a lot more needs to be done in order to enforce accountability of administration through implementation of Citizen's Charters. The government of Uttar Pradesh has felt the need for training of personnel in order to remove obstacles to people's participation and decentralisation. The administration of the Union Territory of Andaman and Nicobar Islands has bemoaned the mindset of the bureaucracy.

On the whole, the governments of Andhra Pradesh, Karnataka and Gujarat appear to have fared better than others in implementing the Action Plan for Effective and Responsive Administration. The government of Andhra Pradesh, in particular, has adopted a systemic and holistic approach through formulation and implementation of 'Vision 2020' for the state as a whole.

None of the deadlines prescribed in the Action Plan (three months for operationalising Citizen's Charters, three months for revamping of procedures for departmental enquiries, six months for streamlining the mechanism for grievance redress, six months for review of legal provisions to enable immediate and exemplary prosecution of corrupt officials, one year for review of laws, etc.) have been met. The Committee set up under the Cabinet Secretary with a few Chief Secretaries from different regions and others to monitor the implementation of the Action Plan has not met for over three years.

CRITICAL ISSUES IN ADMINISTRATIVE REFORMS

At an earlier point, it has been observed that the central question in AR was as to why the system's responses to the periodic initiatives in this field were of such a weak and indifferent quality. Despite such widespread external criticism and comment, and an admittedly serious failure of public trust in the governance machinery, why was the system not responding well to the variety of initiatives being undertaken?

While the apparent reasons seem to be the lack of a political or bureaucratic will, an inability to sustain focus on a prioritised set of agenda points and an inability to exert enough pressure on the system to push through the agreed agenda calls for a much deeper and systematic probe. The present chapter hypothesises that the deeper reasons may be found within, first, the present level of maturity of the democratic system, and second, the level of self-confidence and courage of the various levels of the permanent bureaucracy in facing ground-level realities and in engaging in a dialogue with the citizenry for the resolution of the problems and challenges confronting the government.

The above hypothesis is tested here by examining how the system has behaved in two selected contexts, one of self-governing institutions in transition, and the other of a time-tested principal cadre within the bureaucratic structure.

Regarding the democratic maturity aspect, it may be rewarding to examine the impact of the legal change, the 73rd and 74th Constitutional Amendments of 1992 and 1993 respectively, in force now for a decade, aimed at ushering in stability of elected local self-governing institutions in urban and rural areas. This is an inherently significant case since it extends the democratic principle into the design of institutions covering all localities, based on the strength of a constitutional mandate. It ought to provide a contrast to reforms that are taken up on solely official initiatives of the executive which may not have a similarly strong legal or comprehensive basis.

As regards the capacity of the bureaucracy to cope in the context of the changing environment and high public demands on the administrative structures, an insiders' assessment could be made specifically of the high profile IAS, to which the authors belong/ belonged and which provides a unique nation-wide administrative leadership network based on a federal arrangement.

LEVEL OF MATURITY OF THE DEMOCRATIC SYSTEM

Local self-government has a long history in India: the older among the present municipalities started functioning under the British in the second half of the 19th century, and the Zila Panchayats (District Boards) go back to the 1920s and the village panchayats at least to 1947 (Uttar Pradesh). Their offices were found at a central location in the towns, they raised taxes and fees, charges for services, etc., were provided capital grants, and managed most civic and urban regulation services through their own staff. They had considerable choice to determine budgets and activities and were perceived as effective units of management and public participation. Mayors, chairpersons, councillors and pradhans enjoyed a proud civic role and representative status.

In the post-independence era, though these institutions came to be elected on the basis of universal suffrage, they also got enmeshed in political conflicts. Freely superseded by the state governments for political reasons (technically, for real or imaginary misdemeanours), these bodies were often kept under official administrators for long periods, sometimes for decades. The new Constitutional Amendments provide for mandatory elections, with a gap of no more than six months being permissible between the end of term (or suspension) of one body and the election of its successor local body, under the aegis of the newly provided institution of the State Election Commissions (SEC). Parallel constitutional provisions also apply to the three tiers of panchayats, the rural local bodies at the district, block or sub-district, and village levels. State Finance Commissions (SFC) are now set up every five years to review their finances and recommend the principles for sharing of state revenues with these urban and rural local self-governing institutions, and also for the distribution of the shares between the different bodies. The state governments may also include other matters in their terms of reference.

Beyond these constitutional provisions (the 'virtual world'), a mass of state legislation and government executive orders and departmental instructions (the 'real world' of governance) come into play with respect to their respective powers and functions (an attempt to incorporate standard prescriptive lists of transferred subjects in the Constitution did not succeed, because of stiff resistance from the states, on grounds of autonomy in decision-making); budgetary and expenditure systems and norms; monitoring, appellate and reviewing authorities; reporting; staffing pattern, strength and salary structure; the appointment and control of key officials, who have for some years come to belong to state cadres in the name of quality of recruitment and professionalism; the rules of procedure, rules and bye-laws for conducting the business of the organisation and its committees, as well as for taxation, charges and licence fees, etc; allotment of state discretionary grants for various purposes, especially for capital expenditure; accounting; and audit. More often than not, governments also tend to prescribe conditionalities for use of funds at the time of release of the SFC-entitled shares of the local bodies in state revenues, ignoring the fact that the transfers were meant to strengthen the capacity of these bodies to take their own decisions as self-governing institutions in their respective settings.

Since the situation varies from state to state, it needs to be stressed that generalisations here are to be read with caution. By and large, the recent constitutional changes, however, seem to have (a) not percolated to operating levels (even at state government headquarters and naturally, therefore, not at the town and village level), (b) come rather late in the day, and (c) been superimposed on past legislation, administrative structure and personnel.

The reality of the Constitutional Amendments, however, is very different. The statutes enacted by the states have not significantly altered the functional domain of the so-called self-governing organisations, e.g., the panchayats and municipal bodies. Even after devolving several responsibilities upon these institutions, most of the states have not transferred requisite staff and funds in respect to the transferred 'subjects'. A large number of states have not constituted District Planning Committees (DPCs). In some states, ministers in charge of the district have been made the Chairpersons of the DPCs. Most of the states have not spelt out the powers of the Gram Sabha, nor have any procedures been prescribed for the functioning of this body. Certain states have recently started setting up bodies parallel to the Panchayati Raj Institutions (PRIs), such as the Village Development Committee in Haryana and the Gram Vikas Samiti in Madhya Pradesh.

Thus, the status and authority of local bodies have been so seriously undermined that they have less powers now than at the time of independence. Usual civic functions have been split between many government departments and entities since long: for instance, those relating to distribution of electricity; water and sewerage; roads and other public works; urban planning, regulation and development; public lands; industrial growth and tourism; social welfare, education and health services delivery; and environmental regulations.

These governmental entities have negligible formal or operational linkages with the local bodies or their councils and boards, and function autonomously within their respective government department structures. In fact, these entities work in isolation and do not even consult each other or coordinate their field operations, resulting in the common Indian feature of roads being dug up for one thing after another. Comparable splitting is the norm in the rural settings too, where distance and smallness of far-flung development blocks and villages renders it almost impossible to understand what is going on.

Left with sanitation, street lighting and vendor control functions, dependent on government resources and para-statal agencies for most of the towns' needs, the urban local bodies have a hard time justifying their existence whenever they seek to jack up levy of urban property taxes. It is not a surprise, therefore, that they tend to make the most of the powers that they enjoy and are happy to remain in an antiquated working mode at most points.

In the rural setting, the same is true of most self-governing institutions, except for the district panchayats which have the legacy of the erstwhile District Board as a main agency for taking up the task of delivery of a limited package of rural services and which enjoy limited powers of taxation, fees, etc., since the pre-independence years. The sub-district or block-level institutions originated as government-funded extension centres for carrying the messages of modern agriculture technology and social development programmes and have retained a governmental character in almost all the states, despite their tenuous link with elected office bearers. Village panchayats have a longer history of representation of village interests and internal social order, but in the present era of universal suffrage they have become a highly divisive factor in the village community, more so with large state and centre grants flowing in under various rural development schemes and the provision for simultaneous direct election of village representatives at each of the three tiers of panchayats. In any case, their role in village development and civic services remains largely passive, and their equations with the village community (the Gram Sabha) and the departmental development officials remain largely undefined; therefore, they tend to operate in an environment of bargaining.

These features of distance between the institutions of self-governance and the governmental machinery support the hypothesis that the

Indian democratic system is yet to mature. Further clinching evidence of this is to be found in the lack of trust of the citizenry in the overall working of these bodies, their effectiveness, fairness, impartiality, etc. The perfunctory (often insulting) manner in which appointed officials in these institutions deal with ordinary visitors and the superficial manner in which even their elected chairpersons and office-bearers treat their general and governing bodies, the erratic quality of documentation and record keeping related to meetings and other important functions like budget, taxation and expenditure, absence of access to information, etc., are all pointers to a serious loss of a sense of civic obligation and answerability. These conditions create a hostile environment for AR as such, since the ideas that form part of AR are not yet a part of an agenda of the powers-that-be, even in the institutions of self-governance closest to the lives of ordinary citizens.

CAPACITY OF THE BUREAUCRACY

At this point, the context and situation of a key administrative cadre, the IAS, may be briefly examined from the responsible insider civil servants' point of view, a combination of the serving and the retired being justified on the ground that the joint value of the two perspectives would be greater than of each of the two.

This prominent civil service institution is designed to provide the governmental system with the best possible management and leadership qualities that it may recruit from the national market in a lifetime commitment format. The public expectation is that the individuals manning this cadre would score higher than other groups of officials on a leadership qualities scale.

Traditionally, at whatever point or level they may be placed, responsible civil servants have been regarded as those who understand that their leadership status within the permanent bureaucracy of the country, especially in a newly independent and developing democracy of the size and diversity of India, carries with it a definite legal as well as societal obligation and some prestige among their equals and the citizenry. This professional obligation involves working at all times in a 30-odd year long career in the bureaucracy (*a*) under the Constitution of India, in a regime of rule of law, (*b*) as part of the executive function of the state, (*c*) in a fair, impartial, objective and constructive manner, and (*d*) with standards of absolute, rather than relative, personal honesty and integrity. These may be considered to be part of the 'virtual world' of a classical Weberian set of parameters which continue to retain their relevance as principles, despite repeated failures in practice in the Indian context.

From time to time, various other qualitative elements too have been stressed in the Indian setting: (e) empathy for the common people (the *mai-baap* complex? not faceless?), the weak and poor, (f) physical and moral courage, and perseverance, (g) willingness to sacrifice personal goals (to the vagaries of sudden transfers, for instance), (h) commitment (which had an odious meaning at one time as loyalty to a person in power), and (i) motivation for acquiring knowledge, continuous upgrading of skills, etc.

In the newest listing, elements having to do with the following have been added: (j) transparency in work, (k) openness and wide public contacts, (l) public–private partnership, (m) a degree of activism, (n) acquisition of IT and communications skills, and (o) support to self-help groups, NGOs and democratic bodies (if departmental rules allow).

The confusing factors relate to the vast and complex nature of the 'real world' of bureaucratic setting as viewed from the inside. There is a vast flow of information through the governmental system as well as in the press and publications, but it remains unprocessed and hence difficult to access and use; research and analysis or support from academia or from within is rarely available. Hence, amateurism, hunch and instinct, bias and unexamined views dominate, not analysis and evaluation. Hearsay, politically correct conduct and fads are extremely significant attributes.

The team-coordination function is nebulous. Each slot may be defined, each cog may logically appear to be necessarily a part of the wheel, but the picture is not always clear. It is not merely a question of duplication and overlap. The problem is that the question of 'who is responsible for what' is usually seen as a query about who has the highest right to exercise power in a particular matter legally or otherwise. (Everything requires the Prime Minister's or the Chief Minister's blessings.)

Some aspects of the reality are unpleasant. Criminals, including in politics and power, in society, among contractors and bidders, pose a real threat to many officials who have little assurance of protection or support as government servants may have once been entitled to. Man-made urban agglomerations have horrible slums, some others have serious societal conflicts or dominant groups with vested interests which prevent free working by officials. Earlier to be found as exceptions, the reality is that these forces outside the law and democratic set-up are expanding their empires at present.

Mutual confidence and goodwill within the official class has disappeared, deep divides have come into being, and dialogue is not frank or honest, motives are suspect, and one segment distrusts (even hates and exploits) another. Not many tread the common ground.

Officials must find time for attending meetings. Meetings without agendas in advance are the norm; it remains a matter of guesswork as to why they are called, what commitment may be made, what was the real outcome, and what may have been the per hour cost borne by the tax payer. There is no evidence so far that e-mail access would change all this. Non-attendance on account of lack of notice of an assigned aspect of the participants' task is seen as non-cooperation, and even insult. Many meetings are just disguised forms of coercion.

Communication is usually a one-way street, from the top down; everyone waits for guidance. Yet, the picture of the boss at the top of a line of command and power, as role model, is rather hazy, since lurking somewhere may be the absence of rigour and the presence of extraneous considerations, brokers, influence peddlers, and politicians exercising their muscle.

The modalities and terms of the dialogue with citizens are even more peculiar. The individual hearing of grievance or search for advice on procedures is not easily arranged. The darbar-style 'tahsil day', village day, etc., are the most successful models of public contact and delivery of individual responses. However, this does not add up to a whole system. More successful methods involve a search for family, regional (linguistic or geographic) and social (school friend, club tie or golfing partner) links. Letters and petitions are treated as pieces of paper which no one has time to read, and visitors are quite often told as much. Of course, money talks, and the space for the ordinary public interest has shrunk equally with the increase in this exclusive, private domain. Associations, NGOs and the media are some of the other props which serve as a means of exchange of dialogue. Old-style visibility, fixed modes of accessibility (say, first thing every morning) and pre-announced tours to cover maximum places within the jurisdiction have not survived the pressure from endless meetings and summonses, and the great need to hide!

In this environment, the combination of nominal status, permanence and pension, which are essentially the unique selling points (USP) of public employment, does not provide sufficient strength and motivation to the incumbents. Fear of transfer away from soft headquarters postings in the larger towns also encourages the tendency to play safe. Such locations in close proximity to the powers-that-be also enable individuals to spot possibilities of perks, travel, special jobs, etc.

Since service or peer-group norms are weak as compared to the forces noted above, most individuals go along with the flow rather than face up to the implications of an independent, stand-alone stance. Here too it would be worthwhile to review the cross-cultural reality in order to refine (and, maybe, redefine) the public service character of various bureaucratic institutions and their members.

CONCLUSIONS

There are innumerable challenges in the field of administrative reforms, and many types of actions have been taken or have been proposed/suggested. However, the tremendous inertia of the government systems is still to be overcome. Such inertia and unconcern about building more efficient and accessible structures and working systems in the government perhaps arises from a general feeling that the many partners to the enterprise may be too weak or non-committal to mount a well-coordinated effort. There is also a genuine fear of loss of power or control at the bureaucratic and the political level. A more open and democratic environment in the working of the government would prevent many misdeeds from being planned and/or perpetrated. Self-interests are better protected in a predominantly compartmentalised and inward-looking public administration set-up, more so when it is based on secrecy and limited departmental answerability. How can the impasse be broken? There is a genuine need to candidly understand and spell out the real ramifications and dimensions of the AR deficit, discover the right means to minimise it and move towards a modern administrative system. The credibility of the AR agenda has to be established first.

It may, therefore, be worthwhile to carefully study cases of success as well as failure and learn the right lessons from them. A critical mass of studies is required to be undertaken in order to establish the real opportunity costs of mismanagement and to bring home the fall-out of neglect on this score. There is a need for well-researched and strong evidence to be publicly presented, so that a loud and clear message would register with the administrative system that dysfunctional and closed systems are no longer affordable. Inter-disciplinary panels should review these studies, and be armed with sufficiently strong teeth to recommend, and, if possible, also give effect to the specific changes that are called for. In addition, broad-based experiments in AR also need to be developed. While partial measures, which have a specific context and content, leave a largely symbolic impact, they expend government energy in tinkering with one or another aspect of the AR agenda within a limited, cautious and traditional regime. Such half-measures are not likely to prove effective in bringing about any palpable improvement.

After carefully studying cases of success and failure, therefore, comprehensive experiments should be developed for a total paradigm shift in a few limited settings at a time. Such experiments may cover: the objectives (say, the delivery of specific services, or social support systems); content and prospective approach; agencies, working systems and the functional relationships; backward and forward linkages and system changes required to bring them in alignment from the front office to the board room; responsibility and accountability systems, internal, external as well as democratic; impact; and replicability.

The choice of settings may not be difficult. The decentralisation situation since the Constitutional Amendments of the early 1990s is ripe for such an approach in which an unprecedented need has already arisen for creating entirely new equations for working together (rather than within a traditional framework of hierarchy, turf, confrontation and mistrust).

Given the complex nature of the phenomenon of social deprivation and poverty, the setting of chronically difficult areas, or of people with social handicaps, may be rewarding fields for taking up such comprehensive projects. These may be the areas where traditional and standardised institutional approaches and formal structures have had a limited reach and impact so far. Reforms here may call for a greater degree of realism, freedom to innovate and design non-traditional approaches to AR, in order to bring together different parties and to evolve the requisite programmes, relationships and modes of delivery, as well as to create new working and review systems, which meet the needs of a socially responsible and self-consciously democratic and modern structure of governance.

While the ingredients of these approaches may appear to be the familiar ones, namely, reforms touching upon the laws, the structure, the human resources and the bureaucracy's equations with civil society, the paradigm shift in the approach to AR, as set out above, may generate through reactions and their resolutions relevant knowledge for confidently moving towards a sound, non-stereotyped, future-oriented, systems-wide programme of AR in governance.

NOTE

1. Based on material in Agnihotri and Narula (2002).

REFERENCES

Agnihotri, V.K. and Narula, A.L. 2002. *Department of Administrative Reforms and Public Grievances: Through the Ages.* New Delhi: Department of Administrative Reforms and Public Grievances.

Government of India. 1957. *Report of Team for Study of Community Projects and National Extension Service* (Balwantray Mehta Committee). New Delhi: Government of India Press.

———. 1970. *Report of the Administrative Reforms Commission.* New Delhi: Government of India Press.

———. 1997a. *Action Plan for Effective and Responsive Government.* New Delhi: Department of Administrative Reforms and Public Grievances.

———. 1997b. *Report of the Fifth Central Pay Commission.* New Delhi: Government of India Press.

Maheshwari, S.R. 2000. *Public Administration in India.* Delhi: Macmillan.

CHAPTER 13

NGOs as Partners in the Process of 'Reform': Are They the *Yogis* or the *Bhogis* of Development?[1]

Vithal Rajan

WHY NGOs?

On Saturday, 20 April 2002, the Prime Minister of India inaugurated in New Delhi a national conference on 'The Role of the Voluntary Sector in National Development'. Speaking to a large group of bureaucrats and politicians, with a token sprinkling of Delhi-based *voluntary-wallahs*, he lauded their efforts 'for carving out a space'. Mr Vajpayee wanted the 'relationship of benefactor and supplicant' to be changed 'to one of partnership where the Government acts as a facilitator' (*The Hindu* 2002b). This is all that is to be expected nowadays, including the careful selection of attendees.

Despite the influence of early Gandhian thinking, the development process in India since independence has been designed and controlled by the ruling elites of the country. A 'trickle down' process was to ensure that benefits would gradually improve the lot of the poor. However, even 50 years later, the percentage of the poor stubbornly remains well over 40 per cent of the population. Changing fashions in development theory have now created a mantra out of the concept of 'people's participation', that is upheld by all, the World Bank, the Indian government, and other experts thriving on the development industry, academics, non-governmental organisations (NGOs) entrepreneurs and their foreign donors. However, the concept of people's participation itself means several things to several people, and rarely more than a public audience of development projects, conceived, created and controlled by the various interested elites. Most importantly, since an important component of the funds for these projects emanate from foreign sources, Indian agencies, governmental and NGO alike, tend to fall in readily with exotic superficial concepts of people's participation. This falling in line is made all the easier by the Indian decision-making elites lacking real social practice in people's movements. Even many NGOs which vociferously espouse the 'people's cause', not only depend on the largesse of their foreign donors, but have little contact with grassroots political movements. In fact, they consciously portray themselves as 'non-political'. Hence the power over decision-making remains, as it always has, in the hands of the elites, whatever competing identities they may take over internal struggles for power, prestige or profits.

But let me start with the story of a development mantra that ushered in the NGO as a token partner of government. We all know that part of the current development fashion is the promotion of Participatory Rural Appraisal (PRA) methods, devised by Robert Chambers, an Englishman, formerly of Her Majesty's colonial service in Africa. These techniques are nothing more than an extension of the way British district officers learnt of village realities by sitting under the village tree. Clearly, government officials are happy to go back to a system in which they are in command, but the subtlety lies in packaging it as 'participatory' to suit modern politically correct officialese. The participation of the poor ends with the disgorging of local information to the Sahib, who will, as he always has, take necessary steps, with abundant caution, through proper channels. In development or voluntarism, smart marketing as in business leads the way to success.

Since the word is with voluntary agencies, who are now fashionably involved in several circles of development decision-making (Ramachandran 1999),[2] it may be best to investigate the process by looking at how these advocates of the people practice people's participation in these days of structural adjustment, and compare their efforts with governmental initiatives to promote the same. While rural women's groups have far outstripped expectations in their ability to manage thrift and savings schemes (Rajan 1994), their freedom of action seems to be strictly curtailed by the decisions of elite government officials and NGO leaders. The new managerial innovation of involving local communities in the management of forests, and the technology of watershed development are both seen as empowering, but the actual practice on the ground seems to have the opposite effect. Kerala, the small south-eastern state in India, is well known for its breakthroughs in women's empowerment, and the dramatic lowering of the infant mortality rate, the birth rate and the total fertility rate, now below 1.9. This state is innovating with a new process of 'people's plans', designed and implemented at the local level, but these are still early days (Bandopadhyay 1997). So, while the principle of people's participation is widely accepted, the actual exercise of the principle requires the build up of social practice at the grassroots, much more than theoretical visitations from afar, or from the top down.

The Nellore women of Andhra Pradesh, without ever having heard of Paolo Friere, converted a rather tedious government-run adult literacy programme into a women's movement to oppose the government imposing arrack on their menfolk, most times through powerful contractors, many times as part payment for work done. The Indonesian farmers similarly converted an innocuous Integrated Pest Management (IPM)-learning project into one that demanded peasant rights, rights of the tiller and the landless. From these instances we learn that participation occurs in unregulated ways, surprising the organisers; in ways of self-empowerment and community assertion. At the right historical juncture, the weaknesses of those who rule can be exploited by the poor to win some rights and produce some sustainability at the grassroots.

Indian NGOs, perhaps among the most experienced, have many excellent similar development stories to tell in micro-credit, community health (Arole and Arole 1994), primary education,[3] watershed (Mathew 1995), and afforestation schemes (Arora 1994); but are these micro-successes replicable? We will know only with genuine large-scale, systematic participation of the people, the poor, in self-managed development. Till that happens, we are left only with interesting anecdotes. Western economists and left-wing intellectuals have developed a penchant for development by anecdotes, from 'the Brazil Miracle' to 'Learn from Dai-chai'. Such ideological campaigns have led only to strengthening authoritarian regimes. The goal of people-based development remains illusory, as ever.

Area-wise studies are being conducted today on the impact of structural adjustment programmes on different sectors of the economy. Voluntary agencies have been involved to examine the impact of such changes in economic policies on the poor of this country. There is very little regret on any side at the passing away of unhelpful bureaucratic controls and regimentation. Far from securing the interests of the poor in a socialist, secular state, the control by politicians and bureaucrats of the economy through rules, regulations and licences merely ensured what is popularly known as socialism for the rich and capitalism for the poor. That is, while the interests of Indian businessmen and the rich were taken care of by state policy and their profits grew under state protection, the poor were more or less free to sell their labour power at low wage rates wherever there was a demand. This process strengthened the interests of wealthy and powerful families; the gap between the rich and the poor widened; caste interests and antagonism were enlarged; and the role of a few leading families such as the Nehru family ensured. In the new era that is opening up, well-known assurances and securities for the elite of this country have evaporated, and politicians and businessmen alike are beginning to realise that they have to try new ways for securing their profits and power bases.

Despite the hype that Indians are entering a period of high growth and business and technological success, realistic prognostications are far more pessimistic. The commandist structure of the polity of the country has in no sense been weakened. Major decisions, in fact, any decision of note, flow from the top to the bottom. Administrative and managerial systems remain unchanged and hierarchical. All that is of significance is that the political and administrative elite has decided to share some power, and transfer some decision-making areas, to the business elite in the simple hope that businessmen and industrialists would somehow prove to be more competitive in the world market. While it is clear that the arrogant Indian administrative elite has no skills whatsoever in competing for markets, it is misinformed to think that businessmen are any better. Under the closed-door security offered by the government, Indian business houses till now have grown to positions of great importance and wealth without actually having to compete with the much larger, more efficient, and more powerful transnational corporations of the world. In the economy of scarcity, their main role was the allocation of their products, many times at much higher prices than prevailing elsewhere. Their managerial elite has not learned the skills of simple selling. They will not be able to market their expensive products with inferior technology and without the advantage of economies of scale under competition with the cheaper, superior products of transnational corporations (TNCs), which also have far superior selling abilities. The idea that the nation will grow through an export-led growth strategy is wishful thinking.

From Dr Manmohan Singh to Mr Yaswant Sinha, Finance Ministers doing yeomen service in trying to clean out the tangles of red-tape have still to produce a single worthwhile idea on how the Indian economy is to prove competitive or to modernise itself. Just as the idea of an export-led growth strategy has been going around for the last several decades, so are the ideas for agricultural development that have been dredged up in the plan documents. Changing the profile of agricultural subsidies, or trying to establish small centres to promote organic farming or integrated pest management, fall far short of the kind of decentralised power sharing and encouragement of local planning and growth that is needed in poverty-stricken, environmentally-degraded areas.[4]

If anything, the structural adjustment programmes (SAP) will strengthen the elite, and perhaps produce a broader base for it by bringing into the fore a new class of exporters and businessmen who might be able to take marginal advantage of some openings in the global market. The gap between the rich and the poor will inevitably widen; the middle class and salaried classes will be struck by high inflation; and the divide between the rural and the urban sectors would become even more marked. The present main thrust of the structural adjustment programmes could force India into another form of dependency. Several such unspoken questions linger in Indian minds.

What Price Voluntarism?

In this rather grim scenario, the role of voluntary agencies is to be seen neither as humanitarian nor as non-political. Their movement, if it may be called so, has gone through rather startling transformations: from that of the 'Handmaiden to Government' from the time of independence till the near-famines of the early 1960s through the role of 'The Filmi Rebel' in the heyday of Naxalite upsurge to that of the 'Drab Advocate' of the 1970s and 1980s and today's role of the 'Sarkari'[5] Catalyst.

By and large, the voluntary sector has grown in this country in response to the idealism of many of its citizens and the continuing traditions of constructive work that were emphasised by Mahatma Gandhi as a cornerstone of the freedom movement. The voluntary movement's attempts to support the government in carrying through modern messages of development to the remotest village ended with the failure of the five-year plans to produce marked growth. Turning away from being the handmaiden of corrupt and self-interested politicians, the voluntary movement tried to join the people's protest movements during the 1960s and the 1970s. It was encouraged to do so by the funding agencies from foreign countries, themselves influenced by liberation theology which found its roots among the oppressed peasants of Latin America. With the defeat of the Emergency in India, the voluntary movement had to take stock of its achievements and found that it had gained little by either supporting or confronting the government over the last three decades. Over several workshops called to find out a mutually satisfactory identity, the voluntary movement settled for an advocacy or a catalytic role, but still saw itself as playing a crucial role in the economic upliftment of the poor and in the struggles of the poor to reach self-sufficiency and self-reliance. All of which required economic strengthening of the poor.

However, in the new period that is emerging of American overlordship, Washington perhaps sees a very different role for voluntary agencies worldwide. This is not to say that international voluntary and donor agencies have deliberately become instruments of American policy. However, trends in policy-making, academic thinking and international action programmes also follow fashions which many times are deliberately initiated, as they have been many times in the past to serve wider interests. Over a decade ago, Susan George[6] warned voluntary agencies that they should be a bit more critical of the sudden interest the West was taking in promoting their involvement in development, and that they should ask why this change had occurred. It is difficult from a Third World point of view to dismiss such fears as the paranoia of the weak.

When the World Bank and the IMF speak of governance, for example, they mean simply another set of conditions to be added to the long list of conditions already set out in structural adjustment programmes. Where is 'governance' when neo-liberal globalisation not only leaves out vast swathes of humanity and intentionally weakens the State but also plunges even countries like the erstwhile 'tigers' Korea, Thailand or Indonesia into financial chaos and mass unemployment? Where is governance when the Fund deliberately turns a blind eye to the looting from Russia of billions of dollars in its own hard currency loans? . . . Such disasters as have occurred in Asia, Latin America and the so-called 'transition countries' show that, contrary to the neo-liberal myth, freedom of capital flows, highly leveraged loans and uninhibited Portfolio Equity Investment are not the road to prosperity but to ruin (George 2001).

The break-up of the Soviet Union heralded the twin pincer thrusts of globalisation and privatisation in economic warfare as the preferred mode of conquest in 'postcolonial' society. This direct attack on the sovereignty of weaker states is led by TNCs (far more resource-rich than the East India Company, for example), as a modern follow up to colonial gunboat diplomacy. Resistance to penetration is decried as an effect of the absence of a 'free market', and this in turn is taken as a critical symptom of the lack of human rights and democracy. A lack which must be rectified through the 'free market' before being given 'most favoured nation' status, or other marks of fair dealing.

The processes of globalisation and structural adjustment impact directly on national social welfare schemes of direct benefit to the vast majority of the world's poor. Despite the new formalism of democratic governance, of which participatory process is a part, the actual methods of rule are still very much 'commandist' in reality. The small highly privileged elite at the top controls the vast dispossessed majority through the very processes of reinforcing poverty and making knowledge itself the exclusive prerogative of the elite and the rich. The stability of the system is ensured through using brute force, or more effectively the 'threat' of force over people who have to make regular real-life decisions on the worth of questioning authority, let alone rebelling against it.

The spaces vacated by the government from spheres of social policy are being filled by foreign-donor backed NGOs. The World Bank, the United States government, the European Union, all support, cultivate and elevate NGO leadership. Even authoritarian bureaucracy, once suspicious of NGOs, now prefers to deal with such powerful upper-class individuals. A key insider role in the colonisation of India was played by local 'dalals' or traders. In the recolonisation of the world, what ambiguous role is now marked out for NGOs? Almost all of the Third World in 'postcolonial' times has faced authoritarian, or certainly elite, rule. A promise has been held out that NGOs could be catalysts in the re-emergence of grassroots democracy and civil society resistance to local and transnational elite control. But they have not yet lived up to this promise.

Leadership among NGOs is mostly in the hands of gifted entrepreneurs or charismatic individuals. Little networking exists in reality. Occasional grand NGO conclaves produce little more than ego clashes. At the same time, NGO policies seem to be driven by foreign donors which in turn are influenced by the development perspectives shaped by First World institutes. These perspectives are not unrelated to First World national interests or interests of dominance (Mawdsley and Townsend 2002: 91).[7]

It is in this realpolitik setting that a few courageous activists could experiment with 'participation'. The active middle managers of governance, in government, in business and among NGOs, still see the process as nothing more than an opportunity to voice support for the leader, the employer or the benefactor. To achieve the beginnings of the reality of people's participation a well-defined boundary has first to be created around the 'experimental participatory project'. This boundary has to be well understood by those in authority, and the project needs someone in power having the mandate to make it work. This could perhaps be done on an experimental basis so that the powerful may gauge its usefulness as a 'survival strategy'. And the powerful arbiter has to assure those at the bottom that there will be no penalties for compliance with the new permission to 'speak out'.

THE INNER TRUTH

So how shall we see the NGO intervention? And how may we regard the NGO itself? Is it like a pair of drainpipe trousers round the belly of its fat leader? Or is it truer to see it as a romantic Robin Hood band that somehow has yet to deliver to the poor? Or are these social entrepreneurs only prosaic 'development dalals'? Or is it a benign zamindari? Or is there reality in the fear that NGOs form a 'sixth column' through which the Great Powers are trying to subvert the independence of nations?

Before we can even formulate a suspicion, we must realise there are several kinds of NGOs, several histories. We must not for a start confuse them with genuine 'people's movements', like the famous one led by the late J.P. over 30 years ago, or Medha Patkar's Narmada Bachao Andolan or the Adivasi struggles for recognition of human rights. These are large amorphous movements, held together by a shared ideal or grievance, rather than by the structure of a funded organisation. In a very tell-tale way, power is far more diffused in a people's movement, while it is tightly held in an NGO.

But it is the very hierarchical structure of the NGO, clothed in an aura of empowerment, that has found such laudatory approval from international bodies such as the World Bank, and ready acceptance from the more insightful of governmental circles. Government-organised NGOs (GONGOs) are mushrooming all over the place to empower charismatic leaders and bureaucrats to spend money without being confined to departmental duties or having to shoulder old governmental responsibilities. The Andhra Pradesh government leads in this imaginative exercise,[8] and has already scored a notable success by imitating an NGO initiative to make rice available under the public distribution system to below poverty line families on credit and at export prices![9] This opportunity to do something outside of government has not been lost on aging civil servants looking for a life of power after retirement. The new breed of Retired Officials' NGOs (RONGOs) permit bureaucrats to indulge their fancies. Last year's Czars of Shastri Bhavan (the seat of the Education Ministry) can conveniently jettison their proclaimed ideologies in favour of foreign money to try their hand at primary education. Defenders of the Green Revolution after retirement find safety in organic farming institutes. Upholders of the rights of the forest department, once out of Paryavaran Bhavan (where high foresters sit in Delhi), are equally eloquent about community conservation. Even police officers known to chivvy outspoken democrats when in service speak up for human rights when drawing a pension. Not far behind are the Brahmin-organised NGOs (BRONGOs) whose chief concern is voicing the injustices suffered by Dalits in any conference they can attend, from Berlin to San Diego. The early-bird RONGO, or captured NGO (CANGO), needs a government to tango with an NGO to get an in-service official running it.

So the appearance of several specialist NGOs have now made it imperative to create a taxonomy of voluntary effort which by the way most find very paying. The Business-inspired NGOs (BINGOs) continue to reap corporate benefits by spending tax-deductible money lavishly on adopted villages or media-worthy programmes which can lighten the pages of annual reports and balance out unfavourable public comment. But their reward is nothing when compared with that gained by the Donor International NGOs (DINGOs).

In the structuring of development packages, we see how institutions in a Western country, say, such as the British DFID, research institutions such as IIED or IDS, located in Sussex University, and donor international NGOs such as Oxfam or Christian Aid run as a pack. The fact that aid brings in extra profits through increased trade is openly acknowledged. The Canadian CIDA has always justified its existence on this count alone. The aid research industry is a major source of employment in the West, particularly of a dangerous class of educated unemployables. These, in return for the security of academia, dredge up patent colonial ideology as the new science of development. They are secure in the knowledge that no challenge can come from the Third World intelligentsia who are kept locked into convenient subaltern positions with suitably graded rewards of fellowships, visiting assignments, and invitations to conferences and consultancies. To these rather simple benefits is added the even greater one of pacifying the large body of home-based liberals who are unhappy with the exploitative nature of their society and to whom aid and charity are presented as justifications of overlordship. Many large European donors, styling themselves as 'Christian', though in fact being secular to the point of being non-spiritual, hard-bitten fundraisers, saw aid as an answer in the mid-1960s to the crisis of relevance within the Church and as a way of attracting youth back to the folds of belief. But behind all these apparent and rather pathetic reasons for the convergence of the interests of government, church and academia lies the formidable project of Western civilisation itself, its need to control the people, societies and resources of the Third World, and its lust to destroy other cultures, and other ways of being. It is not only money power that dictates this process, but the psychological legacy of cultural subordination under colonialism. Despite the intellectual glitterati of the Third World vociferously condemning the results of 'orientalist' scholarship, their persistent personal need emerges for recognition by the 'international', meaning, 'Western' community of scholars.

What is alarming is not that the West is developing an armoury of neo-colonial control mechanisms, but that there is so little challenge to rather blatant practices of mixing science with disinformation; persuasive aid money to governments and NGOs and chances of personal promotion to key individuals with scorn and threats towards dissenters; and media-designed calls to conform to 'global', in other words, Western, standards with open relegation of Third World needs and perspectives into subordinated and disconnected positions.

Let us look at historical instances of how the West has governed development policy. Green Revolution scientific ideology was discussed in international workshops and had helped appoint the supporters of such policy in several universities and research institutions througout the world. The Consultative Group on International Agricultural Research (CGIAR) was created at that time not only to help increase food supply in the world, but to support transnational agri-biz. The selling of the Green Revolution to the Third World as a scientific package without which they could not possibly survive is perhaps the best example of how a business opportunity for the West can be presented as aid and as scientific dogma to poor countries. While great oil companies, such as Shell, were already forecasting that the bulk of profits in the 21st century will come from agri-biz, Indian scientists and politicians humbly accepted a strategy which enriched richer farmers in selected areas such as the Punjab, coastal Andhra and Tanjavur where the irrigation infra-structure already existed, created long ago by the British, the Mughals and the Cholas. In furthering the interests of petroleum-based agriculture, the gap between the rich and the poor widened; the Punjab went up in communal flames; around 80 per cent of the rural population of small and marginal farmers and agricultural labour were neglected over a crucial two-and-a-half decades; 100 districts were declared drought-prone and left to endemic hunger with extensive and consequential environmental degradation.

Social forestry projects funded by the World Bank and other international aid agencies have swept the country like a forest fire. They did not promote trees to feed and support the poor but stands of eucalyptus and similar species as raw material reserves for industry. It was only when the indigenous people of Madhya Pradesh took up arms against such plantations that the world's experts started being solicitous about peasants and tribals. Even the phrase 'social forestry' is believed to have been designed in Harvard University as a marketing tool for selling a package to a Third World country as science, as aid and as community help. While readily accepting this half-baked idea, the Indian government never enquired into its own long history of people's managed forestry, never questioned how the British by a legal fiction appropriated all forest lands as government property in the 19th century, disinheriting villagers, peasants and forest dwellers.[10]

We cannot talk about forests without talking about tigers. There is a story doing the environmental rounds in Andhra Pradesh that the Forest Department has more conservators than there are tigers in the state, and this despite the Sri Sailam reserve being the largest of the Project Tiger sites in India. A recent tiger census came to nothing; one believes not a single animal was sighted and the few pugmarks found added to the confusion over numbers.

The three-decade-old project, with India having primary responsibility for saving the tiger, was inaugurated with much fanfare by the international conservation crowd led by the World Wildlife Fund (WWF). Interest in tigers goes back to the time when rajahs and captains couldn't look one another in the eye unless they had killed a number of these beasts in sport. Mughal miniatures attest this fact. John Nicholson of 1857 fame is known to have sabred tigers from horseback. Jim Corbett, after whom our most famous wildlife sanctuary is named, became immortal thanks to the man-eaters of Kumaon. Aristocratic Indians were not far behind. A Maharaja of Bikaner is said to have shot over 3,000, while another Maharaja of Sarguja could kill no more than 1,800, though he festooned forest trees with tiger-signalling telephones and ranged rifles like golf clubs in his hunting jeep. Parkinson's disease disabled his left hand for teacups but not for rifle barrels![11] In fact, killing a tiger was a rite of passage for the ruling classes—from Lord Willingdon who disturbed his entourage's sleep by dragging along a roaring tiger in the last bogie of his train for the morning's shikar to the District Collector or Forest Conservator who would tell tall stories of the 'kill' while patting the glassy-eyed stuffed head of the 12-footer which had almost ended the sahib's career. Even the great royal patrons of the WWF, Prince Philip of England and Prince Bernhardt of Holland, were known as avid shikaris, till they saw their hunting grounds vanishing.

The feudal aristocracy of Europe knew how to preserve game and hang hungry poachers who would eat what they massacred at pleasure. The notorious Brandeis Commission of the mid-19th century brought a European prescription for the control of Indian forests, and by an act of expropriation which far outdid the depredations of Dalhousie's Doctrine of Lapse made the government owner of all forest land. Not that Indian kings in olden days did not have hunting rights in parts of the forests but villagers also had their rights, as did animals in areas designated as 'elephant forests'. There was customary division of forest areas, as attested by the *Arthasastra*, whose author, Kautilya, was not known to give away any rights unless he was forced to do so.

The greatest impact of 'scientific forestry', which disinherited all tribal communities and made them interlopers in their own homeland living under sufferance, was first to destroy the teak forests of the Malabar to feed the Royal Navy, and later wherever axe could reach to help build railway lines and maintain the huge armies of the Empire during the two World Wars. The great Indian forests have shrunk to a fifth of their original size, fast losing their capacity to support animal life or tribal communities. Tribal discontent was suppressed with the ruthlessness of conquest, leading to unquenched discontent among oppressed peoples, later igniting into the Naxalite movement across the country. Murder, extortion, rapine, and constant humiliation suffered by tribals to this day make forest areas a veritable war zone, and hence incapable of being protected.

The elite international environmental NGOs and bodies whose Third World branches glitter with the leaders of the social register can have little patience with the plight of the tribals whom in their own circles they consider as the rascals responsible for poaching. The WWF, with a $300 million annual income, around half of which is spent on conservation, for years followed protectionist policies that Sally Jeanrenaud describes as ethnocentric, ecologically outmoded and self-defeating (Jeanrenaud 2002: 26). As old growth forest loses out to scrub land, fewer animals appear, and more the armed guards that are emplaced to guard emptying reserves. Miserable poverty and governmental oppression of tribal communities are the two best ways for ensuring destruction of forests and the killing of wildlife. Great scarcity drives people to make inroads on their own natural resources, and oppression surely leads to disaffection and tacit connivance with poachers. Anyone who has lived in jungle areas or talked on friendly terms with tribals knows that they are quite aware of the benefits of biodiversity; they know that carnivores maintain a symbiotic relationship with herbivores and that every tiger signifies at least 25 sq. km. of healthy forest, stocked with plant and animal life.

For elite supporters of the WWF, however, their concern is still signified by the cuddly panda whose bamboo forests have been much destroyed by slash and burn cultivation. But there is a lesson here that none has learned. The tribals at fault are supposed to have migrated from their traditional eastern Tibetan homelands a couple of centuries ago. Attracted by the vast profits the British were making in the early half of the 19th century by pushing opium on the hapless Chinese, they grew opium themselves to corner part of the lucrative market. When the Chinese communists under Mao Zedong came to power in 1949, all opium trade was banned. Even as the drug barons left Hong Kong for greener pastures in the West, the tribals took to slash-and-burn agriculture. Clearly, the difficult option here was the introduction of sustainable agricultural methods suited to the region, rather than offering a few jobs as tour guides or teashop owners.

We in India are very much better placed. The agricultural practices of tribal communities are by and large eco-friendly, despite concerted attempts by ICAR staff to wean them away to monocropping and the use of pesticides and hybrids. If many practise *podu* or slash-and-burn cultivation, let it be noted it became dysfunctional only after the forest cover shrank alarmingly under the inroads made by greedy contractors and corrupt or negligent officials. What tribals need is technical and financial support for sustainable mixed farming practices integrated into the forest ecosystem. They need supportive capacity-building for social development and environmental stewardship. Perhaps the Joint Forestry Management programmes and the newer Community-based Management of Forests programmes could teach forest officials, NGOs and tribals to take small steps towards each other in support. What they do not need is further policing or exclusions from tribal homelands.

At last the penny is beginning to drop in high places, mostly because of the potential multi-billion dollar business that could be generated out of medicinal plants in forest areas. Successful extraction of active principles for the pharmaceutical industry may require first-level processing to be carried out in forest villages. The biodiversity of our forests shelters several living gold mines, and we need to partner tribal communities if we wish to get at them.

They can no longer be excluded from their homelands. In fact, neither the forests nor the biodiversity of the country can be saved without tribal communities taking leadership in protecting their own environment (*The Economic Times* 2001).

Several great imperialists have done their best and worst, and departed—the Maharajas, the Mughals, the British, the Nehruvians—the land has borne all, the people even more. The time may now be not to think of great deeds, of leaving our imprint on one and all, but to let the humble and the dispossessed have their time and space. By trusting the simple, we may come to a better understanding of who we are, our land and all the life we share together. Time to heed Ashish Kothari, one of India's best known NGO environmentalists: 'Wildlife conservation and social justice both require us to move towards a model in which local people are central partners in managing and benefiting from conservation' (*The Hindu* 2002a).

CIVILISATIONAL FAULTS AND ACTS OF MADNESS

An assumption that I wish to revert to is the middle-class obsession with 'corruption'. In fact, most critics of NGOs focus on the predilection of a few NGOs to fudge the books. To imagine that NGOs should be as incorruptible as Robespierre when no other sector is, neither religious institutions nor universities, is to be hypocritical rather than unworldly. It is power that corrupts absolutely as Robespierre discovered too late. Now, if the message of 'service before self' is to be adopted by the NGO movement in all sincerity, we may have to try and overcome the civilisational fault of building individualised empires rather than democratic institutions. And we may have to choose 'Big is Beautiful' as a slogan in a country where the masses are victims of elite decisions, including those of *conference-wallahs*. We may not be so self-righteous in priding ourselves on small self-indulgent charitable work. So what should be the new sutra? Since all the sectors of leadership have proved over the last 50 years their clear inability to help the poor or the environment, can NGOs help create a social space for dialogue and decision, involving officials, business managers, academics and grassroots activists? If no one is in charge, can ordinary people come into their own? The United States has produced the Social Venture Network of hundreds of socially concerned corporate houses.[12] England's Prince of Wales has his International Business Leaders Forum, also with a clear social agenda.[13] Why is it so difficult for Indians to cooperate? What will we lose except our egos?

Mr. Vajpayee while lauding the voluntary sector also stoutly defended his Party's role in the Gujarat massacres, I guess to emphasise the voluntary nature of atrocities. While so ably partnering government, can the NGO sector help work out the Atrocity Codes? Amartya Sen has given credit where it is due by pointing out that the Indian government's highly successful Famine Codes found their prototype long, long ago in the foresight of India's famous mad monarch, Mohammed bin Tughlak (Sen and Drèze 1999: 43). Well, can NGOs match this madness today? One case history after another, from the days of the partition to those of Gujarat have shown that 'development' leads to social conflict. Parliamentary democracy of the Westminster Model has sneaked in adversarial confrontation into the fabric of multi-communal Indian life. There were several traditional ways of dealing with potential dispute, fear or jealousy. Essentially all these were ways of seeing both sides of the question at the same time, and being *inclusive* of both sides, or many sides. This accommodation of interests and viewpoints was found to be both devious and inscrutable by upright Englishmen, leading even very good men like Stafford Cripps to dislike cordially the oriental in Mahatma Gandhi. Be that as it may, NGOs could give new life to the injunction to try *sama*, or inclusive dialogue in any dispute, and later, *dana*, or giving in, if dialogue could not resolve the issue, long before resort to adversarial confrontation. Arun Maira calls for dialogue, for an 'alternative means we will use to resolve differences'. A dialogue that will have 'participative formats that facilitate listening, inquiry, and exploration: not speeches from a panel with perfunctory questions-and-answers. We urgently need effective dialogues to help stop the bleeding of our national potential and the lives of our people' (Maira 2002). Why NGOs? Because most of them could have their ear close to the ground and they might hear better if they remembered to keep their big mouths shut.

NOTES

1. Freely translatable as 'ascetics' or 'sybarites' of development.
2. After making the point that all donors are encouraging the involvement of autonomous societies, she reminds us that making 'societies genuinely

democratic and transparent could help us address issues related to leadership and control'.

3. A very successful single-teacher single-room school system has been innovated by the famous Rishi Valley School, Madanapalle, Andhra Pradesh, for educating poor out-of-school children. Sixteen satellite schools are run around the main school campus, and the system is now being replicated for adoption in tribal villages under a special United Nations Children's Fund (UNICEF) programme.

4. See the careful analysis of the Indian economy made by Dandekar (1994). See also trenchant criticism of the failure to reduce poverty by Sankaran (1997).

5. Meaning, in popular derisive terminology, 'government dependent'.

6. During an annual convention of the International Council of Voluntary Agencies (ICVA), at Dakar, Senegal, in 1985.

7. Dr Bala Reddy is quoted as saying: 'I see a direct link between great power and superpower interests and the fashions of development as handed out by the so-called Christian organisations that are affecting the working of civil society in this country'.

8. The Andhra Pradesh Government has innovated by establishing a GONGO, termed rather hopefully as the Society for the Elimination of Rural Poverty (SERP), to implement the Rs 30 billion World Bank-funded District Poverty Implementation Programme (DPIP). The World Bank has also launched similar programmes in the states of Rajasthan and Madhya Pradesh. However, in a recent assessment workshop held at Hyderabad, IT, media and jargon savvy Andhra Pradesh officials outshone their colleagues from other states.

9. *The Times of India,* 20 April 2002. By December 2001, 4,262.89 tonnes of rice valued at Rs 26.5 million had been distributed, of which Rs 24.5 million advanced as credit was recovered by 31 March 2002, benefiting 5,914 self-help groups, covering more than 73,795 families.

10. The voluntary movement in India has vigorously put forward this viewpoint, led by the Centre for Science and Environment and Lokayan, of New Delhi; Samvardhan of Ahmedabad; and others.

11. From recollections of childhood!

12. 'Founded in 1987 by some of the nation's most visionary leaders in socially responsible entrepreneurship and investment, Social Venture Network (SVN) is a nonprofit network committed to building a just and sustainable world through business . . . . SVN promotes new models and leadership for socially and environmentally sustainable business in the 21st century. We champion this effort through initiatives, information services and forums that strengthen our community and empower our members to work together on behalf of their shared vision.'

13. 'As an international non-profit organisation working with some of the foremost global companies and community partners to promote responsible business practices and partnership for development, The Prince of Wales Business Leaders Forum is committed to assisting the United Nations engage

business as an active partner in the "Global Compact" announced by UN Secretary General Kofi Annan in January 1999. Helping to interpret the UN Compact for business including identifying opportunities for dialogue, input and practical engagement in specific areas such as human rights, conflict prevention and working standards . . . . Identifying the areas of common agenda between UN and business in good governance, standards, social development and security.'

REFERENCES

Arole, Mabelle and Arole, Rajanikant. 1994. *Jamkhed: A Comprehensive Rural Health Project.* Jamkhed, Maharashtra: Comprehensive Rural Health Project.

Arora, Dolly. 1994. 'From State Regulation to People's Participation: Case of Forest Management in India'. *Economic and Political Weekly*, 29.

Bandopadhyay D. 1997. 'People's Participation in Planning: Kerala Experiment'. *Economic and Political Weekly*, 32(39).

Dandekar, V.M. 1994. *The Indian Economy 1947–92*, Vols. I and II. New Delhi: Sage.

George, Susan. 2001. 'The Global Citizens Movement: A New Actor For a New Politics'. Conference on *Reshaping Globalisation: Multilateral Dialogues and New Policy Initiatives*. Sponsored by the Central European University, Budapest. 18 October.

Jeanrenaud, Sally. 2002. *People Oriented Approaches in Global Conservation: Is the Leopard Changing its Spots?* London: IIED/IDS.

Maira, Arun. 2002. Chairman, Boston Consulting Group, India. *The Economic Times*. 17 April.

Mathew A.S. 1995. 'Kabbanala, Ralegaon Siddhi and Panipanchayat: A Revisit'. *Administrator*, XL(2).

Mawdsley, Emma and Townsend, Janet 2002. *Knowledge, Power and Development Agendas: NGOs North and South.* Oxford: INTRAC NGO Management and Policy. Series No. 14.

Rajan, Vithal. 1994. 'Power of the Poor'. *Resurgence*, September/October.

Ramachandran, Vimala. 1999. 'External Aid in Elementary Education: A Double Edged Sword'. *Economic and Political Weekly*, 34(50).

Sankaran, S.R. 1997. 'Planning for the Poor: Indian Experience'. The First Dr C.D. Deshmukh Memorial Lecture, 1997. Hyderabad: Council for Social Development.

Sen, Amartya and Drèze, Jean. 1999. *The Amartya Sen and Jean Drèze Omnibus, Poverty and Famines.* Delhi: Oxford University Press.

The Economic Times. 11 May 2001.

The Hindu. 2002a. 5 February.

_____. 2002b. 21 April.

The Times of India. 20 April 2002.

PART III

CORPORATE GOVERNANCE

This part opens with a conceptual chapter by Reed which is followed by Seth's chapter that reviews corporate governance systems in the international context, drawing implications for India. While De Vincentiis and Schmidt look into the European situation and Abell and Reyniers consider participatory firms, Bhattacharyya looks into issues in corporate governance in India.

Reed argues in his chapter that the study of corporate governance is a broad, multidisciplinary field that employs different forms of analysis and draws upon a variety of theoretical traditions. Such characteristics inevitably imply controversy. This chapter sets as its goal the aim of identifying the nature of the disputes in the field. It attempts to fulfil this goal by first distinguishing between three basic approaches to the analysis of corporate governance and then identifying the issues that arise within each of these approaches. In taking up this goal, the underlying intent is to facilitate interaction and greater mutual understanding both within and across the different disciplines which take up the analysis of corporate governance, viz., business ethics, business and related professional disciplines, and various social science disciplines.

Seth proposes in her chapter that it is crucial to understand the genesis of the governance system in a specific national context in order to develop an appropriate yardstick for measuring the potential effectiveness of reform initiatives. She develops in her chapter a model of corporate governance systems based on the theoretical perspectives of property rights, political economy and strategic management. The model highlights the important influence of governance institutions on the governance system of a national economy. This system evolves from a complex bargaining and negotiation process over time among governance institutions. Implications of the model for governance reform are presented and applied in the case of India.

De Vincentiis argues in her chapter that in the global financial market setting competition that is triggered by worldwide economies of scale and scope, heightened by technology and innovation, leads to increased concentration and consolidation. Initially these developments are good for the consumer who enjoys lower prices and goods and services of a better quality. However, once the consolidation battle is over, there is a danger that those global groups will exploit their power in the world market in a traditional oligopolistic fashion. This is the reason why, at least in principle, many recognise that global competition laws enforced by a supranational competition authority dealing with issues such as anti-trust and abuse of dominant positions are required. Markets, notably the financial system, are playing a key role in the global economy. What we clearly experience is a real-time confidence vote of the markets on global companies, national parliaments, governments and central banks. The new market powers mainly stem from the possibility of asset managers (who closely monitor governments and corporate policies) shifting huge investment flows in real-time worldwide. This possibility poses great challenges and high risks. There is a need for supranational surveillance of the working of the global financial system to prevent systemic risk and check possible overshoots, while avoiding distortion effects on resource allocation.

Schmidt shows in his chapter that globalisation or more precisely internationalisation in connection with the liberalisation of the financial markets has led to a restructuring of corporate governance practices. The intention is to create more transparency, comparable conditions of competition and smooth international exchange of capital and goods. In Germany, the newly defined legal frames are accompanied by managerial strategies changing from traditional cooperative and integrative style of business systems and labour relations to a more Anglo-Saxon type of management practice. This chapter analyses the influence of the new norms and regulations, the pressures of stock markets and the rigorous demands of shareholders. It considers the liberalisation and 'financialisation' process in German enterprises and the resistance of the (yet) persisting cooperative structure in the firms with co-determination, trust relations and management by delegation.

The chapter by Abell and Reyniers analyses the participation by employed labour in both the management and the ownership of productive assets of the firm. It discusses the conditions that favour the emergence and survival of employee-owned firms and the inherent difficulties in establishing the inferiority or superiority in terms of efficiency and performance of participatory firms over traditional capitalist firms. The role of government intervention in the observed evolution towards more labour participation is assessed. Top management is introduced as an actor beside labour and capital in an explicit model of corporate governance that sheds light on the evolution of participation.

Bhattacharyya's chapter is concerned with corporate governance in general and with corporate governance initiatives in the financial sector in particular. He discusses corporate governance practices in India, highlighting recent initiatives to improve these practices. The focus of his chapter is on the 'agency problem': This problem refers to difficulties in ensuring that financiers' funds are not expropriated or wasted on unattractive projects. Difficulties arise in formulating contracts to cover all situations that the enterprise may face during its lifetime and in enforcing those contracts in the court of law. Therefore, institutions are developed to protect the interest of financiers. The structure of institutions and their behaviour is governed by the ownership structure of publicly-traded companies, the stage of economic development and the culture and ethos of the society; therefore, corporate governance systems are not uniform in all countries. In India, over the last two years, the government, regulators and business associations have initiated actions to improve corporate governance. All these measures, Bhattacharyya argues, will change corporate practices and corporate financial reporting in India.

GOOD CORPORATE GOVERNANCE IN THE GLOBAL ECONOMY: WHAT IS AT ISSUE?

DARRYL REED

The study of corporate governance (CG) has been enjoying unparalleled attention over the last two decades. This recent surge in popularity, however, should not overshadow the fact that investigators from a variety of academic disciplines have long been concerned about how corporations are run, even if they have not formulated their analysis in terms of 'corporate governance'. One thing that has been constant in the study of CG over the years, however, is controversy. Major disagreements permeate not only the positive (social science) analysis of how policies, institutions and models of CG function, but also the normative (ethical) analysis of how CG should be organised and regulated and the strategic analysis of how to effectively promote change in the desired directions. The primary purpose of this chapter is to examine some of the discussion around what good CG might entail and the basic conditions for the promotion of good governance in the emerging global economy, especially in developing countries.

In taking up these questions, I will proceed in the following manner. First, I will briefly examine the problematic of investigating CG, making two key distinctions that will provide the basis for the subsequent sections: (*i*) three different forms of analysis (positive, normative and strategic), and (*ii*) a range of approaches to conceptualising CG, from the very narrow (best characterised by the Anglo-American model of CG) to the very broad. Next, I examine some of the basic issues that have distinguished broader approaches to the positive analysis of CG from narrower approaches. In the third section, I again contrast narrow and broad approaches to CG, but this time in terms of their normative analysis of key issues. Finally, in the fourth section I argue that if good CG is to be effectively promoted in the global economy, new forms of regulating the activities of transnational corporations (TNCs) and the international economy will have to be developed. More specifically, I contend, only some form of democratically controlled, supranational regulation will probably be capable of effectively regulating TNCs in the global economy and restoring the public policy autonomy to national governments necessary for good governance.

THE PROBLEMATIC OF ANALYSING CORPORATE GOVERNANCE

The conceptualisation and analysis of CG, like all social institutions and practices, is controversial.[1] Such controversy is rooted in the fact that there are different forms and traditions of analysis. These differences, which lead researchers to ask different questions, inevitably result in different analysis of how the policies, institutions and models of CG function, should function and can be more effectively reformed. In this section, I briefly indicate how the controversial nature of these key aspects of the analysis of CG result in a range of understandings of what CG entails.

DIFFERENT FORMS OF ANALYSIS

One key aspect of the analysis of CG involves the fact that it is possible to investigate corporations, like all social institutions, from a variety of different disciplinary perspectives. More specifically, the recognition that the study of CG can be undertaken from three distinct analytical approaches (viz., the positive, the normative and the strategic) is critical in elucidating the complexity and accounting for the diversity in the field (Reed 2002a). Positive analysis, primarily undertaken by the social (and natural) sciences, makes truth claims. It problematises how we can know existing states of affairs and their causes. Normative analysis, primarily undertaken by ethics and political philosophy, makes claims of goodness and correctness. It problematises the criteria by which we (ethically or morally) evaluate people, policies, institutions, effects, etc. Strategic analysis, primarily undertaken by professional disciplines and public policy, makes claims of effectiveness. It problematises how we can most effectively achieve given ends.

The distinction between these different forms of analysis, which can be viewed as complementary, is itself not particularly controversial.[2] What is controversial, however, is the relationship between these different forms of analysis. While aspects of these three different forms of analysis are generally interwoven into all investigations of CG (often as unstated presuppositions), usually only one form of analysis is problematised to any significant degree. What is at issue, then, is the level of support that these different forms of analysis require from each other to produce a cogent argument. Of particular importance for our concerns is the degree to which normative understandings of CG are dependent upon positive analysis for their justification.

DIFFERENT TRADITIONS OF ANALYSIS

Another factor that contributes to diversity and complexity in the study of CG is the existence of different theoretical traditions of analysis. These traditions exist both within specific disciplines such as economics (e.g., neo-classicals, Keynesians, institutionalists, Marxists) and ethics (e.g., virtue ethics, deontology, utilitarianism) as well as across disciplines and forms of analysis (e.g., postmodernism, German critical theory, etc.). These different traditions ensure that there is not only (complementary) diversity across the different forms of analysis, but (conflicting) diversity within them. As a result, the choice of different theoretical traditions for the analysis of CG is invariably controversial. What is at issue, more specifically, are the different ontological, epistemological and methodological presuppositions that characterise these different theoretical traditions.

NARROWER VERSUS BROADER CONCEPTIONS OF CORPORATE GOVERNANCE

The distinctions made above between positive and normative analysis and different traditions of analysis help us in understanding how corporate governance might be conceptualised in different ways. The positive concept of CG can be formally expressed as 'the manner in which corporations are governed', while from the perspective of normative analysis CG can be formally conceptualised as 'the manner in which the corporation should be governed'. Different traditions of analysis, however, combine with different historical experiences of the corporation and different value systems to provide competing (positive and normative) conceptions of corporate governance. It is possible to distinguish a range of substantive (positive and normative) conceptions of CG, extending from the very narrow to the very broad. These conceptions vary with respect to their understanding of: (a) what counts (should count) as a corporation; (b) what governance entails (should entail); and (c) what effects and actors are (should be) relevant objects of consideration. While the formal (positive and normative) concepts of CG are relatively uncontroversial, there is obviously greater controversy surrounding the various (positive and normative) substantive conceptions of CG.

The narrowest conceptions of CG are commonly associated with the most restricted understandings of the Anglo-American model of CG. Historically, this model has been characterised by: (a) a single-tiered board structure which gives almost exclusive primacy to shareholder interests (e.g., the board is elected exclusively by shareholders, shareholders have strong rights grounded in company law); (b) a dominant role for financial markets (both as the major source for investment funds and as a disciplinary mechanism to address the agency problem); (c) a correspondingly weak role for banks (which typically provide a small proportion of investment funds, cannot hold shares, do not have nominee directors, etc.); and (d) little or no industrial policy involving firms cooperating with government agencies (and labour bodies). Broader understandings of corporate governance are typically associated with substantially altered forms of the Anglo-American model or other types of national models of CG (most notably the German and Japanese), but can also be associated with other non-national models (e.g., the model of governance of the Mondragon Cooperative Corporation). In what follows, we examine in more detail what is at issue between broader and narrower conceptions of CG by investigating key issues pertaining to different social realms, viz., the economic, socio-cultural and political. We do this in turn with regard to the positive and normative analysis of CG.

Positive analysis makes truth claims. It problematises how we can know existing states of affairs and their causes. In the field of CG, positive (social science and historical) analysis is used to investigate: (*a*) how corporations are governed; (*b*) the effects of given governance practices and policies; and (*c*) the causal relationships that account for these practices, policies and effects. The various issues relating to the practices, policies and effects of CG can be subsumed under three broad categories, viz., economic performance, socio-cultural activities and effects, and political involvement. While we are primarily concerned with what good corporate governance should entail, it is also imperative to address the issue of how the institutions and structures actually function. This is important not only from the perspective of application, but also in terms of the justification of policies and models, as most normative theoretical perspectives (strict Kantian deontologists aside) do incorporate performance into their evaluation criteria.

ECONOMIC PERFORMANCE

At issue here are a range of closely related factors that potentially affect how (efficiently) corporations are governed. These can be organised under five headings. First, there is the question of ownership and, in particular, changes in the dispersal of ownership among investor-owned firms. For narrow conceptions of CG, such changes are of significance both because they represent a decline in family-controlled firms (which is of interest for a number of reasons) and because they point to a 'democratisation' of the economy. While the basic claim that there has been an increased dispersal of ownership is relatively uncontroversial, claims of 'democratisation' remain controversial. This latter point is vigorously disputed by many investigators operating out of broader conceptions of CG, who argue that (a capitalist) class still exists (Miliband 1969; Scott 1997; Zeitlin 1989). Broader conceptions of CG are also concerned with patterns of ownership among alternative firms (e.g., employee-owned, cooperatives) and the various factors relating to CG that may affect their ability to compete with investor-owned firms (Blair et al. 2000).

Second, there is the issue of control. For narrow conceptions, the dominant issue tends to be whether, or the extent to which, corporations are controlled by management rather than owners. This thesis, of course, was most famously expounded by Berle and Means ([1932] 1968). While it is generally accepted that historically there has been a significant shift in control from owners to management, the extent of this shift, the mechanisms by which it occurs and the criteria for defining control remain controversial (Herman 1981; Kaufman et al. 1995). One recent issue, which is addressed both by those operating out of narrower and broader conceptions of CG, is the degree to which the increased presence of institutional investors has changed the dynamics of control, i.e., whether they 'act like owners' and try to attain and exercise control (Macey 1998). Broader conceptions of CG also find two other basic questions of significance: (a) how patterns and issues of control vary across different (national) models of CG (Franks and Meyer 1997); and (b) how control operates in the case of alternative corporations such as employee-owned firms (Gordon 1998) and cooperative firms (Harvey 1995).

Third, there is the question of agency. This is the dominant issue for most narrow conceptions of CG (Parkinson 1995). The basic point of contention here is whether management runs the corporation: (a) in its own interests as agency theory argues (Ross 1973); (b) in the short- to medium-run interests of shareholders as the market myopia model claims (Blair 1995); (c) in the long-run interest of the firm as stewardship theory claims (Lipton and Rosenblum 1991); or (d) in the interests of consumers as the neo-classical ideal of competitive markets holds it should. Underlying these different positions on the question of agency are a range of factors that potentially influence the decision-making processes of boards. Here, narrower conceptions of CG emphasise such issues as: (a) the composition of boards, e.g., inside versus outside directors, board size, etc. (Bhagat and Black 1998); (b) board structure and functioning, e.g., frequency of meetings, role and composition of board committees (Lorsch 1995); (c) remuneration and incentive programmes for directors and leading executives, e.g., linking remuneration to performance (Bruce and Buck 1997); (d) disclosure (Loss 1985) and accounting standards (Stern and Chew 1997); (e) legal measures for the enforcement of directors' duties (Boyle 1985); (f) the efficiency of capital markets as a tool for disciplining management (Jensen 1988; Schmidt 1985). Broader conceptions of CG, while interested in these concerns as well, also raise a number of other issues including: (*a*) differences between dominant and non-dominant shareholder interests (Herman 1981); (*b*) the influence of the banking system (Mulbert 1998); (*c*) shareholder activism and the role of annual general meetings (Butcher 1995); (*d*) the (watchdog) role of institutional investors and stakeholder directors (Davies 1997; Hillman et al. 2002); (*e*) differences between national and multinational corporations (Hertner 1998); and (*f*) how different aspects (e.g., two-tiered boards) of different forms of CG (e.g., the German model, co-op models) affect the problem of agency (Hopt 1998; Leggett 2002; Teubner 1985).

Fourth, there is the issue of other stakeholders. For narrow conceptions of CG, what is at issue is the degree to which various actors can influence those in control of the corporation—Freeman's (1984) original definition of a stakeholder—and how the response of controlling groups affects corporate performance. Because the performance of the company drives this approach, attention tends to be limited primarily to 'business stakeholders' (i.e., suppliers, distributors, consumers, etc.), especially those who have clear claims to contractual or fiduciary obligations by the corporation and are in a position to (threaten to) litigate. The effects of the corporation's influence on other stakeholders is taken into account only to the degree that they are able (and likely) to organise themselves to put pressure on the corporation. Again, while broader conceptions of CG are also concerned with business stakeholders, they also examine the corporation's effects on a wider range of stakeholder groups, independently of their ability to influence the corporation. Issues here include pollution and other environment impacts, various social impacts (e.g., contributions to urbanisation, social stratification, poverty alleviation, etc.) and the response of corporations and government to these issues through social reporting and auditing (Dierkes 1985) and different approaches to the enforcement of fiduciary obligations, e.g., private litigation, wider board representation, etc. (Reberioux 2002; Teubner 1985).

Fifth, there is the question of the regulation of corporations and industries. At issue here is how different approaches to regulating the corporation (viz., self-regulation, government regulation and market discipline) affect different stakeholder groups. For narrow conceptions of CG, which focus almost exclusively on shareholders, a key issue is the impact regulation (company law, environmental law, labour law, etc.) upon the discretionary powers of management and how this affects their ability to maximise shareholder value (and, possibly, how this in turn effects larger macro-economic indicators such as growth, employment, etc.). Another major issue involves the functioning of capital markets and how effective different approaches to regulating them are in disciplining management and boards (Levine 2000). The third basic issue for narrow conceptions of CG relates to self-regulation and entails discussions of the effectiveness of different approaches to self-regulation. While broader conceptions of CG are also concerned with these three approaches to regulation, they broaden the scope of their concern to include the effects on different stakeholder groups. Thus, for example, with respect to government regulation they investigate the effects of company law not just on shareholders, but employees and other stakeholders. Similarly, with respect to market regulation, they are concerned not only with the ability of markets to discipline managers, but the impact of mergers and take-overs on various non-shareholder groups such as employees, local communities, etc. Broader conceptions are also concerned with comparative analysis, both with respect to the evaluation of different models of corporate governance (Charkham 1994; Kaplan 1997) and different types of corporations (Hansmann 1996).

SOCIO-CULTURAL ACTIVITIES AND EFFECTS

The overarching issues in this area are how corporate activities impact social relations and cultural values and traditions and vice versa. For the narrowest conceptions of CG, the key issue is how cultural values and traditions can affect the performance of the corporation (Gay 2002). This concern is raised both with respect to the cross-national comparison of firms operating in a single country and the problems faced by TNCs operating in a variety of different countries (Mentzer 1999; Sison 2000). Insofar as narrow conceptions focus almost exclusively on board activities, a particular concern that arises is how the composition of boards of directors (e.g., women, ethnic and racial minorities, non-nationals) affects corporate performance (Burke 1997). Such narrow conceptions are generally only concerned with the social and cultural impacts of the firm's activities on non-shareholders in the context of the evaluation of their (potential) costs to the firm, and whether it pays to be 'socially responsible'.

In contrast to narrower conceptions, broader conceptions of CG tend to emphasise the impact of corporate activities on the social and cultural realms (Waddock 2000). Insofar as it is assumed that the board is ultimately responsible for management behaviour, the effects of a full range of corporate activities come under the purview of CG including finance, production, marketing, philanthropy, etc. While an almost unlimited range of issues might arise, key concerns have included the effects of philanthropic programmes in addressing social problems and supporting cultural development, the under-mining of local community values (e.g., through product selection decisions and marketing strategies), contributions to processes of urban decay/regeneration in the inner core of large cities and small towns (e.g., through plant relocation decisions), the promotion of a culture of consumerism, etc. Broader conceptions of CG are also concerned with comparative analysis, both with respect to whether board diversity, investors composition, governance devices and models (e.g., the Anglo-American, the German, cooperatives) affect social responsibility and responsiveness to local community con-cerns (Coffey and Wang 1998; Johnson and Greening 1999).

POLITICAL INVOLVEMENT

What is broadly at issue with respect to corporate political involve-ment are the nature and effects of the interrelations between business, the formal political process and institutions of government and the broader political process and culture. Here, narrower conceptions of CG emphasise the effects of government on business. More specifically, at issue are the effects of government and administrative regula-tions and practices (other than traditional economic policy mea-sures) on the ability of business to compete. In the case of foreign governments what is frequently at issue is how (non-domestic) busi-ness is adversely affected by and often totally unable to compete in the presence of informal processes, questionable procedures and/or pervasive corruption (Kotchian 1977). With respect to national gov-ernments, a key concern has been how the imposition of regula-tions on the activities of corporations operating in other countries (e.g., the Federal Corrupt Practices Act in the US) inhibits the ability of such firms to compete (Geo-JaJa and Mangum 2000).

For their part, broader conceptions of CG switch the emphasis away from the effects of government policy on corporations to the influence of corporations on government and the broader political process. Key issues with respect to the more direct influence that corporations exercise vis-à-vis government include lobbying, campaign financing and influence peddling (Birnbaum 1993; Bowman 1996; Kaufman et al. 1995). Closely related concerns include the nature and effectiveness of measures taken to limit corporate influence over the political realm (e.g., limits on the campaign contributions, lobbying activities, etc.) and comparisons of how different political systems regulate corporate political activity. On the flip side of the coin, broader conceptions are also concerned with how governments respond somewhat proactively to corporate power by trying to compete against other jurisdictions to attract capital. A notable example of this within a country involves the struggle in the US by federal states to attract corporations to incorporate within their jurisdiction, a 'race to the bottom' in which Delaware has been the undisputed victor (Monks and Minow 1995). Recently, with economic liberalisation and deregulation on a global scale, developing countries have become involved in their own 'race to the bottom' to attract foreign capital (Strange 1994). Also at issue for broader conceptions of CG are the (more indirect) effects of corporations on the broader political process through their control over the media (Chomsky and Herman 1988) and their influence on the educational system (Marsh 1995). Key issues here include such phenomena as the promotion of elite and market models of democracy and the generation of a political culture of apathy (Parenti 1995).

ISSUES IN THE NORMATIVE ANALYSIS OF CORPORATE GOVERNANCE

The key form of analysis in determining what constitutes good CG is normative analysis. It makes claims of goodness and correctness and problematises the criteria by which we (ethically or morally) evaluate people, policies, effects, etc. In the field of CG, normative analysis is used: (*a*) to determine the criteria that should be used in evaluating people, policies, practices, institutions, and structures involved in CG; (*b*) to identify factors that may condition the applicability of these criteria; and (*c*) to evaluate these various entities. Again, the issues involved in the normative analysis of CG can be subsumed under three basic categories, viz., economic, socio-cultural and political responsibilities.

ECONOMIC ISSUES AND RESPONSIBILITIES

The general issues in this area are who is an appropriate object of concern with respect to the economic effects of corporate activity, what are the nature and extent of the responsibilities of those governing the corporation to such 'stakeholders' and what is the normative basis of such responsibilities. For the narrowest conceptions of CG, the only valid objects of concern are shareholders (Friedman 1970). The basic obligation owed is the maximisation of shareholder value, with other obligations (e.g., disclosure) primarily understood as auxiliary to ensuring the fulfilment of the primary obligation. The question of the extent of the obligations of boards and senior management, then, is usually understood in terms of two issues, viz., whether they should enjoy the discretion to undertake activities (e.g., corporate philanthropy) which do not directly maximise shareholder value, but may ultimately rebound to the shareholders' interests, and whether they should operate the firm on the basis of the short-term or long-term interests of shareholders. Such narrow conceptions of CG generally ground themselves (tacitly if not explicitly) in some strain of libertarian or utilitarian thought (Reed 2002b).

Broader conceptions of CG may extend the potential objects of corporate obligations to a variety of other stakeholder groups, most notably, employees, consumers, other business stakeholders (e.g., suppliers, distributors, etc.), local communities and society as a whole (Post et al. 2002). Understandings of the nature and extent of the obligations owed to these various groups may vary widely. Some possible responsibilities commonly advocated include paying fair wages, ensuring adequate health and safety standards, providing a humane work environment, producing safe and reliable products, competing fairly, being environmentally responsible, etc. A key overarching concern for broader conceptions of CG, then, is profit strategy. More specifically, at issue is: (a) whether firms should/may employ strategies that seek to maximise profits in ways which go against the spirit of competitive markets (e.g., putting up barriers to market access, seeking out non-competitive market niches, etc.) or must seek profits only through innovation (Miles 1993); and (b) the nature of the constraints under which firms should pursue such profit strategies (e.g., paying fair wages, not producing externalities, etc.). There are a wide variety of individual values (e.g., loyalty, community) and principles (e.g., merit, need, various rights claims), which may be invoked to justify the (non-) existence of particular CG obligations. There is also a somewhat extensive range of moral theories that may be drawn upon both for prioritising different (potential) obligations and providing a more comprehensive justification of the nature of corporate responsibilities, e.g., virtue ethics, utilitarianism, discourse ethics, Rawlsian political theory, etc. Also at issue for broader conceptions of CG is the comparative evaluation of both different models of corporate governance and different forms of corporations (Reed 2002c).

SOCIO-CULTURAL ISSUES AND RESPONSIBILITIES

At issue with respect to this area are the nature and extent (if any) of corporate socio-cultural responsibilities, the appropriate objects of such responsibilities and the normative basis of such responsibilities. For the narrowest conceptions of CG, the answers to these questions are clear and simple. Corporations have no socio-cultural responsibilities. Indeed, the expenditure of any resources in these areas is understood to constitute theft from shareholders (Friedman 1970). Libertarianism generally provides the normative basis for such a position.

For broader conceptions of CG, the nature, extent and objects of socio-cultural obligations may vary considerably. Again, any range of stakeholder groups (from employees to local communities up to society as a whole) may be viewed as potential objects of corporate responsibilities. One way to categorise the nature of such obligations is to distinguish between negative obligations to respect the existing status quo (e.g., to respect local community values, to refrain from or limit activities that will cause undesired social change) and positive obligations that require more active involvement to promote cultural and social development (e.g., support for the arts, education, health, poverty alleviation programmes, etc.). Another approach to categorising such obligations is to determine the form of the obligation, i.e., whether they are seen as primarily philanthropic in nature (i.e., commendable but not required), obligations of charity (i.e., imperfect duties which are required but have no specific object to whom the obligations are owed), obligations resulting from past relationships (e.g., obligations of loyalty) or obligations pertaining to claims of rights and justice. As in the case of economic responsibilities, a wide variety of normative values, principles and theories can be invoked to uphold different types of CG responsibilities. Again, broader conceptions of CG are also interested in comparative evaluations of both different models of corporate governance and different forms of corporations.

POLITICAL ISSUES AND RESPONSIBILITIES

Generally at issue in this area are our understandings of political democracy and the obligations and rights (or entitlements) that corporations have vis-à-vis different stakeholder groups, the state and the political community as a whole. For narrow conceptions of CG, two basic issues tend to dominate the discussion. First, there is the issue of the legal status of the corporation and the rights or entitlements that it should be granted. Narrow conceptions of CG tend to hold that corporations should enjoy the extensive personhood rights (e.g., freedom of speech) that they are guaranteed in the US. Usually, however, support for such a position resorts to legal judgements rather than any normative theoretical argumentation (Bowman 1996; Kaufman et al. 1995).

Second, there is the nature of shareholder rights. Either of two basic approaches is typically adopted here. On the one hand, it is argued that shareholders (should) have ownership rights. These include not only such rights as disclosure, transferability, but also some rights to control over the enterprise (traditionally exercised through the election of the board of directors and the ability to pose questions and introduce resolutions at the annual general meeting). The usual basis for upholding such a position is some form of libertarianism. On the other hand, it is argued that shareholders are not (or should not be viewed as) traditional owners, but merely investors. As such, they do not (should not) have any claims to control, but only claims to have their interests maximised (and the associated rights which help to ensure this, e.g., disclosure, the right to bring suit, etc.). The most common normative basis for this position is some version of (rule) utilitarianism. While it is acknowledged that CG does imply respect for the rights of shareholders, there is little discussion of the need to respect the rights of other political stakeholders. The reason for this is that such narrow conceptions tend to assume that the only other political obligations of corporations are to obey the law (and that the existing law is legitimate).

There tends to be little or no discussion of the criteria for legitimate law and what, if any, special obligations corporations may have when these criteria are not fully enshrined in law (Reed 2002b).

Broader conceptions of CG are generally characterised by a stronger emphasis on the political obligations of corporations and a substantially different understanding of the rights of corporations and shareholders vis-à-vis other groups. With respect to the question of rights, broader conceptions contest the imputation of strong personhood rights to corporations as essentially a legal fiction based on a bad analogy (Greider 1992). As a result they may question the legitimacy of a range of corporate political practices in the formal political realm, e.g., campaign financing, lobbying, influence peddling, etc. Moreover, they may also question the legitimacy of the influence that corporations exert in the broader political process through their control over the media and their ability to influence the education system (Marsh 1995).

Broader conceptions of CG also raise the issue of whether groups other than shareholders (e.g., employees, public interest groups) should have greater opportunities to participate in the governance of corporations. They may advocate increased participation through reforms to the form of corporate governance in traditional for-profit corporations, e.g., worker or public interest representation (McCall 2001; Monks and Minow 1995), or through the promotion of alternative forms of corporations, e.g., cooperatives, employee-owned firms (Ellerman 1999).

Broader conceptions of CG may also raise the basic question of what political obligations corporations might have beyond respecting the law. Perhaps the most glaring issue and the limit case in this regard involves the obligations of corporations when operating in non-democratic environments. More generally, though, it could be argued that insofar as few, if any, governments fully live up to justifiable standards for legitimate law and democratic practice, the obligations of corporations in virtually all instances extend beyond mere observance of the law (e.g., respecting the privacy rights of individuals even when they are not fully enshrined in law). Underlying discussions on this latter issue, of course, is the most basic of normative political issues, viz., the nature of a justifiable conception of the political legitimacy. Broader conceptions of CG may draw upon a variety of theories and traditions of political philosophy for such a conception (viz., contract theory, radical democracy, utilitarianism, Habermasian political theory, etc.) (Reed 1999).

Due to the potential range of normative criteria involved in evaluating CG, different value preferences across populations, different historical experiences of CG in different countries and the potential for significantly different outcomes for different groups of stakeholders under given models of CG, the normative analysis of corporate governance is extremely complex and controversial. Such controversy, it would seem, is likely to ensure that there will never be consensus within any given country about the most desirable model of CG, let alone an international consensus. What is most important, then, in the normative evaluation of CG is not the individual issues noted above, but the larger questions of whether a given population has been able to engage in a truly democratic process to choose what it deems the most appropriate form of CG. Ultimately, the evaluation of what good corporate governance is can only be determined through the democratic process.

STRATEGY AND CORPORATE GOVERNANCE— ENSURING DEMOCRATIC CONTROL

If the democratic nature of the process for choosing the system of CG is the most basic normative concern, then the most fundamental strategic concern must be ensuring that models of CG are freely chosen through a fair process. While there has been much discussion about CG reform over the last two decades, there is good reason to question whether the nature of these reforms has reflected the will of the people or the interests of economic and political elites. In this section, I will outline this concern and what needs to be done to address it. First, I will start by noting that the economic reforms that have been carried out over the last two decades, especially in developing countries, have moved countries in the direction of an Anglo-American model of governance. I will then go on to examine why developing countries are adopting Anglo-American-style reforms. Here I will not only argue that such reforms reflect the interests of international (and some domestic) business and political elites, but that with processes of economic globalisation developing countries have largely been stripped of public policy autonomy, making the Anglo-American model a default option for reform. Finally, I will contend that in order for developing countries to be able to regain some public policy autonomy (and freely choose what the people believe to be an appropriate model of CG), there will have to be more aggressive regulation of transnational business than is currently being proposed.

THE ANGLO-AMERICAN NATURE OF RECENT CORPORATE GOVERNANCE REFORMS

As noted above, the reforms being undertaken in developing countries are largely moving them in the direction of an Anglo-American model (Reed 2002a). There are several possible factors that may help to account for this phenomenon. One has to do with the past experience of the countries themselves. For some countries (e.g., India, Nigeria) there are strong historical ties to the Anglo-American model (e.g., their company law is firmly rooted in British company law) that make further movement in this direction appear natural. Another possible factor is that the lack of success of their previous interventionist models has served to discredit elements commonly associated with other models (e.g., a major role for bank finance, the use of industrial policy). It is also the case that, insofar as the previous interventionist system bred uncompetitive firms, strong financial markets present themselves as an important tool for promoting more competitive domestic firms. While it is an open question whether past failures are directly attributable to the interventionist development strategies in question (Taylor 1991), it is indisputable that key domestic (business and political) actors have presented past failures as a justification for liberalisation and moving towards an Anglo-American model. Business interests generally tend to favour the Anglo-American model and have been outspoken in opposing the adoption of any other models of governance, especially models that provide a role for stakeholder involvement (e.g., employees), like the German model (Confederation of Indian Industry 1998).

Another reason for the move to an Anglo-American model has to do with debt and the influence of international financial institutions (IFIs). Starting in the late 1970s, as a condition for renegotiating loans, IFIs imposed structural adjustment programmes on developing countries. These programmes included a variety of features that induced a move to an Anglo-American model of governance. For one, fiscal cutbacks pressured governments to reduce credit supplies, diminishing the role of bank finance and direct bank influence in governance (e.g., a decreased emphasis on nominee directors) and leading to a much greater role for equity financing. An emphasis on equity financing (and shareholder interests) was also encouraged through requirements that states deregulate financial markets and relax controls on foreign portfolio investment. States were also forced to abandon strong interventionist industrial policy (e.g., licencing regimes, labour market interventions, etc.) and dramatically reduce direct participation in production (e.g., privatisation of national industries). Again, while the wisdom of the structural adjustment programmes can be questioned (Stallings and Peres 2000)—especially as they were applied in the aftermath of the East Asian crisis (Stiglitz 2000)—there is no doubt that they have encouraged developing countries to move in the direction of the Anglo-American model.

Structural adjustment programmes reflect a more general approach by business and political elites to economic reforms. Dubbed by Williamson (1990) as 'the Washington Consensus', this approach advocates liberalising reforms in a range of areas (viz., fiscal discipline, public expenditure priorities, taxation, financial markets, trade, privatisation policy, deregulation, property rights, foreign direct investment, exchange rates). It is this 'consensus' that has shaped not only International Montary Fund (IMF) and World Bank policy, but also the neo-liberal form that processes of globalisation have taken. This neo-liberal character of globalisation serves to promote an Anglo-American model of corporate governance. In the neo-liberal environment, where domestic firms have to increasingly raise funds in equity markets (due to declines in bank capital) and states are seeking to induce foreign investment—foreign portfolio investment to finance domestic firms and foreign direct investment to generate employment and stimulate key sectors of the economy—shareholder interests have to be given priority. This necessitates a liberalisation of capital markets, changes to company law, etc. Similarly, other aspects of the neo-liberal global economy (e.g., trade agreements) undermine the use of interventionist industrial policy associated with non-Anglo-American governance models. In effect, the Anglo-American model of corporate governance is a logical micro-level complement of the macro neo-liberal global economy.

One final point about the 'consensus' needs to be highlighted with respect to governance concerns. This so-called consensus was largely induced by lobbying efforts and negotiations involving large TNCs in developed countries and the dominant economic powers. The TNCs have exercised their influence at the level of the nation-state (e.g., in supporting the Thatcher and Reagan revolutions, in lobbying for trade liberalisation) through the creation of strong business lobbies (e.g., the Business Roundtable in the US, the Business Council on National Issues in Canada), as well as through the establishment of and participation in unofficial multilateral bodies (e.g., the Trilateral Commission, the Bilderberg Conferences, the Mont Pelerin Society, etc.). For their part, the dominant economic powers (e.g., US, Japan, EU) have asserted their influence through multilateral organisations whose participation is (largely) restricted to developed countries (e.g., the G-7, the Organisation for Economic Cooperation and Development [OECD], etc.). Through these organisations, the dominant economic powers have laid the basis for key changes in the international economy, inviting 'participation' from developing countries only after they have reached a basic agreement among themselves (Cox 1987, 1994). These practices have contributed to the widely held perception, as expressed in 'Seattle', that processes of globalisation tend to largely reflect the interests of TNCs in developed countries.

CORPORATE GOVERNANCE, INTERNATIONAL REGULATION AND DEMOCRATIC SOCIETY

At a practical level then, the key normative question is the degree to which the adoption of an Anglo-American model of governance, especially by developing countries, has reflected a truly democratic process. To summarise, there are three particular sources of concern in this regard: (*a*) the influence that TNCs are able to exert in the political realm of developed countries (and through them in the international realm); (*b*) the ability of the governments of developed countries (largely reflecting the interests of TNCs) to determine the nature of the global economy (e.g., trade agreements, investment agreements, etc.), without much regard for domestic public opinion or the concerns of developing countries; and (*c*) the ability of business elites in developing countries to use their influence to channel any resistance against processes of globalisation in ways that largely benefit large domestic firms (Cox 1987; Mukherjee Reed

2001). These three factors come together in ways which allow businesses, especially TNCs, to subvert the formally democratic structures of nation-states to determine the nature of governance reforms in line with their own interests.

With respect to strategic analysis then, while there is a range of strategic issues which of differing importance depending upon the model of CG in question, the basic question is how the processes of selecting and implementing governance reforms can be brought under greater democratic control. In a global economy, it has become increasingly clear that individual states, especially small and/or developing states have lost their policy autonomy to a significant degree (Perraton et al. 1997). This means that the only way that democratic control over the international economy (and the choice of governance models) can be effected is through some form of international regulation. There are two basic options.

One option would be an international approach to regulation working through the current international state system. The obvious problems with the current system include the facts that international agreements are voluntary, their targets are typically non-binding, there are no effective enforcement agencies, states can renounce agreements at any time (as the US has recently done in indicating its intention to no longer abide by the Kyoto agreement) and agreements are not developed through a democratic process, but rather reflect the power and resources that key actors (large states, large business) can bring to bear to influence processes of international negotiation. Reform of the system might involve increasing participation in the development of standards (e.g., as has been occurring with the inclusion of civil society groups in discussions as consultants), the development of regulation in previously unregulated areas (e.g., international anti-trust regulation, etc.), strengthening enforcement mechanisms (e.g., by allowing citizens and civil society groups to sue businesses and governments for damages outside their home country), restricting participation to democratic countries (as is being proposed for the new Free Trade Area of the Americas agreement), etc. (Teubner 1997). While such changes might contribute to more effective promotion of more responsible corporate governance in developing countries, they still suffer from major limitations (Galtung 2000). One key concern is that such reforms do not address a basic feature of a system based upon state sovereignty namely, that states can always opt out of agreements. This situation can create competitive disadvantages for those states that agree to more stringent conditions—including opting for alternative models of governance—and has an inherent tendency to induce a race to the bottom. A second concern is that there is little opportunity for democratic control over the process. In the best case scenario (which often does not hold), democratic participation is mediated through democratically elected national governments. The problem here, of course, is that even when formal democracy exists, business interests are able to exercise considerable influence to affect a government's approach to international policy (including issues of trade, environmental standards, etc.) in inappropriate ways.

Another option would be to move to a system of supranational regulation. A supranational model, conceived along the lines of the emerging European Union, addresses aspects of the international model that are particularly problematic from the perspective of any robust understanding of democracy (Habermas 1999, 2002; Held 2000). One advantage of this model is that it does not permit individual nations to opt out (and thereby helps to inhibit a regulatory race to the bottom). Second, it allows for more effective enforcement of standards as supranational enforcement agencies can help to reduce the influence that individual corporations may have in a particular country (e.g., the European court which allows individual citizens to bring cases that are not adequately resolved by courts in their home country). Third, it includes more direct democratic generation of international norms and standards through supranational legislative bodies (e.g., the European Parliament). Only under these conditions will it ever be possible for societies in developing (and many developed) countries to choose (and sustain) what they believe to be a good model of corporate governance.

CONCLUSION

In this chapter, I have tried to investigate the problematic of understanding what good corporate governance in the global economy entails. I have argued that, while there is a wide range of important normative issues that arise with respect to corporate governance, ultimately the most important determinant of good governance is the manner in which the model of governance has been chosen, viz., whether a given population has had the opportunity to actively engage in the democratic process to determine what they believe to be the best model. Moreover, I have contended that in order for the latter to happen, the influence of corporations over national governments, both directly and indirectly though their influence over their home states, has to be dramatically curbed through some form of democratically controlled supranational regulation. For this reason, the comparative analysis of good governance in democratic societies cannot be viewed merely as an academic exercise, it takes on urgent pragmatic importance. Such comparative studies are essential in helping us to understand how new models of democracy that transcend individual societies can be developed. Without the development of such new forms of democracy, our traditional models of democracy at the national level are doomed to become empty shells.

NOTES

1. While historically corporations have been involved in a range of endeavours (e.g., charitable, educational, etc.), today the concept is most closely associated in the public's mind with large (private-sector) businesses (Monks and Minow 1995). In this chapter, we limit the scope of our investigation to business corporations (i.e., corporations that produce products or provide services that are sold in the market), but recognise that these may take a number of forms (e.g., privately-held, publicly-held, state-owned, cooperatives, not-for-profit development corporations, etc.).
2. While some traditions, most notably postmodernism and communitarian, will question the degree to which it is possible to redeem (universal) claims within each of these forms of discourse, for the most part they acknowledge the distinction between these categories and generally allow for some level of meaningful discourse within them.

REFERENCES

Berle, A.A. Jr. and Gardiner, C.M. [1932] 1968. *The Modern Corporation and Private Property,* 2nd Edition. New York: Harcourt, Brace & World.

Bhagat, S. and Black, B. 1998. 'The Relationship Between Board Composition and Firm Performance', in K.P. Hopt, H. Kanda, M.J. Roe, E. Wymeersch and S. Prigge (eds), *Comparative Corporate Governance: The State of the Art and Emerging Research,* pp. 281–306. Oxford: Clarendon Press.

Birnbaum, J.H. 1993. *The Lobbyists: How Influence Peddlers Work Their Way in Washington.* New York: Times Books.

Blair, M.M. 1995. *Ownership and Control: Rethinking Corporate Governance for the Twenty-First Century*. Washington, D.C.: Brookings Institute.

Blair, M., Kruse, D. and Blasi, J. 2000. 'Employee Ownership: Unstable or Stabilizing?', in M. Blair, D. Kruse and J. Blasi (eds). *The New Relationship: Human Capital in the American Corporation*, pp. 241–88. Washington, D.C.: The Brookings Institute.

Bowman, S.R. 1996. *The Modern Corporation and American Political Thought: Law, Power, and Ideology*. University Park, PA: Pennsylvania University Press.

Boyle, A.J. 1985. 'The Private Law Enforcement of Directors' Duties', in K.J. Hopt and G. Teubner (eds). *Corporate Governance and Directors' Liabilities: Legal, Economic and Sociological Analyses on Corporate Social Responsibilities*, pp. 261–82. Berlin: Walter de Gruyter.

Bruce, A. and Buck, T. 1997. 'Executive Reward and Corporate Governance', in K. Keasey, S. Thompson and M. Wright (eds). *Corporate Governance: Economic Management and Financial Issues*, pp. 80–102. Oxford: Oxford University Press.

Burke, R.J. 1997. 'Women on Corporate Boards of Directors: A Needed Resource'. *Journal of Business Ethics*, 16(9): 909–15.

Butcher, D. 1995. 'Reform of the General Meeting', in S. Sheikh and W. Rees (eds). *Corporate Governance & Corporate Control*. London: Cavendish Publishing Ltd.

Charkham, J. 1994. *Keeping Good Company: A Study of Corporate Governance in Five Countries*, pp. 221–40. Oxford: Clarendon Press.

Chomsky, N. and Herman, E. 1988. *Manufacturing Consent: The Political Economy of the Mass Media*. New York: Pantheon.

Coffey, B.S. and Wang, J. 1998. 'Board Diversity and Managerial Control as Predictors of Corporate Social Performance'. *Journal of Business Ethics*, 17(14): 1595–1603.

Confederation of Indian Industry. 1998. *Desirable Corporate Governance—A Code*. Delhi: Confederation of Indian Industry.

Cox, R. 1987. *Production, Power, and World Order*. New York: Columbia University Press.

———. 1994. 'Global Restructuring: Making Sense of the Changing International Political Economy', in R. Stubbs and G.R.D. Underhill (eds). *Political Economy and the Changing Global Order*. pp. 45–59. Toronto: McClelland & Steward.

Davies, P. 1997. 'Institutional Investors as Corporate Monitors in the UK'. in K.J. Hopt and E. Wymeersch (eds). *Comparative Corporate Governance: Essays and Materials*, pp. 47–66. Berlin: Walter de Gruyter.

Dierkes, M. 1985. 'Corporate Social Reporting and Auditing', in K.J. Hopt and G. Teubner (eds). *Corporate Governance and Directors' Liabilities: Legal, Economic and Sociological Analyses on Corporate Social Responsibilities*, pp. 354–79. Berlin: Walter de Gruyter.

Ellerman, D. 1999. 'The Democratic Firm: An Argument Based on Ordinary Jurisprudence'. *Journal of Business Ethics*, 21: 111–24.

Franks, J. and Meyer, C. 1997. 'Corporate Ownership and Control in the UK, Germany and France', in D. Chew (ed.). *Studies in International Corporate Finance and Governance Systems*, pp. 281–96. Oxford: Oxford University Press.

Freeman, R.E. 1984. *Strategic Management: A Stakeholder Approach*. Boston: Pitman.

Friedman, M. 1970. 'The Social Responsibility of Business is to Increase its Profits'. *The New York Magazine*. September 13.

Galtung, J. 2000. 'Alternative Models for Global Democracy', in B. Holden (ed.). *Global Democracy: Key Debates*, pp. 143–61. London: Routledge.

Gay, K. 2002. 'Board Theories and Governance Practices: Agents, Stewards and Their Evolving Relationships with Stakeholders'. *Journal of General Management*, 27(3): 36–61.

Geo-JaJa, M.A. and Mangum, G.L. 2000. 'The Foreign Corrupt Practices Act's Consequences for U.S. Trade: The Nigerian Example'. *Journal of Business Ethics*, 24(3): 245–55.

Gordon, J. 1998. 'Employee Stock Ownership in Economic Transitions', in K.P. Hopt, H. Kanda, M.J. Roe, E. Wymeersch and S. Prigge (eds). *Comparative Corporate Governance: The State of the Art and Emerging Research*, pp. 387–435. Oxford: Clarendon Press.

Greider, W. 1992. *Who Will Tell the People? The Betrayal of American Democracy*. New York: Simon & Schuster.

Habermas, J. 1999. 'The European Nation-State and the Pressures of Globalization'. *New Left Review*, I(235): 46–59.

———. 2002. 'On Legitimation through Human Rights', in P. De Greiff and C. Cronin (eds). *Global Justice and Transnational Politics*, pp. 197–214. Cambidge, MA: MIT Press.

Hansmann, H. 1996. *The Ownership of Enterprise*. Cambridge, MA: Harvard University Press.

Harvey, B. 1995. 'The Governance of Co-operative Societies', in S. Sheikh and W. Rees (eds). *Corporate Governance & Corporate Control*, pp. 173–80. London: Cavendish Publishing Ltd.

Held, D. 2000. 'The Changing Contours of Political Community: Rethinking Democracy in the Context of Globalization', in B. Holden (ed.). *Global Democracy: Key Debates*, pp. 17–31. London: Routledge.

Herman, E.S. 1981. *Corporate Control. Corporate Power*. Cambridge: Cambridge University Press.

Hertner, P. 1998. 'Corporate Governance and Multinational Enterprise in Historical Perspective', in K.P. Hopt, H. Kanda, M.J. Roe, E. Wymeersch and S. Prigge (eds). *Comparative Corporate Governance: The State of the Art and Emerging Research*, pp. 41–59. Oxford: Clarendon Press.

Hillman, A.J., Keim, G.D. and Luce, R.A. 2002. 'Board Composition and Stakeholder Performance: Do Stakeholder Directors Make a Difference?'. *Business and Society*, 40(3): 295–314.

Hopt, K.J. 1998. 'The German Two-Tier Board Experience', in K.P. Hopt, H. Kanda, M.J. Roe, E. Wymeersch and S. Prigge (eds). *Comparative Corporate Governance: The State of the Art and Emerging Research*, pp. 227–58. Oxford: Clarendon Press.

Jensen, Michael. 1988. 'Agency Cost of Free Cash Flow, Corporate Finance and Takeovers'. *American Economic Review*. May.

Johnson, R.A. and Greening, D.W. 1999. 'The Effects of Corporate Governance and Institutional Ownership Types on Corporate Social Performance'. *Academy of Management Journal*, 42(5): 564–76.

Kaplan, S. 1997. 'Corporate Governance and Corporate Performance: A Comparison of German, Japan and the US', in K.J. Hopt and E. Wymeersch (eds). *Comparative Corporate Governance: Essays and Materials*, pp. 195–203. New York: Walter de Gruyter.

Kaufman, A., Zacharias, L. and Karson, M. 1995. *Managers vs. Owners: The Struggle for Corporate Control in American Democracy*. New York: Oxford University Press.

Kotchian, A.C. 1977. 'The Payoff: Lochheed's 70-day Mission to Tokyo'. *Saturday Review*, 9 July, pp. 7–12.

Leggett, K.J. 2002. 'Membership Growth, Multiple Membership Groups and Agency Control at Credit Unions'. *Review of Financial Economics*, 11(1): 37–46.

Levine, R. 2000, 'Bank-Based or Market-Based Financial Systems: Which is Better?'. Minneapolis MN: Institute of Financial Studies, Carlson School of Management, The University of Minnesota.

Lipton and Rosenblum. 1991. 'A New System of Corporate Governance: The Quinquennial Election of Directors'. *The University of Chicago Law Review*, 187.

Lorsch, J.W. 1995. *Pawns or Potentates? The Reality of American Corporate Boards*. Boston: Harvard Business School Press.

Loss, L. 1985. 'Disclosure as Preventative Enforcement', in K.J. Hopt and G. Teubner (eds). *Corporate Governance and Directors' Liabilities: Legal, Economic and Sociological Analyses on Corporate Social Responsibilities*, pp. 327–37. Berlin: Walter de Gruyter.

Macey, J. 1998. 'Institutional Investors and Corporate Monitoring: A Demand-Side Perspective in a Comparative View', in K.P. Hopt, H. Kanda, M.J. Roe, E. Wymeersch and S. Prigge (eds). *Comparative Corporate Governance: The State of the Art and Emerging Research*, pp. 903–19. Oxford: Clarendon Press.

Marsh, J.L. 1995. *Critique, Action and Liberation*. Albany, NY: State University of New York.

McCall, J.J. 2001. 'Employee Voice in Corporate Governance: A Defense of Strong Participation Rights'. *Business Ethics Quarterly*, 11(1): 195.

Mentzer, M. 1999. 'Two Heads are Better than One if your Company Spans the Globe'. *The Academy of Management Executive*, 13(2): 89–90.

Miles, G. 1993. 'In Search of Ethical Profits: Insights from Strategic Management'. *Journal of Business Ethics*, 12(1): 219–25.

Miliband, R. 1969. *The State in Capitalist Societies*. New York: Basic Books.

Monks, R.A.G. and Minow, N. 1995. *Corporate Governance*. Oxford: Basil Blackwell.

Mukherjee Reed, A. 2001. *Perspectives on the Indian Corporate Economy: Exploring the Paradox of Profits*. London: Palgrave.

Mulbert, P.O. 1998. 'Bank Equity in Non-financial Firms and Corporate Governance: The Case of German Universal Banks', in K.P. Hopt, H. Kanda, M.J. Roe, E. Wymeersch and S. Prigge (eds). *Comparative Corporate Governance*, pp. 445–98. Oxford: Clarendon Press.

Parenti, M. 1995. *Democracy for the Few*. NY: St. Martin's Press.

Parkinson, J. 1995. 'The Role of "Exit" and "Voice" in Corporate Governance', in S. Sheikh and W. Rees (eds). *Corporate Governance & Corporate Control*, pp. 75–100. London: Cavendish Publishing Ltd.

Perraton, J., Goldblatt, D., Held, D. and McGrew, A. 1997. 'The Globalization of Economic Activity'. *New Political Economy*, 2 (2).

Post, J.E., Preston, Lee E. and Sachs, S. 2002. *Redefining the Corporation: Stakeholder Management and Organizational Wealth*. Stanford, CA: Stanford University Press.

Reberioux, A. 2002. 'European Style of Corporate Governance at the Crossroads: The Role of Worker Involvement'. *Journal of Common Market Studies*, 40(1):111–34.

Reed, D. 1999. 'Three Realms of Corporate Responsibility: Distinguishing Legitimacy, Morality and Ethics'. *Journal of Business Ethics*, 21(3): 23–35.

———. 2002a. 'Management Education in an Age of Globalisation: Some Insights from Critical Theory', in C. Wankel and R. DeFillippi (eds). *Rethinking Management Education*, pp. 209–36. Greenwich CT: Information Age Publishing.

———. 2002b. 'Corporate Governance Reforms in Developing Countries'. *Journal of Business Ethics*, 37 (3).

———. 2002c. 'Employing Normative Stakeholder Theory in Developing Countries: A Critical Theory Perspective'. *Business and Society*, 41(2):166–207.

Ross, L. 1973. 'Managerial Strategy for the Future—Theory Z Management'. *California Management Review*, 15(3): 68–82.

Schmidt, H. 1985. 'Disclosure, Insider Information and Auditing: Theory and Practice', in K.J. Hopt and G. Teubner (eds). *Corporate Governance and Directors' Liabilities: Legal, Economic and Sociological Analyses on Corporate Social Responsibilities*, pp. 338–53. Berlin: Walter de Gruyter.

Scott, J. 1997. *Corporate Business and Capitalist Classes*. Oxford: Oxford University Press.

Sison, A.J.G. 2000. 'The Cultural Dimension of Codes of Corporate Governance: A Focus on the Olivencia Report'. *Journal of Business Ethics*, 27(1/2):181–92.

Stallings, B. and Peres, W. 2000. *Growth, Employment, and Equity: The Impact of the Economic Reforms in Latin America and the Caribbean*. Washington, D.C.: Brookings Institution Press.

Stern, J. and Chew, D. 1997. 'The EVA Financial Management System', in D. Chew (ed.). *Studies in International Corporate Finance and Governance Systems*. Oxford: Oxford University Press.

Stiglitz, J. 2000. 'What I learned at the World Economic Crisis'. *The New Republic Online*. Can be accessed at *http://www.tnr.com/041700/stiglitz041700.html*.

Strange, S. 1994. 'Rethinking Structural Change in the International Political Economy: States, Firms and Diplomacy', in Richard Stubbs and Geoffrey R.D. Underhill (eds). *Political Economy and the Changing Global Order*, pp. 103–15. Toronto: McClelland & Steward.

Taylor, L. 1991. 'Economic Openness: Problems to the Century's End', in T. Banuir (ed.). *Economic Liberalization: No Panacea*, pp. 100–147. Oxford: Clarendon Press.

Teubner, G. 1985. 'Corporate Fiduciary Responsibilities and their Beneficiaries: A Functional Approach to the Legal Institutionalization of Corporate Responsibility', in K.J. Hopt and G. Teubner (eds). *Corporate Governance and Directors' Liabilities: Legal, Economic and Sociological Analyses on Corporate Social Responsibilities*, pp. 149–77. Berlin: Walter de Gruyter.

————. (ed.) 1997. *Global Law Without a State*. Aldershot, England: Dartmouth.

Waddock, S. 2000. 'The Multiple Bottom Lines of Corporate Citizenship: Social Investing, Reputation, and Responsibility Audits'. *Business and Society Review*, 105(3): 323–45.

Williamson, J. 1990. *Latin American Adjustment: How Much Has Happened?* Washington, D.C.: Institute for International Economics.

Zeitlin, M. 1989. *The Large Corporation and Contemporary Classes*. Cambridge: Polity Press.

CHAPTER 15

CORPORATE GOVERNANCE SYSTEMS:
AN INTEGRATIVE MODEL AND
IMPLICATIONS FOR INDIA

ANJU SETH[1]

INTRODUCTION

The recent economic crises in various countries around the world have underscored the importance of the link between corporate governance and economic prosperity. For example, an examination of the causes and consequences of the Asian economic crisis in the late 1990s indicates the need for reforms in the corporate governance systems of numerous countries including Thailand, the Philippines, Malaysia, Indonesia and South Korea (Scott 1998). Similarly, the present downturn in the United States stock market can be traced in large part to a crisis of investor confidence in the prevailing governance system and attendant concerns about misappropriation of funds by those who control corporate decision-making. In the light of their important implications for economic health, issues of corporate governance and reform are receiving considerable attention by public policy makers, scholars and managers.

In this context, the question arises: what is *appropriate* corporate governance reform? The purpose of this chapter is to develop a theoretical approach to answering this question, both in the general case and in the specific case of India. Although this is a normative question, an understanding of positive theory is critical to its answer. This chapter takes the view that an essential prerequisite for identifying and evaluating corporate governance reform measures is to understand the genesis of the corporate governance system in which the governance practices are embedded. The corporate governance system that prevails in a particular national context is defined as the set of legal, cultural and institutional arrangements that determine what publicly traded corporations can do, who controls them, how that control is exercised, and how risks and returns from the activities they undertake are allocated. These arrangements include rules and practices regarding property rights, ownership structures, the rights of various stakeholders, the market for corporate control, labour markets, capital markets, product markets, the role of the board of directors, capital structure, voting practices, accounting and control systems, and executive compensation. These rules may be codified in law and regulation but may also prevail as normal practice.

The chapter proceeds as follows. Section 2 introduces a model to explain the observed variations across corporate governance systems that prevail in different national contexts. I briefly illustrate how the model can be applied to understand variations across the US, German and Japanese governance systems. Section 3 builds on the model to discuss the current corporate governance system in India and evaluates corporate governance reforms for this context. The final section offers a conclusion.

AN INTEGRATIVE MODEL OF CORPORATE GOVERNANCE

Why are different nations characterised by significant differences in their corporate governance systems? This section develops a model of the antecedents of corporate governance. An important requirement of such a model is that it must have the power to not only explain governance systems in different national contexts but also to explain the choice of governance mechanisms within a particular governance system. The complexity of the governance construct suggests that it is instructive to use multiple theoretical lenses to facilitate explanation of different aspects of the phenomenon, as well as to have explanatory power across different national contexts. The model presented here draws upon the property rights perspective, the political economy view and strategic management theory to achieve these objectives.

Property Rights, Ownership Systems and Governance Systems

The nature of the property rights associated with corporate ownership is perhaps the most critical feature of a governance system. In general, property rights refer to the set of expectations regarding rights to use, enjoy income flows from, to change the form and substance of, and to dispose of an asset (Furubotn and Pejovich 1974). In the context of understanding corporate governance systems, the property rights perspective calls attention to the following two questions:

1. What rights are associated with ownership of a corporation?
2. What institutions maintain and enforce the rights associated with ownership?

Each of these questions is briefly discussed below.

Control and Cash Flow Rights

The two critical dimensions of the property rights associated with 'ownership' of a corporation are control rights over the firm's decisions and activities, and rights over the cash flows of the firm. Hence, the substance of 'ownership' is the set of expectations of control rights and cash flow rights held by investors. However, investors may not comprise a homogeneous class with respect to these rights. Instead, the nature of the rights held by an investor frequently depends upon the identity of the investor. Governance systems around the world vary with regard to the holdings of different types of entities, i.e., diffused small shareholders, families or individuals with significant control, widely held financial institutions, industrial corporations and the state. The property rights perspective highlights that in different governance systems these different classes of owners may be invested with different rights vis-à-vis each dimension of ownership. It also calls attention to the correlation between cash flow rights and control rights for each type of owner. The magnitude of this correlation may be different for each type of owner, so that, for example, the correlation between control and cash flow rights may differ for institutional owners versus members of the firm's founding family versus diffused shareholders. The pattern of ownership rights in a particular governance system, i.e., the identity of the players, the magnitude of the shareholdings of each type of player (averaged across all firms in the economy), and the nature of each player's control and cash flow rights, is here called the 'ownership system'.

The specification of control and cash flow rights will also vary across corporations within a specific governance system. Therefore, it is relevant to distinguish analytically between ownership systems and ownership structures; the former facilitates inter-system analysis and the latter inter-firm analysis. The 'ownership structure' of a firm within an ownership system refers to the pattern of ownership rights within a firm, i.e., the identity of the firm's owners, the relative shareholdings of each type of owner, and how control rights and cash flow rights are allocated and shared among the different types of owners.

Ownership Systems and Governance Systems

The ownership system of an economy and the firm's ownership structure have a critical influence on the costs and benefits of investment in the economy or the firm respectively, in that they shape the expected returns from this investment. This cost-benefit trade-off obviously influences the incentives for share ownership. But what is the effect on other stakeholder groups? To examine this, it is useful to conceive of the firm as a nexus of explicit and implicit contracts among different stakeholder groups, including employees, customers, debtors, creditors, local communities as well as contributors of capital or owners. Each stakeholder group contributes an essential ingredient for the effective functioning of the firm in return for the appropriate inducement for its participation. The nexus of contracts that represents the firm essentially describes the matrix of inducements and contributions for all stakeholder groups and the nature of their claims on the profits of the firm.

Economic efficiency would dictate that the contracts among different stakeholder groups must exist in balance so that the rights and responsibilities of different groups are clearly demarcated with regard to their claims on the profits of the firms as a going concern, the nature of the potential liability associated with their participation in the firm and their priority in bankruptcy. There is an important interdependence among contracts governing the inducements offered to different stakeholder groups for their contributions. As an example of this interdependence, if the shareholders in a particular ownership system (e.g., the USA) have the status of residual claimants on the profits of the firm, employees would be treated as fixed claimants. Given this interdependence, ownership systems and structures can be considered to influence not only the incentives for share ownership but also the incentives for other stakeholders to participate in the firm. In this sense, the ownership system can be expected to influence the nature of the other components of the governance system that characterises a national economy.

GOVERNANCE INSTITUTIONS AND GOVERNANCE SYSTEMS

The property rights perspective also calls attention to the institutions that govern and control the rights specified in ownership systems. Property rights institutions refer to the structures and rules by which control and cash flow rights over shareholdings are allocated and enforced. However, given the interdependence among property rights of shareholders and rights of other stakeholders, property rights institutions can be properly understood as having a profound influence on the governance system as a whole. Because of this functional equivalence, I do not differentiate between property rights institutions and governance institutions here.

Markets (including capital, labour and product markets as well as the market for corporate control) comprise one important set of governance institutions. The political structure, including the extent to which control rights are in the hands of bureaucrats and politicians and the role of the government in enforcement of property rights, represents a second set of institutions. Financial institutions represent another set. The fourth set consists of the legal rules governing corporate conduct, including disclosure and accounting rules, dividend rights of investors, and rules governing voting for directors, participating in shareholder meetings, bringing lawsuits against the corporation's officers and directors, etc. Firms and their stakeholders, including large private shareholders, top managers, and employees constitute the fifth set of institutions. In those governance systems where other industrial corporations and the state have significant ownership stakes in corporations, they would also be considered as relevant stakeholders of the firm. This ranking of institutions is not intended to imply causal primacy to any institution over another in its influence over the governance system that prevails in an economy. Instead, I consider governance institutions to act as partial substitutes as well as complements in allocating and enforcing the rights they allocate to stakeholders.

The Role of Governance Institutions in the Governance System

The institutions described above have a profound influence on the nature of the governance system in an economy. They allocate rights among different stakeholders and, therefore, may be considered as the architects of the purpose of governance. They influence the types of firms that will emerge in an economy (e.g., family-controlled firms with concentrated shareholdings versus public firms with dispersed shareholdings), so that they shape the ownership system. They generate the monitoring and incentive mechanisms to enforce and maintain the governance system and, therefore, maintain and enforce the rules of the governance game. Thus, for example, the threat of a hostile takeover will have limited potential to limit managerial discretion to appropriate shareholder wealth in an economy characterised by a sizeable population of family-controlled firms with concentrated shareholdings.

In understanding the role of governance institutions in shaping governance systems, it is also necessary to understand the process by which this influence is exerted. Political economy theory and strategic management theory suggest that the specific outcomes observed in the case of a particular economy's governance system and the governance structure of the firm result from a process of political bargaining and entrepreneurial action among the different groups of players in the system, i.e., the governance institutions.

The political economy framework proposes that the intersection of the polity structure and the political life of organisations with the economy and economic life of organisations yield useful insights on how institutions develop (Zald 1970). Governance systems and structures can be analysed in terms of the structure, processes and interaction of four broad sectors: the external political and economic environment, and the internal political and economic environment of the firm. The strategic management perspective highlights the entrepreneurial role of firms in the genesis of governance systems. This perspective views the organisation as a purposive and entrepreneurial entity with specialised unique resources that interacts with and attempts to shape its environment to maintain long-term viability (Seth and Thomas 1994). Firms will have some degree of autonomy to choose and/or alter their ownership structures and, more generally, their governance structures. Firms may be motivated to do so to seek competitive advantage and thereby increase their relative profits over their competitors, or to materially benefit those groups that have control rights at the expense of other classes of owners. These actions influence the nature of the governance system that prevails in the economy.

In the model presented here, complex negotiations among different governance institutions are considered to give rise to the ownership system and the governance system that exist in an economy, but there is recursiveness in the system. In that it accounts for the important role of governance institutions beyond legal rules, the perspective adopted here is somewhat broader than the analysis by La Porta et al. (1999), who conclude that 'existing ownership structures are primarily an equilibrium response to the domestic legal environment that companies operate in' (p. 512). It is also broader than the perspective of Milhaupt (1998), in whose formulation 'the key independent variables in corporate governance are not the legal rules governing financial intermediaries but the broader set of rules worked out among public and private actors concerning control rights over assets'. While the model presented here is consistent with Milhaupt, it also highlights that entrepreneurial actions taken by firms, one of the central governance institutions, can influence other governance institutions (e.g., firms can act to inhibit the market for corporate control or lobby for relaxation of accounting standards and rules), and thereby influence the governance system. I propose that the situation is more complex than represented by a one-way causal relationship between the institutions that shape property rights and the ownership/governance systems of an economy. Instead, corporations are properly understood as not only reflecting the governance and ownership systems in an economy but also influencing the evolution of these systems.

Note that the rules and norms represented by governance institutions may be explicitly or implicitly stated, i.e., they may be codified in law, rules or administrative arrangements or instead may merely reflect the norm of regular practice arising from repeated interactions. Similarly, the responsibility for enforcement may be explicitly or implicitly enjoined. An additional source of complexity arises from the possibility that implicit rules that are reflective of norms of actual practice conflict with explicit rules that are reflective of desired practice. Since the rules arise from an ongoing bargaining process among governance institutions with divergent interests, some degree of non-correspondence between explicit and implicit rules is to be expected in any economy and reflects the critical issues presently under negotiation. In general, therefore, an important question in examining any governance system and considering reforms within that system is the source of the divergence between actual and desired practice. Such an examination assists us in understanding better the power and influence of various governance institutions. Finally, I propose that greater divergence is likely to be observed in emerging economies where there is ongoing, perhaps fierce, negotiation and bargaining about governance rules.

AN INTEGRATIVE MODEL OF CORPORATE GOVERNANCE

The above discussion lays the foundation for an integrative model of corporate governance. Figure 15.1 contains a graphical representation of the model presented here.

Figure 15.1
Corporate Governance Systems: An Integrative Model

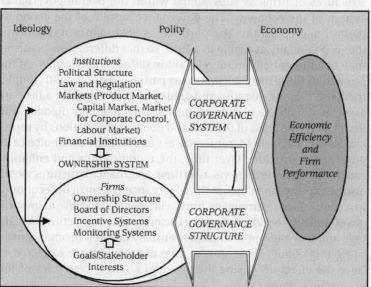

The model proposes that to understand corporate governance systems (at the level of the national economy), it is first necessary to analyse the set of expectations regarding control and cash flow rights that comprise the property rights underlying corporate ownership, i.e., the ownership system of an economy. Since 'owners' and other stakeholders have joint claims on the resources of the firm, the ownership system influences the inducements provided to other groups of stakeholders for their contributions. Social expectations of the system of inducements and contributions to the various stakeholders of the firm are an important dimension of the governance system in an economy. These expectations are shaped by interactions among and within the governance institutions in the economy, i.e., legal rules, markets, financial institutions, the political structure and firms. A bargaining process among governance institutions also shapes the set of mechanisms that arises to achieve this allocation and enforcement. The corporate governance system of an economy, then, embodies the rights of stakeholder groups and the governance mechanisms used to allocate and enforce these rights. Governance institutions influence the nature and substance of the governance system and also enforce the incentives for allocation of resources that is represented by this system.

In a parallel fashion, we can understand corporate governance structures of firms as subsystems within the overall governance system of the economy. The governance system of the economy defines and constrains the portfolio of governance mechanisms that is potentially available to a firm, so that different mechanisms may be differentially more relevant in different economies. At the same time, these mechanisms act as partial substitutes and complements so that the quantity and quality of governance in a firm are associated with the bundle of mechanisms it adopts (Rediker and Seth 1995). The goals of the firm and political negotiations by representatives of stakeholder interests act to influence the choice of its governance structure. Over time, the modifications and enhancements that firms develop vis-à-vis their governance structures would also be expected to influence the governance system of the economy. In a competitive environment, firms will have the incentive to improve governance to build economic efficiency and competitive advantage and will attempt to entrepreneurially develop mechanisms to bring this about. These governance innovations are expected to have the effect of 'raising the bar' and creating new rules of the governance game.

Finally, I highlight that the governance system and governance structure play a critical role in determining the cost of capital and the incentives for investment in an economy and a firm respectively, since they provide the means by which non-controlling shareholders are protected from expropriation by managers or controlling shareholders. Such expropriation can include two types of actions: first, actions that divert resources away from investment (e.g., managerial self-dealing or excessive perquisite consumption); and, second, actions that divert resources toward inefficient investment (e.g., empire building or cross-subsidisation of investment among divisions). The expectations of these types of expropriation would cause rational investors to demand higher returns for their capital or in the extreme case to desist from investing any capital at all. The recent decline in the US stock market following the revelation of improper accounting and inflated profits in a number of major US corporations exemplifies this principle. Thus, the objective of a strong governance system is to create incentives for corporations to maximise their economic efficiency. The largest beneficiary of an effective corporate governance system is the nation as a whole, since improvements in firm performance and reduced cost of capital in the economy aid the nation in domestic productivity and international competitiveness.

Implications for Governance Reform

A number of implications result from this formulation. First, the degree of similarity or dissimilarity in governance systems in different nations will be a function of the similarity or dissimilarity in their governance institutions considered as a whole. At the same time, in the light of the path-dependent nature of the formation of governance institutions and the bargaining process that characterises the evolution of governance systems, at any point in time there are also likely to be significant differences among systems in different national economies and, therefore, differences in the governance issues to be addressed. Table 15.1 summarises some key features of governance systems in the US, Germany and Japan, and indicates the specific governance reform issues that are particularly relevant in the context of each of these systems.

A related implication is that governance reform in a specific governance system may not be relevant in other systems. Instead, the model encourages us to consider governance reforms in the context

Table 15.1
Corporate Governance Systems: USA, Germany and Japan

	USA	Germany	Japan
Ownership System	Cash flow rights: • Thousands of institutions own about half of the total equity market. • Also diffused among a multitude of small stockholders. • Liquid market for holdings. Control rights: • Management and control of firms delegated to professional managers.	Major companies: Strong control by commercial banks via proxy voting on behalf of individual investors who hold cash flow rights. Smaller companies: Norm is family control. Corporate cross-holdings. Limited role of individual investor, illiquid holdings.	Corporate cross-holdings (keiretsu) Shareholdings by major banks. • Cements good relationships and impedes hostile takeovers. Now, general public becoming important source of equity funds.
Role of Governance	Protection of interests of minority shareholders from expropriation by managers.	Protection of interests of multiple stakeholders, primarily lenders and employees. Allow considerable autonomy to management. Strong protection of creditor rights.	Protection of interests of multiple stakeholders, primarily holding companies and lenders. Degree of protection of both shareholder and creditor rights.
Legal Rules	One share one vote rule. Solicitation of proxies by mail. Proportional representation of minorities on boards of directors. Mechanisms to legally safeguard minority investors. Pre-emptive rights to new share issues (to maintain proportional holdings).		
Market for Corporate Control	Relatively active.	Relatively active.	Relatively active.
Governance Reform	Transparency/accuracy of information. Accountability of executives. Incentive systems. Large block-holders: institutions • Effectiveness? • Who monitors the institutions? Monitoring by board of directors.	Banks reconsidering stakes. Shareholders challenging voting rights restrictions. Pressures to improve standards of financial disclosure.	Pressure on corporate–political links. Amendments to Japanese Commercial Code (1992): • shareholder lawsuits • access to company books • independent auditor.

of a specific governance system, since the costs and benefits of changes in any governance mechanism will differ across governance systems. The model cautions that while the experience of reforms in other governance systems is a useful avenue of learning about the costs and benefits of changing a specific mechanism, attempting to piecemeal import reforms from other governance systems without consideration of the systemic nature of the system is likely to be an unsatisfactory solution.

Another implication relates to the process of governance reform. The model highlights that not only are different kinds of benefits and costs likely to characterise different governance systems, the yardstick of what constitutes effective governance is also likely to vary among systems. The task of governance reform is thus particularly complex. In examining potential modifications, it is not enough to merely modify a specific governance mechanism such as accounting rules or director responsibility. Instead, in order to bring about effective change, policy makers must consider the complex interlinkages among governance mechanisms that exist within a governance system and address the potential implications for reform associated with one mechanism on other aspects of the system. It is critical to also reach a consensus of what is desired to be achieved by governance reform. Given the political nature of the bargaining process, arriving at such a consensus is not an easy task.

THE INDIAN CORPORATE GOVERNANCE SYSTEM

I now turn to examining the implications of the model for India. This section first introduces the ownership system and the broader governance system in India and how these have evolved over time. I draw implications from this discussion for governance system reform in the Indian context.

THE OWNERSHIP SYSTEM IN INDIA AND GOVERNANCE IMPLICATIONS

Government policy in the post-independence period to facilitate the development of the small-scale sector had an important effect on the ownership system in India. In 1999, about one-third of the total equity (book value) of the Indian corporate sector was represented by more than 400,000 private limited (closely-held) companies. Only about 7–10 per cent of the approximately 71,000 public limited (widely-held) companies are listed on a stock exchange. Similar to other developing economies, ownership of the public limited companies reflects a high concentration of control rights. Key players in the ownership system include family or business groups, financial institutions, the state, other corporations (including foreign firms), and individual small investors.

BUSINESS GROUPS

A business group consists of a form of corporate organisation where firms are linked together by cross-holdings and pyramidal stock ownership. Typically an individual or family controls such a group. One indication (although an imperfect one) of the relevance of the family/business group organisational form in India is that individuals and non-financial corporations are estimated by various sources to hold more than 50 per cent of total corporate equity. In the case of one of the largest business groups, *Business Standard* reports (23 April 2002) that as of 31 March 2002, the Tata group owns between 25–35 per cent of the shares in group companies such as Tata Steel, Tata Engineering, Tata Power, Tata Chemicals, Tata Tea, Indian Hotels, Voltas, Titan and Trent.

The concentration of control rights in the hands of a business group or family has a number of potential advantages in the context of the Indian business environment. This corporate form is well suited to a wide diversity of business requirements and can ease the problems of operating in a large number of industries. In a developing economy such as India, the internal capital markets that are created by such business groups could provide more efficient capital allocation than the external capital market. However, from a governance perspective, some significant disadvantages may also exist. Foremost is the potential for those in control to entrench themselves with small commitments of personal or corporate capital and to divert corporate resources to end uses that benefit them but are detrimental to the interests of other shareholders. Often, in group- or family-controlled firms, control rights are highly concentrated but there is low correlation between cash flow and control rights. Therefore, controlling owners have both the incentive and the means to expropriate wealth from minority (from the point of view of their control rights) shareholders. Similarly, intra-group transactions can be used to manipulate reported profits and net worth. There is the clear possibility of oppression of the interests of non-wholly-owned subsidiaries and the 'outside' or minority holders of shares of the parent corporation.

Two questions arise. First, what empirical evidence is there regarding the costs and benefits of group ownership? The research suggests that in India this organisational form indeed represents both benefits and costs. Khanna and Palepu (2000) find that affiliates of highly diversified business groups in India outperform unaffiliated firms as well as affiliates of business groups with relatively narrow scope. However, Bertrand et al. (2002) also find that controlling shareholders in Indian business groups divert resources away from minority investors. The second question is: how much does the potential for expropriation of minority shareholders matter? Research on governance in Asian corporations (Claessens et al. 2000) highlights that protection of property rights of minority shareholders are central to explaining the economic value of business groups. Their evidence suggests that group-affiliated firms are valued at higher levels than independent firms when there is no divergence between cash flow rights and control rights. However, the reverse is the case when control rights exceed cash flow rights. Claessens et al. interpret their results to suggest that for group-affiliated firms in general, the expectation of expropriation more than offsets the perceived benefits from group affiliation. Their evidence also shows that small shareholder expropriation occurs to a large extent by families.

Thus, a critical governance problem in the Indian context is to protect minority shareholders from expropriation by business groups where there is divergence between cash flow rights and control rights. What role can and do financial institutions play in mitigating the governance problem of wealth expropriation from non-controlling shareholders? Financial institutions are estimated to hold 15–20 per cent of the equity of Indian firms. By and large, these institutions are state owned with the charter of facilitating economic development; they often undertake the dual roles of lender and shareholder vis-à-vis their corporate clients. It is conceivable that because of this dual role financial institutions could play an important monitoring role (as, for instance, is the case in Germany), but this has not been the case in India. Since the financial institutions are themselves state owned, they have limited incentives to foster wealth creation.

Furthermore, although institutions are entitled to nominate directors on the boards of the companies that they hold stakes in, and, therefore, at least nominally hold control rights proportional to their cash flow rights, the employees of the state-owned financial institutions who serve as nominee directors typically have neither the expertise nor the power to exercise control over decision-making. Thus, financial institutions have neither the incentive nor the ability (although they technically do have the means) to serve a strong monitoring role.

STATE OWNERSHIP

Is state ownership the solution? State-owned enterprises (SOEs) represented 39 per cent of the book value of equity of Indian corporations in 1999. In a developing economy such as India, significant state ownership has potential benefits in industries of strategic significance to the nation. At the same time, a critical issue is again the dissociation of cash flow rights and control rights, since bureaucrats have significant control rights but cash flow rights are dispersed among taxpayers. Since state-owned corporations are essentially subsidised by taxes, there is the strong potential for a focus on economic value creation to be absent. Also, when such enterprises are not forced to meet financial and budgetary constraints, they may lobby for subsidies or protection from competition. Frequently, in such corporations, managers owe their position to patronage, not competence, and employment policies result in overstaffing. The evidence suggests that although there are notable exceptions, the performance record of Indian SOEs on an average is dismal. However, it is instructive to note that in Singapore, state-owned corporations appear to be relatively more focused on value creation. This suggests that checks and balances exist in some systems to create significant incentives for SOEs to focus on value creation, unlike the situation in India.

GOVERNANCE INSTITUTIONS AND THE GOVERNANCE SYSTEM

What is the role of the governance institutions described in the above model in shaping the present governance system? Clearly, the economic reforms enacted by the political structure have been the primary stimuli of change in the right direction. The rule changes (liberalisation of investment, relaxation of licencing rules, elimination of industry restrictions on private-sector investment and reduction of import tariffs and controls) initiated in the early 1990s by the political structure have brought about increased competition in product markets with the salutary effect of creating new incentives to companies to strive towards economic efficiency. Corporate responses to these incentives as well as the entry of foreign portfolio investors have triggered the development of the capital market. To further encourage this development, the Stock Exchange Board of India (SEBI) has introduced a number of initiatives oriented toward protection of shareholders including stronger disclosure norms in initial public offerings, greater detail and frequency of financial reporting to the investment community, and development of a takeover code.

Role of the Takeover Market

Although there does now exist a takeover market in India, it is unclear as to how well it can effectively function as a market for corporate control, i.e., as a disciplinary device to prevent governance violations. The threat of a takeover to replace an inefficient controlling group or management team could provide a powerful incentive for decision makers to act in the interests of all shareholders. However, at the present time, the high level of concentration of control rights that characterises the ownership system in India creates barriers to the effective functioning of the market for corporate control. In fact, the creation of a takeover market appears to have prompted some business groups to increase their holdings in group companies to ward off hostile takeovers. For example, the Aditya Vikram Birla group, India's second largest conglomerate, planned to raise their stake in group companies (Hindalco, Indian Rayon, Indo Gulf Fertilisers & Chemicals and Grasim Industries) to 40 per cent (*The Telegraph*, 6 August 2001). Note also that in this business group, a complex pattern of cross-holdings among group companies suggests that there is a potential divergence between cash flow rights and control rights of the controlling shareholder. For example, three group companies, Grasim, Hindalco and Indo Gulf hold 4.96 per cent, 9.81 per cent and 2.98 per cent respectively in Indian Rayon.

LEGAL RULES AND BOARDS OF DIRECTORS

Legally, the board of directors is the ultimate governing body of a corporation. The board in India has a single-tier structure with board members owing a fiduciary duty of loyalty to the company and its shareholders and a duty of care to the company. The legal system allows shareholders to seek redress for oppression or violation of their rights at the level of the Company Law Board (CLB), SEBI, civil courts, the high court where the company is registered, and the Supreme Court. The CLB and lower court decisions may be appealed to the high courts and Supreme Court. However, the backlogs in the court system cause long delays in resolving disputes.

Various governance institutions have focused attention on achieving stronger monitoring by the board of directors towards more effective governance. The SEBI Committee on Corporate Governance, appointed in 1999, introduced a mandatory requirement for outside, independent directors to represent one-third or one-half of the board of listed companies with a non-executive chairman or an executive chairman respectively. The appointment of an audit committee on the board consisting of a majority of outside directors is also mandatory, and the role and functioning of this committee are specified in SEBI rules. Director remuneration is required to be disclosed, individuals may not serve as directors on more than 10 boards, and shareholders must be provided information about the background and expertise of directors prior to their election. In 1998, the major business association in India, the Confederation of Indian Industry (CII), introduced a voluntary code of best governance practices described in 'Desirable Corporate Governance: A Code', again oriented towards listed companies, with similar recommendations. While these are steps in the right direction, it is unclear that monitoring by the board of directors is a sufficient device to achieve strong governance in the Indian context. As the World Bank Report on The Observance of Standards and Codes (ROSC) states in its Corporate Governance Assessment,

> Although the law provides safeguards to shareholders, there is anecdotal evidence that directors' duties are sometimes followed in letter but not in spirit. The resolutions of the board of directors are often vaguely worded and fall short of giving full information to the owners of the company (Section 5.2, p. 11).

AN ASSESSMENT OF THE CORPORATE
GOVERNANCE CLIMATE IN INDIA

The model of governance systems described above predicts that when the role of a limited number of families in the corporate sector is large and the government is heavily involved in and influenced by business, the governance system does not easily evolve in a manner to protect minority shareholders and, more generally, to protect transparent and market-based activities. Instead, one would expect that under these circumstances, there is the greater likelihood that business interests subvert the judicial system and rule of law for their private gain.

The problem of corruption is documented by the Berlin-based organisation, Transparency International, who ranks India 71 out of 91 countries in their 2001 Corruption Perceptions Index. This Index is based on the perceptions of businessmen, risk analysts and the general public on the degree of corruption among public officials and politicians (Jha 2002). India receives a score of 2.7 on a 10-point scale where 10 corresponds to 'highly clean' and 0 corresponds to 'highly corrupt'. Given limited oversight over corruption, entry into the bureaucracy is often viewed as a ticket to wealth by virtue of the enormous decision-making power it confers upon civil servants. Woefully inadequate salaries, a seniority-based rather than merit-based promotion system, and a rigid decision-making hierarchy compound the problem. Clearly, there are those individual politicians and bureaucrats whose careers are unblemished by corruption. The point is, however, that the system is not geared towards effective functioning of the market for political or human capital.

The evidence, therefore, suggests that in the overall analysis progress has been made towards strengthening the corporate governance climate. At the same time, perhaps it is fair to say that more progress is evidenced in instituting rules than in actually bringing about the discipline of good governance. Witness the recent revelations by Xerox Modicorp, the Indian joint venture between US-based Xerox Corp (68 per cent stake) and the Modi business group (28 per cent stake). In 2002, Xerox Modicorp revealed that it had made improper payments of $700,000 to push its sales to government customers in India. The bribes paid by Xerox Modicorp (and received by some unnamed government functionary) have interfered with the effective functioning of the office equipment product market in India. It is worth noting that these revelations were made in a filing with the US Securities and Exchange Commission (SEC) in the wake of a detailed investigation of the parent company by the SEC, rather than being detected by any monitoring system in India. Thus, the reporting requirements associated with participating in stock markets do not appear to be fully functioning to protect the minority shareholders in India, who jointly own 4 per cent of Xerox Modicorp stock. Finally, the legal rules governing corporations and monitoring by directors appear to be an insufficient deterrent or check to malfeasance.

Thus, the checks and balances that could be represented by a complementary operation of the various governance institutions are presently inadequate to achieve a relatively strong governance climate. I emphasise 'relatively': no governance system can be perfect, since there are costs of instituting stronger governance.

CORPORATE GOVERNANCE: PRINCIPLES OF FUTURE REFORM

If indeed corporate governance is to be viewed as a complex system as suggested by the model presented here, I submit that the most critical issue is to create a climate whereby an effective governance system can thrive and flourish. This requires that appropriate incentives be put in place vis-à-vis each of the property rights institutions described here. Such incentives should be based on enlightened self-interest, so that in the long term there are both significant private gains to be realised from effective governance as well as significant penalties to be borne if misappropriation takes place. In other words, markets—in the broadest sense of the term—must operate more efficiently than at present, with appropriate checks and balances in place to enable the survival of the fittest.

In order for markets to work efficiently, they must be policed in an orderly fashion vis-à-vis both detection of governance violations and timely action. For legal rules to really matter, there must be enforcement. The enforcement power of CLB and SEBI in the matter of investor claims is an important step in the right direction. Another important step towards strengthening the governance system in India could be to establish a special system in high courts to handle governance claims. To be effective, such a system would require judges to have (a) specialised expertise about property rights and the economic consequences of violations of good governance;

(*b*) the infrastructure to move speedily in examining the cases brought before them; (*c*) the power to impose strict penalties for violations; and (*d*) the wherewithal to be insulated from pressures from self-interested parties. The creation of a court system that meets these criteria is not a simple task. However, even if such a system could only handle a subset of governance violations claims, it could greatly assist efficient market functioning and thereby effective governance.

As the model described here implies, addressing the legal system is not enough: other institutions must also be considered. Let us now turn to the political structure and the bureaucracy that act as its administrative arm. Once again, all possible steps should be taken to achieve greater efficiency in the political marketplace. The May 2002 Supreme Court decision requiring electoral candidates to reveal their previous criminal history (if any) and their financial status is a welcome move in this direction. Similarly, as described elsewhere in this chapter, a change in the rules that govern the market for human capital in the case of the bureaucracy is long overdue.

Continuing to foster the development of the capital market to assist investors to make more informed choices, as well as allowing investors a greater range of choices (including access to overseas stock markets) would greatly assist the disciplinary role of this governance institution. Clearly, the availability of transparent and accurate information is critical for any governance system to work, so this must be an avenue of further effort. In addition, a well-developed external capital market also reduces the need for an internal capital market that the business group organisational form represents.

Perhaps the brightest sign on the governance horizon is the entrepreneurial role of Indian companies in 'bonding' themselves to good governance practices and thereby building investor confidence. One mechanism to accomplish this is that firms may themselves choose to participate in a stronger governance regime than that represented by India to credibly signal their good governance practices and thereby achieve a competitive advantage in generating capital. A notable example is Infosys Technologies Ltd., the first Indian company to be listed on NASDAQ and the recipient in 2000 of an award for disclosure transparency from Washington, D.C.-based Institutional Shareholder Services. However, the cost of overseas listing may be prohibitive. Thus, fostering the further development of the Indian capital market so that firms are rewarded by investors for good governance is critical. Similarly, voluntarily abiding by codes of good governance such as that recommended by CII should, over time, act to raise the bar and perhaps act as a self-enforcing mechanism. By virtue of their entrepreneurial actions to seek competitive advantage, firms can exert a potent influence on government reform.

CONCLUSION

This chapter has presented a model of corporate governance systems based on the property rights political economy and strategic management perspectives. A central assertion of the chapter is that only by understanding how and why governance systems came to exist as they did in different national contexts can we develop an appropriate yardstick for measuring the appropriateness of different reform initiatives. The model highlights the important role of governance institutions as having a complementary influence in fashioning the governance system of a national economy. This system evolves from a complex bargaining and negotiation process among institutions and their functionaries over time. It is likely that competitive pressures in the global economy will provide an impetus for greater governance efficiency in all systems. At the same time, reform changes must consider the path-dependent nature of the evolution process and the systemic nature of governance. The model predicts that when institutions and their key functionaries have the incentive and the power to limit the effective functioning of markets in order to derive private benefits, any progress towards governance reform will be slow. Nonetheless, the economic reform process in India has created a powerful impetus for firms to strengthen their competitiveness in order to effectively participate in an open economy. Continuing to foster the development of well-functioning markets that contain strong incentives for governance efficiency is a critical means to bring about further progress.

NOTE

1. I would like to thank participants at the 'Conference on Good Governance in Democratic Societies' held at IIM Calcutta, 25–27 April 2002 for their helpful comments on the chapter.

References

Bertrand, Marianne, Mehta, Paras and Mullainathan, Sendhil. 2002. 'Ferreting Out Tunnelling: An Application to Indian Business Groups'. Working Paper. Cambridge, MA: Department of Economics, Massachusetts Institute of Technology.

Claessens, Stijn, Djankov, Simeon, Fan, Joseph P.H. and Lang, Larry H.P. 2000. 'The Costs of Group Affiliation: Evidence from East Asia'. Working Paper. Washington, D.C.: The World Bank.

Furubotn, E.G. and Pejovich, S. 1974. 'Introduction: The New Property Rights Literature', in E.G. Furubotn and S. Pejovich (eds). *The Economics of Property Rights*, pp. 1–9. Cambridge, MA: Ballinger Publishing Company.

Jha, Nilanjana Bhaduri. 2002. 'Just How Corrupt is India? Read the Numbers'. *Times News Network*. 5 July.

Khanna, Tarun and Palepu, Krishna. 2000. 'Is Group Affiliation Profitable in Emerging Markets? An Analysis of Diversified Indian Business Groups'. *Journal of Finance*, 55(2): 867–91.

La Porta, Rafael, Lopez-de-Silanes, Florencio and Shleifer, Andrei. 1999. 'Corporate Ownership around the World'. *Journal of Finance*, 54(2): 471–518.

Milhaupt, Curtis J. 1998. 'Property Rights in Firms'. *Virginia Law Review*, 88: 1145–94.

Rediker, Ken and Seth, Anju. 1995. 'Boards of Directors and Substitution Effects of Alternative Governance Mechanisms'. *Strategic Management Journal*, 16(2): 85–99.

Scott, Kenneth. 1998. 'The Role of Corporate Governance in South Korean Economic Reform'. *Journal of Applied Corporate Finance*, 10(4): 8–15.

Seth, Anju and Thomas, Howard. 1994. 'Theories of the Firm: Implications for Strategy Research'. *Journal of Management Studies*, 31(2): 165–92.

Zald, Mayer. 1970. 'Political Economy: A Framework for Comparative Analysis', in Mayer N. Zald (ed.). *Power in Organisations*, pp. 21–61. Nashville, TN: Vanderbilt University Press.

CHAPTER 16

ROLE OF GOVERNMENT IN THE FINANCIAL SERVICES INDUSTRY IN THE EUROPEAN UNION: AN INTERNATIONAL PERSPECTIVE

PAOLA DE VINCENTIIS

CONSOLIDATION IN THE FINANCIAL SECTOR: FEATURES, FIGURES AND REASONS FOR THE PHENOMENON

One of the most impressive trends, which marked the development of the financial systems in the 1990s, was the increasing level of consolidation in the banking and financial services industry. A wave of mergers, acquisitions, joint ventures and strategic alliances has in fact given a new shape to the financial sector, deeply modifying the competitive landscape and the drivers for success.

The consolidation trend and its consequences have been broadly analysed in various studies, among which is an extensive report of the Group of Ten released in January 2001 and which focused on 13 industrialised countries.[1] Some figures taken from this report can give an idea of the dimension of the phenomenon:

- in the 1990s, more than 7,600 deals in which a financial firm located in the area under examination acquired another financial firm took place and the aggregate value of these deals amounted roughly to US$ 1.6 trillion;
- by 1998, the assets of the top 20 banks had nearly doubled compared to their level in 1980 and amounted to 40 per cent of the aggregate gross domestic product (GDP) of the area (see Table 16.1);

- both in the USA and in the European Union (EU), the number of banking organisations declined from about 13,000 to 7,000, thus diminishing by roughly 40 per cent.

Table 16.1
Assets of World's Largest Banks to G-13 GDP

	1980	1990	1995	1997	1998
Top 20	19.5%	31.6%	37.0%	38.1%	39.8%
Top 30	25.5%	40.3%	48.5%	51.1%	52.7%
Top 50	35.4%	52.8%	64.0%	69.0%	71.2%

Source: Group of Ten 2001.

Looking at the features of the consolidation process in the financial industry, it is important to say that it was to a large extent a 'domestic' phenomenon and mainly involved the banking sector (Group of Ten 2001). In fact, the great majority of operations took place between banks based in the same nation. More in particular, the actors were very often medium and small firms trying to reach a survival level through aggregation in order to face an environment of heightened competition. This was also the case in the EU, in contrast to the forecasts of rapid internationalisation associated by many researchers and experts with the introduction of the Euro (European Central Bank 2000).

However, the cross-sector and cross-national operations—even if less numerous—cannot be disregarded. In fact from these operations some 'giants' were born whose importance, global coverage, level of market power, and potential for conflicts of interest are the main causes of concern to the public authorities nowadays. The cross-sector mergers and acquisitions (M&A), in particular, led to the creation of 'financial supermarkets' capable of offering almost the entire spectrum of financial services, both to individual investors and corporations, and often on a worldwide basis. The importance of the phenomenon and the related growing concern of the supervisors is very well stigmatised in the words of the General Manager of the Bank for International Settlements:

The maintenance of financial stability used to be relatively straightforward in the days when banks and other financial institutions earned protected rents and supervisors and managers could focus on simple risk measures. Over the last decades, the world has become far more complicated. Firms are running more complex risks, sectoral distinctions are blurring and markets are integrating globally. This has made the task of authorities responsible for financial stability more difficult to define and execute: there are more parameters to be considered, shocks come from many more corners and the manner in which supervisory actions affect supervised institutions is far more complex (Crockett 2001: 1).

As a conclusion to this brief introduction, before exploring the consequences and the risks of the new landscape of the financial world, it is important to answer a preliminary question: what were the stimuli that led to the described consolidation process? A complex mix of factors has been pushing financial firms to look for greater dimension and wider scope of activity.

- **Improvements in Information Technology:** In order to compete effectively, a financial firm nowadays has to bear a high level of fixed costs related to the information technology (IT) equipment. This equipment is indispensable not only to access the financial markets, to participate in the settlement systems and to dispose of real-time information on any kind of relevant news. An expensive IT structure is also needed for processing internal data and for putting in place the new sophisticated risk management systems, whose importance is increasing in parallel with the increasing complexity of the activities carried out. Great fixed costs naturally call for a larger customer base and thus a larger revenue base (European Central Bank 1999). Furthermore, the developments of IT made it possible for financial services providers to reach customers over a wider geographic area, consequently fostering the level of competition and the need to look for higher efficiency through economies of scale.
- **Deregulation:** Over the past decade, all the major industrialised countries have gone through a process of deregulation in the financial sector. As a consequence, the financial intermediaries have gradually being losing their traditional protected environment and higher competition for market shares has been developing in the sector. This again has forced the financial service providers to look for economies

of scale in order to improve their efficiency and to attain a larger customer base or to keep the existing one. Moreover, the deregulation also meant more freedom for the financial intermediaries to expand their activities into sectors that were closed for them in the past. The economies of scope attainable and the possibility of offering a wider range of financial services to the clients were other relevant reasons to look for aggregations (Banca d'Italia 1999).

- **Globalisation:** The internal deregulation process was accompanied by the removal of many barriers to the free movements of capitals and financial intermediaries across borders. These regulatory developments—together with the new opportunities opened by information technology—contributed to the creation of a global financial market setting. In this global setting, the minimum dimension needed to compete—and often to survive—is far higher than it used to be. Thus, the national financial communities were pushed to look for aggregation not only to face the heightened internal competition, but also to protect themselves from the competitors coming from abroad, or to try and expand their activities internationally.[2]

- **Shareholders' Pressures:** The need to improve profitability and efficiency was also fostered by more demanding pressures from the shareholders, represented in increasing percentages by institutional investors. As the profit margins were diminishing for the harsher competition, the financial firms were forced to look for innovative strategies for creating shareholders' value.

OPPORTUNITIES AND THREATS BROUGHT BY THE CONSOLIDATION PROCESS: AN OVERVIEW

The consequences of the described process of consolidation are very complex and difficult to evaluate. The analysis of the stimuli to the process outlined that it was basically an increase in the competitive pressures—coming from different sources—to push the concentration in the financial services industry. More competition is in principle good news for consumers who can enjoy a reduction of prices and a better quality of the services provided. However, once the consolidation battle is over, some relevant risks can emerge.

First of all, the danger exists that global groups will exploit their world market power in a traditional oligopolistic fashion. This would mean, in practice, prices above (or volume below) those prevailing in a hypothetical situation of perfect competition. Whether this scenario becomes a reality or not depends on several factors, among which the most important is the existence of barriers to entry in the sector. We said earlier that the regulatory barriers have been to a large extent removed. However, other important kind of barriers may exist, related to the behaviour of customers and the level of fixed costs needed to operate in a given sector.

A second problematic issue is linked to the cross-sector aggregations. Inside the major groups offering a wide range of financial services, relevant risks of conflicts of interest can emerge. Will a financial analyst be unbiased in his studies and recommendations when the company he works for is very active in trading or asset management or underwriting? Will the stock picking activity in asset management be unbiased when the same company has been unsuccessful in an underwriting operation and has a massive quantity of a certain security in its portfolio?

A third issue is related to financial stability and the risk of systemic crisis. Basically the question is: could the failure of a major global player today create unmanageable consequences? Are there intermediaries who are 'too big to fail' in the sense that their failure could create a dramatic domino effect on the entire sector worldwide?

Finally, another issue is related to the free movements of capital across borders. The markets, and notably the financial system, are playing a key role in the global economy nowadays. What we clearly experience is a real-time confidence vote of the markets on global companies (corporate governance = maximisation of shareholders' value) and our national parliaments, governments and central banks (political governance = fiscal and monetary discipline). The new market powers mainly stem from the possibility of asset managers—closely monitoring governments and corporate policies—to shift huge investment flows in real-time worldwide. This possibility poses great challenges and high risks. The main international crises of the 1990s (the Mexican crisis in 1994, the East Asian crisis in 1997, the Russian crisis in 1998, the e-economy 'bubble' in 2000) clearly show the danger of overshoots and the distortions of resource allocation which can be associated with the massive inflows/outflows of capitals into certain countries or sectors.

THE IMPACT OF CONSOLIDATION ON COMPETITION AND THE BENEFITS/DRAWBACKS FOR THE CONSUMERS OF FINANCIAL SERVICES

The impact of consolidation on the competition in the financial services industry and, consequently, on the prices applied by the intermediaries and on the benefits/drawbacks for consumers depends very much on the features of each particular sector, but in general seems to be negative. In fact, the existence of significant barriers to entry made it possible for the main players to exercise a certain degree of market power in an oligopolist fashion.

This seems to be particularly true for retail banking where presence on the territory and personal relationships are still quite important, making it more difficult for new entrants to acquire market shares. Various researches clearly show that higher concentration in banking markets may lead to less favourable conditions for consumers, especially in small business loans (both in terms of interest rates and quantity of credit available), retail deposits and payment services (Group of Ten 2001).[3]

For different reasons, the situation is similar for the investment banking sector as well. In fact, even if the market for this kind of services is very internationalised, nevertheless, it is dominated by a very restricted group of global players. The same top 10 firms dominate in most geographical markets and in all types of investment banking activities. Table 16.2 is very interesting from this point of view. A quick look at the league tables in the various kinds of services shows a clearly defined dominant group, with impressive market coverage. Their competitive advantage is firmly based on their reputation, on their experience and on their largely superior placing power, thus becoming difficult to contest in the short term. Such a situation necessarily generates an oligopolistic behaviour.

From another point of view, the advantages of the consolidation process for the consumers are questionable because the efficiency gains are questionable. Very often, in fact, the reductions of costs coming from aggregation are more attractive in theory than in practice.

Table 16.2
Top 10 Names in Some Branches of the Financial Services Industry in 1999

International equities underwriting	International IPOs	Financial advisory	International bonds underwriting
Morgan Stanley	Merril Lynch	Goldman Sachs	Merril Lynch
Goldman Sachs	Goldman Sachs	Morgan Stanley	Morgan Stanley
Merril Lynch	Morgan Stanley	Merril Lynch	Deutsche Bank
Credit Suisse FB	Credit Suisse FB	JP Morgan	Salomon Smith Barney
Warburg Dillon Read	Warburg Dillon Read	Credit Suisse FB	Credit Suisse FB
Salomon Smith Barney	Deutsche Bank	Lazard Houses	Goldman Sachs
Deutsche Bank	Mediobanca	Rotschild	Warburg Dillon Read
Lehman Brothers	Lehman Brothers	Warburg Dillon Read	JP Morgan
ABN Amro	Credit Lyonnais	Lehman Brothers	Lehman Brothers
Dresdner KB	Salomon Smith Barney	Dresdner KB	ABN Amro
Aggregate market share			
75.8%	76.1%	88.1%	63.3%

Source: Group of Ten 2001.

When the moment arrives for streamlining and rationalising the combined organisations, the task reveals itself as less straightforward than forecasted, very time-consuming and tense. This is particularly the case when the M&A involves two big companies.

THE POTENTIAL FOR CONFLICTS OF INTEREST IN COMPLEX ORGANISATIONS

The more an organisation is complex and involved in a varied pool of activities, the more risks for conflicts of interest can arise. An area that proved to be quite affected by this problem is the work of research analysts inside financial organisations involved in investment banking activities. A myriad sources of conflicts of interest, in fact, threatens the objectivity of analysts' recommendations in these situations. The underwriting activity, the trading activity and the management of the proprietary portfolio of the investment bank may in fact be significantly influenced by the content of the reports issued by analysts. In particular, positive reports can contribute to the finding and retaining of corporate clients, the successful development of a bond or equity public offering, the amount of trading on a certain security, thus generating commissions and/or capital gains on the proprietary position. As a natural consequence, hard pressures affect the integrity and quality of these reports, unless appropriate organisational mechanisms isolate the research activity from the investment banking activities.[4]

A clear evidence of the problem emerges from the aggregate observation of the analysts' recommendations. According to a study conducted by the US Securities and Exchange Commission (SEC), in the year 2000, less than 1 per cent of analysts' recommendations in securities houses were characterised by a 'sell' or 'strong sell' advice. Similar results are outlined by a research conducted on the Italian market by Consob, the Italian SEC. In the year 2000, the 'sell' recommendations were around 6 per cent of the aggregate amount of the analysts' reports released. Even assimilating the 'hold' recommendations with the 'sell' ones, the percentage rose to 32 per cent, still lagging far behind the share of 'buy' and 'strong buy' recommendations.[5]

More in general, the problem of conflicts of interest comes from organisational complexity and from the parallel involvement in different activities, partly linked to each other and characterised by different levels of profitability. In these situations, in fact, the firm may be tempted to sacrifice the quality of a less profitable activity in order to boost the margins generated by another area. Even when this is not done on a systematic basis, the damage to the customers and the consequent need for protection are clear.

HEIGHTENED RISK OF SYSTEMIC CRISIS?

'Five-hundred-billion-dollar banks and $700-billion financial conglomerates may have been unimaginable a couple of decades ago; now they exist in the United States. Moreover, Japan, Germany, and France all have banks with assets pushing and perhaps soon exceeding a trillion dollars' (Spillenkothen 1999: 2). These words, pronounced during a conference at the Federal Reserve Board in New York, can well introduce the third important issue related to consolidation: the impact of the new dimensions and complexities of the financial intermediaries on the systemic stability.

What happens if one of the big entities born from consolidation fails? How would this failure affect the systemic equilibrium? Are the big players more or less exposed to risks?

Starting from the last question, the answer should be—less. In fact, the greater possibilities of diversification should limit the aggregate risk exposure and the ability of a large firm to absorb shocks should be higher than that of a smaller organisation.[6] Nevertheless, after consolidation, some firms may shift towards riskier asset portfolios and the managerial complexities increase, together with the operating risks. Thus, it is not possible to determine the net effect in general terms. Moreover, as a result of the globalisation of financial markets, the benefits related to geographical diversification are less clear-cut than they used to be.

If the changes in the risk profile of individual companies are difficult to evaluate, the dimension of the major players in today's financial landscape makes their potential failure for sure much more dangerous than in the past. In many cases, a comprehensive intervention by the public authorities would be impossible. Moreover, the interdependency between large and complex organisations has increased over the last decade, mostly through inter-bank loan exposures and over the counter (OTC) derivatives trading. Thus, the possibilities of rapid spreading of crisis have significantly increased. In other words, the failure of one big player could deeply involve many other actors of the financial industry.

HEIGHTENED RISK OF 'FINANCIAL CONTAGION'?

Another relevant challenge posed by the consolidation and globalisation of the financial services industry is linked to the consequences brought by large movements of capitals across borders. As said beforehand, the last decade's financial crisis show how volatile the capital flows can be, with enormous effects on the involved economies. Table 16.3 gives a vivid evidence of the dimension of the problem with reference to the Asian crisis.

The magnitude of the volatility's effect—often driven by and exacerbated by psychological factors—is amplified by the enormous

Table 16.3

Capital Flows in Asian Countries—Net Private Capital Flows in US$ billion

	1996	1997	1998	1999
Indonesia	11.5	−9.1	−9.9	−8.3
Korea	24.9	−21.2	−21.2	7.1
Malaysia	7.9	1.4	0.08	−8.8
Thailand	16.6	−14.1	−16.1	−6.8
Crisis-hit Asia	60.9	−43.1	−46.4	−16.8

Source: Crockett 2000.

quantity of money involved. The sharp increase of the financial assets in percentage of the GDP, the institutionalisation of saving and the removal of many former barriers to free capital mobility have, in fact, significantly increased the gunfire of institutional investors. As a natural consequence, the inflows and the following outflows easily overshoot, with relevant distortions of the resource allocation processes. When the situation of a country or a sector is attractive and promising, a considerable flow of funds tends to move towards it, reinforcing the positive trend. At the same time, however, an excessive liquidity may lead to a less attentive selection of the investment opportunities. The process is rapidly reversed when the first signs of weakness become apparent. The withdrawal of funds takes place at a very rapid pace, worsening the situation.

Moreover, the recent episodes of crisis proved to be particularly prone to contagion. In fact, when a country or a sector shows signs of weaknesses, the new sophisticated risk management systems of professional investors are mechanically required to sell assets in the same asset class. Consequently, the wave of capital withdrawal rapidly spreads to countries and sectors with similar features.

THE ROLE OF GOVERNMENT AND PUBLIC SURVEILLANCE IN THE NEW MARKET CONTEXT

The new features and criticalities of the financial services industry impose a rethinking and reorganising of the surveillance activity from public authorities. The issues are numerous and relevant.

First of all, the international dimension of some global players pushes towards a more intense coordination among national authorities.

In fact, surveillance at a mere national level risks being useless when the field of action of a financial firm extends worldwide. Among the different proposals concerning this aspect, there is even the extreme idea of creating a sort of global supercoordinator in charge of ensuring a level playing field across sectors and across nations, mainly in terms of regulatory, anti-trust and prudential policy.[7] This idea, however, is very difficult to put in practice mostly from a political point of view. The case of the EU failing to agree on a common surveillance authority is a very clear proof of that. A more feasible solution is to strengthen the effort to set common standards internationally through the recommendations of consultative bodies, extending and upgrading the actions of the Basle Committee for Banking Supervision. In parallel, the national authorities should be engaged in a more intense and continuous exchange of information.

Remaining at the international level, an important change would also be required in the institutional role of the main multilateral financial entities: in particular, the IMF and the World Bank. Their role and expertise, in fact, would be particularly appropriate in the detection, prevention and handling of the international financial crisis, in a sort of consultant role. On the contrary, their traditional, more strictly financial role is less crucial than it used to be:

> All of this is an appropriate mission for the IMF and the World Bank in the new financial architecture. Indeed, in some sense it could be seen as their key function: equipping national authorities and private markets with the capacity to handle international financial relations in an efficient and stabilising way. The purely financial role of the two institutions would then be to deal with the much smaller range of cases where market failures led either to inefficient outcomes or to financial instability (Crockett 2000: 14).

A similar problem is created by the blurring of distinctions among different sectors of the financial services industry. The increasing relevance of conglomerates, operating in many different kinds of activities, creates the need for a stronger coordination among sectoral authorities that used to work quite independently. In many countries, in fact, at least three different public surveillance bodies exist: one in charge of banking supervision (usually the central bank), a second one in charge of the insurance sector, a third one in charge of financial markets' and securities houses' control. When more and more financial intermediaries become involved in many sectors at the same time, the very logic of this division is put into question. Thus, one radical choice can be to concentrate the oversight functions together in a single entity, as the UK, Japan and the Scandinavian countries have decided to do. Alternatively, an appropriate coordination is needed in order to minimise the bureaucratic burdens for the supervised firms and in order to avoid the possibilities of regulatory arbitrage.

As often happens, both these solutions present advantages and drawbacks. The single-entity solution seems very attractive, especially in those contexts where domestic financial institutions are widely integrated across sectors. However, this solution raises various questions. The first is related to the attitude a single entity could have when a trade-off between different supervisory objectives exists. For instance, in many cases the need for investor protection can be in conflict with the maximisation of financial stability. In fact, the investors are better satisfied when the competition is higher, but a high level of competition can create instability because of the aggressive behaviour induced in the financial intermediaries. Basically the doubt is: are these kind of trade-offs better solved when the conflicting objectives are assigned to different institutions? Another important question is related to where the concentrated oversight functions should reside. Should they be absorbed by the central bank or should a separate entity be created?[8] The historical expertise and attitude of the central banks, together with the desire to avoid the concentration of too much power into a single non-elected body, suggest the opportunity to appoint a separate entity. This solution has, in fact, been gaining greater consensus in the international debate.

Once the appropriate organisational structure of the oversight functions have been decided, the following problem is how to face the increased systemic risks which can stem from the consolidation and globalisation of the financial services industry. The urgent need for innovative solutions in this field is well testified by the radical revision of the standards proposed by the Basle Committee, to be applied from the year 2006. In the effort of creating a more flexible and risk-sensitive approach, a new philosophy of prudential supervision was born. This new philosophy relies much more than before on the internal risk-management systems devised by the financial intermediaries and much less on the imposition of standardised prudential ratios. Basically, the idea is that the authorities should nowadays control the soundness and reliance of the internal risk-management systems adopted by the institutions, thus forcing a widespread adoption of the best practices in this area. Consequently, the prudential limits to the activities and the risks sustained by the financial firms should not be expressed in general and fixed terms, but related to the risk measures provided by the internal systems for control.[9] This new approach became feasible and was prompted by the tremendous advancements the financial firms made in the risk-management field during the 1990s, following the path opened by a few investment banks. As Greenspan remarked:

> The use of new technology and instruments in rapidly changing financial markets means that some bank balance sheets are already obsolescent before the ink dries. They are not even necessarily indicative of risk exposures that might prevail the next day. In such a context, the supervisor must rely on his evaluation of risk management procedures as a supplement to—and in extreme cases, a substitute for—balance sheet facts. As the 21th century unfolds, the supervisor's evaluation of safety and soundness, of necessity, increasingly will be focused on process and less on historical trends (1996: 2).

This is the core of the new process-oriented regulation as opposed to the previous rules-oriented regulation.

Another measure that would help limit the systemic risk is a greater degree of disclosure and transparency that would in turn allow a stronger market discipline on the financial intermediaries' actions and thus a more effective private-sector monitoring. In fact, 'considerable evidence supports that market discipline is an important force for controlling bank risk taking, especially by largest institutions. This evidence suggests that reinforcing the effectiveness of market discipline would have considerable benefit' (Olson 2002: 4). Under this point of view, a critical aspect is represented by the increasing complexity of financial firms' organisational structures and, more particularly, by the widespread use of special purpose vehicles. The misuse of this latter instrument can create the potential for considerable risk-hiding, as the Enron story vividly proves.

Finally, many proposals are on the table for dealing with the conflicts of interests and the dangers of market abuse. More in particular, the Forum of the European Securities Commissions (FESCO) has been intensely working on the subject and has released two important documents: *Market abuse. Action plan for financial services* (June 2000) and *Measures to promote market integrity* (August 2001). In these papers the attention is focused on the following main issues:

- misuse of material information in relation to financial instruments before that information has been disclosed to the public;
- dissemination of information or trading behaviour which is likely to give false or misleading signals as to the supply, demand or price of a financial instrument.

The measures recommended to avoid these distortions mainly rely on four pillars: disclosure, confidentiality, restrictions on relevant persons, and proper internal organisation. According to the disclosure principle, all inside information should be made public as soon as possible. Before disclosure, however, appropriate mechanisms should be in place to avoid the misuse of the information. In particular, trading restrictions should be applied to the people who possess the information, and the circulation of information inside the organisation should be restricted through the use of the so-called 'Chinese walls'. For instance, the trading area should be adequately separated from other business areas.

However, it should be quite clear that—in this field more than in others—an active cooperation is needed from the firms involved for the sake of market integrity and development. The misuse of information, the dissemination of misleading information, insider trading, and similar sort of behaviours are in fact extremely difficult to detect and to prove from outside. For this reason, the FESCO proposed the creation of a compliance function inside each financial firm; i.e., the designation of one or more persons in charge of:

- preparing a code of conduct outlining the rules and procedures applicable in the organisation;
- identifying and recommending to the executive body the measures needed to ensure compliance with the code of conduct;
- monitoring compliance with all the code of conduct rules and ensuring that the appropriate measures are taken in case of non-compliance.

An adequate independence of the compliance function should be obviously ensured by the management of the firm.

CONCLUSIONS

Globalisation and the new competitive environment brought about by liberalisation is rapidly changing the world of banking and finance. The financial intermediaries cannot earn protected rents anymore, they need bigger dimensions to compete effectively on a worldwide basis and a wider range of services to retain their customers. These needs—in turn—create the stimulus for mergers, acquisitions and strategic alliances at various levels: national and international, intra-sectoral and cross-sectoral.

The resulting wave of consolidation has various upsides and downsides. The question marks and problematic issues are plenty. Will the global players born from the consolidation be able to exploit market power in an oligopolist fashion? Could serious conflicts of interest develop inside the highly diversified 'financial supermarkets'? Do the investors need new and stronger forms of protection? What would be the consequences of a 'major player' crisis? Would these consequences be manageable? Has the risk of systemic crisis through 'financial contagion' significantly increased?

All these questions urgently require a rethinking and reengineering of the role of governments and public surveillance in order to face effectively the changes brought about by the new market context. National and sectoral boundaries do not make sense anymore, global actions and prudential standards are needed, together with an early warning system to detect overshooting situations.

NOTES

1. See Group of Ten 2001. The study—conducted by six task forces—has taken into consideration the 11 G-10 nations plus Australia and Spain. A more detailed analysis of the pattern of consolidation in the European Union (EU) can be found in European Central Bank 2000.
2. 'The liberalisation of financial markets and the accelerating development of information technology has increased competition both within and across industries. In particular, the lowering of geographical barriers and the

increasing integration of financial markets pit against each other banks, insurance and asset management companies that used to operate in segmented markets. In response to this process, financial institutions attempt to improve the efficiency of existing operations and to expand into new markets, trying to build a competitive advantage in a new environment. Mergers and acquisitions (M&A) allow financial institutions to rapidly increase their size and improve their knowledge of new products and markets, thereby allowing them to attempt to exploit economies of scale and scope, to preserve falling margins by increasing market share and to attract new customers' (Group of Ten 2001: 247).

3. However, this situation could soon be affected and rebalanced because the developments in IT and the diffusion of Internet banking are making these segments of the market more contestable.

4. The potential sources of conflicts of interest affecting the work of research analysts emerge very clearly from a testimony of the US SEC:

It has become clear that research analysts are subject to several influences that may affect the integrity and the quality of their analysis and recommendations. There are numerous pressures that exist within full-service brokerage firms, but four potential areas of conflict stand out:

- attracting and retaining clients: the analyst's firm may have underwritten an offering for a company or seek to underwrite a future offering. The analyst may have been part of the investment banking team that took the company public;
- firm profits: positive reports by brokerage firm analysts can also trigger higher trading volumes, resulting in greater commission for the firm;
- compensation: an analyst's salary and bonus may be linked to the profitability of the firm's investment banking business;
- equity stakes: the analyst, other employees and the firm itself may own significant positions in the company the analyst covers (Unger and US SEC 2001: 1–2).

5. Another clear and dramatic evidence of the problems related to the conflicts of interest comes for the case of Enron's failure. In fact, some major global financial players—who had to be aware of the firm's critical situation because of their investment and commercial banking relationships—continued with positive reports on the society's perspective up to the very end of its life. Moreover, the revision of Enron's rating and auditing analysis arrived with an unacceptable delay, clearly signalling a lack of transparency. In the year 2000, the stock price gained 91 per cent, while the Standard & Poor's 500 (S&P 500) lost 9 per cent. Less than one year afterwards, on 2 December 2001, the company filed for bankruptcy because of the losses gradually accumulated and concealed through three partnerships.

6. 'Diversified institutions should be subject to less financial volatility in their earnings and asset quality. Well-managed institutions with a broad customer and product base can typically absorb shocks that might adversely

affect smaller or more specialised firms. On the other hand, if large institutions encounter significant problems, the consequences are obviously potentially more severe and can more easily rise to systemic risk levels. And, market linkages mean that financial shocks can be transmitted much more quickly at home and abroad. The balance, then, seems to have shifted. The probability of a troubling event may have declined as banks have consolidated and diversified, but even the unlikely failure of a large financial institution today could well be more significant than ever before. It seems to me that the size, complexity and systemic implications of some of the banking organisations we jointly supervise create a dilemma with important implications for how we should conduct supervision in the future. Because of the potential impact of these institutions on the health and stability of our financial system, we need to fundamentally strengthen our supervisory approaches and maintain a much better and up-to-date understanding of the financial condition and risk profile of these firms. This will help supervisors anticipate and better cope with the financial disturbances and crises that experience clearly shows will inevitably occur from time to time' (Spillenkothen 1999: 2).

7. 'How to ensure a level playing field internationally, both in terms of regulatory/prudential policy and enforcement? An approach sometimes discussed has been to set up a world financial authority, with powers to set and enforce regulation worldwide. I do not believe such an approach would be either feasible or desirable. It is not feasible, since there is very little chance of sovereign legislatures ceding powers in the regulatory area to a supranational body. And it would not necessarily be desirable. A single regulator could be too monolithic, disinclined to experiment with new regulatory approaches. The rules it would create might not take adequate account of the particularities of the financial sector in different jurisdictions. And insofar as all countries had to agree on regulatory initiatives, there would be a risk of converging on the lowest common denominator' (Crockett 2001: 7).

8. 'The boundaries between financial intermediaries had become thoroughly blurred. Borio and Filosa (1994) were, perhaps, the first to explore the consequences of this for the structure of financial supervision. So one obvious conclusion that was reached was equivalently to place responsibility for the supervision of all financial intermediaries in one institution. But this naturally caused a problem for Central Banks, should they wish to maintain internal control of banking supervision. The logic of placing all supervision under one roof would then require the Central Bank to take responsibility for supervision over activities which lay outside its historical sphere of expertise and responsibility. An even more serious problem, than already exists, would arise of how to demarcate the boundaries between those sub-sets of depositors/institutions which would be covered by the "safety-net" (explicit or implicit), deposit insurance, Lender of Last Resort facilities, etc., and those not so covered. Would the Central Bank really want to take under its wing the responsibility for customer protection in fund management? In practice, much of staff time, even in banking supervision, is taken up with customer

protection issues (other than deposit insurance). Would a Central Bank really want to extend its operational remit to dealing with financial markets and institutions where issues relating to systemic stability were limited, and customer protection of much greater importance, e.g. the pension mis-selling scandal in the UK? So if efficiency and cost saving implied the unification of financial supervision, this suggested placing such a unified body outside the Central Bank' (Goodhart 2000: 18).

9. 'The answer to this dilemma—and the key to effective supervision in the next millennium—seems to me to depend on the extent to which we can successfully develop and pursue the following strategies:

- Enhanced supervisory focus on the quality of internal systems and processes for identifying, measuring, monitoring and controlling risks.
- Active encouragement of banks to continually develop, reassess and upgrade sound risk management policies and practices.
- Substantial improvement in public disclosure by banks and greater reliance on financial markets to discipline and "regulate" bank risk-taking.

That the current capital standard—the 1988 Basel Capital Accord—has become obsolete for many large banks provides a lesson for policy makers. A decade ago, I believe we did the best that we could. Better, more sophisticated risk measurement techniques within the industry did not exist, or at least they were not in sufficiently broad use worldwide. Implementing a more rigorous and economically accurate standard was not practical. Today, though, with the improvements in this area and the dramatically enhanced ability of the industry to maintain and process data, stronger techniques are available—and will be critical in the next millennium' (Spillenkothen 1999: 3).

REFERENCES

Banca d'Italia. 1999. 'Why do Banks Merge?'. *Temi di discussione*. Rome: Banca d'Italia.

Borio, R. Filosa. 1994. *The Changing Borders of Banking: Trends and Implications*. BIS Economic Papers.

Crockett, A. 2000. 'Progress Towards Greater International Financial Stability'. Conference of the GEI Programme. London.

———. 2001. 'Issues in Global Financial Supervision'. Conference held in Singapore.

European Central Bank. 1999. 'The Effects of Technology on the EU Banking Systems'. Frankfurt: European Central Bank. Downloaded from *www.ecb.int*.

———. 2000. 'Mergers and Acquisitions Involving the EU Banking Industry. Facts and Implications'. Frankfurt: European Central Bank. Downloaded from *www.ecb.int*.

Forum of the European Securities Commissions. (FESCO). 2000. 'Market Abuse. Action Plan for Financial Service'. Paris: FESCO.

————. 2001. 'Measures to Promote Market Integrity'. Paris: FESCO.

Goodhart, C.A.E. 2000. 'The Organisational Structure of Banking Supervision'. *FSI Occasional Papers*. Downloaded from *www.bis.org*.

Greenspan, A. 1996. 'Banking in the Global Market place'. Speech delivered at the Federation of Bankers Association. Tokyo, Japan.

Group of Ten. 2001. 'Report on Consolidation in the Financial Sector'. Basel: Group of Ten. Downloaded from *www.bis.org*.

Olson, M.W. 2002. 'Observations on the Evolution of the Financial Services Industry and Public Policy'. Speech at the Center for Study of Mergers and Acquisitions, School of Law, University of Miami, Miami Beach. *Bis Review*, 8.

Spillenkothen, R. 1999. 'Bank Supervision and Regulation in the Next Millennium'. Division of Supervision and Regulation, New York State Banking Department. Downloaded from *www.federalreserve.com*.

Unger, S.L. and US Securities and Exchange Commission. 2001. 'Written Testimony Concerning Conflicts of Interest Faced by Brokerage Firms and their Research Analysts'. Before the Subcommittee on Capital Markets, Insurance and Government Sponsors Enterprises. US House of Representatives.

CHAPTER 17

CONVERGENCE OF DIVERGENCES:
THE CHANGING LEGAL FRAMEWORKS,
FREE MARKET IDEOLOGY AND CORPORATE
REORGANISATION IN GERMAN ENTERPRISES

RUDI SCHMIDT

THE POLITICAL FRAMING

Just as the influential publicists and their pundits had agreed that we would see a new expansion of capitalism, carried on by the old confidence in progress and development, and after the dichotomy of the world order had been overcome, the soap-bubble of the 'New Economy' burst and the high-flown expectations went with it. What had seemed to be almost a natural law of succession in the development of productive power in which the epoch of the predominating information and communication technologies of the 1980s and 1990s would be replaced by the 'life-sciences' led, after the crash of the inflated, speculatively upheld market prices, to the realisation that the 'old' branches of the economy offered perhaps the more dependable profit perspectives after all. In the self-propelled exhilaration of an unending economic dynamic, many market actors were earlier prepared to renounce old accepted certainties of conjectural economic links, for the long upward trend in the United States made the vision of a crisis-free dynamic of growth appear real. The high-profit financial acrobatics of the speculators fostered a belief that a new mechanism of capital gain had been generated, and with America's leap into the new economy, the supposed superiority of 'old-economy' Japanese and German production organisations of the early 1980s was now obsolete,[1] as was any doubt about the traditional principle of 'America first'.

Whether the consequences of September 11 should be considered part of the economic setback described above implying some sort of world-historical divide can meanwhile be doubted, at least in the sense presumed by many observers at first. The US quickly resumed its former practices of unilateral power-politics determined by simple causal thinking habits and selective morality. Behind this 'new' old self-confidence, the American economy has also recovered optimism and is supported by President Bush's huge rearmament programme. It even seems that behind the sign of a new *Pax Americana*, the anti-terror campaign is actually returning to the old objective of containing the Soviet Union, presently Russia. From the spring of 2002 American soldiers have been in the Caucasians (Georgia) and the Central Asian republics around Afghanistan. They could open the way to the long hoped-for access to Asian oilfields and to the routes for its safe transfer by which a greater independence from Arabian oil could be achieved. The newly confirmed politico-military dominance of the US reinforces the economic order too and with that the imposition of the American business system gains impetus.[2]

The US is now at the height of its international power which will probably be relativised only when China or perhaps even Europe can take a place at its side as an equal power. The chief commentator of the *Washington Post*, Charles Krauthammer, expresses this rather drastically:

America won the Cold war, pocketed Poland and Hungary and the Czech Republic as door prizes, then proceeded to pulverize Serbia and Afghanistan and, *en passant*, highlight Europe's irrelevance with a display of vast military superiority. We rule the world culturally, economically, diplomatically and militarily as no one has since the Roman Empire . . . . We control everything else in the world. Can't we let somebody else have a bit of sporting glory?

And he mocks at the same time the nationalistic enthusiasm of his compatriots at the Winter Olympics 2001–2 (*International Herald Tribune*, 22 February 2002).

It is not the conspiracy theory expressed in the Islamic world, which accuses the Christian West (the US and Europe) of wholesale exploitation and oppression of Islamic states, but rather neo-liberalism, the ideology practised above all by the Anglo-Saxon nations, which serves as an explanation for and legitimisation of their economic preponderance. From the ideological justification for the superiority of liberalism and democracy by Fukuyama (1992: 75) to the innumerable treatises of the worldwide dominant neoclassical economics since the decline of Keynesianism, the pure theory of the free market has been preached in unison. 'The dominance of free trade ideology at this millennium-end is nearly absolute' (Dore 2000: 15).[3] The world market, it is true, has developed through technological differentiation and increasing specialisation, but the impetus and the forms of regulation after which it has been formed are politically determined. They are 'the result of political will. They are the salient features of the neoliberal radicalism of Reagan and Thatcher' (Dore 2000: 3). An intense debate has arisen over whether the national state can still be a regulating force over the growing power of the big multinational companies (see for example Altvater and Mahnkopf 1996; Reich 1991).

Yet, inasmuch as the new rules of the world market are made by states, they are still the essential actors in the drama of globalisation norms. Power of course is very unequally divided among the various nations. Because the US since Reagan as the most powerful economy subscribed fully to the neo-liberal economic doctrine ('Reaganomics') and Britain under Thatcher followed, the Anglo-Saxon preference for economic liberalism—by way of the particularly dynamic development of international finance markets—has gained or at least claims predominance everywhere against more societally engaged economic concepts such as those of Japan or continental Europe.

THREE LEVELS OF REGULATION

The development in the international process of liberalisation intensified and since the 1990s is known as 'globalisation'. I define it—in its effects on the individual state—as a process of the 'degovernmentalisation and economisation of society; Dore (2000: 3) calls it, 'marketization plus financialization'.

The new regulation of the economic relations of firms and investors which is the theme of my chapter takes place at three levels:

first, at the international level, i.e., the world market, second, at the regional level, in specific economic zones such as the EU and third, at the national level.

THE INTERNATIONAL REGULATION LEVEL

The forced re-regulation of international finance structures bears the mark above all of the big exporting countries, as well as of several collective actors and institutions, all of which more or less 'freely' take part in forming the result. 'Freely', however, often means just the acceptance of the inevitability of a power gradient between the big and small players. The large states, and the multinational corporations (MNCs) behind them, have an easy time advocating the unlimited freedom of the marketplace, since they stand to gain the most.

> International institutions which seek to achieve genuine, inter-
> national public goods . . . are indeed highly desirable. But those
> institutions can be, and are in the case of the BIS as in that of
> the WTO, shaped not merely by such public good considerations
> . . . but also by the stronger players' appeal to 'level-playing
> field' arguments for rules which minimize all restraints on
> international competition to the clear and disproportional advan-
> tage of their own national firms (Dore 2000: 16).

Among the main actors are the EU which is liberalising its internal market and wants to create equal conditions for competition, the US, Japan, the World Trade Organisation (WTO), International Monetary Fund (IMF), Bank for International Settlements (BIS) and other important world market actors, above all the MNCs, which are the real global players. From the paramount aim of reducing trade barriers and also creating equal competitive conditions—above all for the transfer of goods and funds (the four freedoms of mobility are: of merchandise, money, people and information)—follow all the other measures. However, this does not come about through a centralised act of volition—with maybe the WTO or the IMF at the top—but rather within a structure of reciprocally confirmed and reinforced influence in which the principles are repeatedly communicated and legitimised by the dominant actors. They are finally, in separate decisions made by the respective organisations, transformed into concrete measures. This can be observed well in the process of liberalising the movement of goods and capital.

Since the successive abolition of control over the flow of capital, the demolition of tariff barriers, import quotas, and import-limiting technical standards by the General Agreement of Tariffs and Trade (GATT) process and later by the WTO, the idea of free trade has spread ever further during the last decades. It has been accepted beyond the circle of the old industrialised countries, in newly industrialised countries (NICs) and in many countries on the threshold.[4] One can see this simply on the basis of the number of member countries since the founding of the preliminary organisation in 1947 (signing of the founding declaration), when it had 23 member states; by 2000 this had increased to 140 states. The actual WTO, founded in 1994 as the successor organisation, extended its spectrum of activity to include services (General Agreement on Trade in Services) and intellectual property rights (Agreement on Trade-related Aspects of Intellectual Property Rights). Because liberalisation is being carried out with the intention of creating equal competitive conditions, the WTO must regulate conflicts of interest between its members (Bise 2001). This is especially with regard to distortions of competitive advantage resulting from direct or indirect subvention, and artificial, non-tariff barriers as well as import limitations set up against the rules, like those imposed by the US in 2002 to protect its own steel industry.

Besides these two organisations, the Organisation for Economic Coorpertion and Development (OECD), IMF, World Bank and the G-7 (or G-8) with their world economic forums also play a coordinating and structuring role in the world economy. All of these are dominated by the intensively exporting industrial countries, in spite of the unanimity principle in the WTO.

Another important role is played by the BIS in international standardisation, the new regulation of capital relations. The BIS is presently working on new refinancing rules, above all for granting risk-graded loans and dependent on this for the minimum amount of internal capital security for banks. Because in consequence these new rules should not only make the risks associated with banks more visible and calculable for capital investors but also for borrowers, they will have a great practical effect, especially on the business of small- and medium-sized firms. Until now banks gave loans to firms with interest rates dependent on bonitary state but always supported internally with 8 per cent of their own capital; in future the amount of internal capital involved will be graded according to risk.

While until now it was mostly the long experience of the loan officer responsible for an industrial branch or firm which determined the general estimation of a debtor's risk, the new rules require an external rating procedure which will cost medium-sized firms from 15,000–20,000 Euros. Unrated firms will still get loans but will have to accept higher interest rates or else seek private capital sources such as private equity funds or risk their luck on the share markets (Gerke et al. 1995; Kerwer 2000; Chew 1997).

A second area of conflict has appeared at the Basel Commission in the form of differing assessments of the relative importance of long- and short-term loans. The Anglo-Saxon representatives on the Commission—which the majority of the members tend to be— would like to make long-term loans more expensive. This has met with stiff resistance from German and Austrian government representatives. In the American type of firm policy based on short-term gains, long-term financing does not play any essential role, and is also considered rather risky in the dynamic up-and-down environment of enterprise policy. In addition, procurement of liquid assets in American companies depends more heavily on stock markets than bank loans. In Germany and Austria, with rather long-term-oriented firm policies, financing by loans is still fundamental, and that is especially true for medium-sized enterprises which are generally not stock companies and, therefore, in the great majority depend on long-term loans from banks (see Deeg 1999; Gerke et al. 1995). The required rating and the intended cost increase of long-term credit threatened the competitiveness of German and Austrian firms and provoked a major intervention on the part of German Chancellor Schroeder in November 2001, by which the completion of the agreement was delayed and is now expected to be resolved only in 2003.

What form the agreement will then take is at present hard to foresee. Probably the financing of medium-sized businesses will be more costly than before. With that there will be more pressure to seek other ways of financing. And with the increased coercion of rating, probably accounting procedures will also be made similar to international standards in Europe in the direction of the International Standard Accounting system (ISA) which is to be made the EU standard. Company accounting will in future be not only uniform, but also more transparent and comparable which will make loaning money easier for banks as well as make risk-assessment easier for private investors. Also here there is a conflict between European states and the US. European companies which want to be on the New York exchange in order to access the American capital market and increase their share value have to use the American Generally Accepted Accounting Principles (GAAP), which do not conform to the ISA standards in several important aspects. Critics claim that the Enron bankruptcy was not only not prevented but actually first made possible by GAAP standards. That view strengthens the position favouring European accounting standards, although the conclusion of the dispute over competing accounting standards is still an open matter.

Besides the normative restructuring by international institutions, there is also an informal pressure at work to radically equalise the various capital relationships in European countries. This pressure is exercised particularly by the large pension funds, hedge funds and investment banks, which have long been the object of critical public attention and discussion. These large capital investors are constantly in search of new and profitable investment opportunities.[5] The more risk and profit-conscious among them seek above all firms—underpriced because of not preferred concepts—which they can then restructure or disassemble and later sell at a good profit without consideration of the interests of employees or other shareholders. They, like the banks, are interested in uniform assessment standards, greater transparency, etc., in order to conduct their business better and more calculably.

THE EUROPEAN REGULATION LEVEL

The policy foundation of the European Union is the creation of a uniform internal market within the framework of economic and currency union, according to the 'principle of an open market-economy with free competition' (see Title II, Article 2 and Article 3a, EU Treaty). Corresponding to this comprehensively conceived objective, the current pressure for liberalisation exercised by European institutions is the strongest-acting factor at work in the new regulation of legal frameworks for the European economic actors. It is acting especially to create an internal market,

> which is characterised by the elimination of barriers to the free movement of goods, persons, services and capital between member states; a system which protects competition from

misrepresentation within the internal market and promotes the uniformisation of country-internal legal statutes, in as far as this is necessary to the functioning of the common market (see Title II, Aricle 2 and Article 3a, EU Treaty).

In further sessions of the Council of Europe these goals were made firmer; for example, at a meeting in Lisbon in March 2000, the minister presidents agreed to make the EU the most competitive and dynamic knowledge-based economic area of the world. They further agreed to introduce an accelerated legislative process for securities markets and to create an internal financial services market by 2005.

In this area, the European Commission and Council of Ministers have introduced a number of new regulations with the intention of pulling down national protective barriers and making easier the cross-border activity of economic actors. One of the most important consequences of this liberalisation policy is the retreat of the state from the economy. This has occurred, and is continuing, through direct privatisation of, for example, state energy, communication and transport monopolies, and through scaling back the rights of governments to intervene in the market of corporate control, as well as indirectly through deregulation of existing state-sanctioned norms. The granting of rather long transition periods, however, has led to variable speeds of compliance with which the single national states are prepared to act on the demands presented by liberalisation. Great Britain, in consequence of Thatcherism, has thus progressed quite far in privatisation and deregulation, while France with its tradition of centralisation and tendency towards nationalistic economic policies is farthest behind. Even today it resists opening its electricity, gas, railroad, etc., to private competition. Other countries, such as Germany, occupy a middle position.

The European Commission intervenes in this either on the basis of its legal rights or upon request by the Council of Ministers or the European Parliament, but also often upon complaints filed by market participants themselves. Thus for example the Commission ordered after a complaint made by German private banks in Brussels the separation of private banking business from that conducted in the public interest by the German state-supported public regional and savings banks. The private banks had complained of unfair competition due to the lower capital requirement for the public banks which results from the state's liability or guaranty authority and the so called 'institutional burden'. A similar case is the Commission's challenge to the practice of setting obligatory book prices in the German-language book trade.

My thesis is thus that the liberalisation policy of the EU Commission, because of its clear and comprehensive form inspired by the WTO principles, as well as its inner dynamic, enjoys a legitimacy and effectiveness superior to a policy of the mere conservation of traditional or national specifics. Its dynamic force is supported by the experience of more advanced liberalisation, especially in capital markets, gained in the Anglo-Saxon economic sphere, which out of self-interest also exerts pressure for the adoption of its regulatory forms elsewhere in the EU. Thus, for example, the attempt failed to anchor in the new EU law on workers' councils, and in the new 'enterprise constitution' for the European stock corporation the traditionally strong position of employee rights in Central Europe, because of the neo-liberal opposition of England and Spain. It is, therefore, feared by the unions in Germany that workers' rights will be degraded because international companies there increasingly try to adopt the European regulatory form in order to escape employee participation. But this has not yet been observed as a strong tendency.

REGULATION AT THE NATIONAL LEVEL

At the national level, regulation of capital relations can be distinguished as *reactive* or *autonomous measures*. The reactive measures apply the internationally-made regulations or once applied, change them to conform to newer ones. In Germany, on which I focus my attention here, this kind of measure is surely the most frequent. The autonomous measures on the other hand are those which anticipate developments in the liberalisation of capital and economic relations, and try to prepare the way for the liberalised market by taking appropriate steps, also to prepare these firms against the unwelcome effects of liberalisation.

The German Federal Republic has for many years and without respect to party politics assumed the pioneering role in European integration. To promote this process, German governments have repeatedly tried to overcome hesitation in the integration process with financial concessions. Since German reunification in 1990, the financial basis of this policy has changed considerably: in the last

12 years nearly 1 trillion Euros have gone into the East-German Laender, aid which has been financed largely on credit. In this way a gigantic debt has accumulated which has in 2002 caused a warning to be issued from Brussels. But it is not only the financial problems of the Federal Republic which make it harder to pursue further the usual agricultural and regional structure policies of the past, to say nothing of carrying them over to the new member countries of Eastern Europe.

Under Federal Chancellor Schroeder, an economic and constitutional rethink has also occurred. The government appears only now to have noticed, with a certain disconcertment, how many of its rights have been transferred in the meantime to the European Commission, and how small the nation's room for manoeuvre has become. This has led among other things to rather important problems with the federal state structure of Germany. Politically autonomous regions in fact do not occur within the two-level EU organisational concept (national level–EU level) which markedly resembles the centralist self-image of states like France and Italy. Therefore, recently in Germany the demand has become loud for certain functions to be given back to the single states or regions, i.e., the Laender, according to the principle of subsidiarity, and that also with reference to the system of public finance and the market for corporate control.

Besides these political and constitutional problems, a transformation in economic politics in Germany has also become apparent. While the previous (CDU/FDP–conservative/liberal) Federal government pursued rather a liberalistic, i.e., Anglo-Saxon market principle, carrying through at an early date the liberalisation and privatisation of the media market, the energy sector and the railroads, the present government has taken note of the existing excesses in the use of these opportunities by the large multinationals or national monopoly concerns. It has been critically observed, and not just in Great Britain, that EDF (Electricity of France) uses the liberalisation of the electricity market in Britain and Germany for acquisitions and market consolidation, while the French state has always strictly refused to create the same conditions in the home country. Meanwhile, local and long-distance trains in the possession of French-dominated companies are running in Germany, while in France itself the Société Nationale des Chemins de Fer Francais (SNCF) holds an unchallenged monopoly over all rail routes.

The strongest long-term impression on German politics, however, was probably made by the hostile takeover of the Mannesmann concern by the British Vodafone (see Hoepner and Jackson 2001). In Germany Mannesmann was the model for the successful conversion of an old heavy industrial concern (steel, pipes and machines) into a modern IT enterprise which, with its mobile telephone division, could even outperform the former state giant Deutsche Telekom. Even though the legitimacy of the takeover was unchallenged, the fact is still irritating that in many other European countries enterprises which now participate without scruple in such mergers, acquisitions, and even do not rule out unfriendly takeovers, are themselves protected from takeovers by specific measures. Among these are voting-rights limitations, so-called state 'golden shares' (e.g., as in France), state merger-permits as in Italy, or the right of a board of directors to take special precautions to avoid hostile takeovers. By means of a special law meanwhile the regulation of the 'market for corporate control' has been strengthened in Germany; a firm's management can protect it more easily from takeovers through provisional resolutions taken by the board and shareholders' assembly. Here, thus, a certain deliberalisation has set in, and the fall of Germany from the top of developments back to a middle position. The law is newly criticised by the EU Commission which wants to establish a liberal regulation of the market.

The same change in attitude was also instrumental in the Federal government's intervention against the plans of the Basel Commission for a reform of loan financing. The conflict of the Anglo-Saxon capitalist concept with the German idea of economics was here even more apparent than in other areas. The German enterprise landscape, strongly oriented to medium-sized firms not noted for the most part on stock exchanges, is far more dependent on long-term loans, while the usually larger stock corporations in the US finance themselves largely through the stock exchange. Because of the different firm structures and financing traditions, in Germany a three-sector bank system—private banks, cooperative banks, and public savings and regional banks—was established, in which above all the savings banks assumed the financing with loans to small- and medium-sized enterprises. The large private banks have largely withdrawn from the business of financing medium-sized companies because of low interest margins on such loans.[6] Their complaint before the EU Commission of unfair competitive practice has meanwhile been resolved together by the Commission and the federal government in such a way that the liability of guaranty authority

(*Gewaehrstraegerhaftung*) of the state runs out after a transitional period, and the so-called 'institutional burden' (*Anstaltslast*) is to be counted in future as a subsidy.

Tax legislation is one of the central policy areas left to national sovereignty after EU treaties. In a few European states it is used—in economic areas relevant to taxes on firms and capital investors—as a competitive strategy. Thus, the British Channel Islands or Luxemburg, for example, where low capital gains tax or none at all are paid, attract much capital which has 'fled' from other countries. Holland encourages the keeping of holdings of multinational concerns by giving massive tax breaks, as does Ireland. The financial centre of London is so attractive for expert foreign personnel because, among other things, they pay no taxes—as long as they don't take up permanent residence there.

It was thus by a political, autonomous option for change in tax legislation that the federal government made it possible for large firms to sell their holdings in other enterprises tax-free, in order to favour consolidation and growth processes, concentration on the main business activity of firms, and the future oriented resizing of companies. The demand for this action had come for a long time from outside Germany, because the reciprocal participation of many German banks and enterprises in the business of the others had prompted the accusation of the country being an impenetrable castle, a 'Germany Ltd.' (Deutschland AG). The large reciprocal participatory packages were never sold, above all because such sales would have been liable to a 50 per cent tax. From the tax break it is hoped that not only an increased attraction for foreign investments will result but also a more efficient redirection of companies' attention to the relevant core business (for the various consequences of this policy see Hoepner 2000).

Another field in which the German government acts 'autonomously' is the reform of business management and surveillance practices, and the modernisation of shares law proposed by a government commission (Baums 2001). From the Anglo-Saxon viewpoint, German shares law is shareholder-unfriendly because it is thought to give management an unacceptable level of freedom, which results in the particular long-term orientation typical of the investment and business policies of German firms. As economists point out again and again, managers are more interested in the preservation of their jobs, i.e., in the long-term survival of the firm, an interest the employees also share, than in the profitability of the invested capital. In order to minimise this divergence of interest vis-à-vis shareholders, many large corporations have meanwhile gone over to paying greater portions of managers' salaries in the form of shares or share-options and/or bonuses dependent on profit levels.

Moreover, the federal government in 1999 instituted a governmental commission for the reform of corporate governance. It has made a range of suggestions for improving 'corporate governance, above all in the functioning of management bodies, their cooperation and the surveillance of their behaviour' (Baums 2001: 6). The purpose of this commission, which presented its report in summer 2001, was not only to consider the requirements of capital markets, but also to 'take into account the rightful interests of all stakeholders' (Baums 2001: 1). The commission in its report suggested, on the one hand, changes in the various laws relevant to firms, and on the other, made proposals which were not legally binding but to be enacted in the form of obligatory information about the observance of rules formulated in the 'Corporate Governance Codex'. A permanent commission is to watch over and report on the observance of the Codex and possibly make suggestions regarding its further development.

The commission's numerous proposals strengthen above all the right to information of share purchasers and globally the surveillance powers of boards of directors and shareholders' assemblies. At the same time the requirements made of board members are raised, conflicts of interest caused by multiple board-mandates limited, and the answerability of boards to the shareholders' meetings increased. Stronger requirements to publicise possible conflicts of interest have been set up, share deals by manager-stakeholders will be more sharply checked ('insider deals', 'director's deals', etc.), a higher level of transparency, frequency and liability to publicity will be demanded of firm accounting. These and more suggestions for improvements have been developed by the commission after considering the rules and viewpoints of other countries, especially considerations of the reform commission for corporate law of the British Economics Ministry. Some of these suggestions have meanwhile met with acceptance; others, especially the proposed changes to laws, will probably be passed during the next legislative period after the elections of the coming autumn.

To sum up the activity of the German federal government towards restructuring capital market relations and German enterprise law, the following can be said. On the one hand, it corresponds to the internationally imposed liberalistic world-market concept, although in Europe it cannot claim any more to be in a pioneering role in all areas, but rather, having also its national interests at heart, is hesitating in part due to critical disagreement with EU Commission and with the other European partners. On the other hand Germany is involved in modernising its legal and institutional framework so that international capital exchange to its benefit is not hindered, but made easier. In contrast to the French state, however, there is little if any interference in the restructuring of firms as a result of the new economic configuration, but rather only limited and indirect influence exercised through the framework of preconditions. One could thus speak of a process of internationalisation and liberalisation tempered by the strong German participatory tradition. Whether this will lead in the end to a modified 'Americanisation' or to a separate European way is still uncertain.

There is no doubt that in the beginning of the 21st century as well, there does exist more than one modern capitalism (see Crouch and Streeck 1995) and for the immediate future there will be 'divergent capitalisms' (Whitley 2000). The prediction for the long run is controversial. Wolfgang Streeck (1995) agrees with Michel Albert's (1991) pessimistic assumption of the less well-performing Anglo-American model of capitalism outcompeting the better performing 'Rhine Model'.

> Globalisation discriminates against modes of economic governance that require public intervention associated with a sort of state capacity that is unavailable in the anarchic world of international politics. It favors national systems like those of the United States and Britain that have historically relied less on public-political and more on private-contractual economic governance, making them more structurally compatible with the emerging global system, and in fact enabling them to regard the latter as an extension of themselves (Streeck 1995: 27).

> There are good reasons to believe that the normative pressure on German firms exerted at international, European and national levels, in concert with the interventionist power of the financial markets, has become so strong that the cultural and social divergences in the various forms of capitalism will further diminish—but not disappear.

These arguments will be strengthened when looking at the growing difficulties of Germany to reorganise its well-performing welfare system becoming more and more unsustainable in the future; also the average ratio of economic growth (GDP) in the last years were remarkably less than in USA or the UK. On the other side, one may predict a retardation of the integration of the European free market, taking into consideration the enormous effort to assimilate the seven former socialistic states of Middle-East Europe to the EU level after their gaining membership in 2004. And at least nobody knows if after the war against Iraq the USA really remains a political and economic superpower of the world, which was the precondition to make war without the backing of the United Nations (UN).

Summarising these facts, there are many uncertainties for predicting the future of capitalism. Nevertheless more arguments are to be heard for an adaptation of divergent capitalisms in the long run. For Germany the most probable development will be that the big firms, especially the MNCs dependent on the stock market, will follow more or less the shareholder value orientation and short-termism, transparency rules and international corporate control, whereas the huge number of small- and medium-sized enterprises—more than 90 per cent of the firms with two-thirds of the whole employees—which are not integrated in the stock market, will follow the German tradition of close contacts to the 'house bank' and to the stakeholders. The labour relations in these firms are based on trust and codetermination, with a labour force of high-skilled workers, long-term strategies and products of high quality. Thus we will get a rift between the big MNCs and the small- and medium-sized firms, one on the way to an international model of Anglo-Saxon-orientated free market capitalism and the other following the 'Rhine Model'.

NOTES

1. See Piore and Sabel 1984 or Fukuyama 1995, also the 'lean production debate' of the early 1990s (Womack et al. 1990) or many other authors praising the coherent society of 10–15 years ago with fewer conflicts and more cooperation (such as Dore 1988).
2. The war against Iraq, initiated in March 2003, can be understood as a perpetuation of this principle in an openly aggressive manner.
3. To trace how it has become so, see Yergin and Stanislaw 1998.

4. For historical development see Djelic 1998; James 1996, 1997; Kitschelt et al. 1999; Scherrer 1999.
5. The amounts in question are huge: the investment volume of pension funds in the US is currently estimated at $11,000 billion, in Japan at $3,100 billion and in Great Britain at $1,700 billion. The volume of the new pension funds in Germany with 250 billion Euro looks quite modest by comparison (*Frankfurter Allgemeine Zeitung*, 10 April 2002). But there are also 12,000 billion Euro in investment funds worldwide (*FAZ*, 6 April 2002).
6. By way of comparison, in 2000, the return after taxes on bank capital loaned by the German *Sparkassen* (Savings Banks) was on average 5.6 per cent, by the *Volksbank* and *Raiffeisen* (cooperative) Banks even only 3.7 per cent; capital return at the *Deutsche Bank* however, was 18 per cent, at UBS 21.5 per cent, and at British Lloyds even 31.8 per cent (from *FAZ*, 25 February 2002).

REFERENCES

Albert, M. 1991. *Capitalisme contre Capitalisme*. Paris: Edition du Seuil.

Altvater, A. and Mahnkopf, B. 1996. *Grenzen der Globalisierung. Oekonomie, Oekologie und Politik in der Weltgesellschaft*. Muenster: Westfaelisches Dampfboot.

Baums, T. (ed.) 2001. *Bericht der Regierungskommission Corporate Governance. Unternehmensführung—Unternehmenskontrolle—Modernisierung des Aktiensrechts*. Koeln: Dr. Otto-Schmidt.

Bise, M. 2001. *Die Welthandelsorganisation (WTO). Funktion, Status, Organisation*. Baden-Baden: Nomos.

Chew, D.H. (ed.). 1997. *Studies in International Corporate Finance and Governance Systems. A Comparison of US, Japan and Europe*. New York, Oxford: Oxford University Press.

Crouch, C. and Streeck, W. (eds) 1995. *Modern Capitalism or Modern Capitalisms?* London: Francis Pinter.

Deeg, R. 1999. *Finance Capitalism Unveiled. Banks and the German Political Economy*. Ann Arbor: The University of Michigan Press.

Djelic, M.L. 1998. *Exporting the American Model. The Post-War-Transformation of European Business*. Oxford: Oxford University Press.

Dore, R. 1988. *Taking Japan Seriously*. London: Athlone and Stanford: Stanford University Press.

————. *Stock Market Capitalism. Welfare Capitalism. Japan and Germany versus the Anglo-Saxons* . Oxford: Oxford University Press.

Fukuyama, F. 1992. *The End of History*. New York: The Free Press.

————. 1995. *The Social Trust, the Social Virtues and the Creation of Prosperity*. New York: The Free Press.

Gerke, W., Bank, M. and Neukirchen, D. 1995. *Probleme deutscher mittelstaendischer Unternehmen beim Zugang zum Kapitalmarkt. Analyse und wirtschaftspolitische Schlussfolgerungen*. Baden-Baden: Nomos.

Hoepner, M. 2000. 'Unternehmensverpflichtung im Zwielicht. Hans Eichels Plan zur Aufloesung der Deutschland AG'. *WSI-Mitteilungen*, 53(10): 655–63.

Hoepner, M. and Jackson, G. 2001. *Entsteht ein Markt fuer Unternehmenskontrolle? Der Fall Mannesmann und seine Implikationen fuer institutionellen Wandel in Deutschland*. Unpublished Paper. Koeln.

James, H. 1996. *International Monetary Cooperation since Bretton Woods*. New York: International Monetary Fund.

———. 1997. *Rambouillet, 15. Nov. 1975. Die Globalisierung der Wirtschaft*. München: Deutscher Taschenbuchverlag.

Kerwer, D. 2000. *Governance by Standardisation: The Case of Credit Rating Agencies*. Unpublished Paper. Bonn: Max Planck Project Group on the Law of Common Goods.

Kitschelt, H., Lange, P., Marks, G. and Stephens, J.D. 1999. *Continuity and Change in Contemporary Capitalism*. Cambridge: Cambridge University Press.

Piore, M.J. and Sabel, C.F. 1984. *The Second Industrial Divide: Possibilities for Prosperity*. New York: Basic Books, Inc.

Reich, R.B. 1991. *The Work of Nations*. New York: Alfred A. Knopf, Inc.

Scherrer, Chr. 1999. *Globalisierung wider Willen? Die Durchsetzung liberaler Aussenwirtschaftspolitik in den USA*. Berlin: Edition Sigma.

Streeck, W. 1995. *German Capitalism: Does It Exist? Can It Survive?* MPIFG Discussion Paper 95/5. Koeln. (Also published in C. Crouch and W. Streeck [eds.]. 1995. *Modern Capitalism or Modern Capitalisms?* London: Francis Pinter).

Whitley, R. 2000. *Divergent Capitalisms: The Social Structuring and Change of Business Systems*. Oxford: Oxford University Press.

Womack, J.P., Jones, D.T. and Roos, D. 1990. *The Machine that Changed the World*. New York: Rawson Associates.

Yergin, D. and Stanislaw, J. 1998. *Commanding Heights: The Battle Between Government and the New Market Place that is Remaking the Modern World*. New York: Simon and Schuster.

CHAPTER 18

THE EMERGENCE AND VIABILITY OF PARTICIPATORY FIRMS

PETER ABELL AND DIANE REYNIERS

Efficient production typically requires cooperation, but cooperation opens the possibility that some of the cooperating parties have an opportunity to exploit others, using means that reduce the total output. The 'governance' structure of a company is the means it uses to combat and control output-reducing exploitation. In this chapter, we discuss the governance of worker-controlled and capitalist firms. Exploitation in worker-owned firms takes the form of a free rider problem where workers do not put forth the efficient amount of effort. In a capitalist firm, the exploitation we focus on is that by the top management.

We offer some explanations for the pattern of worker ownership in industries and identify where worker-owned firms may have efficiency advantages. Efficiency in this context is typically defined as profitability, but while profitability is the appropriate measure for a capitalistic firm, it can be argued that the efficiency concept is trickier for worker-owned firms. Workers may want to trade off profit or income for better working conditions or better social relationships.

ORIGINS OF WORKER OWNERSHIP

A vast amount of literature advocates the participation by employed labour in both management (i.e., decision making) and ownership of the productive assets of firms. The reasons given for advocating labour participation of either or both sorts are varied, ranging from superior efficiency and performance (compared to capitalist firms) to issues of distributive justice and human rights. If 'participation' does indeed give rise to superior performance, however, we must ask why the competitive forces inherent in market economies have not (so far at least) selected the superior form.

When considering the success or failure of the worker ownership model, it is instructive to contemplate how worker-owned firms emerge. Employee buy-outs are popular as a privatisation method in Central and Eastern Europe and Russia where the employee-owned firm is seen as a compromise between the socialist and capitalist forms of organisation. In firms threatened with closure, management and unions often engage in 'concession bargaining' with the aim of ensuring survival and preserving employment. This then leads to whole or partial employee ownership with workers receiving shares and seats on the board in exchange for voluntary wage cuts. Russell (1985) suggests that this amounts to 'sowing the seeds of employee ownership on exceedingly infertile ground'.

It would be difficult to argue that labour participation in either ownership (equity) and/or management is a predominant practice anywhere, except where it has been introduced under the auspices of the law (e.g., *Mittbestimmung* or co-determination in Germany) or tax inducements. In the US, for example, over 12,000 organisations (Blasi et al. 1996) are currently making some use of Employee Share Ownership Plans (ESOPs), and over 10 per cent of 'workers' hold stock in the companies in which they work, but it is generally recognised that tax breaks have played a significant role in the generation of these statistics.

Is the relatively low incidence of 'labour participation' in both management and ownership (in the absence of inducements) attributable to (*a*) poor productivity or performance, (*b*) the existence of non-competitive forces preventing, in some way, the natural emergence and evolution of participative firms, or (*c*) [and related to (*b*)] a slow learning process where the above statistics may provide some indication of the early stages of an evolutionary process?

The question of first importance is whether or not participation (of whatever sort or degree) does indeed have a discernible impact upon performance, however measured. In this respect it is natural to look in the direction of systematic research. But even then, as we shall see, drawing conclusions is not at all easy. In an ideal research design the effects of 'participation' would be detected by taking a sample of otherwise identical start-ups, some adopting 'participation', others not, and studying their performance henceforth. In practice, research is far from this ideal.

It, furthermore, could conceivably be the case that the impact of participation 'induced' by regulation could be different from that of 'spontaneous' participation and could be heterogeneous by sector, capital intensity, and so on. If, for instance, performance effects arise from labour motivation, they may only show up in labour-intensive sectors.

FIRM OWNERSHIP STRUCTURES

According to the 'theory of the firm' literature (e.g., Hart 1995), firms exist because of the inevitable incompleteness of contracts. It is impossible to stipulate what each party in a bilateral contract will have to do under all possible circumstances. In the absence of a firm, any operation would have to somehow hang together by a number of these bilateral or multilateral contracts among input suppliers. Firms also contract, but resolve the incompleteness issue by systems of corporate governance which mean allocation of authority, rights and duties, and rules of ownership. Owners are residual claimants who have the formal right to monitor and control (make decisions), the right to contract with all input providers including the right to hire and fire employees, and the right to delegate and sell these rights.

Hansmann (1988) defines a 'stakeholder' as anyone who transacts with a firm either as a customer or as a supplier of an input such as labour (workers) or capital (investors), and claims that generally firms are owned by one and only one type of stakeholder who enters into bilateral contracts with the other stakeholders. There are thus two classes of stakeholders, those who own the firm and those who are linked to the firm by market transactions.

In what follows, when we mention capitalist firms we mean publicly-held firms. In such firms, equity is owned largely (with the exception of equity holdings by top management) by individuals who have no other relationship with the firm. In what sense, then, do these shareholders own capitalist firms? In theory, they monitor management but they typically have very little decision-making power. They do not get involved in contracting directly but delegate all decision making to the management or the board of directors. They have no *de facto* control and are in reality not very different from moneylenders. Hence there is a clear separation between who receives the residual earnings and who controls the firm. Top management, because it has control, can manipulate residual earnings and exercise some discretion in the allocation of rents.

What is a worker-owned and worker-run firm? In such a firm employees jointly control the use of assets and the distribution of residual earnings through an egalitarian, democratic voting mechanism (Putterman 1984). Only individuals who work in the organisation have control rights, usually on the basis of one person one vote. Workers can and generally will, however, decide to have a managerial elite, elected from among the workers or hired from outside, which processes information and makes at least some of the decisions. Closest to this model are the Kibbutz movement and the Mondragon network of cooperatives. Note that equity ownership by workers is not necessary under this definition. It is difficult to classify firms on the basis of what proportion of equity is owned by whom. Would it be necessary for workers to own all or a majority of the equity? Are managers classified as workers for these purposes? Is dispersion of ownership among all workers important? One could imagine all sorts of setups with workers providing some or all of the capital and getting either a fixed return on capital (while residual earnings are distributed in some other way) or a share in residual earnings. A large variety of arrangements exist in between worker-owned and capitalist firms. How would one classify, for example, small family-owned businesses where the workers are owner-managers?

When do we call a firm worker-owned and when do we say an ownership structure is capitalist? There doesn't appear to be a single answer to this question in the literature. Ownership structure involves at least two dimensions: (a) who has claims on the firm's assets and (b) who has the power to control the use of the assets. It is argued that for efficiency reasons one party should both own the assets and control the use of the assets. Clearly, having control over asset use without entitlement to residual earnings does not encourage the use of control to maximise earnings. This simple observation suggests that purely worker-owned and purely capitalist firms should perform better than (a) 'participatory' firms where workers are not necessarily entitled to a share of residual earnings but have a degree of control, and, (b) 'profit sharing' capitalist firms where workers are entitled to bonuses proportional to profits but have no decision-making power. The former type includes large German companies where co-determination is imposed by law, employees occupy half the seats on the 'supervisory boards', and have a say in hiring and firing senior management. The latter type is more common among American companies.

Figure 18.1 gives us a rough and ready indication of the various types of participation available by combining varying levels of labour participation in both management and ownership. The horizontal axis may represent participation by labour in the (non-contracted) residual control of assets, while the vertical axis may depict the participation by labour (i.e., those who work in the firm) in residual (non-contracted) remuneration, though the latter participation can arise without ownership.

The diagram also indicates some of the possible institutional arrangements located on either axis which can all be found in one place or another. Although not all possibilities are neatly captured in such a simple diagram, it does enable us to locate the traditional capitalist firm somewhere near the origin (i.e., external capital owners with *de jure* managerial control and remuneration) and what we might term producer cooperatives at the top right hand corner (i.e.,

Figure 18.1
Labour Participation

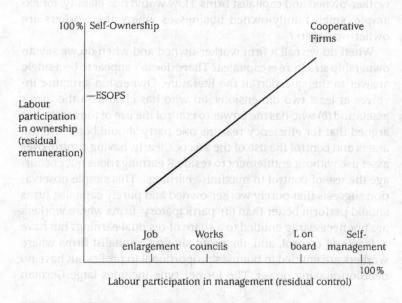

with self ownership and management). Twentieth-century historical experience in Organisation of Economic Cooperation and Development (OECD) countries (with perhaps the partial exception of the Anglo-Saxon countries) seems to indicate, first, a drift (often in stepwise movements) along the horizontal axis (increasing managerial control being vested with labour) and, second, a drift up the vertical axis (increasing ownership to labour). One can, thus, detect a net move up the diagonal away from the 'pure' capitalist firm. We should hasten to add that this story, as presented, is palpably under-nuanced, but probably contains a broad truth. It has, however, as we noted above, been significantly propelled by a framework of regulative injunction and tax inducements. The counter-factual question may accordingly be posed as to whether or not we would have witnessed something similar even in the absence of this framework. Has the state sometimes anticipated what competitive forces would have procured anyway? Or, indeed, has it perhaps stepped in where competitive forces would have failed? There are scholars and practitioners who lament any moves from the bottom left hand corner of the diagram, feeling that they are associated with efficiency losses. So let us now turn in this direction and discuss some of the factors relevant to the success or failure of participatory firms.

COMPLEXITY OF MANAGEMENT

An argument in favour of capitalist firms is that in such firms control is centralised. In democratically organised worker-owned firms with participation in decision making and diffusion of power there is a problem of dilution of responsibility. Even when there is centralisation of control, workers can exert pressure on managers only through the democratic process, which is subject to the free-rider problem. On the other hand, workers are likely to have an enormous informational advantage over shareholders in capitalist firms when it comes to knowing when pressure on management is warranted.

Another relevant issue is the quality of managers. If workers elect the management, what are the chances they will end up with talented, experienced managers with valuable business connections? Are worker-managers as competent as managers hired by capitalist firms? When management tasks are routine and firm operations relatively uncomplicated managerial talent may matter less.

The Free-Rider Problem

Holmstrom (1982) analyses the problem of team production where individual effort cannot be observed and joint output is shared among agents. He shows that under these assumptions there is no sharing rule, such that in a non-cooperative game, with team members choosing effort levels, the Nash equilibrium is Pareto optimal. In other words, inefficiency results from the free-rider problem. However, if we ease the constraint which states that joint output has to be distributed among all members, it is possible to resolve the inefficiency. For example, group penalty schemes in which workers only get paid if the team achieves the Pareto optimal output eliminate the inefficiency. But how could such a rule be implemented in a worker-owned firm? Suppose the target (efficient) joint output is not reached, what happens to the output which is reached? In a capitalist firm the owners would appropriate this output. In a worker-owned firm, workers would anticipate that the output will be shared, which brings us back to the original free-rider problem. The conclusions from Holmstrom's analysis are incontrovertible in the setting he outlines. However, if we relax the rather severe assumption of total unobservability of effort, it is possible, at least in a dynamic setting, to overcome the free-rider problem and generate Pareto optimal outcomes. In this context, Kandel and Lazear (1992) suggest the adoption of appropriate human resource policies, encouraging team spirit and solidarity.

Monitoring

Monitoring is one way of attenuating the free-rider problem. Monitoring technology is an important factor in the choice of organisational form. Is it easier for workers or for a supervisor (who may get the residual earnings) to monitor? Mirrlees (1976) states that it is not obvious that a symmetric solution in which workers engage in horizontal monitoring, possibly whilst performing productive tasks, is inferior to an asymmetric solution (cf. Alchian and Demsetz 1972) in which one person is assigned the monitoring task. One can indeed envisage scenarios where workers are able to monitor and motivate each other more effectively than management could. This possibility seems to be particularly acute in the Alchian and Demsetz setting of team production where individual productivity is very hard to measure since several workers are involved in production and their output is not merely the sum of the separable outputs of each worker. In principle, an outsider can observe team output but probably can only speculate about each individual team member's abilities and contributions. Workers have an informational advantage in disentangling marginal products.

If workers cannot monitor each other they could (democratically) appoint a monitor, but the problem arises as to how the monitor will be incentivised and/or monitored himself. In capitalist firms this issue is (partially) resolved by giving the monitor a share of the residual earnings. There is no reason why a similar arrangement could not work in employee-owned firms, although there is of course the problem of how much authority the monitor in a worker-owned firm should have. If he can hire and fire workers, to what extent is the firm still democratically organised?

Worker-owned firms (partnerships) with elected Chief Executive Officers (CEOs) are prevalent in professional service industries (e.g., accountancy, investment banking, advertising, law, medicine, headhunting, consultancy). Monitoring and evaluation of professional employees by non-professionals is difficult in these fields since the employees' tasks require a significant amount of autonomy and the quality of the output is not always easy to assess. Mutual monitoring may be relatively easy although whether sufficient levels of monitoring can be expected, given that typically shared claims in profit are diluted, is debatable. But then these problems are not foreign to capitalist firms.

Size

Self-monitoring by workers is easier when the firm is small. Partnerships are generally small, certainly in comparison to car manufacturing firms, for example. Interestingly, over the past two decades, some partnerships which have grown very large (thousands of partners located all over the world) have changed their organisational and management structure.

It is a well-known result in game theory that the severity of the free-rider problem per se as well as its potential remedy in an infinite horizon setting depends on the size of the group. The likelihood of generating cooperation in a dynamic model through horizontal monitoring and an appropriate organisational culture also depends on group size. It is perhaps not surprising, then, that average productivity increases due to profit sharing have been found to be larger for small companies (Kruse 1993).

Larger firms benefit comparatively more from hierarchy and authority. Collective decision-making is fraught with difficulties unless there are relatively few decision makers. Yet there are examples of very large and successful worker-owned firms, e.g., Publix Super Markets (over 120,000 employees) and United Airlines (close to 100,000 employees) which are majority-worker owned. The John Lewis Partnership with 57,000 members is Europe's biggest worker-owned business. It has no external shareholders and distributes a significant proportion of its profits to its employees in the form of bonuses.

Sometimes cooperatives are set up precisely because of the advantages they bring in terms of size. This is the case when a cooperative takes the form of a collective of self-employed individuals, e.g., farmer cooperatives. Such collectives have the advantages of size in purchasing and marketing, and larger clients prefer contracting with large collectives to writing lots of individual contracts (Russell 1985). We are forced to conclude that size per se is not necessarily a good predictor of the success or failure of worker-owned firms.

HOMOGENEITY

Self-monitoring is easier for a group of workers doing the same job or when jobs are regularly rotated. The larger the extent of specialisation and division of labour which limits worker interaction, the more difficult it is for workers to monitor each other. On this basis, one would predict that partnerships of individuals in the same profession, doing tasks requiring the same sort of expertise, would be more successful than multidisciplinary partnerships comprising, for example, accountants, lawyers and consultants.

Aside from the monitoring issue, heterogeneity amongst workers (e.g., with respect to age, skill level, tasks, degree of risk aversion) almost inevitably leads to conflicting interests. These conflicts form a central problem for governance in a worker-controlled firm. Economists often simplify their models by supposing that all workers are identical and, therefore, have identical interests. This is a sensible strategy for some purposes—in particular to make a start on analysing the reactions of the firm to external stimuli. It is not a sensible strategy for examining governance problems: its effect, indeed, is to assume the greater part of the problem away. If workers have identical interests (and identical perceptions), the voting structure in the company does not matter—whatever the voting structure, the vote will go the same way.

In an actual worker-controlled company, however, interests will typically diverge—the voting structure will matter. The first question we ask, therefore, is what worker control means in these terms—how do the (many) workers whom we assume to have many different characteristics arrive at their choices? What are the procedures for collective decision-making? The essence of the problem is easily seen by supposing that there are two groups of workers, As and Bs, whose interests conflict. Any A, however, has interests identical with those of any other A, and vice versa.

Consider a proposal, which, put into effect, has a present value V_a for each A and V_b for each B and a present cost of C_a for each A and C_b for each B. The proportion of As is a. It can be assumed that for the proposal under discussion, present value exceeds present cost, i.e., that

$$a(V_a - C_a) + (1 - a) + (V_b - C_b) > 0$$

so that adoption of the proposal would potentially increase the welfare of all members of the firm. The question, though, is whether the voting structure of the firm will allow it to be adopted.

That there is room for doubt about this is clear from the simplest model of voting structure: one worker-one vote. Suppose, for example, that $V_a > C_a$ but $V_b < C_b$. As will vote for the proposal, Bs will vote against. Whether it is adopted or not will depend, in this simplest case, on whether As or Bs are in the majority. But the proposal is good for the 'firm', regardless of who is in the majority. Settling conflicts by authority (as in a capitalist firm) rather than democratically is likely to be less costly.

Of course, this is a simple model. Within the firm, side payments can be made (as would be possible in the case above), or issues tied together, so that proposals put to the vote have a positive 'net present value' (NPV) for all voters. But then, who sets the agenda?

We conclude that the more heterogeneous the workforce, the more likely it is that the firm will be organised in capitalist fashion. It is interesting to observe that the industries in which worker ownership has been successful consist of firms with narrowly-defined activities assuring homogeneity of tasks among workers. Plywood cooperatives are a much-quoted example of worker-controlled firms which implement equal pay and where workers hire the management. Other examples are the taxi industry and the refuse collection industry in the San Francisco Bay Area (Russell 1985). In some cases the heterogeneity problem is solved by assigning ownership and control rights to one (homogeneous) class of workers, e.g., Egged, the Israeli bus company, is owned by its drivers and other workers are hired without receiving an ownership claim. In the plywood cooperatives only workers, not management, own equity.

Homogeneity of interest amongst owners of a firm is also important in terms of decision making or delegating control. In a capitalist firm, investors have identical interests, i.e., maximisation of the firm's NPV. Hence, as the agent of the shareholders, the management of a capitalist firm is supposed to maximise the net present value of the firm. In addition, the mechanism by which owners are rewarded is very clear-cut; returns are divided transparently in proportion to the amount of capital invested. How should residual earnings in a worker-controlled firm be divided? And what is the management of a worker-owned firm supposed to do? Maximise residual income per worker? Are higher wages more important than employment security? What about investment? How much of the profit should be retained and re-invested? Worker-owned firms are often said to under-invest because of the horizon problem created by making ownership contingent on employment. Projects with short payback periods are prioritised over projects with higher NPV.

EFFICIENT RISK BEARING

In capitalist firms owners can diversify and hold small quantities of shares in a number of firms. This is not possible in the worker-owned firm. In addition to having a large fraction of their wealth tied up in one company, employees in such firms incur a very substantial risk by holding a job in the same firm (although employment is likely to be more secure than in a capitalist firm). One reason to expect higher wages in worker-owned firms is that a wage premium is paid to compensate for higher risk. In general, labour costs are indeed higher in firms with profit-sharing arrangements (Kim 1998).

The fact that workers tend to sell shares to outsiders as soon as possible is disappointing to proponents of worker ownership. Risk avoidance, however, provides one reason to do so. If workers sell their shares to outsiders and start hiring non-member labour, the worker-owned firm is transformed into a capitalist firm (Ben-Ner 1984; Vanek 1977).

Principal-agent theory suggests that profit sharing (and by extension the likelihood of worker ownership) depends on the degree of control the agent has. Hence, the extent to which firm profitability is (perceived to be) under workers' control is important here. In sales, for example, if repeat business is important and the salesperson's effort determines the amount of repeat business, an optimal profit sharing arrangement will (depending on the degree of risk aversion) tend towards a franchise arrangement. Similarly, when workers' effort is a determining factor in the success of the company, and if economic conditions are stable, worker-owned firms are more likely to thrive.

MOTIVATION

Some versions of efficiency wage theory predict that anticipation on the part of workers of better treatment and a more congenial organisational culture will enable worker-owned firms to attract better workers. It seems plausible that long-term tenure is more common in worker-owned firms. This in itself may have positive effects on organisational culture. Notions of fairness may increase workers' commitment to an organisation. Akerlof (1982) discusses this type of reciprocity norm in his paper on labour as gift exchange. Also, the psychological cost of being monitored by a co-worker is likely to be lower than that of being monitored by a supervisor. In addition, employee involvement increases workers' identification with the firm, which is likely to translate to increased productivity (Korsgaard et al. 1995).

We do not intend to review in any detail the vast literature that attempts to assess the impact of labour participation (in both management and ownership) on motivation and, therefore, productivity. This has been carried out by many others before, most recently by Doucouliagos (1995), though it is, unfortunately, true to say that much of the research leaves an awful lot to be desired and, as a consequence, it is only with caution that any general conclusions can be drawn. In particular, the majority of studies are cross-sectional and suffer from a selection bias. Not surprisingly, researchers have reported all manner of results, positive, negative and negligible, about the impact of participation upon various measures of performance.

Research into the functioning of producer cooperatives (the top right-hand corner of Figure 18.1) is also indecisive. Outstanding examples exist, like some of the Israeli kibbutzim and the Mondragon group of cooperatives in Northern Spain, but most observers seem to feel that special nationalistic sentiments underpin their relative success. The early experience of the former Yugoslav 'self-managerial socialist market system'—despite its very special features—is also sometimes paraded as a positive exemplar but, once again, sharp differences of opinion coexist amongst those who have studied this historical period.

In the face of these various results, it is perhaps best to rely upon systematic meta-analysis and follow Doucouliagos who finds a small interactive effect of the participation in both management and ownership upon 'firm productivity'. Others have over the years found similar results (Conte and Svejnar 1990; Rosen and Quarrey 1987, Winther and Marens 1997). Cable and Fitzroy (1990) were probably the first to report this sort of finding. Some studies find larger and independent effects, both positive and negative. Furthermore, the existing research does not allow us to easily access the possible effects of 'participation' across the full range of variation implied by the two axes in Figure 18.1. From a theoretical standpoint an interactive effect of both types of participation upon performance would make considerable sense. Increased opportunity for participation in decision making is expected to have a larger effect if workers also own a larger fraction of the firm; increased worker ownership is expected to be more productive if workers have more control.

Labour versus Capital Intensity

If labour's share in total costs is relatively small, then even if productivity increases with worker ownership, the effect of this increase on firm profit will be small. If, on the other hand, having a committed work force is crucial (maybe because human capital is more important than physical capital), the advantages of worker participation and ownership are more pronounced. Workers who have no

control or ownership are less likely to make firm-specific investments in human capital (e.g., acquiring organisational knowledge)
which would lock them in. Long-term ownership (not shares which
can be sold immediately) and participation in firm decision-making
may be needed to encourage such investments.

Worker-owned firms are rare in industries with high capital requirements due to 'the wealth obstacle'. The owners of the firm, as
the contracting party, have to be able to compensate hired inputs in
adverse conditions. While this may be possible for suppliers of capital such as machines, equipment and buildings, as these assets can
be sold, this is not true of labour. In addition, principal-agent theory
tells us that owning capital assets is superior to renting because of
the inefficiency in monitoring the use of depreciable assets. All of
this suggests that capital-intensive firms (e.g., in manufacturing)
are more likely to be investor-owned, whereas worker-owned firms
are more likely to exist in labour-intensive industries.

It is often claimed that large transaction costs are incurred when
capital suppliers are not the owners of the firm, i.e., they are lenders.
One wonders whether the asymmetric information problem alluded
to here is really all that serious, whether the worker-controlled firm
is debt financed or financed by non-voting outside equity. What is
the nature of the putative transaction costs and are they really that
high? It is possible to have outside shareholders in a worker-owned
firm as long as these shareholders can be reasonably sure that
workers will not exploit them and eat up the firm's assets. But would
workers abscond with the capital or make risky decisions? This does
not seem terribly likely if they have a long-term interest in the survival of the firm and in securing their employment.

Worker-owned firms may have liquidity problems, but why can't
they borrow? Why do they face insuperable costs of raising capital?
Of course, all the ways of raising capital available to a worker-owned
firm are also available to a capitalist firm, but a worker-owned firm
cannot issue voting equity. If control is of value to shareholders,
then a worker-owned firm will have to pay for the absence of control rights either through having a lower valuation of its equity or by
paying higher dividends. It is hard to believe, however, that non-
voting equity in a worker-owned firm is that much inferior to equity
in a capitalist firm. Non-voting shareholders would have no control
over the decisions of the firm and no right to hire or fire management, but is this situation all that different from that of shareholders
in a large dispersed capitalist firm?

TOP MANAGEMENT

In this section we explore the idea that the persistence of the capitalist mode of organisation arises from the exercise of power by the top management. Capitalist firms with dispersed shareholdings are essentially controlled and run by top management. Top executives have enormous discretionary powers and the extent to which they pursue their reputed objective of maximising value to shareholders is debatable. Current mechanisms of corporate governance (e.g., the common practice of the CEO appointing external non-executive directors to the board, CEO's sitting on each other's remuneration committees, etc.) allow the management to appropriate residual earnings as long as shareholders receive some threshold return. Executive compensation seems to be determined not so much by guidelines offered by the principal-agent theory as by greed bounded only by the possibility of shareholder revolt or public outrage (which might lead to regulation). A recent paper puts forward this view of managerial power to skim rents (Bebchuk et al. 2002) and discusses the various ways in which executive compensation practices deviate from optimal incentive pay. Compensation packages are usually designed to shield executives from downside risk. Stock options are a case in point.

In our simple model we assume that there are three types of stakeholders in the evolutionary process—capital, labour and (top) management. We hope the justification for including top management as an independent group will become evident as we proceed, but a few initial remarks might be appropriate. In a pure capitalist system (bottom left-hand corner in Figure 18.1), where risk-bearing capital hires (contracts with) labour (at a market clearing wage rate) and retains any post-contractual residual rights to both control and remuneration, (top) management is technically but one of the categories of contracted labour. Likewise, in a pure 'cooperative system' (top right hand corner in Figure 18.1) the roles of labour and capital are reversed and management is now a category of labour which hires capital. In either case the role of (top) management, as a particular interest group, does not (in theory) enter the picture. However, there is, in our view, ample evidence (see below) which should lead us to the conclusion that 'top' management should be treated as a group with its own distinct objectives or interests in any evolutionary dynamics.

It is clear, from a conventional theoretical standpoint, that if firms are envisaged as more or less successfully seeking to locate and then to sustain their not easily replicable advantages, then we are speaking of, at least temporarily, sustained monopoly power. No less a luminary than Larry Summers recently opined that 'the central driving force of the new economy is the force of monopoly power'. It is generally difficult to explain why competitive firms do not undermine, through entry, exit and emulation, any existing competitive advantages. But if they do not, then the issue is: would one expect 'participatory arrangements' to be selected in a world of imperfect competition?

Although monopolies have been around for a long time, the 'new economy' may be driving us in the direction of even more monopolies (i.e., sustainability). The drift up the vertical axis of Figure 18.1 does seem to coincide with the founding of the new economy. Developments in information technology often imply large fixed costs (development costs) but low variable costs. Match this with the possibility of network consumption effects which cause barriers to entry to increase further and the likelihood of contestation is substantially diminished. Certainly, there appears to be a quickened interest in regulating monopoly power. In the last decade, for example, the number of mergers reported to the anti-trust authorities has doubled, and in the EU it has increased four times.

In contrast to the perfectly competitive world, rents in the world of sustained competitive advantage are captured for sufficiently long periods for issues about their distribution to become of motivational consequence within the firm. An evolving economy is best envisaged in terms of a perpetual struggle to grasp the significantly lasting rents occurring from a flow of both exogenously and endogenously generated opportunities. The competitive process is one of protecting rents that are not quickly competed away within the confines of a motivationally significant time horizon. Thus, the division of significantly sustainable rents between capital, labour and (as we shall argue) top management becomes of central significance in the portrayal of evolutionary dynamics. We can, without too much imprecision, construe the distribution of rents as equivalent to the distribution of residual remuneration in Figure 18.1.

Residual claims in a capitalist dispersed firm are tradable. This obviously lowers the incentive to monitor as 'exit' is much easier than 'voice'. In theory, the advantage of a public company is that monitoring by shareholders is not strictly necessary. There are substitutes for monitoring in the form of the market for corporate control. Managers are claimed to be in a contestable market due to the potential threats of hostile takeover bids, and this is believed to limit the potential for 'embezzlement'. However, if management is sufficiently entrenched, takeovers can be blocked.

In practice, shareholders (especially if they are a dispersed group) or their representatives, the board of directors, do not seem to make substantial investments in monitoring the management and largely relinquish control to top executives. They thereby forego the opportunity to exercise the one clear right they have, namely removing bad management. This is not to say that shareholders behave irrationally. They face a trade-off between large shareholding, which would give them an incentive to monitor, and small shareholding which allows for risk diversification and resulting lower capital costs. From this perspective, agency costs in the form of managerial opportunism may not be all that high, especially when gathering and sharing information is difficult for shareholders. One wonders, though, whether the fact that top executives can write their own paychecks is not a sign of ineffective corporate governance in general. If the top management can determine their own compensation, can they also not pursue strategies that are not value-maximising for shareholders?

Interestingly, there does not appear to be a significant relationship between ownership concentration and profits (see, e.g., Demsetz and Lehn 1985). Indeed, it is difficult to argue that concentrated ownership in continental European fashion outperforms America's and Britain's dispersed ownership model. Diffusion of ownership may not be all that harmful to shareholders. It has to be said, though, that the empirical literature on ownership concentration focuses either on whether there is one large shareholder or on the percentage of shares owned by, say, the top 10 shareholders. These variables may not capture enough information, as the distribution of shareholdings may be important.

In any case, we feel justified in hypothesising that in the capitalist system (bottom left hand corner of Figure 18.1), characterised by the quest for sustained competitive advantage, where equity owners are dispersed and ill-organised (perhaps because of free-rider problems), the top management is able to capture a significantly large proportion of any sustained rents.

Labour, with no rights to residual remuneration, has little power to wrest the rents away from management. How does all of this shape any evolutionary selective dynamics? We might note that surveys have time and again found evidence that (top) management is resolutely opposed to labour participation at the higher levels of management decision-making ('the right to manage' is the ideological epithet which is characteristically invoked), though they seem more relaxed about participation in ownership and even participation at lower levels (e.g., consultation). The latter, of course, impinges upon the 'right to manage' of the lower management much more than on that of the top management. While in the last decade or so the top management has by and large welcomed labour (including their own) participation in equity, it has been vociferous in supporting the roll-back of legally imposed high level participation in management (witness the strong objection to clauses on worker directors in the European Fifth Directive).

Our argument rests heavily upon the assumption that a rent-seeking and sustaining economy benefits top management if they can secure *de facto* rights to residual control. What evidence is there stating that managers do manage to extract rents in capitalist economies? As far as we know there is no definitive study which unequivocally establishes their success in this respect, let alone whether or not their remuneration rewards their appropriate contribution to the creation of any rents. Certainly gross statistics are suggestive. For instance, Table 18.1 depicts the ratio of CEO remuneration to manufacturing employee remuneration. The ratios are large and display significant variability across countries. It would be difficult to explain this variability other than in terms of the different institutional frameworks that impinge upon rent extraction. Certainly, any attempt to invoke varying managerial productivity is likely to flounder. In particular, it is difficult to believe that the difference between, say, Switzerland and the US, is attributable to differing productivity. There is, however, some indication of a pattern; the US—a country with little or no 'participation'—is markedly exceptional but the rest of the figures suggest that the European countries (where 'participation' is to some degree developed) tend to have a lower ratio than the others. One cannot make too much of this, but maybe rent extraction by management is more difficult in the presence of 'participation'.

We are sometimes told that we are living in the age of globalism where competitive market forces cut across national boundaries, equalising returns everywhere. Table 18.1 lends little credence to such arguments, at least at the moment. If we concentrate upon the US, the most extreme country represented in Table 18.1, then the chosen ratio has changed from 42 in 1980 to 84 in 1990 and now stands at 475.

Table 18.1
CEO Total Remuneration as a Multiple of Manufacturing
Employee Total Remuneration (1999)

Argentina	44
Belgium	18
Brazil	49
Canada	20
France	15
Germany	13
Italy	27
Japan	11
Mexico	46
Netherlands	17
Spain	17
Sweden	13
USA	475
Switzerland	11
UK	24
Venezuela	50

Source: *www.aflcio.org/paywatch/ceopay.htm.*

Some research is strongly suggestive in respect of rent-extraction by top management. Crystal (1991) suggests that *de facto* CEOs set their own pay with a weak constraint set by share prices (he calls it 'skimming'). Thus, for him the world of optimal contracting—even in near competitive conditions let alone in non-competitive ones—is remote. Bertrand and Mullainathan (2000) largely agree. They say: 'In poorly governed firms the skimming view (pay for luck and little charge for options) fits better whereas in well-governed firms, the contrasting view fits better (filtering out luck and charging for options)' (p. 2). Core et al. (1999) also find that less effective boards lead to increases in CEO compensation. Hallock (1997) in a similar vein finds that firms with interlocking boards of directors give higher salaries to their CEOs.

So let us henceforth assume that attempts to control the distribution of rents significantly shape the selection process in a capitalist economy. Furthermore, as argued above, this is particularly so in the 'new economy'. A simple model may help to understand the impact of 'participation' upon this distribution. How should we model the effect of labour participation on the generation of rent (R)? Participation here comprises 'control' (C) and share of residual rent (S). C having an impact on S complicates matters. We assume that up to a point, R is increasing at a decreasing rate in S because of the motivational effect of S on labour. However, since a large S is indicative of labour's high level of C, it is conceivable that R will eventually decrease in S. Hence we assume the relationship between R and S pictured in Figure 18.2. Self-interested management wants to maximise $(1 - S)R$. It is easy to see that this implies that if management has a significant amount of control and can determine S it will choose a sub-optimal level of S. Let R be maximised at S_0 and $(1 - S)R$ at S_M. We need to prove that $S_0 > S_M$. We know that

$$\frac{\partial R(S_0)}{\partial S} = 0 \text{ and}$$

$$(1 - S_M) \frac{\partial R(S_M)}{\partial S} - R(S_M) = 0 \text{ or } \frac{\partial R(S_M)}{\partial S} = \frac{R(S_M)}{1 - S_M} > 0.$$

Figure 18.2
Labour Participation and Rent Distribution

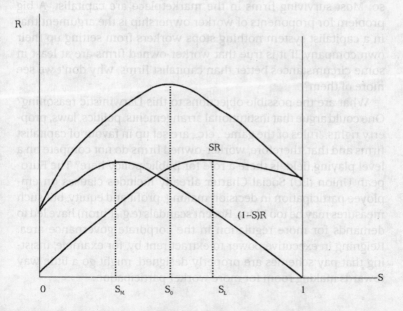

Since R is concave we conclude that $S_0 > S_M$. We can show similarly that labour's remuneration SR is maximised at $S_L > S_0$. This illustrates the conflict between labour and management with respect to the degree of labour participation. It seems unlikely that optimal rents can ever be achieved. Bargaining theory would suggest that a contract could be negotiated in order to attain maximum rent, but whether this would be enforceable must be open to question. If, in addition, we assume that management has a taste for control and prefers a low S, the problem is clearly exacerbated. Furthermore, if 'good' managers exit firms where labour has managed to move nearer to (or beyond) the joint optimum, then participatory firms may also experience a managerial deficit. It does seem that under reasonable assumptions rent seeking agents will undermine any supposition that evolutionary forces will deliver an optimal level of participation.

CONCLUSIONS

According to a popular economic Darwinistic argument, optimal ownership structures will naturally emerge. Workers can choose to work for conventional capitalist firms and they overwhelmingly do so. Most surviving firms in the marketplace are capitalist. A big problem for proponents of worker ownership is the argument that in a capitalist system nothing stops workers from setting up their own company. If it is true that worker-owned firms are at least in some circumstances better than capitalist firms, why don't we see more of them?

What are the possible objections to this Darwinistic reasoning? One could argue that institutional arrangements, politics, laws, property rights, 'rules of the game', etc., are set up in favour of capitalist firms and that, therefore, worker-owned firms do not compete on a level playing field. Is there a role for public policy here? The European Union (EU) Social Charter already includes clauses on employee participation in decision making, profit and equity, but such measures may be too blunt. Recent scandals (e.g., Enron) have led to demands for more regulation in the corporate governance area. Reigning in executive power to extract rent by, for example, insisting that pay schemes are properly designed, might go a little way towards making room for more worker participation.

Our discussion here has a weakness in that it doesn't explain why we start out with capitalist firms. Our analysis does show, however, that inertia and the top management's incentives imply that changes towards more worker participation are unlikely unless imposed. It is difficult to draw the conclusion that history has conducted an experiment and found labour participation wanting.

REFERENCES

Akerlof, G. 1982. 'Labor Contracts as Partial Gift Exchange', *Quarterly Journal of Economics*, 97: 543–69.

Alchian, A.A. and Demsetz, H. 1972. 'Production, Information Costs, and Economic Organization', *American Economic Review*, 62: 777–95.

Bebchuk, L. Fried, J. and Walker, D. 2002. 'Managerial Power and Rent Extraction in the Design of Executive Compensation', *University of Chicago Law Review*, 69: 751–846.

Ben-Ner, A. 1984. 'On the Stability of the Cooperative Type of Organisation', *Journal of Comparative Economics*, 8: 247–60.

Bertrand, M. and S. Mullainathan, S. 2000. 'Do CEOs Set their Pay? The Ones Without Principals Do'. Working Paper 431. Industrial Relations, Princeton University.

Blasi, J., Conte, M. and Kruse, D. 1996. 'Employee Stock Ownership and Corporate Performance among Public Organisations', *Industrial and Labour Relations Review*, 50: 60–79.

Cable, J.R. and Fitzroy, F.R. 1990. 'Productive Efficiency, Incentives and Employee Participation: Some Preliminary Results from West Germany', *Kyklos*, 33: 100–123.

Conte, M.A. and Svejnar, J. 1990. 'The Performance Affects of Employee Ownership Plans', in A.S. Blinder (ed.), *Paging for Productivity: A Look at the Evidence*. Washington D.C.: Brookings Institute.

Core, J.E., Holthausen, H.W. and Larcker, D.F. 1999. 'Corporate Governance, Chief Executive Officer Compensation and Firm Performance', *Journal of Financial Economics*, 51: 371–406.

Crystal, G. 1991. *In Search of Excess: The Overcompensation of American Executives*. New York: Norton.

Demsetz, H. and Lehn, K. 1985. 'The Structure of Corporate Ownership: Causes and Consequences', *Journal of Political Economy*, 93: 1155–77.

Doucouliagos, C. 1995. 'Worker Participation and Productivity in Labour-managed and Participatory Capitalist Firms: A Meta-analysis', *Industrial and Labour Relations Review*, 49: 58–77.

Hallock, K.F. 1997. 'Reciprocally Interlocking Boards of Directors and Executive Compensation', *Journal of Financial and Quantitative Analysis*, 32: 331–44.

Hansmann, H. 1988. 'Ownership of the Firm', *Journal of Law, Economics and Organization*, 4: 267–304.

Hart, O. 1995. *Firms, Contracts and Financial Structure*. Oxford: Oxford University Press.

Holmstrom, B. 1982. 'Moral Hazard in Teams', *Bell Journal of Economics*, 13: 324–40.

Kandel, E and Lazear, E. 1992. 'Peer Pressure and Partnerships', *Journal of Political Economy*, 100: 801–17.

Kim, S. 1998. 'Does Profit Sharing Increase Firms' Profits?', *Journal of Labor Research*, 19: 351–70.

Korsgaard, M.A., Schweiger, M. and Sapienza, H.J. 1995. 'Building Commitment, Attachment and Trust in Strategic Decision-making Teams: The Role of Procedural Justice', *Academy of Management Journal*, 38: 60–84.

Kruse, D.L. 1993. *Profit Sharing: Does It Make a Difference?* Kalamazoo, Michigan: W.E. Upjohn Institute for Employment Research.

Mirrlees, J.A. 1976. 'The Optimal Structure of Incentives and Authority Within an Organization', *The Bell Journal of Economics*, 7: 105–31.

Putterman, L. 1984. 'On Some Recent Explanations of Why Capital Hires Labor', *Economic Inquiry*, 22: 171–87.

Rosen, C. and Quarrey, M. 1987. 'How Well is Employee Ownership Working?', *Harvard Business Review*, 65: 126–32.

Russell, R. 1985. 'Employee Ownership and Internal Governance', *Journal of Economic Behavior and Organization*, 6: 217–41.

Vanek, J. 1977. *The Labour Managed Economy: Essays*. Ithaca: Cornell University Press.

Winther, G and Marens, R. 1997. 'Participating Democracy May Go a Long Way: Comparative Growth and Performance of Employee Ownership Firms in New York and Washington State', *Economic and Industrial Democracy*, 18: 393–422.

CHAPTER 19

ISSUES IN CORPORATE GOVERNANCE IN INDIA[1]

ASISH K. BHATTACHARYYA

INTRODUCTION

The fundamental question of corporate governance is how to assure financiers that they get a return on their financial investment (Shleifer and Vishny 1996). Berle and Means observed that by 1932 'entrepreneurial capitalism' had given way to a system of 'financial capitalism' where owners and professional managers who ran the corporations were not the same. According to them, separation of ownership and management also leads to a separation of ownership and control (Berle and Means 1932). This gives rise to the agency problem because the 'utility' of professional managers seldom converge with the 'utility' of owners. The agency problem perspective or the principal-agent paradigm fits into the view that modern corporations are run by professional managers who are unaccountable to dispersed shareholders. The agency problem arises, first, because financiers cannot write complete contracts to cover all events that might arise during the operation of the firm. Second, though as a general rule residual right of control on physical and intangible assets rests with owners, in case of a firm owners (financiers) cannot enforce their residual right. The general rule does not work because shareholders are not qualified or informed enough to decide what to do in a situation not covered in the contract *ex ante* (Hart 1991). Enforcement of residual right of control becomes more difficult because of the 'free rider' problem and because small shareholders usually do not take active interest in improving the performance of the firm. As a result, managers end up with significant residual right of control, which they use to pursue projects that benefit them, rather than financiers (Boumol 1959; Jensen 1986; Marris 1964; Williamson 1964). Under the principal-agent paradigm, the two most important issues are 'adverse selection' and 'moral hazard'. Corporate governance mechanisms should ensure selection of right managers, alignment of managers' interests with those of financiers, and appropriate monitoring and control of managers. Provision of 'appropriate incentives aims to align managers' interests with those of financiers, particularly shareholders. Monitoring and control is made with the board of directors by a large shareholder, a large creditor or the market for corporate control (Vives 2000).

In the past, the separation of ownership and control surfaced in India only when in the later part of the 19th century 'managing agency system'[2] emerged as the most appropriate system for managing joint stock companies (Bhattacharyya 1973; Ghosh 1987; Roy 2000). At the later stage of the managing agency system, managing agency firms assumed control of the companies they managed. The directors of the companies were gradually deprived of all effective powers and the interests of shareholders received little consideration. The seriousness of the problem can be gauged by the fact that the managing agency system of corporate governance was completely abolished in 1970. Subsequently, until liberalisation, corporate governance was not an issue in Indian corporate management.

In India, traditionally, business families that are usually promoters of those companies also manage them. In the colonial period capital for industry was severely and perpetually scarce (Roy 2000). Mostly, fixed capital in large-scale industry came from own sources of funds or from borrowings from within a small set of people known to each other. Consequently, large-scale industry came almost entirely from communities that had specialised in trading and banking activities. Thus, industrialisation in India was led by 'business families' based on community lines. The dominance of old business families continued even after independence. After independence in 1947, India followed the policy of 'partnership capitalism' with centralised planning and state dominance. Over the period, government nationalised major commercial banks, established development financial institutions (DFI), specialised financial institutions, and nationalised insurance companies. The financial system came predominantly under state control. The government followed the policy of 'command and control'. This led to the accessibility of centralised resources to established business families and groups, powerful and capable of diverting the same for expansion of their business empires. New business families with the necessary financial and political clout, capable of taking advantage of the existing system and exploit it, emerged on the business scene. 'The centralising powers of the public sector have been used in recent years to strengthen organised private industry, and in some cases to help the process of extreme centralisation of private economic power' (Bagchi 1998: 327).

Though major investment in Indian joint-stock companies came from state-owned financial institutions, the management and control remained with promoter business families. Financial institutions rarely interfered in the management of those companies. Bagchi writes:

> Over the years, in the course of the business activities of public term-lending institutions and other investing agencies such as the Life Insurance Corporation, the General Insurance Corporation and the Unit Trust of India, the public sector has become the chief shareholder and creditor of many, if not most, term-lending institutions. In some cases, they have become even the majority shareholders. Yet the public sector financial agencies have refused to exercise any real control over these enterprises and seem to have intervened only to carry out the partisan objectives of powerful politicians in the Central Government. In a recent notorious case, the Reliance Industries which had grown explosively through a combination of dynamic entrepreneurship and clever manipulation of the regulatory functions of the Government was to acquire the control of a major engineering and construction group, viz., Larsen and Turbo, through the active co-operation of public sector banks and term-lending institutions (1998: 327).

Small investors did not show much interest in the capital market. Limited liability was formally recognised in 1860 and the Bombay Stock Exchange (BSE)[3] was formed in 1875. However, the BSE could not grow because the state provided the long-term capital and promoters did not want to offer any significant shareholding to the general public in the fear of losing control. For the Indian capital market, 1977 was the watershed year. Bagchi writes:

The rise of Reliance is, however, significant in another respect. The group has been able to raise far more capital through shares and convertible debentures than practically all other firms or conglomerates in Indian history. But the achievement of the group is not unique in this respect. It is an aspect of the deliberate fostering of an equity capital market through all kinds of special favours granted to investors. But there is yet very little control over insider trading and other practices which have been subjects of a considerable amount of regulatory activity in capital markets of advanced capitalist countries (Bagchi 1998: 328).

In the pre-liberalisation period, promoters had no real accountability for funds entrusted to them. Financial institutions had significant investments in equity and loan of joint-stock companies, but they did not behave like owners. They did not participate, passively or actively, in the control and governance of those companies. Promoters behaved like owners, and they managed and controlled the companies. Therefore, there was virtually no separation between ownership and control as suggested by Berle and Means (1932). The corporate governance problem, if any, was similar to that suggested by La Porta et al. (1999). Promoters had 'control rights' much in excess of 'cash flow rights' and they expropriated the interest of dispersed shareholders. 'There's little doubt that for decades, there have been plenty of business families that have treated their empires like personal property, other shareholders be damned' (*Business Today* 2002: 147). In fact, during the 'license raj',[4] business groups picked up all licences that came in their way and went into unwarranted diversification. In the absence of any requirement to present a 'consolidated financial statement', groups created a complex network among group companies (pyramid structure) to control a large number of companies without any significant investment. Investors were deprived of information on group performance. However, in practice, there was no information asymmetry between owner-managers and other large investors. Financial institutions could call for any information they required to control and govern companies. The oppressed group was minority shareholders. However, in the absence of any significant investment by that group, corporate governance did not receive due attention. The Companies Act 1956 was amended from time to time to protect the interests of 'minority shareholders', but the compliance was unsatisfactory. The issue of corporate governance has come to the central stage of corporate management since liberalisation in 1991.

INDIAN CORPORATE SECTOR—THE TREND

India adopted the policy of economic liberalisation in 1991. The policy initiatives include withdrawal of government from business through disinvestment; reduction of government investment in nationalised commercial banks to 33 per cent; reduction of government investment in financial institutions; encouragement to private (including foreign) initiatives in banking, insurance and other services, manufacturing and infrastructure sectors; reduction in the importance of central planning and dismantling of the 'control and command' system; and the establishment of appropriate regulatory authorities to enhance standards of regulatory norms and to ensure compliance. The new economic policy is a policy of 'participative capitalism' with the dominance of the private sector. The process of structural adjustments is yet to be completed.

The new business environment provides opportunities and threats to the Indian private sector. They have the opportunity to decide their own corporate strategy, but they have to operate in a competitive environment. The stability and growth will depend on the ability to compete in the product market and also in the capital market. The new policy has widened the composition of the Indian industry. New business opportunities have emerged in areas like information technology, telecom, media, entertainment and retailing. In the past decade, in the new environment, many old business houses could not retain their leadership position. Many of them were split into independent constituent units and many sold or closed down some businesses in their fold.

Many multinational companies (MNCs) have registered or strengthened their presence in the Indian economy. New joint ventures or 100 per cent subsidiaries have been established in the last decade. The MNCs, which have been present in India for long, are hiking their stakes in Indian ventures or buying them out completely. 'According to estimates there are about 95 companies with foreign promoter's holding in excess of 51% and many of these are actively considering the de-listing option, thereby converting their Indian ventures into fully owned subsidiaries' (*The Economic Times* 2002: 16).

INDUSTRIAL FINANCE—THE CURRENT TREND

The capital market achieved significant growth during the period 1989–90 to 2000–1. During this period, the annual turnover at the BSE increased from Rs 1,348 million to Rs 47,758 million. Similarly, the number of listed companies increased from 2,275 to 5,937. According to the World Development Indicators 2000 (World Bank), market capitalisation as a percentage of the gross domestic product (GDP) increased from 12.2 per cent in 1990 to 41.3 per cent in 1999. The Securities and Exchange Board of India (SEBI) was constituted on 12 April 1988. In 1996, a dematerialised form of settlement was introduced. Derivatives trading began in June 2000. However, this period also witnessed a few major scams. Growth of the capital market changed the shareholding pattern of listed companies.

The debt market in India is not developed (Patil 2002). Therefore, public limited companies in India mobilise only a small portion of their fund requirements through debt instruments. In the year 1995–96, 88 per cent of the total funds raised from the capital market was through equity and the balance 12 per cent was raised through debt instruments. In 2001, only 21 per cent of the total amount borrowed was through corporate bonds (*Economic Survey*, Government of India 2001–2: 108).

The NSE in one of its reports discussed the dependence of the corporate sector on the securities market. It said:

The securities market is now a far more important source of finance compared to the traditional financial intermediaries for the corporate sector. It is poised to dominate the future of corporate finance in India, thanks to reform in the securities market. The 1990s witnessed emergence of the securities market as a major source of finance for trade and industry. A growing number of companies are accessing the securities market rather than depending on loans from financial institutions (FIs)/banks. The corporate sector is increasingly depending on external sources for meeting its funding requirements.

There appears to be a growing preference for direct financing (equity and debt) to indirect financing (bank loan) within the external sources (NSE 2001).

This is corroborated by the *Economic Survey*:

Turning to the source of debt financing, two strong regularities may be noted. The largest one-tenth of firms have the least dependence (17 per cent) on institutions. At the same time, they have the highest dependence on corporate bonds (25 per cent). This suggests that for the largest firms, the securities market had become a major source of capital, and that they are able to dis-intermediate financial institutions by directly accessing the markets (*Economic Survey*, Government of India 2001–2: 109).

The NSE report (NSE 2001) analysed the shareholding pattern of public limited companies. The analysis of the shareholding pattern of 536 companies listed on the NSE shows that on an average promoters hold nearly 50 per cent of total shares. Though the non-promoter holding is more than 50 per cent, the Indian public held only 17.5 per cent and the public float (holding by foreign institutional investors, mutual funds, Indian public) is at best 27 per cent. There is not much difference in the shareholding pattern of companies in different sectors. Private corporate bodies hold 62 per cent of shares in companies in the media and entertainment sector. The promoter holding is not strikingly high in respect to companies in the information technology and telecom sector. An analysis of the top 54 companies listed in the BSE, based on market capitalisation, reveals that promoters' holding varies between 22 per cent and 85 per cent and public holding varies between 1 per cent and 40 per cent. Investment of financial institutions in the equity of the top 54 companies varied between 0.15 per cent and 30 per cent. It is less than 10 per cent in 38 out of 54 companies. The debt component in the capital structure has reduced over the years. The debt equity ratio at 2001 was 0.90 as against the ratio of 1.74 in 1992 (*Economic Survey*, Government of India 2001–2: 108).

In accordance with Reserve Bank of India (RBI) norms, banks' exposure to the capital market by way of investments in ordinary shares, convertible debentures and units of mutual funds (other than debt funds) should not exceed 5 per cent of the total outstanding advances as on 31 March of the previous year. Therefore, in India, commercial banks do not invest in equity of joint stock companies. Effective from 1 April 2000, the exposure ceiling in respect to an individual borrower was reduced from 25 per cent to 20 per cent of the banks' capital fund.

The trend in the shareholding pattern and capital structure shows that the dependence of companies on financial institutions is reducing. The trend is likely to continue, and in times to come, investment of financial institutions in Indian public limited companies will drop significantly. Perhaps those institutions will focus on loan portfolios, rather than investing in corporate equities with long-term perspectives.

LEGAL PROTECTION TO INVESTORS AND OTHER STAKEHOLDERS

The Companies Act 1956 provides voting rights to equity shareholders, the providers of risk capital. Each share carries one vote. Till recently, companies were not allowed to issue equity shares with differential rights. However, the Act was amended in 2000 enabling the central government to frame rules regarding the issue of equity shares with differential voting rights. A member can exercise his voting rights through 'proxy'. However, a proxy has no right to speak at the meeting. Shareholders appoint directors by using their voting rights at the annual general meeting (AGM). In 2001, the government framed rules under which, for certain specified businesses, resolutions might be passed through postal ballot. As in other parts of the world, small investors do not use their voting rights or proxy effectively. In most situations, the owner-manager and large shareholders mobilise proxy in their favour.

Creditors have the right to ask for the company to be wound up in case of non-payment of their dues. However, the procedure is cumbersome. It is expected that proper 'bankruptcy' and 'foreclosure' laws will be in place within a year.

The labour laws in India protect the rights of the employees in the organised sector. At present, there is no exit policy, and an establishment with 100 or less employees can be closed down without the prior permission of the government. Enterprises employing more people are required to take the government's permission for closing down the establishment. The government has proposed the relevant labour laws to allow companies to close down the unit without prior permission if the number of employees is 1,000 or less. This proposal is facing resistance from political parties. However, it appears that the government will be able to bring in the reform with some modifications.

The interests of other stakeholders are protected under different civil and criminal laws. Environmental policies and environmental laws are evolving. However, compliance to those laws is not satisfactory.

Thus, the Indian situation fits into the observation of Hellwig (2000: 122) that the outside shareholders' contractual protection is the weakest among all the parties that are involved with the firm.

ROLE OF FINANCIAL INSTITUTIONS—THE TREND

Corporate governance literature discusses at length the role of the banking system in the governance of firms in Germany and Japan (Aoki and Patric 1994; Cable 1985; Charkham 1994). Generally, the literature presents the positive role of banks in those two countries. However, the contemporary literature contradicts earlier findings (Edwards and Ogilview 1996; Weinstein and Jafeh 1998).

In India, financial institutions and banks definitely played a crucial role in industrial development as they did in Japan and Germany. However, because those were state-owned institutions, they neither played an active role in monitoring and governance, nor earned rent. With the reduction of government investment in financial institutions and banks, the character and behaviour of those institutions are likely to change.

In August 1998, financial institutions identified the following areas where the nominee director would have to pay special attention to:

1. financial performance of the company;
2. payments due to institutions, government, statutory authorities, intercorporate investments and deposits;
3. investments in subsidiaries, loans to subsidiaries;
4. award of contracts;
5. mergers and acquisitions;

6. expansion and diversification, hiving off or transfer of divisions, subsidiarisation and desubsidiarisation;
7. changes in articles of association; appointments of chairman/managing director and/or reappointment or change in terms of appointment;
8. setting up of joint ventures;
9. framing dividend and bonus policy;
10. framing preferential issue of equity to promoters' group, raising of funds through rights issues or term loans/debentures; and
11. appointment of committees such as audit review committee, management of committees and appointment of concurrent auditors (*Financial Express* [Mumbai] 18 August 1998).

Thus, financial institutions intend to participate actively in the control and governance of publicly-traded companies. However, it is likely that they will redefine their role when government investment in their own capital structure will reduce significantly, and they themselves will face the problem of corporate governance.

With the reduction in investment in equity and increase in the proportion of loan investment, financial institutions will behave more like large creditors, rather than owners of publicly-traded companies. There are several reasons why financial institutions resort to passive control (Vives 2000). They will exit from an underperforming company and will enforce collaterals to realise payments rather than spending resources for improving the performance of the company. There are several reasons to predict this change in behaviour. First, they will not be willing to spend the resources required to improve the performance of the company because of the 'free rider' problem. Second, as the recent trend shows, financial institutions will not have any significant shareholding in those companies in the future and, consequently, will find it difficult to influence the operating and financial decisions of the company. Third, the loan portfolio of financial institutions will continue to be secured by collateral. With legal reforms that are on the agenda of the government, enforcement of securities will be easier. However, the effectiveness of the role of financial institutions will depend on the ease with which they will be able to enforce collaterals. Experience in other countries supports the argument that the repossession of assets by creditors is often so difficult that creditors renegotiate loans, rather than resorting to bankruptcy proceedings (Shleifer and Vishny 1996).

LARGE SHAREHOLDERS

The trend in shareholding patterns shows that promoters will continue to hold substantial voting rights in Indian publicly-traded companies. They will continue to control the management of the company. Thus, 'control rights' will be much in excess of 'cash flow rights'. The Indian situation is not unique. 'In short, heavily concentrated shareholdings and a predominance of controlling ownership seems to be rule around the world' (Shleifer and Vishny 1996: 28). Members of promoting families manage most Indian companies. 'With the exception of the Tatas, all major enterprises in these groups are headed by the members of the promoting families; and the succession to the top leadership of a group is normally synonymous with the succession in the family' (Tripathi 2002: 143). The situation is unlikely to change in the near future. However, there is a visible trend—family members of this generation come to the helm after receiving relevant education and training. Thus, while in the US and other countries professional managers manage companies, in India management rests with the promoters or the group with concentrated shareholding.

If a wholly-owned firm is managed by the owner, he will make the operating decisions which maximise his utility. The decisions involve not only the benefits he derives from pecuniary returns but also the utility generated by various non-pecuniary aspects of his entrepreneurial activities. If the owner-manager sells equity claims on the corporation which are identical to his, agency costs will be generated by the divergence between his interest and those of outside shareholders. Prospective minority shareholders realise that the owner-manager's interests will diverge somewhat from theirs. Therefore, the price they will pay for shares will reflect the monitoring costs and the effect of divergence between the manager's interests and theirs (Jenson and Meckling 1976). Consequently, the cost of capital to the firm increases. Therefore, it is in the interest of the dispersed shareholders to install an appropriate monitoring system to monitor the decisions of the owner-manager. Even if owner-managers do not like to have a monitoring and control system, it is in their interest to signal that an adequate and effective monitoring system is in place. This will help them to mobilise resources from the capital market at a lower cost of capital.

Evidence all over the globe suggests that for companies which are managed by professional managers, large shareholders play an active role in corporate governance (Shleifer and Vishny 1996). The situation is different in India. The management of companies rests with owner-managers and not with professional managers. Therefore, the issue in corporate governance is how to monitor and control owner-managers. Financial institutions, at least for some time to come, will hold large blocks of shares in public limited companies. Therefore, they can play the role of large shareholders. However, as discussed earlier, they are unlikely to assume the responsibility. They are likely to behave like other institutional investors as regards their equity portfolio. On the positive side, they may not take a short-term view as is usually being taken by institutional investors. Their decisions will provide information signals to the capital market. Financial institutions holding equity will be privy to boardroom discussions and, therefore, will have better information as compared to institutional investors. Therefore, their decisions will provide stronger signals. It will facilitate improving the governance of publicly-traded companies.

An interesting development that is expected to catch the attention of academics and managers regarding corporate governance in present public-sector enterprises is the coming down of government shareholding to 26 per cent in those companies. The strategic partner in whose favour the government will transfer a large part of its holding will hold the largest block of shares. Therefore, the strategic partner will hold the management and control of the company. It will be interesting to observe how the government and the large shareholder will then define their roles in the control and governance of those companies. There is potential for conflict between the interests of the government and the interests of the strategic partner.

THE INDIAN MODEL OF CORPORATE GOVERNANCE

Corporate governance models aim to reduce the agency cost by improving the monitoring system. In the USA and European countries, the corporate governance system focuses on enhancing the effectiveness of the board of directors and the efficiency of the market for corporate control. Key elements in the system are 'independent directors' and 'transparency' in corporate reporting. In Germany the 'Hausbank' system operates. In addition to loans and the direct ownership of equity, German banks are able to vote the proxies of customers' shares. In Japan, 'main banks' play a dominant role in the governance of publicly-traded companies. The main bank, in addition to providing a loan to the company holds a block of equity. Therefore, it can exercise considerable influence on the company. In Japan, companies do not favour the induction of 'independent directors' to the board. Germany has a two-tier board of directors—'supervisory board' is different from the 'management board'. In addition to shareholders, other stakeholders are also represented on the supervisory board. In other parts of the world, the 'unitary board' model is prevalent. Researchers are yet to establish which model of corporate governance is the best.

Corporate governance models evolve around the environment in which companies operate. In India, companies will continue to be managed by promoter-managers. Financial institutions are expected to resort to 'passive control'. Therefore, the governance structure of Indian companies should have an effective internal monitoring system. The Indian Companies Act 1956 provides for a 'unitary board'. Shareholders elect directors at the annual general meeting. However, in the absence of 'proportionate voting', nominees of majority shareholders get elected to the board. Although the Companies Act provides an option to use the system of 'proportional representation', most companies have not responded positively. A recent amendment to the Companies Act stipulates that the board of a public company with a paid up capital of Rs 50 million or more, or 1,000 or more small shareholders may have a director elected by them. A small shareholder is a shareholder who holds shares of a nominal value of Rs 20,000 or less. Many question the practicability of this provision. Therefore, directors are predominantly nominees of promoters who hold significant, if not majority, voting rights in the company.

The Government has amended the Companies Act 1956 in 1999, 2000 and 2001, to incorporate a number of provisions that are expected to raise the level of corporate governance in India.

The central government has notified the establishment of Investors' Education and Protection Fund effective from 1 October 2001. The fund shall be utilised to create awareness among investors and protect their interest. The fund will be created out of amounts in unpaid dividends accounts of companies, the application money due for refund and matured deposit with companies. The amount in those accounts which have remained unclaimed and unpaid for a period of seven years from the date they become due for payment, shall be credited to the fund.

In order to enhance transparency and accountability, a new pro-vision has been introduced in the Companies Act, which requires the inclusion of 'Directors Responsibility Statement' (DRS) in the report of the Board of Directors. The DRS will indicate that:

1. In preparation of the annual accounts, the applicable ac-counting standards had been followed along with a proper explanation relating to material departure therefrom;
2. The directors had selected and applied such accounting policies consistently so as to give a true and fair view of the state of affairs of the company and the profit and loss ac-count of the company for that period;
3. The directors had taken proper and sufficient care for the maintenance of adequate accounting records so as to safe-guard the company's assets and to prevent and detect fraud and other irregularities; and
4. The directors had prepared the annual accounts on a going concern basis.

A new provision has been introduced requiring every public com-pany with a paid-up capital of Rs 50 million or more to constitute a committee of the Board of Directors known as Audit Committee. It will consist of not less than three or more directors as decided by the Board. Two-thirds of the members shall be other than the man-aging or whole-time director. The meetings of the committee shall be attended by auditors, internal auditors and the director-in-charge of finance who can participate in the meeting but without any vot-ing rights. The committee shall discuss the internal control system, scope of audit, auditors' observations and review the half-yearly and annual financial statements before submission to the Board. The recommendation of the committee shall be binding on the Board. If the Board does not accept the recommendation, it will record the reasons for it and will communicate the same to the shareholders through its report. The chairman of the committee is required to attend every AGM of the company to provide clarification on matters relating to audit.

A recent amendment of the Companies Act 1956 has reduced the ceiling of the number of companies in which an individual can hold the office of director from 20 to 15.

The government had formed a committee, headed by Mr R.D. Joshi in 2002, to suggest changes urgently required in the Companies Act 1956. The committee has proposed various measures to raise the level of corporate governance. One of the recommendations is that the management and the statutory auditors should be imprisoned for a period not less than one year and not exceeding 10 years if they are found to have been involved in fraudulent accounting practices. Similarly, the government had appointed a committee, headed by Mr Naresh Chandra, to examine various corporate governance issues. Its focus was to improve the quality of audit and the quality of corporate financial reports. The committee has proposed various measures to enhance the independence of auditors and strengthen the monitoring system.

In 2000, the SEBI issued a Code of Corporate Governance,[5] which is expected to work best within the governance structure stipulated in the Companies Act. The Code is applicable to listed companies. The Code focuses on the role of non-executive directors and independent directors. It requires that 50 per cent of the board of directors should be non-executive directors. The number of independent directors would depend on whether the chairman is executive or non-executive. In case of a non-executive chairman, at least one-third of the board should comprise independent directors and in case of an executive chairman at least half the board should comprise independent directors. The Code requires the formation of various committees, most important of which are the audit committee and the remuneration committee. The scope of the audit committee is very wide and covers almost every aspect of audit and corporate financial reporting. It shall have a minimum of three members, all of whom are to be non-executive directors with the majority being independent, and with at least one director with financial and accounting knowledge. The chairman of the committee shall be an independent director. The remuneration committee shall have at least three directors, all of whom should be non-executive directors.

The 'Code' ensures that non-executive and independent directors get the right information by stipulating the board's procedure and the minimum information to be made available to the board. The Code requires providing forward-looking information in the form of 'management discussion and analysis'. Further, a separate section on corporate governance should be included in the annual reports of the company which is in the nature of a compliance report on corporate governance.

As in the Western model, the Indian model also relies on the external mechanics for corporate governance. It expects that the market for capital control will play an important role in corporate governance. The SEBI has put in place a code on 'Takeover and Substantial Acquisition of Shares' to enhance the effectiveness of the market for corporate control. It has also introduced interim financial reporting on a quarterly basis and the submission of key information to stock exchanges on real-time basis. In order to improve the quality of corporate financial reports, over the past two years the Accounting Standard Board (ASB)[6] of the Institute of Chartered Accountants of India (ICAI) has issued 13 new 'accounting standards'. With the issuance of new standards, the total number of accounting standards issued by the ICAI comes to 28. The ICAI has also initiated policy measures such as 'peer review', and the setting up of a 'Financial Report Review Panel', to improve the quality of audit. The panel would *suo moto* look into the published accounts of different organisations. Similarly, the government has decided to set up a Serious Fraud Investigation Office (SFIO). It is conceived as a multidisciplinary unit capable of investigating corporate white-collar crime.

These and other initiatives are expected to put in place an appropriate corporate governance structure for publicly-traded companies in India.

IMPLEMENTATION ISSUES

It will not be easy to implement the SEBI Code of Corporate Governance because an adequate number of individuals, qualified to be appointed to the board, are not available. The SEBI Code stipulates that an individual cannot join boards of more than 10 companies. The provision aims to ensure that directors allocate adequate time to each company in which they are directors. However, to implement this provision at least 3,600 individuals are required for listed companies if each company plans to have six independent directors on the board. The appointment of independent directors serves the purpose of building shareholders' confidence by issuing signals to the market that the company has an internal mechanism to monitor the decisions of owner-managers. Therefore, unless independent directors are publicly known for their professional attainments and values, the purpose of signalling the capital market will not be achieved. Companies will like to choose individuals who hold the right public image. The market for such individuals is too small. Companies that have a very good track record in corporate governance will attract the right individuals to their board. As a result, those companies which need to significantly improve corporate governance will not be able to get individuals who are qualified to act as directors. There are companies which do not want to improve the effectiveness of the supervisory function of their board. They will induct individuals in their close circuit as independent directors and will use the situation to camouflage their intentions.

Another problem is to motivate independent directors to spend adequate time in understanding and managing the business. At present, the Companies Act 1956 stipulates a ceiling on the remuneration that can be paid to outside directors. The remuneration depends on the profit of the firm. Usually the amount is inadequate to motivate professionals to join the board of directors of public limited companies. Further, in order to ensure accountability, the Companies Act 1956 stipulates that directors are individually responsible for the non-compliance of corporate and other laws and for frauds perpetrated by the company. Those stipulations act as a strong demotivating factor for qualified individuals to join the board in the first place.

The theoretical debate on how independent are independent directors is yet to be settled. In practice, the incumbent management nominates independent directors. It is difficult for them to act objectively and overcome subtle pressures from the management. Therefore, overreliance on independent directors may not provide the desired result. Moreover, independent directors can only provide 'checks and balances'. They usually do not get involved in formulating the corporate strategy. Ideally, they should not become a direct party in corporate decisions, because if they participate in decision-making their independence gets obscured. An individual who is a direct party to a decision cannot objectively review the same. There is a potential for independent directors to support suboptimal decisions with which they are comfortable, because they may not understand finer points of complex models due to a lack of business understanding.

The SEBI Code emphasises monitoring and thus compromises on the managerial enterprise. Corporate governance literature provides enough evidence to show that control by large shareholders acts against the initiative and enterprise of the incumbent management. Although in India large shareholders are not likely to exercise control, control by independent directors might work against the initiative and enterprise of owner-managers. On the other hand, the lack of monitoring gives rise to serious agency problems. The trick is to attain the right balance which is essential to improve the productivity of resources while minimising the agency cost. There is nothing in contemporary literature which points towards a universally appropriate governance structure. According to the literature, the proper balance in constituting an effective governance structure depends on various factors, particularly the nature of the business and the size and the regulatory environment in which firms operate.

CONCLUSIONS

Recent initiatives should improve corporate governance in India. The level of transparency in corporate reporting and information flow to the capital market will improve. Adequate and timely information will improve the effectiveness of 'passive control' by financial institutions and other large shareholders. However, development of the market for capital control will depend on the availability of funds. Financial institutions and banks should be allowed to finance takeovers. The activity level in the market for capital control is low. The number of hostile takeovers in the past is negligible.

The SEBI Code by itself may not bring about the desired outcome until implementation issues are resolved. The SEBI is currently in the process of reviewing the code of corporate governance and the takeover code to improve their effectiveness.

As in other parts of the globe, in India too there are proponents for the 'stakeholder society theory' of corporate governance. According to the theory, corporate governance refers to the design of institutions to make managers internalise the welfare of stakeholders in the firm. Stakeholders include employees, customers, suppliers, the local community and managers. Though the 'stakeholder society' concept is superior to the 'shareholder value' concept at the normative level, many suspect the practicality of the concept.

However to take such a stance would be hasty. First, in trying to implement the stakeholder society, managers will lose focus and will be able to rationalise any action on the supposed benefits for some of the stakeholders. The outcome most likely will be a higher autonomy for the manager with more freedom to pursue private benefits of control. Second, the sharing of control may result in a loss of decisiveness. In practice, managers would consider the welfare of stakeholders that have power, forming with them an alliance of insiders that would tend to expropriate other stakeholders. At the same time managers would try to influence regulations to promote ideas of a stakeholder society to gain more autonomy (Vives 2000: 15–16).

Researchers should also investigate whether Indian corporate practices support the 'stakeholder society theory' or if it is just rhetoric.

The adoption of the Western system is good as a starting point, because international investors from the West are comfortable with the system. However, India needs to develop its own system taking into consideration the Indian ethos and business environment. The next decade will be important for researchers to collect adequate information on the experience of initiatives taken by the government, regulatory authorities, the ICAI, and the business associations to improve the governance of Indian public limited companies.

| NOTES

1. Suggestions and assistance received from B.V. Phani and Sadha Laxmi, both Fellow Programme students at the Indian Institute of Management Calcutta, is gratefully acknowledged.
2. In the managing agency system, joint stock companies used to appoint firms with experience and specialisation in business management to manage the company for a very long period. Each firm used to manage a large number of companies. 'By 1951 there were some 36 managing agency firms—including the Birlas, Dalmias, Singhanias and the Tatas—controlling more than 600 industrial concerns, most acquired from departing Britons' (*Business Today* 2002: 161).
3. The Bombay Stock Exchange is the oldest stock exchange in India. Though the exchange has lost much of its former glory with the creation of the National Stock Exchange (NSC), it is still the most important stock exchange in India.
4. Licence raj refers to the pre-liberalisation era, when the establishment of new units or substantial extension of existing units in specified industries

required a licence from the Government of India. The Industries (Development and Regulation) Act, 1951, which empowered the government to licence originally applied to 37 industries. In 1953, its scope was extended to cover eight additional industries and in 1957 another 34 industries were brought within the purview of the Act. 'In general, the licensing system worked in such a way as to provide a disproportionate share in the newly licensed capacity to few concerns belonging to the large industrial sector. In fact, in the past, maximum benefit of licensing system went to a few larger industrial houses' (Ghosh 1987: 365).

5. As per SEBI guidelines, all Group A entities of the BSE or those in the S&P CNX Nifty index as on 1 January 2000 had to comply with the corporate governance norms by 31 March 2001. By 31 March 2002, all listed entities that have a paid up share capital of Rs 100 million and above have to meet corporate governance norms and by the end of the next financial year (April 2002–31 March 2003), all listed companies have to follow suit.

6. In India accounting standards are being issued by the ASB constituted by the ICAI. The ASB has representations from the government, SEBI, RBI, academia, business associations and others who have an interest in corporate financial reporting. The ICAI is committed to harmonise the Indian accounting standards with the international accounting standards being issued by the International Accounting Standards Boards (IASB). The ICAI has planned to bridge the gap (in terms of numbers) between Indian accounting standards and international accounting standards (IAS) within the next two years. The government has recently (2001) constituted a National Advisory Council on Accounting Standards, which advises the government on the applicability of accounting standards to limited liability companies.

REFERENCES

Aoki, Masahiko and Patric, Hugh. 1994. *The Japanese Main Bank System: Its Relevance for Developing and Transforming Economies*. New York: Oxford University Press.

Bagchi, Amiya Kumar. 1998. 'Public Sector Industry and the Political Economy of Indian Development', in Terence J. Byers (ed.). *The State, Development Planning and Liberalisation in India*. Delhi: Oxford University Press.

Berle, A., Jr. and Means, G. 1932. *The Modern Corporation and Private Property*. Chicago: Commerce Clearing House.

Bhattacharyya, Dhires. 1973. *Understanding India's Economy—Volume 1*. Calcutta: Progressive Publishers.

Boumol, William.1959. *Business Behaviour, Value and Growth*. New York: Macmillan.

Business Today. 2002. The Board Through the Ages. *Business Today*. 20 January.

Cable, J.R. 1985. 'Capital Market Information and Industrial Performance'. *Economic Journal*, 95: 118–32.

Charkham, Jonathan.1994. *Keeping Good Company: A Study of Corporate Governance in Five Countries*. Oxford: Clarendon Press.

Economic Survey, Government of India. 2001–2002. *Economic Survey 2001–2002*. New Delhi: Economic Division, Ministry of Finance, Government of India.

Edwards, J. and Ogilview, S. 1996. 'Universal Banks and German Industrialisation: A Reappraisal'. *Economic History Review*, 49: 427–46.

Ghosh, Alok. 1987. *Indian Economy: Its Nature and Problems*. Calcutta: The World Press Private Limited.

Hart, Oliver D. 1991. ' Incomplete Contracts and the Theory of the Firm', in Oliver E. Williamson and Sidney G. Winter (eds). *The Nature of the Firm, Origins, Evolution and Development*, pp. 138–58. New York: Oxford University Press.

Hellwig, Martin. 2000. 'On the Economics and Politics of Corporate Finance and Corporate Control', in Xavier Vives (ed.). *Corporate Governance, Theoretical and Empirical Perspectives*, pp. 95–136. Cambridge: Cambridge University Press.

Jensen, Michael.1986. 'Agency Costs of Free Cash Flow, Corporate Finance and Takeovers'. *American Economic Review*, 76.

Jensen, M. and Meckling, W. 1976. 'Theory of the Firm: Managerial Behaviour, Agency Costs, and Ownership Structure'. *Journal of Financial Economics*, 3: 305–60.

La Porta, R.F., Lopez-de-Silanes and Shleifer, A. 1999. 'Corporate Ownership Around the World'. *Journal of Finance*, 54: 471–517.

Marris, Robin. 1964. *The Economic Theory of Managerial Capitalism*. Illinois: Free Press of Glencoe.

National Stock Exchange Limited (NSE). 2001. *Indian Securities Market*. A Review. Vol. IV. Mumbai: NSE.

Patil, R.H. 2002. 'Reforming Indian Debt Markets'. *Economic and Political Weekly*, 2–8 February, pp. 409–20.

Roy, Tirthankar. 2000. *The Economic History of India 1857–1747*. Delhi: Oxford University Press.

Shleifer, Anderi and Vishny, Robert W. 1996. *A Survey of Corporate Governance*. Cambridge: National Bureau of Economic Research. Working Paper No. 5554.

The Economic Times. 2002. MNCs Want Solo Act. *ET 500—The Changing Face of India Inc. The Economic Times*. March.

Tripathi, Dwijendra. 2002. 'Whither Family Management'. *Business Today*. 20 January, p. 143.

Vives, Xavier. 2000. 'Corporate Governance: Does it Matter?', in Xavier Vives (ed.). *Corporate Governance, Theoretical and Empirical Perspectives*, pp. 15–16. Cambridge: Cambridge University Press.

Weinstein, D. and Jafeh, Y. 1998. 'On the Costs of a Bank Centered Financial System: Evidence from the Changing Main Bank Relationships in Japan'. *Journal of Finance*, 53: 635–72.

Williamson, Oliver. 1964. *The Economies of Discretionary Behaviour: Managerial Objectives in a Theory of the Firm*. Englewood Cliffs, NJ: Prentice-Hall.

THE EDITORS

Surendra Munshi is Professor of Sociology in the Sociology Group of the Indian Institute of Management Calcutta. He has researched and taught in India and abroad in the fields of classical sociological theory, sociology of culture and industrial sociology. His current research interests include good governance and 'excellence' as a managerial objective.

Biju Paul Abraham is an Assistant Professor in the Environment Group of the Indian Institute of Management Calcutta. His teaching and research interests include issues related to public policy, administrative reforms and good governance. He has also worked on international governance issues, especially decision-making within the World Trade Organisation.

THE CONTRIBUTORS

Peter Abell is former Director and founder of the Interdisciplinary Institute of Management at the London School of Economics and Political Science. He is also Visiting Professor at the Copenhagen Business School. He is the author of several books on cooperation and papers on organisation, rational choice and methodology.

V.K. Agnihotri, IAS, is currently Secretary, Ministry of Parliamentary Affairs, Government of India. His areas of interest include public policy, rural industries, panchayati raj, good governance, economic reforms, and primary education. He has several publications to his credit including *Skills for Effective Administrators*, *Environment and Development*, *Public Policy Analysis and Design*, *Dimensions of the New Economic Policy* and *Socio-Economic Profile of Rural India*.

Asish K. Bhattacharyya is Professor of Finance in the Finance and Control Group of the Indian Institute of Management Calcutta. He has research interests in corporate governance, corporate financial reporting and business valuation. He is the author of *Principles and Practice of Cost Accounting* and *Financial Accounting for Business Managers*.

R.K. Dar IAS (Retd.), Former Secretary to Government of India, was till recently the Chairman of the first State Finance Commission of the newly created state of Uttaranchal. He has edited a book titled *Governance and the IAS: In Search of Resilience*. His research interests include bureaucracy, federal systems and decentralisation.

Abram De Swaan is Research Professor (Universiteitshoogleraar) at the University of Amsterdam. He has published among others *In Care of the State: Health Care, Education and Welfare in Europe and the USA in the Modern Era*. His most recent work is *Words of the World: The Global Language System*. At present his research interests are social policy, social identifications, and the rivalry and accommodation between language groups in a transnational perspective.

Paola De Vincentiis is Assistant Professor in the Faculty of Economics of the University of Turin. She is the author of *The Money Market* and *The Bond Market*.

Prem Shankar Jha, a noted journalist, was the Information Adviser to the Prime Minister of India in 1990. He has a number of books to his credit, including *India: A Political Economy of Stagnation, Management of Public Enterprises in Developing Asian Countries, In the Eye of the Cyclone: The Crisis in Indian Democracy, Kashmir 1947: Rival Versions of History* and *The Perilous Road to the Market: A Political Economy of Reform in Russia, China and India*.

Angela Liberatore works in the Directorate General for Research of the European Commission on issues related to governance and citizenship and was involved in the preparation of the Commission's White Paper on Governance in the Working Group on 'Democratising Expertise'. Her research interests include European integration and governance, democracy, conflict resolution, sustainable development and risk management. She is the author of *The Management of Uncertainty: Learning from Chernobyl*.

Luke Martell is a Senior Lecturer in Sociology at the University of Sussex. He is the author of *Ecology and Society*, the co-author of *New Labour: Politics after Thatcherism* and *Blair's Britain*. He is the co-editor of *The Sociology of Politics, Social Democracy: Global and National Perspectives*, and *The Third Way and Beyond: Criticisms, Futures and*

Alternatives. He has published papers on socialism, neo-liberalism, social movements, and New Labour.

Kuldeep Mathur is Professor at the Centre for Political Studies and Academic Director of the Centre for the Study of Law and Governance at the Jawaharlal Nehru University. He has published on public policy processes, bureaucracy, decentralisation, and state-society relations. Among his recent publications are *Development Policy and Administration and Policy* and *Technocracy and Development: Human Capital Policies in India & the Netherlands*.

Vithal Rajan is Volunteer Chair of the Governing Body of the Confederation of Voluntary Associations which works through community empowerment for harmony between poor Hindu and Muslim communities living in urban and rural areas of India.

Darryl Reed is Associate Professor in the Division of Social Science at York University and the Co-ordinator of the Business & Society Programme. His current research interests are the field of business and society, including corporate governance, community economic development, business ethics, and development ethics. He has published in several journals including the *Business Ethics Quarterly, Journal of Business Ethics, Business Ethics: A European Review,* and *International Journal of Social Economics*.

Diane Reyniers is Professor in Management and Director of the Interdisciplinary Institute of Management at the London School of Economics. Her research interests are in the fields of operations research, management, mathematical sociology, and economics. She has published papers in *Journal of Mathematical Sociology, Journal of Computational Economics, International Journal of Game Theory, European Journal of Operational Research, International Game Theory Review,* and *British Journal of Sociology*.

Manfred Roeber is Professor of Public Management at the University of Applied Sciences for Technology and Economics in Berlin. He has a number of research projects to his credit and has written several books and papers in refereed journals and books. His recent publications include as co-author *Berliner Verwaltung auf Modernisierungskurs* and *Hauptweg und Nebenwege* and as co-editor *Moderne Verwaltung fuer moderne Metropolen*.

Rudi Schmidt is Professor of Sociology at the University of Jena. His fields of research include sociology of work and economy, industrial relations, transition of societies in Europe, sociology of management and white-collar workers, modernisation of industry and production systems. His recent publications include as a co-author *Betriebliches Interessenhandeln* (in two volumes) and as a co-editor *Managementsoziologie*.

Anju Seth is Professor of Strategic Management at the University of Illinois at Urbana-Champaign. She is interested in research issues in strategic management that can benefit from a multidisciplinary approach, particularly drawing from economics and finance. Her papers have appeared in *Strategic Management Journal, Journal of International Business Studies, Review of Economics and Statistics, Managerial and Decision Economics, Journal of Management Studies, Journal of Management Inquiry, Journal of Applied Corporate Finance, California Management Review,* and *Handbook of Business Strategy.*

Anup Sinha is Professor of Economics in the Economics Group of the Indian Institute of Management Calcutta. His academic interests, both in terms of teaching and research, are in the areas of economic development and macro-economic policies. His recent publications include (as co-editor) *The Challenge of Sustainable Development: The Indian Dynamics.*

Hellmut Wollmann is Emeritus Professor of Public Policy and Public Administration at Humboldt University, Berlin. His major research fields include public sector reforms (with a focus on local government), evaluation research and institutional transformation of former socialist countries. His recent publications include as editor *Evaluation in Public Sector Reform* and as a co-editor *Local Democracy in Post-Communist Europe* and *Comparing Public Sector Reform in Britain and Germany.*